THE GHOSTS OF GUERRILLA MEMORY

The Ghosts of Guerrilla Memory

How Civil War Bushwhackers
Became Gunslingers in the
American West

MATTHEW CHRISTOPHER HULBERT

The University of Georgia Press   *Athens*

© 2016 by the University of Georgia Press
Athens, Georgia 30602
www.ugapress.org
All rights reserved
Set in Berthold Baskerville by Graphic Composition, Inc., Bogart, GA
Printed and bound by Thomson-Shore
The paper in this book meets the guidelines for
permanence and durability of the Committee on
Production Guidelines for Book Longevity of the
Council on Library Resources.

Most University of Georgia Press titles are
available from popular e-book vendors.

Printed in the United States of America
20 19 18 17 16 P 5 4 3 2 1

Library of Congress Control Number 2016947160

CONTENTS

ACKNOWLEDGMENTS

For some time now, it has been considered cliché to write about various debts owed to esteemed colleagues and supportive loved ones. In fact, academic acknowledgements—and especially those preceding first books—have seemingly progressed to a point where it has become a cliché nouveau even to poke fun at the *idea* of hackneyed acknowledgments. But as I reflected on my experience with this book, two things became quite clear: first, that no historian ever writes a book by himself or herself, and second, with that maxim in mind, there is simply no way to avoid the unavoidable. So here goes: over the many years spent researching and writing *The Ghosts of Guerrilla Memory*, I ran up a debt from my mentors, colleagues, friends, and family that would make Congress collectively blush.

My "mission control" in Athens was second to none and I cannot thank them enough. John Inscoe is an extraordinary historian, a model advisor, and a cherished friend. Without his counsel and (near superhuman) patience, it is safe to say you would not be holding this book. As the dean of the "dark turn" in Civil War history, Stephen Berry's imprint on this book is undeniable—and I cannot even begin to explain how much of a good thing that is. The insights provided by Kathleen Clark and Stephen Mihm concerning guerrilla memory's place in the "bigger picture" of the American experience have been both eye-opening and invaluable.

As series editors go, Amy Murrell Taylor is a top gun. She has taken exceedingly good care of me and this project from start to finish. Better still, over the last two years, my interactions with Amy, with editor-in-chief Mick Gusinde-Duffy, and with everyone at UGA Press have confirmed again and again that UnCivil Wars is the perfect home for guerrilla memory.

And here is where things start to get a little embarrassing—not on account of the quantity of authors, editors, peer reviewers, commentators, and colleagues that are deserving of my profound thanks for one reason or another, but on account of how spoiled I have been to work with and among such a generous, talented group of scholars in the first place: Bill Blair at the *Journal of the Civil War Era*, Lesley Gordon at *Civil War His-*

tory, Susanna Lee and Katherine Charron at North Carolina State University, and Anne Marshall, Ken Noe, Megan Kate Nelson, LeeAnn Whites, Aaron Sheehan-Dean, Victoria Bynum, Brian McKnight, Brian Miller, Christopher Phillips, Barton Myers, Jim Broomall, Jim Cobb, T. J. Stiles, Kevin Levin, Bruce Nichols, Robert Poister, Trae Welborn, David Thomson, Andrew Fialka, Matthew Stanley, and the late (and dearly missed) Tom Dyer. Joseph Beilein also belongs on this list for several reasons—but I am proudest of our work on *The Civil War Guerrilla: Unfolding the Black Flag in History, Memory, and Myth*, a volume we coedited while still in graduate school.

Outstanding intellectual balances are one thing, and financial ones quite another. Writing about the Missouri-Kansas borderlands from an office in Georgia was not always easy, but a number of institutions and people made my research possible. Many thanks belong to the Frances S. Summersell Center, the Willson Center for Humanities and Arts, the Institute for Humane Studies, and Greg and Amanda Gregory, benefactors of the Gregory Graduate Research Fund at the University of Georgia. Additionally, it was—and always will be—my distinct honor to have been named a Dissertation Completion Fellow by the Harry Frank Guggenheim Foundation for 2014–2015. Their faith in guerrilla memory has been most gratifying and afforded me crucial time for writing and revision.

Both my immediate family—my parents, Jerry and Becky, and my sister, Victoria—and my family-in-law—Jack, Peggy, Lindsey, and Ed—have been inexhaustible in their support of me and this project. This is especially true of my parents, who have bestowed more love and support on me—and shown more interest in a bunch of long-haired, revolver-toting bushwhackers—than I ever had a right to expect. For this, I am truly grateful.

Not everyone meets his future wife on the first day of graduate school, let alone in the office next door. In this regard, I count myself among the luckiest few. Kylie is a marvelous historian in her own right and a powerhouse in the classroom. But she is also my favorite hiking companion (along with our pointer-beagle mix, Cooper), my most trusted editor, my sturdiest support, my closest confidante, and my best friend. I love her dearly. This book is for her.

THE GHOSTS OF GUERRILLA MEMORY

INTRODUCTION

The Borderlands of Memory

In 1884 *Century Magazine* heralded its coming series, "Battles and Leaders of the Civil War." The assortment of personal recollections, historical treatments, and battlefield analytics promised to be a thorough, scholarly, and objective accounting of all things Civil War. Perhaps most important, the contributors to the series included the era's heaviest hitters: P. G. T. Beauregard, John Bell Hood, George McClellan, Oliver Otis Howard, Ulysses S. Grant, and even the much embattled James Longstreet. Through the minds and pens of these men, virtually every state that had seen significant action in the national bloodletting was to receive serious attention.

Enter Samuel Langhorne Clemens, alias Mark Twain.

As first revealed by J. Stanley Mattson in the late 1960s, *Century* editors intended Twain's contribution—an autobiographical portrayal of the early days of Civil War Missouri—to "supply a missing link in the Series."[1] From the beginning of the war, guerrillas and irregular violence had plagued Missouri; so, minus the major battles and iconic commanders of the Eastern Theater, responsibility for the state was delegated not to a prestigious general like Grant or McClellan or even to a colonel. Instead, it fell to the author of "The Celebrated Jumping Frog of Calaveras County" and *The Adventures of Tom Sawyer*.

The magazine's editors got precisely what they should have expected from Twain: an uproarious account of the ill-conceived, ill-equipped, and ill-fated "Marion Rangers." But Twain's comedy starring the would-be band of bushwhackers with whom he had apparently served for all of two weeks in 1861 did the state of Missouri's commemorative cause no real favors. "Indeed, that Mark Twain's contribution was regarded by *Century* editors as basically suspect," Mattson concludes, "seems obvious from the fact that it alone was cut from the subsequently published four-volume edition of the collected essays of the Civil War series."[2] In the simplest of terms, Missouri found itself symbolically cast out from the "mainstream" war the series purported to chronicle.

But for all it lacked in scholarly frills, Twain's "The Private History of a Campaign That Failed" demonstrated in its own darkly humorous and incisive way that Missouri's Civil War experience had been anything but regular or typical—and perhaps it had never belonged among the pages of *Battles and Leaders* to begin with. "Out west there was a good deal of confusion in men's minds during the first months of the great trouble," Twain began. Unlike other states that had allegiances to either the Union or the Confederacy, in Missouri "it was hard for us to get our bearings." Twain eventually fell in with a crew of equally confused young men who dubbed themselves the Marion Rangers; they patrolled the farms and meadows of their neighborhood, searching for things to fill their stomachs and pretty girls to pester. As Twain put it, "It was an enchanting region for war—our kind of war."[3]

"The first hour was all fun," according to Twain, "all idle nonsense and laughter." But the adrenaline rush of going to war—inasmuch as the rangers ever actually went to war—quickly faded. By only the second hour of his first tour of duty, Twain recalled somberly, "nobody said a word." So from the very start, the rangers were a disaster of a guerrilla band. One man, Bowers, habitually slept in the saddle; his horse, able to recognize when its rider had nodded off, "would reach around and bite him on the leg." "Next," Twain noted, "nobody would cook." To the young men of Missouri's best farming families, "it was considered degradation." As a result, "we had no dinner." When the threat of combat finally reached them, the rangers became distraught: "It was a rude awakening from our pleasant trance. The rumor was but a rumor—nothing definite about it; so, in the confusion, we did not know which way to retreat." This was a very serious problem for the company. "The question was," Twain replayed for readers, "which way to retreat, but all were so flurried that nobody seemed to have even a guess to offer." Luckily for the rangers, a man named Lyman stepped forward and offered what seemed like a brilliant solution. "He explained in a few calm words that, inasmuch as the enemy were approaching from over Hyde's prairie, our course was simple: all we had to do was not to retreat *toward* him." "Any other direction," Lyman proudly posited, "would answer our needs perfectly."[4]

After several close encounters with actual military service, Twain and the other rangers finally saw combat—or something akin to it. Camping in a corncrib, the men ambushed a hardly visible soldier on horseback as he approached their camp in a downpour. As Twain looked down on the dying man, with "his white shirt-front" all "splashed with blood," something sinister occurred to him. "The thought shot through me that I was a murderer; that I had killed a man—a man who had never done me any harm." "That," he recorded, "was the coldest sensation that ever went through my marrow." Moments later, Twain learned that other members of the company had fired, too; blame, it seemed, could at least be divided between them all.[5]

Even that did little to soothe Twain's aching conscience. "It seemed an epitome of war," he concluded of the event, "the killing of strangers against whom you feel no personal animosity; strangers whom, in other circumstances, you would help if you found them in trouble, and who would help you if you needed it." This realization soured Twain's outlook on military life, and his campaign "was spoiled." "I could have become a soldier myself if I had waited," he concluded. "I had got part of it learned; I knew more about retreating than the man that invented retreating."[6]

It isn't difficult to surmise why *Century* excluded "The Private History" from its bound edition of *Battles and Leaders*. In just a few pages, Mark Twain, a man with virtually zero credible military experience, had called the entire meaning of the Civil War into question and placed a bull's-eye on its glorious legacy. Given our purposes, though, the story is particularly interesting for two reasons. First, in a broad sense, nothing could illustrate more clearly than Twain's farcical contribution to an otherwise self-important series that recollections of the Civil War were (and still are) the products of both their individual origins and the (man-made) processes of memory—processes that work unceasingly to smooth over minor inconsistencies, fault lines, and rough edges to form a palatable, consensus-driven, collective version of events. Second, when these differences proved too great or the edges too rough, as in Twain's case, they were simply excluded or suppressed altogether. The story of the Missouri-Kansas borderlands simply did not—and could not—look like those coming out of Virginia, Tennessee, Pennsylvania, Georgia, or the Carolinas; its residents experienced the Civil War on unavoidably different terms than the rest of the divided nation.[7]

With these points as a foundation, we can begin to give shape to the term "guerrilla memory" itself. At its most fundamental level, guerrilla memory represents the collision of Civil War memory with the realities of irregular warfare in Missouri and Kansas. In the mainstream culture, the Civil War would come to be remembered as a vast sequence of battles, with a turning point at Gettysburg and a culmination at Appomattox. But in this guerrilla theater, the Civil War had been a vast sequence of home invasions and a general breakdown of law and order. My purpose is to analyze the cultural politics behind how Americans have remembered, misremembered, and re-remembered narratives of guerrilla warfare in rhetoric, historical scholarship, literature, and film, at reunions, and on the stage. By probing how memories of the irregular war were intentionally designed, created, silenced, updated, and even destroyed, this book pieces together a more realistic idea of how controlling the way we collectively remember the past has translated into controlling the way we collectively understand the present. And along the way I analyze the roots of a historiography that, until recently, treated the irregular war in two bizarrely divergent ways: (1) not at all; or (2) as somehow the epitome and indictment of war itself.

Writing in the wake of the Vietnam War, Michael Fellman offered the first serious treatment of the Missouri-Kansas guerrilla conflict in the late 1980s. By cataloging the region's counternarrative wartime experience— one Fellman himself called "the war of 10,000 nasty incidents"—*Inside War* became an instant classic of Civil War scholarship. But the book's underlying political motives (that is, the damning connections it drew between the behavior of Civil War guerrillas and American GIs in Southeast Asia) came with a steep historical price. In the end, Fellman concluded that irregular combatants had essentially been young men infected with bloodlust; a self-serving, nihilistic, and sometimes even sociopathic demographic without genuine ideological roots to anchor the violence they unleashed on their communities. It became an accepted fact that guerrillas lacked any real influence over the outcome of the war, and they were relegated again to the fringes of its history for nearly two decades.[8]

In 2009 the publication of Daniel Sutherland's award-winning *A Savage Conflict: The Decisive Role of Guerrillas in the American Civil War* finally reopened the discussion. By charting the activities of irregular combatants in every region afflicted by war (from the Deep South to Appalachia to Missouri and Kansas), Sutherland shed crucial new light on the ways in which guerrilla warfare affected both morale on the homefront and policy decisions in Washington and Richmond, influences that gradually accumulated to help shape the overall outcome of the conflict. With this newfound legitimacy in mind, historians such as LeeAnn Whites and Joseph M. Beilein have blueprinted the ways in which men, women, and children all participated in the irregular conflict as companies bound by kinship and community; their turn toward "Household War" combines the scope first used by Fellman with the legitimacy achieved by Sutherland and reveals the extent to which the division between homefront and battlefront was always an artificial distinction.[9]

The segregation of homefront violence—that is, of various types of guerrilla warfare—from traditional concepts of battlefield violence (the efforts of formal armies and war departments) has served a broader moral purpose that is unmasked through a study of guerrilla memory. On one hand, this distinction has effectively "othered" irregular violence as uniquely uncivilized and awful; on the other, it has preserved the glories of the regular war by robbing it of its own true awfulness in memory. Such is the commemorative sleight of hand that renders a raid resulting in four deaths more objectionable than a day's battle costing thousands of lives. In blending homefront and battlefront, however, we must be cautious to avoid oversimplification. This is not simply a means for painting a more generic portrait of war as uniformly terrible. Instead, it is an opportunity to rethink and then to preserve the specific contexts of specific stories on equal footing.

This is crucial for the story I aim to tell because to write on guerrilla memory is to tell a story within a story about a war within a war. The irregular conflict may have seemed a sideshow to those whose eyes were glued to the news from Antietam, for example. But it was the only war that really mattered to those it touched, and it was a war with its own brand of violence, its own cast of characters, and its own strains of memory. And it is the latter that I most wish to focus on. I make no attempt in this study to rethink our basic understanding of wartime events. I do seek to explain how those wartime events created different kinds of collective trauma and thereby different commemorative needs.

The makers and keepers of these irregular traumas and commemorative needs went by many names: guerrillas, bushwhackers, Jayhawkers, Red Legs, and homeguard, to name a few. America had a long tradition of guerrilla combat. European colonists first learned the practice of *La Petite Guerre* from Native Americans in seventeenth-century conflicts such as King Philip's War (1675–1678)—tactics the white settlers eventually turned on their indigenous teachers during the Seven Years' War (1754–1763) between England, France, Spain, and their respective Native allies. With the American Revolution came the rise of men such as Francis "Swamp Fox" Marion and Daniel Morgan, commanders well known (and celebrated) for irregular stratagems, fighting from the bush, and frequently eschewing the orchestrated madness of men marching directly into enemy fire. In the first half of the nineteenth century, Americans further honed their irregular skills against Natives, Mexicans, Mormons, and, in the case of the Missouri-Kansas border feud of the 1850s, against each other.

When dealing with the Civil War specifically, historians often divide guerrilla combatants into a top-down hierarchy based on official Confederate affiliation and ideology. They distinguish between cavalry raiders (such as Nathan Bedford Forrest, Joseph Shelby, and John Hunt Morgan), partisan rangers (such as John Singleton Mosby), and bushwhackers (such as William C. Quantrill, Samuel Hildebrand, Champ Ferguson, and Marcellus Jerome Clarke, better known as Sue Mundy).[10] Such categorization serves a basic organizational purpose, but as Daniel Sutherland aptly reveals, wartime guerrilla violence had actually cast a much taller shadow—both in terms of geography and diversity of participants—than these labels might imply at first sight.[11] Because irregular warriors typically had little use for official rosters or reports, it is virtually impossible to precisely calculate how many guerrillas operated during the Civil War.

Regardless of how many fought or what we call them, in the guerrilla theater these belligerents ruled. The back roads, hamlets, and households of the homefront replaced standard battlefields and war departments; entire families of men, women, and children, regardless of age, sex, or ideological affiliation, stood in for regular soldiers; and all manner of violent encounters, from ambuscade, arson, and rape to murder, massacre, and torture, took the place of Napoleonic maneuvers and pitched battles. No consistent moral economy of bushwhacking existed to keep untold numbers of civilians, let alone powerful chieftains such as William C. Quantrill or "Bloody Bill" Anderson, in check. Family fought against family, neighbor struggled against neighbor, and the Civil War took on hyperlocal, hyper-personal qualities as it unfolded at the community level. Within this environment, the rules of regular warfare applied only sporadically, if at all, and irregular violence—the fuel of guerrilla memory in the postwar period—operated as the status quo.

Since its publication in 2001, David Blight's *Race and Reunion* has reigned as the seminal work in Civil War memory. The book provides a large-scale blueprint for the allegorical "war after the war" in which ex-soldiers, pundits, politicians, and propagandists of all sorts crossed pens to establish a definitive narrative of the war and to ascribe an ultimate legacy to four years of death and destruction. Blight consolidates the opposing camps into three major groups based on their interpretations of the conflict and, most importantly, how those interpretations would shape the postbellum sociopolitical landscape. Therein, he identifies a bloc of "White Supremacists" whose motives seem apparent, a bloc of "Reconciliationists" interested in expedited national reunion, and a bloc of "Emancipationists" hoping to use Union victory as a springboard for racial progress. In the end, *Race and Reunion* illustrates how Reconciliationists allied themselves with White Supremacists against the Emancipationists for sake of a quicker reconciliation process at the expense of newly freed slaves, black veterans, and racial egalitarianism in general.[12]

More recently, in *Remembering the Civil War: Reunion and the Limits of Reconciliation* (2014), Caroline Janney takes up Blight's premise and modifies it by drawing a more complex distinction between definitions of "reunion" and "reconciliation." Historians, she contends, have lost sight of the differences that fundamentally separated the two terms. While the former simply required the political restoration of the Union, the latter required combat veterans themselves to let go of lingering war-related hostilities and adopt interpretations of the war potentially at odds with their personal views. So while reunion was an undeniable political fact by 1877, Janney remains much more skeptical about the overall adoption of reconciliatory feelings, however in line with white supremacy Union veterans may or may not have been after the war.[13]

Without question, these are estimable studies of Civil War memory, each thoroughly researched and imminently valuable in the classroom. And it really should not surprise us that powerful generalizing models of this sort are necessary to deal in such sweeping narratives. That said, when units of historical measure become this large, they also become problematic. For books operating on this scale to function properly, their authors must assume that most Americans shared a collective–or at least similar enough–wartime experience to unite them, or at the very least to understand each other, during Reconstruction and afterward. Thereby, despite their differing conclusions, *Race and Reunion* and *Remembering the Civil War* actually constitute opposite poles of the same model for studying memory writ large, one in which untold atypical memories–or "irregular recollections," as I call them–are obligatorily lost to the pruning and streamlining of history.[14]

Rather than using guerrilla memory to shine light into the cracks of this extant model, we will start anew. The past is infinitely complex and this study aims to project a more accurate version of it by not trying to discover the middle ground capable of accounting for it all at once. Too much of the edges are lost in the search process and, as the guerrilla theater illuminates, the edges are where so much of the action took place. Instead, my intention is to add a new layer of complexity to the war's memory by simply releasing that which already exists but has, over time, been condensed, marginalized, overlooked, or forgotten.

With this in mind, chapter 1, "The Nastiest Bits," analyzes irregular warfare as a "war within the war" by harnessing five individual vignettes to provide a kaleidoscopic, constellated sense of the range and diversity of memories in the guerrilla theater. These micronarratives range from an Irish immigrant delivering milk to Lawrence, Kansas, on the fateful morning of August 21, 1863, to a besieged German community laying an ambush of their own for prowling Confederate bushwhackers–they include men and women, native-born and immigrant, black and white, adult and adolescent. These sagas ultimately underscore the atypical nature of the Civil War in the borderlands and exemplify how many veterans of irregular violence refused to conform to broader trends in commemoration and remembrance.

Very much in response to that refusal, chapter 2, "An Irregular Lost Cause," chronicles ex-Confederate and Democratic fire-eater John Newman Edwards attempting to design and construct an "irregular" Lost Cause for the state of Missouri—the unrivaled capital of the guerrilla theater. Edwards feared that the combination of Missouri's Border West location and its failure to formally secede during the war would isolate the state from the rest of the ex-Confederacy culturally and politically. This chapter blueprints how Edwards attempted to fabricate a southern identity for Missouri in the postwar period, regardless of what residents themselves chose to remember, by way of a retrofitted Confederate fighting past in his 1877 magnum opus, *Noted Guerrillas, or, The Warfare of the Border.*[15]

Chapter 3, "Rebooting Guerrilla Memory," begins the first "post-Edwardsian" phase of the guerrilla memory story. It traces the thematic evolution of several memoirs published by ex-guerrillas from 1903 to 1930. In the 1870s and 1880s, the "irregular" Lost Cause created by Edwards had intentionally isolated guerrillas from regular soldiers in order to make them the most diehard of all Confederates. By the turn of the century, however, the partisan usefulness of Edwards's narrative waned; in turn, guerrillas-turned-authors desired to reintegrate themselves into mainstream southern society. This chapter explores how they wielded ideas and symbols of both the New South economic movement and the Lost Cause memory movement to "reboot" guerrilla memory.

In connection to this rebooting effort, chapter 4, "Getting the Band Back Together," investigates the annual reunions held by the remnants of William C. Quantrill's command from 1898 to 1929. This chapter contends that the motive elements behind the guerrilla reunions matched almost exactly the goals of the memoirists featured in chapter 3—that is, these "irregular encampments" intentionally mimicked the activities of regular veterans' meetings as a way to establish a longer-term place for guerrilla memory in twentieth-century southern society. In tandem, these chapters also make a strong statement about the intersection of race and social hierarchy in the postbellum South: that the Quantrill Men, all of whom were white and harbored clear Confederate sympathies, understood such a memorial makeover to be necessary for the endurance of their legacy accentuates that "whiteness"—even in a moment typically portrayed as when the white half of the "color line" resolidified in support of Jim Crow—simply was not enough to guarantee acceptance or remembrance.

While male ex-guerrillas employed memoirs and reunion celebrations to put a more accessible veneer on their Civil War experiences (without ever actually changing the content beneath that new shimmer), a vital part of the process involved venerating women as the gatekeepers of the main-stream Lost Cause. As suggested in chapter 5, "The Gatekeepers' Conundrum," however, women–especially those who belonged to the Missouri Division of the United Daughters of the Confederacy–had their own plan in mind. This chapter outlines how female borderlanders, unable to stand by any longer in the shadows of male memory, attempted to infuse the Lost Cause movement they managed with elements of their own wartime experiences; and, equally important, it reveals how their efforts to re-remember *might* have altered public perception of the guerrilla theater for more than a century.

Attempts by pro-Confederates to wield guerrilla memory for partisan purposes did not go unnoticed across the border. Chapter 6, "The Unionists Strike Back," takes stock of how Unionist residents of the guerrilla theater–most often in Kansas–responded to Edwards's *Noted Guerrillas* and the unmistakably pro-Confederate memory narrative it glorified and disseminated. From burlesque theatrical productions to early histories of the Missouri-Kansas guerrilla war to published memoirs and fictional stories, this chapter details how memory narratives were thrust into direct competition with one another and how different generations of Unionists tried to topple the enduring legacy of John Newman Edwards and the culture of remembrance that clung tightly to it.

As should now be clear, the plotline of guerrilla memory is not linear, but a mechanism of interconnected, moving parts. The first six chapters of this book involve typical residents who refused to forget, political pundits who re-remembered for them, the best-known bushwhackers clinging to commemorative relevance, pro-Confederate female activists, and oft-overlooked Unionists who balked at efforts to remember Confederate atrocities as "real war." Together, these chapters examine how forces located *within* the Missouri-Kansas borderlands attempted to carve out and control legacies of guerrilla warfare that would allow them to control the legacy of *their own* Civil War experiences. But these overlapping stories are also the prologue of another significant narrative, one in which an external force–the custodians of which cared little for the internal wants and needs of the guerrilla theater–was enacted on the legacy of guerrilla warfare. This was to be a legacy of "westernization" and, through it, of "Americanization."

The movers and shakers of the commemorative camps chronicled by Blight and Janney worked very hard to establish an understanding of the Civil War with which many Americans are still quite familiar. Through popular literature, histories, and later film, these eastern interests effectively differentiated guerrilla warfare from the "mainstream." Of this, *Battles and Leaders* serves as a case in point. Then again, even the most powerful collective memory narratives could never completely erase events known so well as the Lawrence Massacre of August 1863 or men so notorious as William C. Quantrill, William "Bloody Bill" Anderson, Cole Younger, or the James brothers, Frank and Jesse.

Rather than eliminating this history, I suggest that ideas of the western frontier were employed to re-remember them into another cultural place and its corresponding geographic space: the Wild West of the American imagination. Twain's efforts to buck the tide of Civil War glorification notwithstanding, even he could not escape it. His characters in "The Private History," with their lassos and six-guns and bowie knives, showed clear signs of their author having internalized some of the westernization of guerrilla memory. But even slightly westernized guerrillas were unacceptable, and just to be sure, *Century* editors similarly excommunicated the piece.

While it may not seem so at first sight, the westernization of guerrilla memory has left an enormous impression on the ways Americans have conceived of and remembered the Civil War since it ended. To fully understand this influence, we need to first reimagine the geographic scale and purpose of the war itself. At present, proponents of the "New Civil War in the West" are doing just that. Their work explores how and why the tendrils of the Civil War reached farther and farther westward to connect both ends of the continent; it investigates the Indian wars as extensions of Union and Confederate campaigns, how competing concepts of manifest destiny influenced Union and Confederate policy makers, and how the goals of Reconstruction coincided and conflicted with the quest to establish an American empire in the West.[16]

Therefore, instead of examining the guerrilla theater as subordinate Civil War territory, territory so often lost to the streamlining of previous models, this book shifts our angle of historical vision, reconstituting the Missouri-Kansas borderlands as the geographic center of a nation engulfed in a multipronged conflict over abolition and empire. From here we can see the Civil War's true nature more clearly than we can from Virginia or Georgia. It was a war, after all, fought over the future of the West, a war in which the first raft of legislation passed by a Republican Congress included the Pacific Railroad Act, the Homestead Act, and the Morrill Land Grant Act.

Located at the fulcrum of this contest to determine the core identity of a nation (literally) spanning from sea to shining sea, the borderlands functioned as the portal in which the alchemy of memory could remake the discarded irregulars of the war in the East into the heroes of the war in the West. Household warfare was never intended to be waged by whites against other whites. This arrangement gave both sides a way out: it helped explain away the violence in the war for abolition and rebranded it as suitable in a war for empire. The larger American project had always been to make the West safe for free white settlement, white commerce, and white industry while maintaining a scrupulous distance from the violence (some of it justified, some of it unjustifiable) that would be necessary to make that happen.[17]

Put another way, the manipulation of guerrilla memory allowed heavily vested commemorators of the regular war to remember it as they saw fit. The outcast guerrillas of Missouri and Kansas became iconic gunslingers so that they could be swept under the same memorial rug as the "cowboys" who actually were Indian killers. The victims of uncivilized modes of irregular violence transitioned from respected white families to unwanted Native Americans; said violence could then be justified as a tool for forcibly installing civility on the western frontier. Thus, when all was said and done, the guerrilla theater, once on the fringes of both conflicts, became the place where northerners, southerners, and westerners could all watch the memory of the *entire* struggle play out.

The first phase of this process of "Americanization through westernization" is chronicled in chapter 7, "Guerrillas Gone Wild in the West," which maps out how once-prominent Confederate figures such as Frank and Jesse James were posthumously transformed into icons of the Wild West. This chapter biographically juxtaposes Jesse James with well-known western outlaw Henry McCarty (AKA "Billy the Kid") while simultaneously chronicling the factors—from outlaw histories and dime novels to Wild West shows—that led most Americans to believe that James genuinely had more in common with the Kid than his original Civil War compatriots.

As an expansion, both chronologically and technologically, of the themes found in the previous chapter, chapter 8, "Black Flags and Silver Screens," appraises how guerrillas—for the most part Confederate ones—have been depicted on film from the 1920s to the present. This chapter asserts that many of these films—from *Renegade Girl* to *The Woman They Almost Lynched* to *The Outlaw Josey Wales* to *True Grit*—have erroneously been categorized as "westerns" as part of the process of cultural exportation described in chapter 7. A reassessment of these films helps us recapture their true origins and forces us to reconsider what exactly a "Civil War movie" even is. More importantly, this chapter outlines the process by which certain realities of Civil War combat were sanitized and sold back to the American people, becoming a celebration of frontier American ass-kicking rather than an indictment of American ways of war.

In an epilogue, "Notes from the [Disappearing] Guerrilla Theater," I provide a firsthand account of my travels in "guerrilla country"—from Centralia and Lawrence to graves, historic homesteads, and monuments. More than anything, this is an attempt to relate how the story of guerrilla memory narrated throughout this book has (or has not) manifested itself in the everyday lives of Missourians and Kansans; moreover, my travelogue also shines a light on how contemporary scholars of the Civil War have allowed the guerrilla theater's commemorative pitfalls to devalue its broader importance. To forget about the borderlands (again) is to ignore that they were once a critical commemorative bridge between the two geographic fronts of a much larger fight for a true national identity . . . and that so little of that structure remains intact because the places where the "dirty work" of memory happens are rarely, if ever, preserved as evidence for posterity. We do not typically think to remember the facility that produces the bomb; we only try to control the narrative of why it was dropped. It is the same with the production of collective memories.

While pulling former Confederate guerrillas back into the context of their Civil War service, I will address key questions of representation in memory: How did the relegation of the most infamous guerrillas to the realm of western pop culture affect guerrilla memory as a whole? Why do Americans seem more comfortable with ex-bushwhackers as gunslingers

and cowboys and bank robbers than as participants in the war that saved
the Union and emancipated millions of African American slaves? How
does the broadest possible legacy of the war change when the abolition of
nonwhites and the conquest of nonwhites were simultaneous goals?

Such questions require clear answers. Until they are answered, our
national Civil War narrative will remain intentionally and unfortunately
incomplete. So begins this history of guerrilla memory.

ONE

The Nastiest Bits

There were scores of little camps scattered over Missouri where the same thing was happening. These camps were composed of young men who had been born and reared to a sturdy independence, and who did not know what it meant to be ordered around by Tom, Dick, and Harry, whom they had known familiarly all their lives, in the village, or on the farm.

—Mark Twain, "The Private History of a Campaign That Failed"

Late in the summer of 1862, G. W. Ballow offered his thoughts on the untamed nature of war in Missouri. "I am happy to state," he informed a friend, "that guerrilla warfare is rapidly playing out in all parts of Missouri."[1] Ballow, as it turned out, was not much of a clairvoyant; the sky still represented the virtual limit for irregular activity in Missouri. Even the massacres at Lawrence (1863) and Centralia (1864)—easily the best-known incidents of the Missouri-Kansas guerrilla conflict and arguably of the entire Civil War—only constituted drops in a deluge of violence that left both states nearly drowned. In reality, counties, towns, hamlets, and neighbors hitherto bound by communal interest or kinship ties stood bitterly opposed and remunerated blood with blood.

All of this bloodletting leads to an obvious question: why Missouri? What couldn't an insider such as G. W. Ballow see about his native soil that allowed—if not encouraged—guerrilla violence to germinate at such a prodigious tempo? What could have made the state's populace so obstreperous for such an extended period of time? While it would be easier to assume that something nefarious was in the water (and many Kansans at the time might have agreed), this chapter actually begins with a brief run-down of the state's history, one equal measures natural, political, and cultural: its geography, its agriculture, its peoples, and how their life cycles produced—and replicated—the tendencies that seemingly primed men, women, and children for an explosion of irregular violence.

This chapter aims to sample the borderlands' stock of guerrilla memory straight from the barrel, unfiltered and uncut. This is not to suggest that "unfiltered" means more objective or historically accurate—only more accurate in terms of how people desired their experiences be remembered by posterity. Accordingly, the vignettes around which the chapter revolves are relayed mostly as narrative and with minimal interruption of perspective. This is because great weight will be placed on how these stories were designed to sound, their adherence to the local and to family matters, and what emotional and intellectual responses they were penned to elicit—confusion, misstatements of fact, fabrications, and all. The vast majority of analysis, both individual and comparative, will come toward the end of the chapter.[2]

These memory narratives, encountered at their original proofs (or as close to them as possible), will also serve as a comparative benchmark for the rest of our trek through the history of guerrilla memory. Subsequent chapters will chronicle the collectivization, the reboots, the evolutions, and the elisions of that story—but these developments only realize their full effect if we are able to recall the design, the lack of polish, and the intent beneath each individualized account. Put another way, we must not lose sight of the units with which traumas in the guerrilla theater were first experienced, first measured, and first remembered.[3]

In 1803 a special envoy acting on behalf of President Thomas Jefferson purchased a tract of western land ranging from Canada to the Gulf of Mexico. These negotiators had originally intended to acquire only the city of New Orleans from France—but the cash-strapped regime of Napoleon Bonaparte made an offer the Americans simply could not refuse. In dire need of capital to continue his military campaigning, the soon-to-be-crowned emperor abandoned plans to establish new colonies in North America and liquidated the vast Louisiana Territory. Surveyors soon carved the Missouri Territory from this broader landscape.[4] By 1821, owing to the compromise of a year prior that bore its name, Missouri officially entered the Union as a slave state. The decision to allow the spread of slavery westward proved fateful; it began a chain reaction of violent disputes that would not cease until the entire nation plunged itself into civil war.[5]

Centuries before such political wheeling and dealing gave way to the rumbling of cannons, forces of the natural world had determined that Missouri would be a place utterly defined by its waterways: the Mississippi

River and the Missouri River. Their tides made the land exceptionally fertile for agriculture; their currents provided transport for both man and the fruits of his labor; their intermingling with the shore created natural trade centers around which urban dwellings could multiply. No matter their distance from the banks of either artery, Missouri's residents were *all* river people—and their life cycles ebbed and flowed as such.[6]

From ancient basins in the Upper Midwest, the Mississippi River courses south through Minnesota and Wisconsin toward the Gulf of Mexico. The waterway that Abraham Lincoln hailed as the "Father of Waters" cleaved its way between Iowa and Illinois before rounding the northeastern corner of Missouri. Then as now, the river formed Missouri's entire eastern border. Positioned along this riverine boundary, Saint Louis marks the spot where the Missouri River collided with the Mississippi and from which Missouri's most developed network of railways commenced. The city also harbored the largest urban population in an overwhelmingly rural state. These characteristics made Saint Louis a thoroughfare for all manner of immigrants hoping to prosper along both rivers—but particularly those of German or Bavarian descent. After escaping the political upheavals and economic inequalities of Europe, these family farmers came in search of cheap, arable land and the ability to own it for themselves. They had little sympathy for slavery and consistently championed free labor.[7] Thus, despite the fact that a significant cluster of slave owners resided in Saint Louis when the Civil War broke out, the city and its surrounding counties represented Missouri's greatest stronghold of wartime Unionism and Republican support.[8]

After gathering in Montana's share of the Rocky Mountains, the headwaters of the Missouri River push east into North Dakota before turning southward into the Midwest. Flowing through South Dakota and then bisecting Nebraska and Iowa, the river eventually courses into Kansas City on the state's western border—at nearly the same latitude as Saint Louis. Though lacking in the railroad infrastructure of the East, Kansas City constituted a major trade outlet for the western territories. As an emanation point for the Santa Fe and Oregon Trails used by pioneers to reach Kansas, New Mexico, Colorado, Utah, Oregon, and California, it was also an outpost of sorts for travelers to the far frontier.

Perhaps more importantly, Kansas City's location involved it in a pair of extremely violent, interconnected conflicts. On one hand, Missouri's

State of Missouri - 1860

Atchison, Nodaway, Gentry, Harrison, Mercer, Putnam, Schuyler, Scotland, Clark

Holt, Andrew, De Kalb, Daviess, Grundy, Sullivan, Adair, Knox, Lewis

Buchanan, Clinton, Caldwell, Livingston, Linn, Macon, Shelby, Marion

Platte, Clay, Ray, Carroll, Chariton, Randolph, Monroe, Ralls

Kansas City, Jackson, Lafayette, Saline, Howard, Boone, Audrain, Pike, Lincoln

Johnson, Pettis, Cooper, Moniteau, Callaway, Montgomery, Warren, St Charles

Cass/Van Buren, Henry/Rives, Benton, Morgan, Cole, Osage, Gasconade, Franklin, St Louis, St. Louis

Bates, St Clair, Hickory, Camden, Miller, Maries, Jefferson

Vernon, Cedar, Polk, Dallas, Laclede, Pulaski, Phelps, Crawford, Washington, Ste Genevieve, St Francois, Perry

Barton, Dade, Greene, Webster, Wright, Dent, Iron, Madison, Reynolds, Bollinger, Cape Girardeau

Jasper, Lawrence, Christian, Texas, Shannon, Wayne, Scott

Newton, Barry, Stone, Taney, Douglas, Howell, Oregon, Ripley, Carter, Stoddard, Mississippi, Butler, New Madrid

Mcdonald, Ozark, Pemiscot, Dunklin

N
W — E
S

- ● Major Cities
- +—+—+ Railroads
- —— Major Rivers
- ////// Little Dixie

0 20 40   80   120   160
Miles

Map by Andrew Fialka

The state of Missouri, by county, on the eve of the Civil War. The region known as "Little Dixie" paralleling the Missouri River was home to many of the state's most active irregular combatants. Data courtesy of the Minnesota Population Center. *National Historical Geographic Information System: Version 2.0.* Minneapolis, Minn.: University of Minnesota, 2011. Map by Andrew W. Fialka.

internal debate over slavery remolded the sectional crisis of North versus South to fit a contest of East versus West. In much the same way that Saint Louis was a mainstay of Unionism, Kansas City functioned as its pro-Confederate counterpart. On the other hand, Kansas City's situation along the Missouri-Kansas border placed it at the center of a strife that raged long before boisterous South Carolinians ever lobbed a shell at Fort Sumter. The people in and around Kansas City had clashed with the likes of John Brown, they had massacred Kansans along the Marais des Cygnes— and they had even sacked the antislavery town of Lawrence, Kansas, in 1856. It would not be a coincidence that the counties nearest Kansas City— Platte, Jackson, Clay, Ray, Cass, and Lafayette—produced many of Missouri's most diehard guerrillas, the Andersons, Jameses, and Youngers among them.[9]

At Kansas City the Missouri redirects toward a junction with the Mississippi in Saint Louis, meandering through the state's central corridor. This stretch of counties—coined "Little Dixie" on account of its high concentration of pro-Confederate slaveholders—was renowned for rich soil and violent origins. Here second- and third-generation Missourians managed farms; their forebears, land-hungry homesteaders from Kentucky and Virginia, had opened the territory for settlement by force, clearing tree and Indian from the land with equal vigor. Subsequently, in the 1830s, they clashed violently with Iowans over coveted farmland along the Missouri-Iowa border and waged a war against Mormon settlers, eventually driving the latter from western Missouri. In the 1840s and 1850s, most of these pioneering families threw their support behind the institution of slavery. On average, the number of slaves owned per household in Little Dixie resembled the Confederate South, though variations in crop selection produced a key difference.[10]

Whereas the cotton, rice, and indigo plantations of the Deep South thrived on slave labor, profitable agriculture along the Missouri River did not depend on slavery. Most of the people in these counties, slave owners or not, harvested bushels of cereal grains (corn, wheat, oats, and rye) by the hundreds and thousands. They also raised livestock and produced various types of hemp. Still others cultivated tobacco, typically with the aid of human chattel, but not always. Agricultural diversity begot competition between free and enslaved laborers—and ensured a collision of worldviews. Expressed another way, this arrangement forced free-laboring farmers, native and foreign-born, to toil in unusually close prox-imity to their neighbors' slaves. Moreover, it placed them in the shadow of an inherently violent, paternalistic culture founded on the very institution that provided their economic competitors with said labor advantage in the first place. Over time, combined with the region's propensity for partisan bloodshed, these interwoven social and economic tensions made Little Dixie a ticking time bomb of irregular violence.

The dual concentration of slaves and self-identified "southerners" in Little Dixie notwithstanding, the overwhelming majority of cotton grown and ginned in Missouri blossomed well south of the Missouri River. Much of this area was known as the Ozarks, so named for the mountain range that juts up and across Missouri's southern border. Rail lines from Saint Louis only stretched a few counties into this lower third of the state—locales where slavery did exist, but in much more isolated instances than in the rest of Missouri. And not unlike members of communities nestled in the Appalachian Mountains of North Carolina, Ozark residents fash-ioned their own mountain culture unique to the region—mores exempli-fied by local feuds and vigilantism (most notably the "Bald Knobbers" of the 1880s). As Union forces occupied (and plundered) mountain neigh-borhoods, locals balked and tempers flared. In retributive raids, pro-Confederate bushwhackers such as William Wilson—the guerrilla on whom the eponymous lead character of *The Outlaw Josey Wales* (1976) was based—clashed regularly with federal troops to defend their homes and families.[11]

All things considered, by 1860 Missouri was a state in name only—an unstable dot on the political map, cobbled together from distinct terri-tories. Kansas City was a world apart from Saint Louis. The Ozarks re-sembled neither. Political inflection even within Little Dixie could vary by the mile, even by the boundary between neighboring farms. These were places and spaces with life cycles defined by their local geographic fea-tures, with their own ideologies, social hierarchies, religious devotions, and cultural traditions. So when the matter of secession came to a head and the influence of Saint Louis—with its disproportionate population and diversity, its industrial might, and its corresponding political clout—over-rode the state's more rural pro-Confederate contingents, Missouri took on the appearance of a place at war with itself.

On one side, antebellum governor and proslavery advocate Claiborne Jackson desperately wanted to deliver Missouri for the Confederacy.

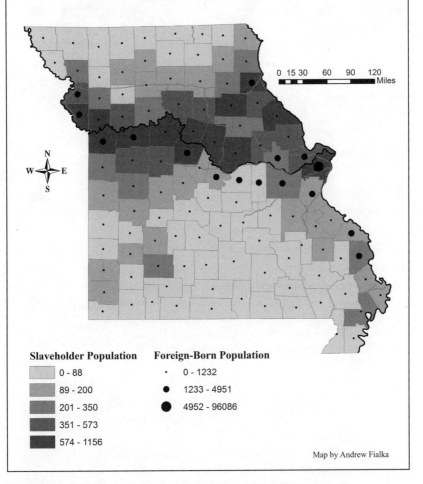

Slaveholder Population vs. Foreign-Born Population
Missouri - 1860

0 15 30   60   90   120
Miles

N
W—◆—E
S

Slaveholder Population

	0 - 88
	89 - 200
	201 - 350
	351 - 573
	574 - 1156

Foreign-Born Population

·	0 - 1232
●	1233 - 4951
●	4952 - 96086

Map by Andrew Fialka

Slaveholder population vs. foreign-born population in Missouri, 1860. Conflict
between slaveholders and foreign-born residents unfolded all over the state, but most
of all in Little Dixie. Not coincidentally, irregular violence followed a similar pattern.
Data courtesy of the Minnesota Population Center. *National Historical Geographic
Information System: Version 2.0.* Minneapolis, Minn.: University of Minnesota, 2011.
Map by Andrew W. Fialka.

Slave Population - 1860

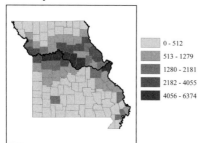

	0 - 512
	513 - 1279
	1280 - 2181
	2182 - 4055
	4056 - 6374

Cereal Grain Production - 1860

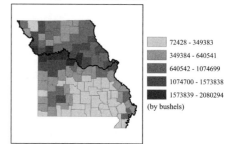

	72428 - 349383
	349384 - 640541
	640542 - 1074699
	1074700 - 1573838
	1573839 - 2080294
(by bushels)	

Hemp Production - 1860

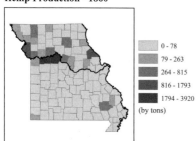

	0 - 78
	79 - 263
	264 - 815
	816 - 1793
	1794 - 3920
(by tons)	

Ginned Cotton - 1860

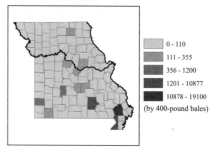

	0 - 110
	111 - 355
	356 - 1200
	1201 - 10877
	10878 - 19100
(by 400-pound bales)	

Missouri crop diversity and slavery, 1860. Crop diversity in Missouri included grains, cotton, hemp, and tobacco—and of all these crops, the institution of slavery coincided with cotton the least frequently. Data courtesy of the Minnesota Population Center. *National Historical Geographic Information System: Version 2.0.* Minneapolis, Minn.: University of Minnesota, 2011. Map by Andrew W. Fialka.

When the state convention, led by Republicans from Saint Louis, voted against an ordinance of secession, Jackson called up the state militia anyway. He headquartered them at "Camp Jackson" on the outskirts of Saint Louis—a move that outraged prominent Unionists. On the other side was Nathaniel Lyon. As commander of the federal arsenal in Saint Louis, Lyon understood both the importance of holding the city to the Union cause and thereby the potential danger of a pro-Confederate force gathering on its doorstep. In response, Lyon captured Jackson's militia (sparking a riot in the process) and forced the governor to flee. At Neosho, Missouri, Jackson gathered a select group of state legislators and prompted them to vote for secession. The Lincoln administration effectively ignored the decree, declared Jackson a traitor, and reset the state government.[12]

As these macro-level political events unfolded, the situation on the ground was much more complicated. Pro-Confederates did dominate the territory around Kansas City while Unionists ruled in the vicinity of Saint Louis. But supporters of each cause were dispersed throughout the rest of the state. In this way, it embodied a near-perfect microcosm of the Republic's existential crisis as the Civil War began. Except in Missouri, regular military campaigns, marked by very early Confederate victories at Wilson's Creek and Lexington in 1861, quickly yielded to irregular warfare. This was a stage set for guerrillas—and the Toms, Dicks, and Harrys occupying the camps described by Twain took to it with unprecedented ferocity.

With a working knowledge of Missouri's backstory now in hand, the point of this chapter is to tell stories—admittedly not with the concern for their accuracy that one might expect. By design, this approach allows the residents of those towns and hamlets to speak for themselves—not simply to explain the blood they shed but to explore how and why they constructed those explanations. Observing the war from the vantage of their memories, we can begin to understand the kaleidoscopic quality of Civil War memory in the guerrilla theater, a place where violence tended to be hyperlocal and hyperpersonal and where commemoration was never so pronounced as it was in places such as Virginia. And only after first diagnosing why it was so difficult for veterans of irregular warfare to create metanarratives of it can we assess the products of their alternative approach to remembering: a patchwork of anarchic images and half-resolved traumas that could never be either fully celebrated or fully forgotten.

Without hallmark battlefields such as Manassas, Gettysburg, Antietam, or Shiloh, the war along and around the Missouri-Kansas border crystallized from an incalculable number of local, unpublicized, though still politically inflected conflicts.[13] Thus, distinctions between "the battlefield" and "the homefront" were not just blurred but impossible—and pointless—to demarcate. In a letter demonstrative of such, one Union soldier wrote to his wife that the execution of guerrilla combatants had become so pedestrian they were now doubling as social soirees. He remarked, rather casually given the circumstances, that a sizable gathering of local ladies had recently attended—and apparently very much enjoyed—the hanging of an accused pro-Confederate bushwhacker in town. Though unnamed, the short-lived life of the party had allegedly been one of "Holtzclaw's gang."[14]

Broadly speaking, the borderland's profusion of guerrilla violence had left it without a standard, battle-driven narrative to guide commemoration efforts for either side. Nor could Missouri or Kansas brandish an archetypal icon or "Marble Man" on which to hang popular mythologies in favor of the Union or the Confederacy. If one could imagine taking core samples from the landscape of memory in post–Civil War Virginia, Georgia, or Pennsylvania, the results would demonstrate a substantial degree of political, ethnic, and especially thematic uniformity. Within such specimens, the likes of Robert E. Lee, Ulysses S. Grant, and William Tecumseh Sherman, along with service in their acclaimed armies at Gettysburg, Richmond, and Atlanta, would feature prominently. But the scenes featured in this chapter, in addition to underlining the guerrilla theater's abundance of domestic strife and shortage of signature battles, reflect a distinct mixture of ethnic diversity, internal political division, border hostilities, and a sense not merely of violence but of consistent *violation*: an Irish immigrant delivering milk to Lawrence, Kansas, on the fateful morning of August 21, 1863, recalls the chaos of the great raid with vivid detail; an immigrant shopkeeper shot and then saved from guerrillas by the quick thinking and acting abilities of his distraught wife; a second-generation German farmer plots the chronology of blood-soaked events that led to a final stand against blitzing guerrillas in Saline County; a Unionist-turned-Confederate farm boy swept up by volatile neighborhood politics recounts several bloody encounters with a homeguard unit in Montgomery County; and, finally, the daughter of a farmer records her father's recollection of the morning a mysterious visitor appeared at the kitchen table—a timorous Union man claiming to be the sole survivor of the massacre at nearby Centralia. At once these sketches emphasize the atypical DNA of the Civil War borderlands; and, more important still, they underscore precisely how the very type of "damnable guerrilla warfare" G. W. Ballow assumed would disappear actually flourished and eventually went on to dictate the ways Missourians and Kansans could and would remember the war for decades after Appomattox.

Ultimately these stories focus on the experiences of individuals and small familial networks; ergo, whenever possible, I take full stock of the provenance and personal details of the men, women, and children involved. This is an effort not to just illustrate the various means through which their accounts have survived but also to tease out as much of their wartime worldviews as possible. Because for these people, events witnessed and survived in their own homes, backyards, and fields, along the muddy creek beds of their farms, and down the moonlit back roads of their neighborhoods trumped news from faraway battlefields or the exploits of demigod commanders in the East. This matters a great deal because the noncollective quality of this experience was not without cultural ramification. Collective memories are *not supposed to be accurate.* They are designed to have elisions, to comfort and explain the sometimes inexplicable. Following periods of intense turmoil and loss—and the guerrilla war excelled in the creation of both—memory often serves as a vehicle for collective emotional healing and reconciliation.[15] But each forthcoming vignette will lend testimony to the idea that many borderlanders could not or did not partake in the process of remembering in a way that alleviated wartime traumas; instead, the particular features and characteristics inherent to guerrilla warfare, as experienced by individuals, remained intact and intimately shaped the landscape of postbellum remembrance.[16]

Sounding the Alarm at Lawrence

In 1837 William Brown was born in Dublin, Ireland. Virtually nothing is known of his childhood years, save for the unfortunate fact that they coincided with what the Irish solemnly call *an Drochshaol*, or "the bad times." Beginning around 1845, widespread potato blight decimated subsistence crops across the island and left the bulk of Ireland's already impoverished population in a state of shock, ruin, and starvation, which lasted nearly seven years. In the wake of one million dead, a hopeful William struck out for the United States at the age of seventeen.[17] Census records fail to note the port of immigration, but odds are good that a boot-worn dock in the harbors of New York or Boston supported his first steps onto American soil. In 1859 William made two life-altering decisions: he married his wife, Jane, to whom he would remain joined for more than half a century, and he settled with her on a dairy farm in Wakarusa, Douglas County, Kansas, a small community on the outskirts of Lawrence. The newlyweds celebrated the birth of their first child, Thomas, in 1860 and in seven years had welcomed three more children—Elmer (1863), Willard (1865), and Emma (1867)—into the world. Though they subsequently disappeared from available records, census data published in 1920 indicated that William, eighty-two, and Jane, seventy-eight, were still married and in possession of the dairy business that had afforded them a front-row seat to the mayhem of fifty-seven years prior.[18]

On September 27, 1909, William dictated his firsthand knowledge of guerrilla chieftain William Clarke Quantrill's infamous raid on Lawrence, Kansas, to pseudohistorian William E. Connelley. The handwritten account survives today on just a few slips of weathered paper. Connelley's work made little effort to mask his anti-Confederate bias or his personal ax to grind with the ghost of Quantrill, which bordered on obsession. The Lawrence Raid marked the height of Quantrill's infamy, so it should come as little surprise that Connelley took great interest in William's account (though he later failed to cite it). In *Quantrill and the Border Wars* (1909), which was supposedly a historical account of Quantrill's life and partisan career, Connelley described the guerrilla commander as a "gory monster" whose "baleful shadow" had fallen on and tainted all that shared his "kindred blood." "In cruelty and thirst for blood," Connelley advised, "he towered above the men of his time"—in the end concluding that as a result of Quantrill's apparently genetic disposition for evil, "widows wailed, orphans cried, maidens wept, as they lifted the lifeless forms of loved ones from bloody fields and bore them reeking to untimely graves."[19]

While few would canonize William C. Quantrill for his role in the war, his August 21, 1863, surprise attack on Lawrence, Kansas (accompanied by hundreds of Confederate guerrillas), admittedly lacked Connelley's "supernatural" flare. In reality, the ambush claimed the lives of about two hundred townspeople and locally stationed Union troops.[20] Reported motivations for the surprise assault typically straddle partisan faults. On one hand, the August 13 collapse of a makeshift Union prison building in Kansas City, in which the female relations of several guerrillas—including the sister of William "Bloody Bill" Anderson—were maimed or killed, is most often presented by pro-Missouri factions as the spark that finally set off Quantrill and his men.[21] On the other hand, pro-Kansas elements often contend that Quantrill and his men were simply brigands, habitually on the hunt for mischief, plunder, and innocent blood. A definitive explanation remains elusive.[22]

In any event, William Brown's narrative began early on the day in question. Duty, or perhaps fate, enjoined him, then an industrious, twenty-six-year-old dairy farmer, to make an early start that morning to deliver milk in and around Lawrence. In the midst of this, he spied a large party of horsemen on the move but assumed unwittingly—like most of his neighbors—that the mounted party was simply the "Second Kansas" on patrol and went about his business. Shortly thereafter, he recalled, the riders suddenly broke formation and then moved through the town from opposite directions. As these unnamed strangers opened fire, the milk seemed suddenly less important. Gunshots rang out, and William likened the cacophony of pistols to "several firecrackers gone off all at once." Very quickly, he and his customers realized, or so he claimed, that Quantrill's notorious band of Missouri bushwhackers were on the prowl in Lawrence.[23]

Though probably stunned by the morning's turn of events, William warned a nearby neighbor of the pending danger. Much to his surprise, though, this particular man—a storekeeper named Dulinski—ignored such warnings and countered haughtily that Quantrill's men were his friends; they might raise hell in Lawrence, but they would do him no harm. Leaving the impudent Dulinski behind, William instructed another neighbor, named Ginerich, to "ride for his life" and raise an alarm along the way. True to his word, Ginerich rode to another townsman, John Connelly, and beseeched him to warn the citizens of nearby Clinton. More cautious than Ginerich, Connelly refused. On the edges of town, other panicked scenes overlaid a gruesome soundtrack of hooves thundering, percussion caps exploding, the pleading of women, and men gasping their last as they died. A young woman, Sally Young, rode toward Lawrence on horseback. An "old preacher" begged her to halt and take shelter. For reasons unexplained, the steadfast Young replied that she "would go if she was killed for it" and spurred her horse forward.[24]

Perhaps emboldened by the young woman's resolve, William next rushed to the house of a local militia captain some six miles south of Lawrence and then to another captain's residence eight miles southwest of the besieged town. By the time approximately nineteen men had been assembled to offer some form of resistance, the guerrillas were already making their exit. At this point, it dawned on William to return home. He found his house charred and empty. After a hasty trek to the nearby Longley residence, he found his wife, Jane, alive and well, the situation notwithstanding. Despite Mrs. Longley's pleas, however, guerrillas had pummeled and then shot her husband five times. He died later that day. Though William never admitted as much to Connelley, had he cancelled or even delayed his morning departure it seems unlikely he would have lived to tell the tale.[25]

All around town, a fine line seemed to separate the lucky from the dead. One elderly citizen, known to locals as "Grandpa Holmes," locked horns with a guerrilla and miraculously survived. When one of Quantrill's men stood ready to gun Holmes down, the old man suddenly wrestled away his revolver and pitched it over a nearby fence. This sudden burst of courage enraged his would-be assailant, who proceeded to beat Holmes savagely. Nevertheless, fists trumped bullets as the guerrilla mistakenly left the old man for dead. Far less fortunate was Dulinski. He had fatally misgauged the depth of his relationship with Quantrill's men. When a small detachment of bushwhackers ordered him to line up along a nearby fence rail, the previously cocksure shopkeeper started to lose his appetite for fast friends and danger. Failure to comply would cost him dearly. In an inebriated state, the raiders shot their former "friend" dead on the spot. According to William, who concluded his brief narrative on a hypothetical note, had the guerrillas not executed Dulinski, the townsfolk of Lawrence would have probably killed him anyway, on account of his traitorous behavior.[26]

A Wife Intervenes

William Brown was not the only immigrant who remembered the day Quantrill and his band of "notorious criminals" took the town by storm. Wilhelm Kroll (better known as William Kroll to his American friends and neighbors) was born in 1829 in Koblenz, Germany, along the ship-laden banks of the Rhine. Aboard the *Fidelia*, he left Germany for the United

States in late 1852 to escape the scornful gaze of unhappy in-laws; his wife of three years, Margaretha, and the couple's two-year-old daughter, Lena, joined him in New York in 1854. Later in the 1850s, while living in Kansas City, the Krolls owned and operated a mercantile business on the Missouri River. Long-simmering racial troubles in Kansas City momentarily boiled over when Wilhelm rented the second floor of the family storehouse to African American dance organizers; when a disgruntled master attempted to whip a slave who had snuck off to attend the party, Wilhelm interfered on behalf of the slave. Soon after, someone set fire to the building. Wilhelm got the message and by 1860 had moved his family to Lawrence, Kansas—a locality more in line with their antislavery attitude. In 1860 and 1863, Wilhelm and Margaretha welcomed the births of two boys—Louie and Edward, respectively—both of whom would survive the infamous Lawrence Massacre as infants.[27]

It took more than a century for any written version of Wilhelm Kroll's narrative to surface; before his death, Wilhelm passed an oral account of the story to his son, Edward, who then relayed it to his own daughter, Ruth. Ruth Kroll—by then known as Mrs. E. L. Cochran—donated the account to the State Historical Society of Missouri in 1967. Oral transmission followed by years of dormancy did not strip the story of lurid detail. According to the Kroll family narrative, Kansas had long been harassed by "bands of guerrilla raiders" and "outlaws from far and near." But in 1863 William Quantrill determined to "wipe out Lawrence" once and for all. Early on the morning of August 21, Quantrill and more than four hundred of his men—"all mounted and heavily armed, grim, dirty, drunken without mercy"—fell on the antislavery stronghold and commenced to slaughtering twenty-one Union soldiers encamped there. Some of the soldiers were trampled to death in their beds by guerrillas on horseback, while others were shot down as they emerged, half asleep, from tents to investigate the sudden commotion.[28]

After finishing off this small military installation, Quantrill and his company, which included the Jameses, Youngers, and Yeagers, "rode through the little town, killing, looting, burning, and shooting as they went." Wilhelm and Margaretha were awakened suddenly by a scout. Their first reaction was to wait out the raid in the safety of their basement. That plan met a quick end: guerrillas set the Kroll residence ablaze. After literally smoking Wilhelm out of his home, the raiders apprehended him at gunpoint. He, along with six other Kansans, was "lined up, backs to a wall or building, and shot." In the instant that powder became smoke, Wilhelm's body slumped to the ground. But the bullet had only grazed his skull and, before the guerrillas could discover his possum act, Margaretha began dragging her husband's "corpse" away from the melee, wailing and moaning all the while to deflect their attention. She hid him under a feather bed and was "not molested further" on account of her carrying on. Owing much to his wife's acting prowess, Wilhelm remained safely hidden until the attack ended. He did, however, recall becoming so overheated and thirsty that he resorted to drinking his own sweat.[29]

As the horrific sequence of events began to unfold around their household, the Kroll children—ages twelve years, three years, and three and a half months—were whisked away and hidden along a nearby river. (The account makes no mention of who actually spirited the children to safety.) But as Margaretha struggled desperately to save her husband's life, she did so under the macabre assumption that her children had been burned alive in the fire that had driven them from the basement. Only after the raid did she discover their true whereabouts.

By mid-morning, Quantrill and his men exited Lawrence; behind them, they left a ghastly scene: "the bodies of men, some of them partially burned away, were lying in all directions." Nearly everything in the Krolls' store had been stolen or scorched—what remained was given as aid to survivors of the massacre. One such survivor, a quick-witted local boy, had allegedly saved his life by posing as a Confederate sympathizer; as one of Quantrill's men tied his horse to begin pillaging a home, the boy offered to hold a fellow rebel's horse. As soon as he had taken the reins, the nameless youth leapt onto the horse and sped away to safety. Most of the business district in Lawrence, along with dozens of homes, had been torched, and "the moaning and crying of the grief-stricken people was heard from all sides." Even weeks after the raid, residents of Lawrence remained overly suspicious of another attack. When a burning haystack caused a young boy to sound a false alarm, townspeople used boats to cross the river and fled wholesale into surrounding thickets.[30]

Despite their hardships, the Kroll family remained in Kansas and prospered. In 1866 and 1869 they welcomed two new additions to the family, Nellie and Ida, and by 1870 the Krolls boasted a net worth of $5,500. Wilhelm died in 1887 at the age of fifty-eight, but Margaretha survived and told their story for almost another thirty years. According to her grand-daughter, she had always "pined for the old country," but the outbreak of World War I nixed any chance of ever returning.[31]

Cleaning Up "the Dutch"

Horns touted a frantic alarm: "bushwhackers were in sight." The fast-approaching guerrilla unit, resolute in their desire to "clean up the Dutch," had spent the previous night in nearby woods. Louis Meyer's narrative recalled that an equally determined cohort of German immigrants, fiercely loyal to the Union, nervously laid in wait for the guerrillas along a wooded road. The "bushwhackers," as Louis tagged them, all rode "fine black race horses" and called to mind "a set of demons just simply a-flyin."[32] The impending collision of arms and ideologies that he dubbed "The Battle at Emma, Missouri" easily rivaled the intensity of violence inherent to any major engagement in the East. "There was a struggle," Louis wrote, "which no pen can describe." By his count, the freshly dispatched corpses of twenty-five German men littered the road—now the site of their ambush gone awry. The bodies of the dead had been mutilated, each skull method-ically crushed by musket or club. True to their intention, the guerrillas had left no wounded to tend.[33] While graphic, such exchanges between pro-Confederate guerrillas and pro-Union Germans were not uncommon. As outsiders in a border state already torn asunder by internal division, Meyer and his countrymen struggled to assimilate smoothly. Many guer-rillas despised the presence of German immigrants—whom they crudely labeled "the Dutch"—for a pair of interconnected reasons. Foremost, they hated the Germans because they were German. Moreover, many German families, like the ones Louis referred to in his recollections, had not been in the United States long before siding with the Union. In the eyes of Mis-souri's Confederate guerrillas, these Germans amounted to an intruding horde of foreign mercenaries and economic competitors.

Louis A. Meyer was born in Saline County, Missouri, in 1853. His par-ents, August Meyer and the former Henrietta C. Walkenhorst, had each been born in Hannover, Germany. August immigrated to the United States in 1848, and Henrietta arrived shortly thereafter, in 1850. Census records confirm that the Meyers lived in the area with several other German fami-lies, and, like most of the first- and second-generation German residents of

Saline County, they were farmers. With little love for slavery or the peculiar institution's tendency to stifle the free labor of industrious immigrants, they remained steadfast for the Union as war broke out between the states. On November 6, 1878, Louis married Maria Ehlers, who would be his wife for forty-nine years. Maria, or Mary as she came to be known, was the daughter of Christian Heinrich Ehlers and the former Christina Evert. She was born in Lafayette, Missouri, in 1862, but both of her parents hailed from Hannover, Germany. Christian, known as Henry in Louis's account, arrived in New York aboard the *Vanhiesdorldt* on July 2, 1846. Though Mary was several years younger than her husband—too young, in fact, to recall anything of the events he described firsthand—her father played an unfortunately tragic role in the story.[34]

According to Louis's story, written in the early 1920s, hostilities between local Germans and Confederate guerrillas first boiled over amid the sweltering summer heat of 1862. The neighborhood's Unionist homeguard implicated a local man for heisting dry goods. Rather than turn the suspected pilferer over to law enforcement, guardsmen executed him on the spot. The owner of the dry goods store had been a German man named Meineke; the brother of the accused (and executed) thief swore an oath of vengeance against the entire local "Dutch" population. Not long after, "the raids began." On July 13, 1862, an initial retaliatory raid had produced four German corpses. On October 5, 1862, a German baptismal party was ceremoniously lined up and shot. Only the hysterical pleading of his wife spared the presiding reverend the fate of his congregants. As grievous as the events seemed to Louis and his neighbors, the German community of Saline County had not yet seen the worst. The raids continued for another two years.[35]

On August 14, 1864, guerrillas struck particularly close to home. In the process of ransacking a hemp factory, they gunned down the facility's owner. The deceased, Henry C. Ehlers, would have become Louis's father-in-law in 1878. "The last raid and the worst one" came weeks later, on October 10, 1864. Louis attributed the attack to the "Guandrel [Quantrill] gang," which had "committed the most horrible atrocities the world ever heard of during the war." Women shrieked and sobbed as they fought in vain to hinder the "beasts" from "assaulting them." Neither daylight nor public setting did much to temper the guerrillas' sexual advances. "All women were criminally attacked, some had to serve five men." Old age offered little in the way of refuge. "Some old women were 75 years old, but were still attacked." More than a dozen houses were put to the torch; an old man, attempting to wait out the raid in the secrecy of his corn crib, was literally "roasted alive." Along with the elderly, the infirm were offered no quarter. A debilitated man was simply shot in bed as his home blazed and collapsed around him. All told, twenty-three men, almost all of them German, fell slaughtered in the barrage.[36]

In the wake of all the burning, killing, rape, and plunder, the German residents of Saline County were, quite understandably, traumatized. A state of fear and paranoia henceforth governed the community's activities—husbands and fathers kept watch with regularity, families coalesced to find strength in numbers, and some even took to a life of exile, hiding out in the forest full-time. Louis's memory of the final raid also brought the narrative full circle: in their state of heightened alertness, the Germans scouted a party of guerrillas, signaled their approach by horn, and waited for what they must have thought would be a viable surprise attack. As we already know, they were badly mistaken—fatally so, in fact. The blood-stained events of their childhoods notwithstanding, Louis and Mary Meyer refused to abandon Missouri after the war. Still living in one of Saline County's heavily German neighborhoods, Louis died in 1927. Mary—in spite of delivering the couple's thirteen children—lived considerably longer. She died in 1951 at the age of eighty-nine.[37]

Encounters with the Hometown Militia

Penned in 1877, the narrative of James H. Rigg chronicled the plight of another neighborhood gripped by fear, partisan division, and appalling violence; one where "strife" reigned in "nearly every household." Born in 1842—and therefore of prime age for service when the war broke out—James lived on his father's farm in Montgomery County, Missouri. Though many of the Riggs' neighbors angrily deemed the election of Abraham Lincoln an unconstitutional act of war against the proslavery South, James's father, John, a Virginia transplant born in 1814, found no illegality in Lincoln's ascension to the presidency.[38] The Rigg farm, while not extravagant, afforded the family a decent living. In 1860 census records indicate that John, along with his wife, the former Thomasin E. Hunter of Saint Louis, Missouri, owned $1,560 in real estate and possessed a personal estate worth $610. They had lost their other three children in infancy (1840, 1846, and 1849). Thus, with the well-being of his only son and property in mind, John Rigg seemed content to sit out the war, though his family's neutrality may have represented siding with the Union to many of their more radical neighbors.[39]

According to James, everything changed when Union troopers murdered a group of outspoken, pro-Confederate neighbors in 1861. The Missouri State Militia, the group responsible, was commanded, he submitted, by "low, vile men" who "delighted in fighting unarmed citizens"—the sort of men who made careers of pillaging, arson, and murder. In an effort to isolate James from such nefarious characters, his father shipped him off to boarding school. Draft registration records from 1863 to 1865 listed James as eligible for conscription but do not indicate that he was ever called to duty. His schooling kept him out of the service as planned but actually did little to spare him encounters with the state militia. Still on the warpath, James next offers that the militia gunned down Reverend George L. Sexton for preaching in a pro-secession neighborhood. Though shot and left for dead, Sexton managed to survive the night. Militiamen revisited the wounded preacher the next morning; he did not live to describe their second meeting.[40]

Militia had driven bushwhackers from their homes in Montgomery County. Each man, armed nearly to the teeth, carried a heavy rifle and three to five Colt Navy revolvers. James alleged that a fluke encounter with these outcast guerrillas landed him on a shortlist of suspected pro-Confederate spies; as he rode alone down a rural back road, the militia was quite pleased to intercept him. Now in the militia's custody, he was taken to the house of Colonel Tate, a well-known Confederate sympathizer. Unfortunately for the colonel, his daughters were present for the unwelcome visit. Violations of feminine honor "to [sic] obscene" for James to fully describe in good conscience took place as militiamen caught sight of the "two intelligent and beautiful young ladies there." One of the girls was "brought out into the yard by four men and her clothing stripped off her while twenty or thirty men stood by laughing and screaming with delight." "At the same time," the colonel's second daughter "was being abused in the house."[41]

Suddenly the militia's picket sounded a warning: a company of bushwhackers was advancing toward the Tate residence. Their debauchery cut short, the militiamen plundered what they could from the house before beating a hasty retreat. They made off with clothing, gold, jewelry, silverware, razors, spectacles, knives, scissors, and an assortment of other domestic valuables. Despite his claim that "such things were occurring in every neighborhood almost every day," the drama of that afternoon stuck out in particular, likely because "the militia were frightened away from here before they committed an actual murder." And, in a twist of fate too ironic for fabrication, the nearing force that militia pickets had spied—the group of rough-and-ready Confederate bushwhackers that had inadvertently saved the lives of James, Colonel Tate, and his family—turned out to be an unarmed funeral procession. Though he had momentarily found good fortune, James and the Missouri State Militia would meet again shortly.[42]

Returning from Readsville—the second leg of a trip to procure medicine for his bedridden mother—James posed that he and his riding companion, an old man named Jones, were waylaid by militiamen. In the heat of the moment, James was thrown roughly from his mount, Royal Charlie. Knocked unconscious by the fall, he vaguely remembered his attackers lifting both his watch and, more importantly, the medicine before leaving him for dead. As he regained his senses, a morbid scene awaited him. The "poor old man" was "lying on his back in a pool of blood." His former companion's white hair was "clotted with gore." Mr. Jones was "entirely dead." Not a single bullet had touched James. The incident later appeared in the local newspaper, where headlines touted a great victory. Militia leaders reported the attack as a crushing blow against a large force of Confederate bushwhackers.[43]

Though a younger man at the time of his trouble with the militia and still only in his thirties when he set them to paper, James summed up his wartime experience with concise clarity: "These were days of terror." Moreover, he claimed only to tell of "what occurred in our own neighborhood." "In other sections of the state," he continued, things had been "much worse." He measured terror in peculiar units—from the number of homes burned to the degrees of suffering shared by men, women, and children. Such dark times a decade behind him, James married Susan A. Snethen in 1874, and the couple had two children, William and James Jr. Both boys labored on the Rigg family farm from which their father had fled to avoid the war. After surviving numerous run-ins with the Missouri State Militia, James H. Rigg died in 1924, outliving Susan by two years.[44]

Massacres and Breakfast

On September 27, 1864, another unusually large band of Confederate guerrillas, this time under the direction of William "Bloody Bill" Anderson, collided with Union soldiers on two separate occasions. Each meeting ended in massacre. The first encounter involved Anderson and approximately eighty of his men. In the process of disrupting rail traffic in Centralia, Missouri, Anderson and company captured a passenger coach belonging to the North Missouri Railroad. Aboard were some twenty to thirty Union soldiers, almost all of whom were promptly removed from the train and executed. A placard near the site of the old depot in Centralia contends that the Federals were not armed and therefore were unnecessarily murdered. Regardless, the event marked only the beginning of a bloody day for Union men stationed in the area. Later that afternoon, Bloody Bill and a much larger force of guerrillas—between three and five hundred—sprang a lethal trap on members of the Thirty-Ninth Missouri Infantry. Anderson and his men used dense foliage and a network of deep creek beds to conceal their mass along three sides of an open field. Meanwhile, a smaller group of guerrillas intentionally provoked the Thirty-Ninth into chase and lured them into the field. Led by Anderson, the guerrillas poured from the tree line and caught the Federals in a deadly vice. In the face of guerrillas charging rapidly on horseback, Union companies dismounted to make their final stand with single-shot carbines. For nearly all of them (including the major in charge), the decision proved fatal. Between 120 and 150 Union soldiers were killed in the rout.[45]

Mary E. Lakenan's recollections of these events, what she called "The Bill Anderson Massacre," were remarkable in two ways. First, with the exception of Lawrence, the majority of guerrilla raids—though typically smaller than the action at Centralia—lacked written accounts, especially when so few potential witnesses had survived to produce them. The second and much more engaging reason is that Mary was born in 1886, more than two decades after hostilities at Centralia had ceased. She was the only child of Theodore J. Lakenan of Callaway County, Missouri, and the former Miss Henrietta Cauthorn of Virginia. The couple married in 1883 and celebrated the birth of their daughter Mary in Mineral, Colorado, three years later. Mary's alleged memory of Bill Anderson and the violence at Centralia undoubtedly stemmed from her father's knowledge of the bloodletting. But although Theodore was nineteen years old in 1864 and virtually lived next door to the battlefield in neighboring Callaway County, he had not witnessed any of the fighting, either.[46]

At the time of the massacres, he lived on a farm owned by his father, Joseph G. Lakenan. In addition to Theodore, Joseph and his wife, Mary (for whom Mary E. is presumably named), had three daughters, all his juniors. Joseph owned an impressive $8,000 of real estate in Callaway County—a net worth that might explain how his only son avoided any discernible military service. However he avoided soldiering, the federal census published in 1860 listed his occupation as "ranchman."[47] As his work on the farm kept him close to home, it makes sense that Theodore, along with his father, would have been around to hear the harrowing tale of a bedraggled Union soldier who randomly happened on the Lakenan family doorstep—and on September 28, 1865, just a day after the massacres, no less. In exchange for a hot breakfast, the battle-weary Federal—apparently convinced that he was the only survivor of the previous day's second conflict—relayed his account of the ambush, the ensuing slaughter, and his narrow escape.[48] In this capacity, Mary Lakenan's narrative constitutes a sort of family oral history, albeit a secondhand one. That notwithstanding, it would be a mistake to quickly dismiss the account for want of a firsthand genesis. Regardless of how Theodore and then Mary came upon or formed their memories of the massacres, they believed, internalized, and preserved them just the same. However detached in terms of physical reality Mary might have been from the fighting of September 27, 1864, when she chose to record her father's boyhood reminiscences for future progeny, the account still constituted the way she and members of her family had remembered the war in Missouri for decades.

The unnamed narrator began his version of what transpired that day with a less-than-glowing description of the guerrillas' commander, the aforementioned Bloody Bill Anderson. He labeled Anderson a "desperado" hell-bent on revenge—an implication likely meant to strip him and his guerrilla fighters of ideological credibility. As previously noted, one of Anderson's sisters had died when a Union prison collapsed in Kansas City, Missouri, about two weeks before the Lawrence Massacre. According to the Federal, George Todd, another prominent guerrilla lieutenant, had gone at Anderson's request to meet the trainload of doomed soldiers at the depot in Centralia. Todd and the other guerrillas mercilessly mowed down the Union troops as they stepped from the abducted coach. (That the soldier was alive and able to break bread with the Lakenans in the first place would indicate he had clearly not attended the day's first massacre personally.)[49]

After their successful raid, Anderson and his men chose to fight the responding companies of Union soldiers in a nearby field. Before chaos descended, Anderson barked at his guerrillas to "hold their horses' reins in their teeth and to charge the enemy." They lurched forward "with a revolver in each hand, riding around and around in circles, shooting with both guns." Against such an audacious charge, the Lakenan's soldier fled and never looked back. Assuming no other men had escaped the assault, the runaway Union soldier managed to hide in the woods. He spent a painfully long night in the forest before creeping up to the Lakenan home, swapping a story for breakfast, and then apparently returning to the army.[50] In truth, between twelve and twenty-four men probably survived the attack. Even today, exact figures are suspect.

Records indicate that Theodore and Henrietta Lakenan were married on October 9, 1883, in Audrain County, Missouri. By 1886, though, they had relocated to Colorado, which had only been a state for ten years. In 1910, when Theodore died at the age of sixty-five, the family had been living in Boulder, Colorado. Though alive at the time of Theodore's passing, Henrietta subsequently disappeared from census records; her date of death is simply not available. Data published in 1920 places Mary, thirty-three years old and unmarried, in Manhattan, New York, where she lived in a boardinghouse and taught school. Though her original account is not dated, it seems likely that she first produced a hard copy during this period. She died in 1981 at the old age of ninety-five in Crossville, Tennessee—but her memory of "The Bill Anderson Massacre" lives on.[51]

Assessing Trauma and Processes of "Repair"

Where even the most detailed chronicle of life extinguished or domesticity shattered may fall short of recapturing the truly intimate traumas of guerrilla warfare, patterns derived of individual memory nonetheless make up an intellectual atlas of the afflicted. Dissected in terms of time, place, space, and authorial self-conception, these narratives—equal parts rancor, heartbreak, and crippling anxiety—unwittingly yield the inner workings of a process through which vulnerable human beings, made so by years of unprecedented suffering, produced and preserved meticulously detailed and intricate memories.

At their most geographically expansive moments, these stories culminate in settings of town or county. More often than not, they recall events anchored to the most local of settings. They are the tales of a war as told by individuals representing communities within communities—the milk route of an Irish immigrant interrupted by massacre; the paranoia of a German neighborhood nearly annihilated by its own desperation; the frantic attempts of a wife to save her spouse from a violent end; the misfortunes of a young man drawn calamitously closer and closer to death by his own attempts to escape military service; and the random genesis of an oral history shrouded in mystery but proudly adopted and sustained by one family for almost a century.

From this vantage point, the space used by each vignette, as a slice of the guerrilla war, represented a conscious choice in which the architect of a memory narrative determined an appropriate unit of measure. Linked directly to these spatial parameters were culturally constructed conceptions of place. Battles from Manassas to Gettysburg to Chickamauga— now ground revered by visitors en masse—unfolded in the fields of *someone's* farm, but the specific farmers or families themselves are typically irrelevant to subsequent annals of victory, defeat, valor, and soldierly sacrifice. The guerrilla war, by contrast, was born in and thrived on exactly that type of personalized environment, one in which a single man or family might be remembered for generations because of blood spilled in a garden, back porch, field, or barn. Such an unusual proximity of combat space to personal place—place being theoretically defined as a locale like "home," to which individuals attached themselves via deeply cultural, personal bonds—resulted in a war fought more on (and to the detriment of) the borderland's domestic territory than anywhere else in the divided nation.

Among this upended backdrop of homes and hamlets ravaged by lawlessness and bushwhacking, extraordinary levels of ethnic tension and the presence of women further alienated the experiences of those touched by guerrilla warfare from their enlisted counterparts. Unlike soldiers operating under the authority of a government-installed commander or moving (albeit often badly) in strategic unison with other wings of the army, overly independent guerrilla combatants were often left to choose for themselves who or what constituted an enemy target worth striking. Freedom in the form of mobility allowed specific neighborhoods, many of them ethnically arranged—such as Louis Meyer's predominantly German community—to become the frequent destinations of revenge-seeking bushwhackers not personally beholden to a wider war effort. Simultaneously, the random quality of guerrilla tactics—from roadside ambush to raids on homes and churches—also provided for what, at least on the surface, seems a strange gender dynamic. On one hand, besides the occasional nurse or high-ranking officer's wife, publicized clashes between bulky armies in the regular theater of war did not directly involve women intentionally in the line of fire. Therein, mothers, sisters, and wives were not normally present when their sons, brothers, or husbands were killed in action. On the other hand, as was made painfully clear by memories of the irregular war—Meyer's, Kroll's, and Brown's especially—women in the guerrilla theater frequently stood by and suffered alongside men on the front lines even as body counts surged at an alarming rate.

Relative to common narratives of the Civil War, then, the by-product of this formula was a savage and abnormally domestic variety of violence. Initially spurred to saddle and gun by some semblance of ideological allegiance to the Union or Confederacy, the unique circumstances of guerrilla warfare temporarily transformed men. Fighting in the presence of (and often for the lives of) their wives and children, or even just against a long-hated "foreigner," previously peaceful farmers, clerks, and ranchers apparently found the motivation to mutilate corpses, execute church congregations, and gang-rape women. Presented in this context—as a series of anomalous atrocities from the furthest reaches of civilized society—the guerrilla war was a self-contained phenomenon fought in but somehow separately from the *real* Civil War, with its plethora of honorable subplots and its heralded heroes.

But if the narratives of William Brown, Wilhelm Kroll, Mary Lakenan, Louis Meyer, and James Rigg are in any way bizarre or exceptional, it is only for the fact that they intentionally recall, with vivid detail, the absolutely nastiest bits of the Civil War. In this sense, of equal if not greater import is what these vignettes do not recollect or, perhaps more appropriately, what they do not attempt to fabricate. Granted, they do all highlight experiences that most newly reunited Americans would have just as soon buried alongside the dead and that more than a few probably lacked the psychological stability to stomach unfiltered. But none make any appreciable effort to locate, insert, or otherwise dilute the experiences of war as remembered within prevalent (and admittedly tempting) narratives of the regular war that stressed gentlemanly honor, female valor on the homefront, mutually earned commemoration, and eventually reconciliation. Rather than burying the very worst of what could be remembered about the war, they preserved it. In doing so, they maintained a local, noncollective remembrance in the face of more collective, statewide, or national narratives that might have helped mitigate and even censor the brutalities of the guerrilla war for posterity. That said, given the postwar scenarios that faced many ex-guerrillas and their families, their memories would probably appear stranger had they immediately tried to forget about or whitewash the previous five years.

Returning home from distant battlefields, possibly missing an arm, leg, or eye, and trying to forget about or block out the gruesome particulars of a past full of suffering, death, and possibly defeat was one thing. At worst, veterans of the regular war—even the losers—could glean solace from powerful mythologies, fraternal organizations, and support networks designed after the fact to make sense of and validate their sacrifices. But forgetting about a husband murdered, a house put to the torch, a church congregation executed, or a daughter raped by assailants who still lived down the road—if not next door—was another matter.

In February 1871 the *Leavenworth Bulletin* reported on just such a case. Conover Ainsworth, a former Kansas jayhawker, professed his love to a woman from Jackson County, Missouri. The young lady—whose name the paper redacted from the story—angrily rebuffed Ainsworth's "tender passions." Apparently, he had personally burned down her pro-Confederate family's home during the war; seven years later, she did not forgive or forget. "The rejection, combined, doubtless, with many a bloody memory he would gladly obliterate, so worked upon the fiery jayhawker of the past, that, in a fit of despair, he ended his life." Ainsworth took a bottle of poison "almost in sight of the spot where the adventure we have alluded to occurred," pulled the stop, and imbibed for the last time.[52]

To many of the men, women, and children in Missouri and Kansas who took in and fought the Civil War from their porch steps, the guerrilla war and its aftermath represented the status quo as they knew it—and neither the signatures of Robert E. Lee and Joseph E. Johnston, nor the efforts of later partisan propagandists, could wipe clean such a backlog of intensely personal violence. As such, the authors of these vignettes essentially bypassed the quickest means of superficially rehabilitating their grim wartime records. Instead of consciously re-remembering a different version of the war as many would have liked to imagine it, they remembered their own versions of the war—the war that was "regular" to them as they had experienced it. However, as the following chapters will illuminate, this phenomenon would not stop a range of other interested parties from trying to re-remember the war *for them.*

TWO

An Irregular Lost Cause

> And then he swore us on the Bible to be faithful to the State of
> Missouri and drive all invaders from her soil, no matter whence they
> might come or under what flag they might march. This mixed us
> considerably, and we could not make out just what service we were
> embarked in; but Colonel Ralls, the practiced politician and phrase-
> juggler, was not similarly in doubt; he knew quite clearly that he had
> invested us in the cause of the Southern Confederacy.
> —Mark Twain, "The Private History of a Campaign That Failed"

Of pro-Confederate guerrillas in the Missouri-Kansas borderlands, pug-
nacious newspaperman-turned-author John Newman Edwards had this
to say:

> He saw that he was hunted and proscribed; that he had neither a flag nor a
> government; that the rights and amenities of civilized warfare were not to be
> his; that a dog's death was certain if he surrendered even in the extremest
> agony of battle; that the house which sheltered him had to be burnt; the father
> who succored him had to be butchered; the mother who prayed for him had
> to be insulted; the sister who carried food to him had to be imprisoned; the
> neighborhood which witnessed his combats had to be laid waste; the comrade
> shot down by his side had to be put to death as a wild beast—and he lifted up
> the black flag in self-defence and fought as became a free man and a hero.[1]

After taking this statement into account—with its seemingly firsthand
knowledge of irregular trauma—it might surprise more than a few readers to learn that Edwards was not himself a guerrilla, at least not as we
typically conceptualize them. During the war, he rode with Confederate
general Joseph Orville Shelby, not the likes of Quantrill, Anderson, or
Holtzclaw. Edwards raided no homes; he lit no torches at Lawrence, took
no scalps at Centralia, nor did he hoist any black flags. Yet, as author of
Noted Guerrillas, or, The Warfare of the Border (from which the excerpt above
is taken) the former cavalryman's expertise was anything but regular or
official.

As soon as the war ended, ex-Confederates took to the production of commemorative propaganda. They churned out histories that apotheosized Robert E. Lee, Thomas "Stonewall" Jackson, Albert Sydney Johnston, and other elite characters, to help cope, at least on paper, with a society shattered by hundreds of thousands dead and an economy ruined by the demise of slavery. But Edwards tread on ground where other architects of memory dared not ply their commemorative trades. In his writing throughout the 1870s, peaking with the publication of *Noted Guerrillas* in 1877, Edwards focused gaze and pen on arguably the rowdiest, most reviled figures the Civil War had to offer: Missouri's pro-Confederate bushwhackers. For them, he proclaimed, "there was no funeral."[2] But to further his partisan agenda, he had much more than a funeral in mind— he would sculpt their legacy to accouter Missouri with its own "irregular" Lost Cause. In the arena of postwar memory politics, John Newman Edwards *did* hoist the black flag; here, he was every bit the guerrilla.

The notoriety of guerrillas such as William Quantrill, Bloody Bill Anderson, and Jesse James notwithstanding, Edwards stood virtually alone in utilizing their memory as a combined cultural-political tool in the 1870s. Historians have generally presented the efforts of southern whites to explain the war and culturally restore the region as a consolidated movement—"the Lost Cause"—that revolved around a standard set of ideas and characters. As such accounts often go, in the early 1870s a core faction of upper-crust southerners, coxswained by Virginians, stepped forward to lift the spirits of despondent southerners and, more importantly, to halt the social and cultural changes unleashed by Confederate defeat that were eroding the antebellum powers of elite planters—that is, *their own* antebellum powers.

With ex-Confederate general Jubal Early at the helm, these Virginians founded the Southern Historical Society (SHS) in 1869 and, in 1876, began publishing the *Southern Historical Society Papers* (SHSP). Under the guise of history, they worked to establish a metanarrative of the war starring key protagonists such as Lee and Jackson. Southerners could point to these heroes as idols of manly virtue and martial valor in efforts to convince themselves that such attributes had been worth the fight. For their part, SHS organizers, many of whom were former commanders themselves, could invoke the increasingly legendary profiles of Lee, Jackson, and company to explain defeat on face-saving terms. Essentially, Early and his copropagandists held that the Confederacy had fallen in defense of antebellum southern culture and envisioned themselves as the keepers of its legacy. In short, they were the guardians of a cause lost but not forgotten—unless, of course, an occasional bout of "selective amnesia" suited their purpose, as General James Longstreet learned the hard way.[3]

At first glance, Edwards seems merely to have been shifting attention from one group of dedicated Confederates to another, the former based in the Eastern Theater, the latter in Missouri. But as Twain's amusing case of confusing allegiances makes clear in the epigraph, the issue of the state's status within Dixie required sorting out—or "phrase juggling," as Twain might put it—prior to any meaningful junction with the Lost Cause movement. Geographically, Missouri did not just represent a crossroads—it *was* a crossroads of the South and the West. This arrangement instilled in its residents a hybrid sense of culture; a medley of southern traditions conformed to the realities of western frontier life. It also greatly complicated Missouri's regional status after the war. Here pro-Confederates had openly dedicated themselves to the cause in a state on the outskirts of the Deep South that never seceded from the Union and in which a majority of able-bodied men had voluntarily donned the Union blue. Without the shared experience of secession or a similar wartime narrative, Missouri essentially lacked the bond of nationalism that otherwise connected—for better or worse—the eleven states of the fallen Confederate nation. Thus its shortfall of wartime credibility left the door open for the state to be seen as a western outsider, as a Unionist imposter, or perhaps both.[4] As ex-Rebels throughout the South coalesced and took stock of their situations, especially with regard to political reclamation, Missourians faced the very real possibility of ostracism.[5]

Reexamined in the light of this identity crisis, partisan intent runs rampant through Edwards's melodramatic prose. The missing funeral he decried was actually a commemorative lacuna—and not simply for Missouri's overlooked guerrilla warriors, but for the state itself. Beneath his literary sleight of hand lurked a significant payload, half cultural, half political: he penned *Noted Guerrillas* to aid Missouri's pro-Confederate minority in their (and his) postbellum struggle to secure a heritage that would ensure the continuation of antebellum connections to the proslavery wing of the Democratic Party. But such a process required much more than providing Missourians with an assemblage of folk heroes or extracting moral victories from defeat. It entailed assimilation; it entailed overcoming the stigma of wartime Unionism; it entailed becoming southern by way of retroactively joining the Confederate States of America.[6]

To achieve these ends, Edwards designed and deployed explanations for defeat that underscored the dedication of bushwhackers to the Confederate cause by actually detaching them from its government and, as a result, from a war department unwilling to attain victory by any means necessary. He also conjured a variant construct of southern honor that prioritized justified homicide and killing efficiency. Earning honor the guerrilla way meant taking life up close and without hesitation or remorse. These concepts gave bushwhackers free reign to kill and destroy throughout the pages of *Noted Guerrillas* in ways that would not have been immediately familiar to eastern audiences. And by Edwards's logic, they were why guerrillas had no "flag" and claimed not the "rights of civilized warfare": doing anything—anywhere—to win the war cost guerrillas the ability to be treated like regular combatants, but such a sacrifice made them the most diehard Confederates of all. Even "honorable soldiers" in the regular Confederate army seemed to recognize the distinction. Many deserted, Edwards offered in the book, to "become desperate guerrillas" that they might "avoid the uncertainty of regular battle and know by actual results how many died as a propitiation or a sacrifice."[7]

From the start, Edwards's grand, cohesive narrative—one tailor-made to vouch for a linear, Confederate fighting past—belied the fundamental realities of household warfare and the fractured environment of remembrance it produced in Missouri. After all, it was the failures of people such as James Rigg and Louis Meyer, along with other untold veterans of the guerrilla theater to recall their experiences collectively that prompted Edwards to fabricate commemorative uniformity in the first place. This chapter delves beneath that uniformity to recover the blueprints of Missouri's irregular Lost Cause and, in doing so, makes sense of the political struggles that necessitated them. Before beginning our excavation, I would only ask that we keep this in mind: no matter how sonorous his efforts to reimagine war in the guerrilla theater for his readers, the end result of Edwards's maneuvering and manipulating of memory was, and remains, inherently and deliberately misleading. We must not lose sight of these facts when reading between the lines of *Noted Guerrillas*, because to forget them is precisely how Edwards intended for us to remember.

Portrait of John Newman Edwards, circa 1870s.
Though a former member of Confederate general
Joseph O. Shelby's Iron Brigade, Edwards appeared
as a respected newspaperman and political
pundit in the 1870s. Image from Jennie Edwards,
ed., *John Newman Edwards: Biography, Memoir,
Reminiscences, and Recollections.* Kansas City, Mo.:
Jennie Edwards, 1889.

Organizing Causes

The Southern Historical Society employed a simple strategy. Step 1: elevate a top-down coterie of venerable ex-Confederates to folk hero status. Step 2: as part of the glorification process, detach these figures from responsibility for defeat, physical ruination, and hundreds of thousands of lives snuffed out. General Robert E. Lee sat atop this hierarchy, while contemporaries such as Thomas "Stonewall" Jackson, Nathan Bedford Forrest, Albert Sydney Johnston, and James E. B. "Jeb" Stuart followed him in a line of succession that lauded cavalier officers and aristocratic planters as the ultimate embodiments of southern manhood, honor, and masculine self-worth. From the beginning, this memorial propaganda likened upper-echelon officers to Christian crusaders who had defended the South in its time of greatest peril; moreover, its pronounced focus on Virginians, leadership within the Army of Northern Virginia, and lofty planter-class culture denoted a specific target demographic among elite Upper South society. These notions of southern cultural superiority became popular talking points for Lost Causers in the East, but they ultimately provided little comfort to white Missourians—some slavers, others not—who had also gone down with the Confederacy's allegorical ship.[8]

Edwards adopted the same approach of top-down deification to commemorate and propagandize his guerrilla subjects. The main difference, however, was that the characters in *Noted Guerrillas* were local to the guerrilla theater and could, therefore, be presented as specifically vested in the

socioeconomic and political affairs of pro-Confederates there. In place of
the newly sainted Lee, William Clarke Quantrill ruled the bushwhacker
pantheon. As a true man of action, Edwards wrote, "Quantrell [*sic*] did
not enquire which side he should defend; brave, the weaker; Southerner,
the Confederacy; sincere, the right. His position made his creed."[9] Hence,
he became the chieftain of chieftains; the "central figure" of the guerrilla
theater and "towered aloft amid all the wreck and overthrow and massacre
that went on continually around and about him." Better still, Quantrill was
"to the Guerrillas their voice in tumult, their beacon in a crisis, and their
hand in action. From him sprang all the other Guerrilla leaders and bands
which belong largely to Missouri and the part Missouri took in the civil
war." As Jackson, Forrest, Johnston, and Stuart followed Lee, so too was a
who's who of notable Missouri bushwhackers arranged beneath Quantrill.
"[George] Todd owed primary allegiance to him, and so did [Ferdi-
nand] Scott, Haller, [Bloody Bill] Anderson, [Andy] Blunt, [Dave] Poole,
[Cole] Younger, [Morgan] Maddox, [John] Jarrette, the two James brothers—Frank and Jesse—[Oliver] Shepherd, [Dick] Yager, [William] Hulse,
[William] Gregg—all in fact who became noted afterwards as enterprising
soldiers and fighters."[10] In effect, by consolidating Missouri's guerrilla war
to Quantrillian origins, its history became a history of Quantrill—now a
linear and immanently more controllable sequence of characters, battles,
and events.

Ignoring that bushwhackers had openly killed neighbors, destroyed
crops, burned homes, and pillaged from their local communities, Edwards
used a constant stream of extravagant prose, mythological metaphors, and
biblical inferences to romanticize the behavior of his guerrillas. George
Todd was "the incarnate devil of battle," and as Quantrill's "thunderbolt,"
his fighting prowess matched that of Scipio or Spartacus. William H.
Gregg resembled "a grim Saul among the guerrillas" while Dave Poole
brought to mind "an unschooled Aristophanes of the civil war"—a warrior
who "laughed at calamity and mocked when any man's fear came." Then
there was Bill Anderson: "Mortal bullets avoided him. At desperate odds,
fortune never deserted him. Surrounded, he could not be captured. Outnumbered, he could not be crushed."[11]

As would become typical throughout the book, Edwards saved the best
for Quantrill, blanketing him with supernatural abilities not unlike the
Lost Cause literature that strove to outfit Lee with a Christlike aura. At

William Clarke Quantrill, circa 1860s. One of the few authenticated likenesses of Quantrill from the war years; since the 1860s, personal descriptions of the guerrilla chieftain have varied greatly, some with or without a mustache believed to have been a retroactive addition. From Harrison Trow, *Charles W. Quantrell: A True Story of His Guerilla Warfare on the Missouri and Kansas Border during the Civil War of 1861 to 1865.* Edited by J. P. Burch. Vega, Tex.: J. P. Burch, 1923.

times, Edwards contended, Quantrill rode with a "pale face" reminiscent of the Angel of Death in both purpose and efficiency. In another episode of *Noted Guerrillas*, the guerrilla captain foresees his own death in battle—but, despite premonitions of doom, continues to fight anyway. As a martyr in the biblical sense, then, the book insinuated that he gave his life to save the southern people. Despite not having witnessed it firsthand, Edwards set the scene of Quantrill's death in 1865, distraught Catholic nun and all, down to the last detail: "A Sister of Charity at the bedside put a glass to his lips, but he did not drink. She heard him murmur once audibly—"Boys, get ready!"—then a long pause—then one word more—"Steady!"—and then when she drew back from bending over the murmuring man she fell upon her knees and prayed. Quantrell was dead!" Even as Quantrill died, according to Edwards, he led his men against their Yankee oppressors. But lest readers imagine he had been a normal soldier finally brought low by his enemies, Edwards summed up Quantrill as "a living, breathing, aggressive, all-powerful reality—riding through the midnight, laying ambuscades by lonesome roadsides, catching marching columns by the throat, breaking in upon the flanks and tearing a suddenly surprised rear to pieces; vigilant, merciless, a terror by day and a superhuman if not supernatural thing when there was upon the earth blackness and darkness."[12] Whether he really put stock in such claims or not, these sensational outbursts were how Edwards remade Quantrill and his subordinates into the larger-than-life spokesmen for *his* history of the guerrilla theater and its unique version of the Civil War.

Guerrilla Honor

Operational similarities between Edwards and his counterparts at the Southern Historical Society did not translate into like-minded expressions of honor. The Virginians saturated their accounts of the war with high-handed ideas of gentlemanly conduct and civilized combat. In this regard, as in most, Lee stood above the rest. The general's purported sense of duty, implacable discipline, and unyielding Christian piety became the stuff of legend—a man whose portrait had not found its way onto the walls of untold homes and schoolhouses by coincidence. And as a leader among leaders, these characteristics represented a set of standards intended to underscore how paternalistic planters had led the fight to preserve southern culture but never compromised the principles that allegedly made it so superior to that of the crass Yankee invader.[13]

Edwards espoused a very different construct of southern honor. (Here it is worth noting that Edwards likely imagined *his own* honor as fitting the mold of Lee, but he had a political goal to accomplish and business was business.) The job of the soldier, he asserted, amounted to the simple act of killing opponents and notching victories—regardless of target, tactic, or perceptions of fairness. Take, for example, a scene from *Noted Guerrillas* in which a gruesome ambush was carried out near Cassville, in Barry County, Missouri. Disguised in Federal uniforms, Quantrill and his men approached an unwitting column of twenty-two Union militiamen. "By the side of each Federal," Edwards explained, "a Guerrilla was to range himself, engage in conversation, and then, at a given signal, blow his brains out." At Quantrill's signal, the bushwhackers opened fire on their victims and "it was as though a huge hand had suddenly opened and wiped clean out a column of figures upon a blackboard."[14] Accounts of the war such as this—numerous throughout the book—prioritized irregular violence and what Edwards deemed necessary (and thereby justified) savagery over Victorian rituals that had done nothing to actually achieve victory.

During the war, the manner in which bushwhackers had waged household warfare—their résumés replete with cases of ambush, torture, murder, rape, and arson—made them a public relations nightmare for the Confederate high command. After the war, Edwards's celebration of these traumas only further ostracized bushwhackers from their regular war counterparts. Most telling in this regard are the ways in which each side's honor code accounted for full-on massacres. Edwards described the August 1863 Lawrence Massacre as "a day of darkness and woe." "Killing ran riot," he related matter-of-factly, as "the torch was applied to every residence . . . the air was filled with cries for mercy . . . [and] on every breeze came the wailing of women and the screams of children."[15] Although cautious in his presentation of gory detail—falling well short of Ambrose Bierce's penchant for what Stephen Cushman dubs "pornographic gore"—Edwards conceded the savage nature of the massacre but considered it a great victory—and better still a legitimate one—for pro-Confederates.[16] By contrast, SHS propagandists wanted nothing to do with such barbarism; they went out of their collective way to ignore a massacre overseen by Lost Cause icon and Ku Klux Klan founder Nathan Bedford Forrest at Fort Pillow, Tennessee, in 1864. Men under Forrest's command slaughtered more than two hundred black Union soldiers as they attempted to surrender—hardly a display of idealized southern benevolence.[17]

But Edwards's guerrillas couldn't slaughter enemies of the South with empty hands. "In an organization where skill with a pistol was a passport to leadership," he suggested, Quantrill "shot with a revolver as Leatherstocking shot with a rifle." Being the bushwhackers' weapon of choice, then, the revolver proved as useful to Edwards as a symbol of guerrilla honor as it had been to bushwhackers during the war. "Before a battle," he revealed, "a Guerrilla takes every portion of his revolver apart and lays it upon a white shirt, if he has one, as carefully as a surgeon places his instruments on a white towel. . . . He touches each piece as a man might touch the thing that he loves." As a tool designed for death dealing, it represented justified homicide within the community.[18] Edwards's story of Cole Younger is particularly illuminating:

Coleman Younger—a boy having about his neck still the purple track a rope ploughed the night the Jayhawkers shot down his old father and strung him up to a black jack—spoke rarely and was always a great deal in the woods. What was he doing, his comrades began to enquire, one of another. He had a mission to perform—he was pistol practicing. Soon he was perfect, and then it was noticed that he laughed often and talked a great deal. There had come to him now the intrepid gaiety which plays with death. He changed devotion to his family into devotion to his country, and he fought and killed with the conscience of a hero.

He changed devotion to his family into devotion to his country, and he fought and killed with the conscience of a hero. In other words, Younger derived honor from the ability to protect his slave-owning, southern family. That protection ultimately required Confederate victory (the success of "his country"), which required him to wield his revolver quickly, efficiently, and without remorse. Later in *Noted Guerrillas*, his practice paid macabre dividends in the form of a revolver kill at "seventy-one measured yards"–stunningly long even by modern standards.[19]

Like his revolver, the bushwhacker's horse also carried heavy metaphorical weight as an emblem of guerrilla honor. Inherent to nearly every skirmish, raid, or violent confrontation throughout the book, Edwards presented Quantrill and his men as master horsemen. This equestrian aptitude, when coupled with the persona of the unparalleled gunfighter, helped transform Missouri's guerrillas into folk heroes one hoped not to meet in combat, real or imagined. Edwards declared that "much horse-craft was also theirs"–concluding that if readers could "create a centaur out of a Buchephalus," the idea would be "fixed of their swiftness and prowess." John Jarrette "was, *par excellence*, a soldier of the saddle"; Bill Anderson could "swing himself to the earth and pick up a pistol" as he charged at full gallop because "horsemanship and prowess seemed as natural to the Missourian as aristocracy and the sea were to Venice"; and Quantrill rode "like he was carved from the horse beneath him."[20]

But *Noted Guerrillas* did not just depict a one-sided relationship between a bushwhacker and his mount. "He [the guerrilla] would often go unfed himself that his horse might have corn and [would] frequently take all the chances himself of being shot that his horse might come out of a place unhurt." Accordingly, guerrilla horses appreciated such thoughtfulness: "Well authenticated instances are on record of a Guerrilla's horse standing guard for his master," Edwards recounted, "and on more than one occasion, when cut off from his steed and forced to take shelter from pursuit in fastness, well nigh inaccessible, the Guerrilla has been surprised by the sudden appearance of his horse, no more desirous than himself of unconditional captivity."[21] Paramount here is how Edwards replaced the traditional Lost Cause portrait of an elite cavalier horseman with a character more befitting of Missouri's irregular wartime experience: a pro-Confederate rider who brought hell by way of hooves to the enemy.[22]

Within Edwards's system of guerrilla honor, vendetta functioned as the cordage that bound together the deadly troika of bushwhacker, revolver, and horse. Stories such as that of Cole Younger avenging a father slain by Union assassins appeared regularly in *Noted Guerrillas*. These narratives, hyperbole-laden as they might be, signified how Missourians—both civilian and soldier, to whatever extent the two can be separated in the guerrilla theater—had sacrificed for the Confederate war effort, even if the Confederacy proper failed to count them among its dead. In 1862, for instance, two of Bill Anderson's sisters were imprisoned by a special group of federal soldiers formed to "persecute women and prey upon noncombatants." Eventually, the prison building collapsed and killed several women, one of the Anderson girls included. As a result, Edwards argued that foreign disruption of southern communities *created* men like Anderson and the vendettas that allegedly fueled their irregular campaigns.[23]

Chief among these "creation anecdotes" was the murder of William Quantrill's older brother by Kansas jayhawkers in 1856. While the brothers slept along the banks of the Little Cottonwood River, "thirty armed men rode deliberately up to the wagons where the Quantrells were and opened fire at point-blank range." "The elder Quantrill," Edwards alleged, "was killed instantly, while the younger—wounded badly in the left leg and right breast—was left upon the bank of the stream to die." In Edwards's telling of the story, William eventually recovered and took his vengeance: he infiltrated the company of Kansas men, befriended them, and then, one by one, killed them. Every one of the men who'd gunned down his brother received a single shot to the forehead from Quantrill's revolver.[24] The fact that this murdered brother was entirely fictitious mattered little to Edwards. The slain phantom served a pivotal role: he became the catalyst for Quantrill's gory baptism as a bushwhacker and put the "chieftain of chieftain's" guerrilla honor on full display.

Detachment from Defeat

Framing defeat on constructive terms for the conquered Confederacy understandably represented priority number one for Jubal Early and the Southern Historical Society. If Lee, Jackson, and their heroic peers could not be separated from blame for the South's ruination in the eyes of the public, efforts to mythologize them would be futile. So in rhetoric approaching the absurd, the Virginians transformed Lee's crushing defeat at Gettysburg (July 1863) into a net positive and a powerful engine of pro-southern propaganda. To cleanse the general's reputation of any tactical fault, SHS polemicists relied on two main excuses.

First, they saddled virtually all of the responsibility for defeat on the back of General James Longstreet. Despite years as a workhorse commander for the Confederacy, Longstreet made an easy scapegoat. Not only had he supposedly failed to follow Lee's specific orders on the second day of battle at Gettysburg, he'd also defected to the Republican Party following the war. Had Lee's battle plans been followed, Early and company shrieked, the Confederates would have achieved victory at Gettysburg; in turn, momentum would have propelled them to total victory and independence. Historian Gaines Foster notes that this explanation was particularly appealing to the Virginians because "it allowed them to believe success had been possible" and, invoking Faulkner, that "for the Virginians it was not yet dawn on 2 July, Longstreet was not yet late, and it all still hung in the balance."[25]

Second, SHS advocates were quick to highlight a vast disparity in manpower. Sometimes called the "overwhelming numbers scenario," this line of explanation alleged that southern soldiers had actually outfought their Union counterparts on a man-to-man basis. The North, however, had simply marshaled too many men for the South to overcome.[26] Overwhelming numbers left the masculinity of defeated southern combatants intact and stole a small moral victory from the closing jaws of Reconstruction and the racial reordering of American society. Both of these factors helped the SHS define Confederate defeat on terms most favorable to elite southerners; in the process, they provided any necessary sanitization or rehabilitation to the reputations of Lee and his subordinates.

To wash his noted guerrillas clean of the stigma of defeat, Edwards intentionally separated them from the failed Confederate government, its War Department, its most famous commanders, and their armies. One might judge this a wrongheaded ploy if the fundamental goal of Edwards's irregular Lost Cause was to provide Missouri with a Confederate heritage—but it actually pillared the most powerful statement he could offer on the unending devotion of bushwhackers to the cause. This statement required readers to understand that Quantrill and company had been utterly unique within the annals of Confederate military history. So from nearly the beginning of *Noted Guerrillas*, Edwards made the case that to love the goals of the Confederacy did not always mean one loved the leaders or policies put in place to achieve them.

A fabricated 1863 conversation between Quantrill and the Confederate secretary of war in Richmond hammered this point home. "Quantrell," Edwards submitted, "asked to be commissioned as a Colonel under the Partisan Ranger Act." The guerrilla pled his case: "The warfare was desperate, he knew, the service desperate, everything connected with it was desperate; but the Southern people to succeed had to fight a desperate fight." In reply, the secretary "suggested that the war had its amenities and its refinements, and that in the nineteenth century it was simple barbarism to talk of a black flag." Stung by the rebuke, "Quantrell's blue eyes blazed" and he let fly a verbal volley:

Barbarism, Mr. Secretary, means war and war means barbarism. Since you have touched upon this subject, let us discuss it a little. Times have their crimes as well as men. For twenty years this cloud has been gathering; for twenty years—inch by inch and little by little those people called the Abolitionists have been on the track of slavery[;] for twenty years the people of the South have been robbed, here of a negro and there of a negro; for twenty years hates have been engendered and wrathful things laid up against the day of wrath. The cloud has burst. Do not condemn the thunderbolt.

At this, Edwards continued, the "War Secretary bowed his head" and Quantrill commenced to picking apart the bureaucrat's delusional understanding of what stood between the South and victory:

Who are these people you call Confederates? Rebels, unless they succeed; outcasts, traitors, food for hemp and gunpowder. There were no great statesmen in the South, or this war would have happened ten years ago; no inspired men, or it would have happened fifteen years ago. To-day the odds are desperate. The world hates slavery; the world is fighting you. The ocean belongs to the Union navy. There is a recruiting officer in every foreign port. I have captured and killed many who did not know the English tongue. Mile by mile the cordon is being drawn about the granaries of the South, Missouri will go first, next Kentucky, next Tennessee, by and by Mississippi and Arkansas, and then what? That we must put gloves on our hands, and honey in our mouths, and fight this war as Christ fought the wickedness of the world?

When Quantrill had finished, the secretary asked, "What would *you* do, Captain Quantrell, were your's [*sic*] the power and the opportunity?" "Do, Mr. Secretary?" Quantrill began. "Why I would wage such a war and have such a war waged by land and sea as to make surrender forever impossible. I would cover the armies of the Confederacy all over with blood. I would invade. I would reward audacity. I would exterminate. I would break up foreign enlistments by indiscriminate massacre. I would win the independence of my people or I would find them graves."[27]

In reality, Quantrill—who was a native of Ohio and owned no slaves before the war—*had* journeyed to Richmond with the hope of acquiring a regular army commission.[28] Richmond turned him down, and no record has been left of the conversation (which freed up Edwards to craft one from thin air). Ironically, though, this failure on Quantrill's part to become part of the mainstream Confederacy during the war greatly bolstered Edwards's ability to commemorate him after it had been lost. In the few brief sentences Edwards concocted as Quantrill's aforementioned response, he illustrated how elite Confederates had brushed aside a plan to "protect the southern people at any cost" for the sake of their own "civilized" reputations. In doing so, the secretary of war made Edwards's case once and for all that guerrillas had been the most diehard Confederates of the entire war: men who had been willing to fight and kill on whatever terms or ground necessary to secure victory, men who had never really surrendered, no matter the fate of Richmond or its officials.

Conveniently for Edwards, several top Confederates, including Lee, had been on record as strongly disapproving of guerrilla warfare and ultimately fearing that, results aside, their "lack of discipline" would reflect poorly on the entire army.[29] Even the renowned Confederate raider John Singleton Mosby—known as the "Gray Ghost" during the war—sought to shield himself from what he considered the stigma of Edwards's bushwhackers. In a letter, Mosby labeled bushwhacker Jesse James a "lady killer" (and not in the complimentary fashion James would have preferred) and found equal disgust with Quantrill.[30] Through Quantrill's story, Edwards implied that men such as Lee and Mosby had shunned the most

effective forms of irregular violence during the war with grave consequences for the South; now he called on readers not to make the same
mistake with how guerrillas should be remembered.

The Legacy of a Legacy

To fully assess the short- and long-term impacts of Edwards's work on
Missouri's Civil War legacy, we must recognize that his efforts belonged
to a much broader discourse of regional politics and contested rights of
remembrance. As support for Reconstruction waned, the presidential
election of 1876 illustrated that no political power existed capable of simultaneous dominance in the North and the South. This situation left various factions—often violent ones at that—in each region clawing for power.
Ex-Confederates, Northern Democrats, Scalawags, and Radical Republicans all vied to make their preferred visions of the postwar South become
reality and to define what might be the war's ultimate legacy.[31]

As a Democratic fire-eater looking to establish southern credentials for
a non-Confederate Missouri, Edwards balked at Radical Reconstruction
and its congressional vanguards—albeit from afar or, oftentimes, vicari-
ously through the experiences of other ex-Confederate states. Just before
the war, Missouri's slave population accounted for less than 10 percent of
its total population; slaveholders constituted less than 3 percent of its total
free population. Even so, the behavior of Missourians toward their former slaves, however few they numbered relative to the Deep South, actually forced the federal government to supervise the state with Freedmen's
Bureau agents—making it one of only two Union states to earn that dubi-
ous distinction. In fact, the case can certainly be made that some Missourians actually brought the harshest, and *only*, acts of Reconstruction over-
sight down on themselves.[32]

In spite of Missouri's benign Reconstruction experience—and, in many
ways, to compensate for it having been so benign—Edwards railed in his
editorials as if all residents of the state had been stripped of their rights
and livelihoods by tyrannical Republican overlords: "Radicalism has no
principle. . . . Everything that was venerable and sacred in the country,
it has taught the people to despise. As far as it could it has defamed and
derided the constitution." Since the war ended, Edwards concluded, the
states "have been treated as conquered provinces" and their peoples like

"abject criminals in the exercise of outrageous power."[33] His partisan rhetoric revealed the sorts of real-world circumstances Edwards needed to spin with *Noted Guerrillas*; in particular, it exposed his understanding that to link Missouri with the rest of the suffering South, he needed to forge a shared experience of federal oppression that allegedly stemmed from the war.

On the political spectrum, Edwards described himself as a Bourbon Democrat who stood against tariffs, prohibition, greenbackism, protectionism, corruption, labor party—or, for all intents and purposes, against anything he considered remotely radical. He strongly supported states' rights and recoiled from nearly any type of federal intervention.[34] Luckily for Edwards, many former slaveholders in Missouri shared his displeasure with the precedent set by the federal usurpation of local authority to own and manage their human property.[35] Grasping how Missouri's geographic alignment influenced the politics of its more conservative inhabitants, Edwards shrewdly framed this sense of disgust for the federal government as both an issue of states' rights *and* opposition to the perceived foreign (eastern) oppression of traditional western rights. In other words, he repackaged Missouri's western quirks to help bolster the state's case for southernness.

The importance of this repackaging process is difficult to overstate. As illustrated in the previous chapter, residents of the guerrilla theater typically refused to concede their individualized memories of irregular violence; they naturally abstained from national trends of remembrance and would not consciously re-remember a war they had not experienced for the sake of assuaging sectional animosities. Herein was the true effectiveness of Edwards's creation: it did not really require them to annul their own personal experiences; it simply collected and consolidated the pro-Confederate ones for the benefit of outside, political appearances. This version of the guerrilla war, as a linear sequence of interrelated events (all orbiting Quantrill and his men in one way or another), would not have been at all familiar to those who had actually survived it. But had those same survivors flipped to nearly any individual page or section of *Noted Guerrillas*, the individual anecdotes—midnight raids, men stranded in the brush, homes burning—would have been instantly recognizable.

To some extent, then, politically disgruntled Missourians (i.e., former slave owners and Democrats) were primed and cocked for Edwards's rendering of the guerrilla theater because he allowed them to have their cake and eat it too, at least temporarily. On one level, his narrative *did* re-remember irregular violence in a collective way on behalf of pro-Confederate borderlanders who otherwise would not have done so. As we have seen, *Noted Guerrillas* rearranged their individual experiences together on a far more complicated scaffolding—a new context that hammered away at the state's record of wartime Unionism and covered up notions that Missourians had been "weak" on slavery. On another level, though, while Edwards's depiction ordered irregular traumas in collective fashion, his method of collectivization still allowed for Missourians to retain their individualized memories; it did not alter the circumstances, endings, or significances of their specific stories. Put another way, the irregular Lost Cause Edwards constructed for Missouri re-remembered guerrilla warfare collectively as a series of *noncollective* events with Quantrill and company as leading spokesmen.

Elsewhere in the South, paramilitary groups such as the Redshirt organizations or the Ku Klux Klan rose to prominence as the physical enforcers of the Democratic Party; they coerced electoral unity through intimidation and physical violence.[36] Neither the fact that southern states responded violently to the shockwaves of political and social upheaval that followed Confederate defeat nor the opportunity to harness similar paramilitary sentiment in Missouri would have escaped Edwards. And it would not have been all that difficult for him—Missourians did not want for their fair share of extralegal politicking. All told, the state's lack of a federally mandated Republican government in the 1870s (consolidated through military occupation) arguably sparked more violence. After the war, the bulk of Missouri's pre–Civil War slaveholders still lived in Little Dixie. This combination of factors afforded a close-knit, highly disgruntled minority the chance to usurp political control by force—a situation perfectly ripe for partisan bloodshed.

Edwards not only understood the finer points of paramilitary politics, but by way of past experience, he understood how to fan the flames with pen and press. Prior to publishing *Noted Guerrillas*, he had spent years glorifying the criminal exploits of bushwhackers-turned-bandits Frank and Jesse James. His popular editorials warped the James brothers into post-war Robin Hood figures: outraged southern patriots who used crime to fight back against the oppression of Reconstruction. In *Jesse James: Last*

Rebel of the Civil War, Pulitzer Prize–winning biographer T. J. Stiles goes so far as to say that with Edwards's assistance, James operated as a pro-Confederate terrorist throughout much of the 1870s. This relationship with the James Gang involved tweaking or even ghostwriting politically charged letters for Jesse that detailed the prosouthern, pro-Confederate, pro-Democratic intent behind his robberies.[37] In one such note, printed in October 1872, James made his political position quite clear: "Grant's party has no respect for anyone. They rob the poor and rich, and we rob the rich and give to the poor. . . . I will close by hoping that Horace Greeley will defeat Grant, and then I can make an honest living, and then I will not have to rob, as taxes will not be so heavy."[38]

To our discussion of his irregular Lost Cause, though, Edwards's stint as the James brothers' personal publicist is noteworthy because it allowed the editorialist to hone the rhetorical tactics he would later employ on a much grander scale in *Noted Guerrillas.* It is no coincidence, then, that the earliest origins of the book—an 1872 article titled "Quantrell"—were penned in this period. "No good reason exists," Edwards contended in the brief article, "why the truth shall not be told of one who, brave and steadfast to the end, died as he had lived, a fearless Ishmaelite." Of course Edwards was writing of William Clarke Quantrill—and in ways that should now sound very familiar: he was the guerrilla with "the most deadly hands with a revolver in all the border" who could "lean from the saddle and snatch a pebble from the ground" while riding at "a furious gallop." Bill Anderson was a "tiger let loose" and George Todd "mingled no melody with his murder," but Quantrill's "power to command was unquestioned"; "he was unlike them all, just as he was greater than them all."[39]

Edwards's fondness for rococo rhetoric clearly predated *Noted Guerrillas,* but the success of his editorial work in the early 1870s made clear that something else did, too: he had a readymade audience. Well aware of the wants and needs of his readers by 1877, Edwards could afford to flaunt wartime guerrilla violence because he knew it would resonate with them—that it would spur them to support his cause the same way it had drawn them to the defense of the James boys. In this context, Edwards's irregular Lost Cause should be viewed both as a literal guerrilla movement against Republican control within the realm of a broader Lost Cause that eschewed direct political action and as a counternarrative segmentation of that mainstream Lost Cause centered on the Missouri bushwhacker.

But was it successful? Did it actually influence politics in the way Edwards hoped?

To answer this question is to evaluate the legacy of a legacy, and to do so, we must examine the reputation of its architect in tandem with political patterns and electoral results in Missouri. As a result of long-term alcoholism, Edwards died in 1889; his personal popularity both in Missouri and abroad dovetailed with the reception of *Noted Guerrillas*, by far his best-known book. In an anthology of articles, letters, and obituaries compiled by his widow, Jennie, dozens of personal tributes from Democratic leaders, newspapermen, and pundits proclaimed his contributions. Congressmen, adjutants general, and judges from New York to Missouri and from Chicago to Richmond paid their respects to the architect of Missouri's irregular Lost Cause. In doing so, they verified his status as a prominent political voice within both state and national Democratic circles.[40]

One obituary from the *Jefferson City Tribune* (Jefferson City being Missouri's state capital and the seat of its legislature) trumpeted that the "prince of journalism was dead," while another from the *Richmond Conservator* blazed that "his pen was a power in the journalistic field of Missouri and his influence even extended beyond her lines." The *Columbia Herald* argued that Edwards had "been a positive force in Missouri journalism for twenty years" and that "no one connected with newspapers has, during that period, impressed his personality so strongly upon public affairs." Perhaps most telling of all, the *Blue Springs Herald* labeled Edwards's death a "great loss to the Democratic Party."[41]

While the showman in Edwards no doubt would have enjoyed such high praise from his partisan peers, his own gauging of success would likely have been influenced most by happenings at the ballot box. In an 1887 editorial for the *Kansas City Times* titled "On Democracy," Edwards proudly recalled how his beloved Democratic Party had historically recovered from impending ruin to defend the founding principles of the United States. Labor, Whigs, Federals, carpetbaggers—all had threatened to overthrow the established hierarchy of southern politics but had ultimately failed.[42] So a decade after the release of *Noted Guerrillas*, he clearly believed that the fight had again been won, the carpetbaggers sent packing (however few found their way to Missouri), and order restored.

The state's gubernatorial and presidential election returns verify Edwards's declaration of victory: they underscore a prosouthern, pro-

Democratic power shift that coincided closely with the development of the irregular Lost Cause between 1872 and 1877. For ten years beginning in 1861, Missouri's voters (minus Confederate holdouts) elected Republican governors, while for two years beginning in 1871 a Liberal Republican reigned in Jefferson City. In 1873, however, the election of Silas Woodson signaled a turn toward Democratic governors that lasted until 1909.[43]

At the national level, in 1864 and 1868, Missouri's electoral votes were cast in favor of Republican candidates Abraham Lincoln and Ulysses S. Grant, respectively. In 1872 Missourians favored Liberal Republican and Democratic nominee Horace Greeley at the polls. But with the selection of Samuel Tilden in 1876, Missourians communicated a clear and growing connection with conservative candidates and supported a succession of Democrats—Tilden, Hancock, Cleveland, Cleveland, Cleveland, Bryan, Bryan—that continued until the turn of the twentieth century.[44]

Naturally Edwards cannot, and should not, be credited with anything near sole responsibility for Missouri's postwar lurch toward the Democratic Party and the appearance of southern electoral uniformity. But in outfitting the state with a Confederate past, he played a role worthy of recognition in the "southern-ization" of its politics. The shift had occurred on Edwards's watch, so to speak—during the peak period of his propagandizing about guerrillas—and, for better or worse, his narrative of the irregular war has been considered a foundational "history" by countless readers. With *Noted Guerrillas* in mind, it is no coincidence that chapters of the United Daughters of the Confederacy thrived (and continue to operate) in western Missouri where the guerrilla conflict burned hottest.

Thus on May 5, 1889, when the *Kansas City Times* eulogized, "It is not derogation to other good and brave men to say that the death of no man in Missouri would cause genuine pain and grief to so many and so different persons as that of John N. Edwards," and concluded that "Nor will the memory of any be so cherished," one is left to wonder if the memories so cherished were of Edwards—or if they were quite literally those he had created.[45] Either way, in the long run, the success of Edwards's narrative left its real-life protagonists in a difficult position. As the next pair of chapters will illuminate, when the political usefulness of being a "noted guerrilla" in the Edwardsian fashion faded, so too did the luster of being a hyperviolent outcast from the mainstream lineage of the Lost Cause.

THREE

Rebooting Guerrilla Memory

> Then trouble broke out between the corporal and the sergeant, each
> claiming to rank the other. Nobody knew which was the higher
> office; so Lyman had to settle the matter by making the rank of both
> officers equal. The commander of an ignorant crew like that has many
> troubles and vexations which probably do not occur in the regular
> army at all.
> —Mark Twain, "The Private History of a Campaign That Failed"

In 1870 the notorious bushwhacker Samuel Hildebrand published his personal chronicle of the guerrilla theater. *The Life of Samuel Hildebrand*, which is generally believed to have been the first such guerrilla memoir, presented readers with bloody tales of enemies slain, vendettas fulfilled, and terror unleashed in the Ozarks of southern Missouri and northern Arkansas. Gritty and vainglorious, the book was undoubtedly an attempt by Hildebrand to line his pockets. But the account, composed with the help of an editor (Hildebrand himself likely was not literate), is also an important bellwether in our discussion of guerrilla memory because it made no discernible efforts to ingratiate its subject to regular ex-Confederates or to sanitize his narrative for mainstream consumption. In other words, Hildebrand basked in the uniqueness of his wartime experience; he remained wholly unapologetic for the acts of irregular violence he had committed on behalf of the Confederate cause, whether its "historians" in Richmond cared to claim him or not. And given his track record, they did not.[1]

The book failed to produce the financial windfall Hildebrand had imagined—or even a small portion of it. So he supplemented his income by other, more nefarious means. In 1872 these dealings prompted a group of U.S. marshals, led by John H. Ragland, to track the "terror of St. Francois and Washington counties" to a hillside camp on the outskirts of Pinckneyville, Illinois. Ragland and his deputies understandably approached with caution—Hildebrand was no stranger to gun play and harbored no qualms about killing. As one newspaper put it, "When he [Hildebrand] takes a dislike to a man he lies in wait for him on the road-side or near a field, and thinks no more of putting a bullet through a man's heart than shooting a squirrel." Moreover, it was widely believed that he kept "the tally of his victims by cutting notches in the butt of his rifle," which he had christened "Kill-Devil." Thus odds were good that Hildebrand would not greet the marshals kindly. The posse was in luck: they caught the ex-bushwhacker off guard—cooking his dinner—and took him into custody without incident. On the ride back to Pinckneyville, however, Hildebrand had second thoughts about going along quietly. He pulled a large knife and viciously stabbed Ragland in the leg. The lawman was forced to send a bullet crashing through his prisoner's skull.[2] Hindsight would make this a fitting death for an unrepentant old bushwhacker such as Sam Hildebrand. Times were changing, and with them, patterns of remembrance.

The defeated South slowly but steadily recovered. Houses were rebuilt, social hierarchies reestablished. As white southerners became increasingly proficient at violently disenfranchising African Americans, the Democratic Party returned to electoral prominence in the ex-Confederacy— and in its postwar additions, Missouri and Kentucky. Former slaveholders used sharecropping (a system that legally coerced workers through habitual debt) to regain control over black laborers, despite constitutional amendments supposedly verifying their newfound freedoms. Owing to these developments, within just a few decades of *The Life of Samuel Hildebrand*'s debut, a new wave of guerrilla memoirists would emerge with a very different sort of story to tell. In fact, they came forward with narratives designed to update and replace the "outsider" status flaunted by Hildebrand and codified by John Newman Edwards in *Noted Guerrillas.*

This gravitation back to the mainstream should not come as a major surprise. Before the war, many of Missouri's deadliest bushwhackers had actually hailed from the state's most established families: the Jameses, the Youngers, the Nolands, the Walkers. Landed, affluent, and politically connected, these were the sons of men who sat atop the social hierarchy— the young princes of Missouri society's proslavery segment. With defeat came a new set of circumstances; those who survived the irregular conflict accepted the novelty status appended by *Noted Guerrillas* because it reaffirmed their masculinity and their southernness, and brought them great notoriety in the process.

By 1900, though, this narrative had fallen out of vogue. Edwards was long dead, his fight to southernize Missouri largely won. Consequently, the political usefulness of the guerrilla as Confederate outcast had greatly diminished, and the idea of being outsiders lost its original luster for the men in question. So they tried to do something about it. Former bush-whackers Cole Younger (1903), William H. Gregg (1906), Andrew Walker (1910), Hampton Watts (1913), John McCorkle (1914), Kit Dalton (1914), Joseph Bailey (1920), Harrison Trow (1923), and George Cruzen (1930) penned their own accounts of life in the guerrilla theater to establish a new place for themselves on the *inside* of early twentieth-century south-ern society.[3]

In effect, former guerrillas needed to reboot how they could and should be remembered. But for as much thought as Edwards had put into de-taching them from the mainstream Confederacy and its legacy in the short term, it would prove no easy task for these bushwhackers-turned-memoirists to shed their ties to his commemorative creation. In the spirit of Twain, these were more of the "troubles and vexations" unknown to the Civil War's "regular" soldiers. With an eye to the future, Quantrill's men now had to recontextualize their wartime experiences to reflect changes in southern gender roles, race relations, and commemorative attitudes. This is not to say that twentieth-century guerrilla memoirs were any more historically accurate than *The Life of Samuel Hildebrand* or *Noted Guerrillas*—anything but, in most cases. Instead, what we observe in this chapter is a memory narrative being retooled for a new, longer-term purpose: perpet-ual remembrance.

Remus versus Rapist, New South versus Lost Cause

Late in 1886, Henry W. Grady addressed the New England Society in New York on race and the economy of the "New South." Often dubbed the spokesman of this new—and supposedly improved—Dixie, Grady be-gan his remarks by stating, "There was a South of slavery and secession—but that South is dead. There is a South of Union and freedom—that South, thank God, is living, breathing, [and] growing every hour." Next he turned to racial discord. "But what of the negro?" Grady petitioned his audi-ence, "Have we solved the problem he presents or progressed in honor and equity towards the solution?" The question was rhetorical; Grady's answer was a resounding yes. Of black southerners, he opined, "We have found out that in the general summary the free negro counts more than he did as a slave," and that every citizen of the New South needed to "put business above politics."

The rosy portrait Grady painted of New South race relations more or less ignored the truth of the matter—that militant white supremacy had inundated the region with racial violence. But if southerners planned to rebuild the South sans slavery, they needed someone like Grady to shape its postbellum image for outsiders. So in a calculated bid to attract those outsiders—that is, sought-after northern investors—and their all-important capital for the interconnected projects of southern industrialization and market development, Grady outlined this duplicitous framework in which the South was not particularly sorry, or ready to apologize for slavery, but would at least acknowledge and embrace the new economic opportunities revealed by its eradication. "The South found her jewel in the toad's head of defeat," he declared, but he maintained that the region "had nothing to take back."[4] Grady's explanations for defeat and his plans for the future met with critical acclaim from both northern and southern audiences.[5]

As promarket boosters in Missouri and elsewhere busied themselves with the economic foundations of the New South, Joel Chandler Harris, a newspaper editor in Atlanta, provided southerners with the tools needed to cover up the racial strife Grady conveniently ignored: Uncle Remus, Br'er Rabbit, Br'er Fox, Br'er Bear, and the infamous Tar-Baby. Known for his supposed mastery of the "negro dialect," Harris's stories of Uncle Remus, which involved the elderly ex-slave relaying folk stories about the Old South to a young white boy, quickly became favorites among supporters of the Lost Cause. Through Remus and his Aesopian tales—one even involving the former slave rescuing his master from a Yankee sharpshooter during the war—Harris recast the violent, slave-addicted South of the antebellum period into an idyllic place where white plantation masters and their black charges lived and worked together in harmony. In doing so, he also constructed the archetype of a loyal, but above all else, sexually docile black man to explain that the South's race problem had never really been a problem at all before the Civil War.[6]

The alleged loyalty of Uncle Remus notwithstanding, danger lurked around nearly every corner for black residents of the New South. Without the institution of slavery to govern the behavior of African Americans, extralegal violence became the new mechanism of choice for white south-erners.[7] Between 1899 and 1903, some 455 African American men and women died at the hands of lynch mobs. Between 1914 and 1918, another 264 black southerners were lynched, and between 1919 and 1923, extra-legal violence claimed still 273 more. As noted by historian Glenda Gil-more, accusations of rape against black men functioned as the excuse for much of this butchery. Put another way, lynching became a tool for sup-pressing the African American vote, and black men supposedly raping white women became a surefire way to recruit a lynch mob. In 1915 D. W. Griffith's *The Birth of a Nation*—a technologically groundbreaking film that had the unfortunate side effect of making southern white supremacy and vigilante violence an international sensation—only made life more pre-carious for black southerners as political fire-eaters such as James K. Var-daman, Coleman L. Blease, and "Pitchfork" Ben Tillman literally "built careers" around this system of "rape-politics."[8]

So how were southerners—whose race problem was anything but re-solved at the turn of the century—to make sense of this racial paradox that pitted the economic and political needs of the New South against the social and cultural ideals of the Lost Cause? How could white south-erners simultaneously have bridged their racial divides while basing a system of extralegal politics on the notion of justified violence against black southerners? Simply put, they internalized a crude but stunningly powerful model of representing black identity. This dichotomous para-digm contrasted the loyal, gentle Uncle Remus figure with the disloyal, ungrateful, lustful, interracial rapist. Former Missouri guerrillas writing between 1900 and 1930 took full notice of the popularity these stereo-types enjoyed and put them to work in their own narratives.[9]

In 1870 Samuel Hildebrand happily recounted the wartime executions of numerous black men, free and slave, always under the justification that they were dishonest, disloyal, murderous, or otherwise subhuman. Toward the end of *The Life of Samuel Hildebrand*, he updated readers on the state of a young black child he had abducted after killing the boy's father. After the war ended, he wrote, "The negro boy I had taken from Free Jim in St. Francois county still remained with me; he was free, I suppose, but he seemed to prefer good living and light work to 'free starvation.'" While few if any Missouri bushwhackers were advocates of "progressive" race relations, Hildebrand's hard stance is critical for two reasons. First, he includes *zero* instances of black men cast as sexual predators or interracial rapists. Second, he was unready to concede *any* merits of emancipation, which in his mind only resulted in "free starvation."[10]

In his 1903 memoir, Cole Younger gravitated away from Hildebrand's antiquated viewpoints; he admitted that emancipation had been a just end to slavery, but he also qualified his confession by discrediting the true motives of Jayhawkers. According to Younger, most of the raiding Kansans had shown little genuine interest in abolishing slavery and had spent most of their time plundering the private property of law-abiding, slave-owning families like his own. *The Story of Cole Younger* recalled the account (quite familiar to James-Younger enthusiasts) of a twelve-year-old boy being tortured and eventually murdered by Union troops for refusing to divulge the whereabouts of his father, a well-known Confederate sympathizer. But in Younger's version of the story, "[a] negro servant who had witnessed the seizure of his young master, had fled for the timber, and came upon a party of a dozen of us, including Quantrill and myself. As he quickly told us the story, we made our plans, and ambushed at the 'Blue Cut,' a deep pass on the road the soldiers must take back to Independence." Only with the help of a loyal slave, Younger noted, were Quantrill and his men able to avenge the innocent boy's death.

Younger later recounted how a "faithful negro servant" named "Aunt Suse" had been interrogated and tortured in the family's barn by Unionists on the prowl for anti-guerrilla intelligence. Despite the ordeal, Aunt Suse allegedly refused to give up information about the Younger brothers' activities or whereabouts. Yet again, a slave remaining loyal to a Confederate master—even when confronted by potential freedom or mortal danger—was meant to imply that black slaves and white masters had lived together harmoniously before and even during the Civil War. As such, Younger's memoir also implied that southern race relations in the postwar period were equally harmonious.[11]

Andrew Walker's 1910 memoir, *Recollections of Quantrill's Guerrillas*, continued with the trend of loyal, even pro-Confederate, African American characters. Early in his account, Walker reported an incident involving a pair of hated abolitionists named Ball and Southwick that actually predated the formation of Quantrill's guerrilla band or even the beginning of the war. These antislavery forces (from across the border in Kansas) had been patrolling slave-laden areas of Missouri and then emancipating—that is, stealing—enslaved blacks from white masters. In response, slaveholders and their neighbors established posses or counter-patrols to protect their human chattel. "We had been home only a few minutes," Walker wrote, "when neighbor Liggett came, bringing word that Ball and Southwick had been discovered skulking in the brush." In this particular case, the alleged *source* of Liggett's intelligence turned out to be much more interesting than the information itself. "Liggett owned an idiotic negro," Walker continued, who had seen the two men in the woods and then "whipped for home as if pursued by devils" and on arriving "announced: 'Mars' Jim, I's found dem bobolionists [*sic*].'"

Walker then decided to set out looking for the abolitionists discovered by Liggett's loyal slave and to take his "best and most trusted slave," Ben, with him on the hunt. Walker remembered that "on arriving in the woods a wicked impulse seized me." He recalled the exchange as follows:

> *Walker:* Ben, don't you want to go with me and bushwhack them Feds?
> *Ben:* Yes, Mars' Andy
> *Walker:* Will you shoot one?
> *Ben:* Yes, I doan lak' 'em nohow.

According to Walker, when the shooting started, Ben's nerves got the better of him and he fled. "Ben was full of regrets that he hadn't stayed with me," he noted, continuing that Ben's "intentions were good, but his legs just wouldn't stand."

Later in his memoir, Walker addressed the connection of John Noland—an enslaved African American man—to Quantrill's band of guerrillas and the infamous raid on Lawrence, Kansas, in August 1863. Many accounts, including Walker's own, contend that Noland served as an advance scout for Quantrill's forces before they descended on Lawrence. Because of Noland's race, Quantrill and his lieutenants believed he would not draw the same degree of suspicion as other bushwhackers. With that in mind, Walker characterized Noland as "a negro, and a brave, resourceful fellow." No black man, he continued, "ever fought with us as a regular member of the band, but John would have done so had Quantrill consented." Walker's narrative implied that Noland wanted to fight full-time with Quantrill's men, but Quantrill valued him too highly as a spy to allow it. Walker concluded, "so John operated with us only as a trusted spy; but he is today a member of our organization." In this way, Walker's memoir promoted a specific portrait of enslaved African Americans: trustworthy, loyal, and, at times, willing to spill blood on behalf of the men such as Walker who literally owned them.[12]

Writing just a few years after Walker, John McCorkle imbued his memoir with much the same sentiment, including a story about a faithful "negro woman" saving Cole Younger from a Union ambush. But while Younger and Walker only included stereotypes in keeping with the tradition of loyal slaves and amicable race relations, McCorkle composed his narrative to feature both halves of the dichotomy. *Three Years with Quantrill* matched Rube, the loyal Remus figure, against "the notorious negro" Jack Mann. According to McCorkle, while they were chasing a supply wagon, several bushwhackers captured a free black man named Rube. Before they could execute him, Rube pleaded to speak with Captain George Todd, who, by chance, was in command of the guerrilla company. As Todd caught sight of him, he proclaimed, "by God, it's Rube!" and added "Boys, the first man that hurts this nigger, I will kill." Todd later explained that Rube, a local barber, had saved him from Union capture in 1862.

On the same page that readers are introduced to Rube, whom the bushwhackers referred to as Todd's "pet nigger," Jack Mann also makes his first appearance. McCorkle offered that Mann was well known to white southerners for aiding Jayhawkers in Missouri and, more importantly, for being "exceedingly insulting to the Southern people and especially the women." In one case, McCorkle even suggested that Mann had undressed himself before the wife of Dick Maddox—one of Quantrill's most faithful followers. Insults directed specifically at southern women undoubtedly implied crimes of a sexual nature. Shortly thereafter, McCorkle reported that Mann's guards could not stand his presence and shot him. The execution apparently prompted a brawl among the other guerrillas—several of whom had wanted to personally dispatch the "black fiend."[13]

Penned in 1923, Harrison Trow's memoir provided another clearly differentiated example of the racial themes presented by Younger and McCorkle. He recalled, "The only prisoner I ever shot during war was a 'nigger' I captured on guard at Independence, Missouri, who claimed that he had killed his master and burned his house and barns." Trow wrote that he "shot him in the forehead just above the eyes." And, to make sure the runaway slave was dead, he shoved his finger into the bullet hole and then shot the slave again in the foot. Years later, Trow recounted that he rather miraculously "met the 'nigger' whom I thought dead" in a saloon, where the reunited duo supposedly joked and shared a friendly drink. The event—unbelievable as it seems—was meant to illustrate that the South (or at least the *white* South) had moved past slavery; that, as Henry Grady had remarked in 1886, southerners needed to place business before politics and old grudges.

Not to be outdone by McCorkle, Trow also included the story of a loyal slave saving the life of Cole Younger. According to Trow, while a company of Union soldiers descended on the Younger homestead, "an old negro woman—a former slave—with extraordinary presence of mind blew out the light, snatched a coverlet from the bed, [and] threw it over her shoulder." She ordered Younger to "Get behind me, Marse Cole, quick," and then snuck him out of the surrounded house. In Trow's estimation, the loyal slave became a hero: "Unquestionable [*sic*] a rebel negro, she was persecuted often and often for her opinion's sake, and hung up twice by militia to tell the whereabouts of Guerrillas. True to her [Confederate] people and her cause, she died at last in the ardor of devotion."[14]

Written in 1930, George Cruzen's manuscript, "The Story of My Life," built on the dichotomy of stereotypical black characters employed by McCorkle, Trow, and company. Cruzen's narrative included multiple examples of African American men serving in the capacity of "extras"—as cooks, stewards, and field hands. But on more than one occasion, even these seemingly unimportant characters were critical to constructing a comparative statement concerning race and the guerrilla war. The first African American characters to appear in Cruzen's account are loyal at best and ignorantly harmless at worst. For instance, readers encounter a "faithful negro man" who, with the aid of his enslaved wife, "always fed us [Cruzen and his fellow bushwhackers] and helped us the best they could" on behalf of their white, pro-Confederate master.

Later in the text, however, Cruzen recalled a night in which "some white Feds with two cannons" accompanied by "about 1000 nigers [*sic*]" came looking for him and his men. Luckily for Cruzen, the guerrillas' camp was mostly empty when the group of black and white Union men arrived. But, he fondly remembered, "our negro boys there said they were scared to death and shure glad when we got back that night." In other words, Cruzen suggested that the "negro boys" owned or held captive by the guerrillas were glad that they had not been rescued by an interracial assemblage of Federal troops. For their loyalty, these men, along with the black would-be quartermaster mentioned above, were the ideal variety of southern African Americans. For their apparent disloyalty, the thousand black men who helped invade the guerrilla camp are the *only* African American characters that Cruzen labeled "nigers" instead of "negros."[15]

A far cry from the racial rhetoric of Samuel Hildebrand, ex-guerrillas writing in the twentieth century responded directly to their new sociopolitical and economic surroundings. With disparate cues delivered by the likes of Henry Grady, Joel Chandler Harris, D. W. Griffith, and proponents of rape politics, these guerrilla memoirists eagerly employed African American identity models that had been specifically constructed by the economic boosters of the New South, the cultural leaders of the Lost Cause, and the partisan figureheads of Jim Crow politics. In doing so, the former bushwhackers purported that their protection of white women long predated the postwar lynch mobs. But Younger, Walker, Watts, and the rest also understood that southern women were much more than the token damsels of a violent political arrangement—female activists wielded real power in the postwar South, and guerrilla memory needed their help.

Courting Rituals, Guerrilla Style

While Confederate guerrillas such as Quantrill, Anderson, Younger, Hildebrand, Wilson, James, Todd, and Holtzclaw are undoubtedly Missouri's dominant Civil War memory export, the state was ironically also home to the first branch of the United Daughters of the Confederacy (UDC). The Daughters decorated Confederate graves and sent birthday cards to veterans; they educated children on the virtues of the Old South and the Confederate cause, and they would react swiftly and viciously to anyone who called the purity of those virtues into question. Most important of all, they spearheaded fund-raising efforts for Confederate monuments in cemeteries, parks, and town squares throughout the South. For instance, when the Jefferson Davis monument was unveiled in Richmond, Virginia, in 1907, the Daughters claimed to have covered some $50,000 of its estimated $70,000 price tag (more than $1,000,000 in contemporary currency). Thus, as the ranks of the war generation began to thin in the 1890s, the women of the UDC essentially usurped leadership from their male forebears. By 1903, when Cole Younger published his memoir, the Daughters were formidable power brokers in Dixie as they utterly dominated both the traditions of the Lost Cause and the movement's finances.[16]

As we know, Missouri failed to officially secede from the Union in the 1860s, but it suffered no corresponding dearth of female-led commemoration. Perhaps *because* the state had not seceded, women in Missouri attempted to compensate with memorial fervor, often in the form of UDC activity. In the late nineteenth and early twentieth centuries, chapters of the UDC sprang up all across Missouri. Higginsville, Sedalia, Saint Louis, Columbia, Kansas City, Springville, Booneville, Marshall, Slater, Jefferson City, Moberly, Independence, Mexico, Bridgeton, Saint Joseph, Hannibal, Keytesville, Clinton, Warrensburg, and Cape Girardeau were all home to at least one chapter; larger venues such as Saint Louis–despite its reputation for wartime Unionism and abolitionism–often hosted several simultaneously. Westerly locations or not, members of these Missouri chapters considered themselves very much a part of the national organization and its commemorative mission.

According to literature published by the John S. Marmaduke Chapter of Columbia (which listed eighty-three active members in 1924), the "business" of the Daughters was at once "historical, benevolent, educational, and social." They sought to "honor the memory of those who served and those who fell in the service of the Confederate states"; to "protect and preserve the material for a truthful history of the War Between the States"; to "assist descendants of worthy Confederates in securing proper education"; and, not coincidentally, to "record the part taken by southern women in patient endurance and hardship and patriotic devotion during the struggle as in [their] untiring efforts after the war during the Reconstruction of the South to fulfill those sacred duties of benevolence toward the survivors and toward those dependent upon them." With those objectives in mind, the UDC in Missouri compiled wartime histories, spearheaded fund-raisers for monuments and assistance programs, helped operate the Confederate Veterans Home at Higginsville, maintained and decorated grave sites, hosted annual conventions and banquets, and even performed matronly duties for the Order of Kappa Alpha–a fraternity at the University of Missouri founded on the principles of Robert E. Lee and the southern cavalier.[17]

Unlike most other ex-Confederate states, the unpredictable nature and domestic setting of irregular warfare in Missouri had mandated that the mothers, daughters, sisters, aunts, and wives of bushwhackers live and work on the front lines of the guerrilla war. A slew of historians have recently illustrated how women not only lived amid guerrilla warfare but were often participants—and willing ones at that—in the violence. These historians correctly interpret the guerrilla theater as a venue of "house-hold war," a system in which women operated most often in the capac-ity of quartermasters and intelligence gatherers; they equipped their men in the bush with clothing, food, ammunition, information, and emotional support. And these women, many of them Daughters, had no intention of letting their own service to the Confederate cause be neglected or forgot-ten in the postwar period. "Few monuments," women of the UDC in Mis-souri lamented, "have arisen to tell future generations of the heroism and grandeur of the women of the South."[18]

To that end, in 1913 the Missouri Branch of the United Daughters of the Confederacy published a collection of seventy-four essays titled *Reminis-cences of Women in Missouri during the Sixties.* As one might expect, contribu-tions covered a wide range of topics, but the vast majority of them revolved around events that had transpired on the homefront, most of which had stemmed from the guerrilla war. Mrs. William H. Gregg recalled that her mother-in-law wore her jewelry concealed in the breast of her clothing to avoid rampant acts of theft committed by Union men. Eventually, though, "they finally discovered the watch chain about her neck," "tore her dress open," and "robbed her." Mrs. M. E. Lewis remembered the day that General James Lane and his men "loaded six mules and horse wagons with the goods from the stores in town" and then torched the town before returning to Kansas. Mrs. J. A. B. Adcock recollected that because of his friendship with Quantrill, Federals had twice attempted to execute her father in the brush, but he escaped both times before taking up permanent exile in the woods to avoid capture. Mrs. N. M. Harris cited an encoun-ter between a pro-Union Jayhawker and a young girl in which the intrud-ing Kansan ordered the girl to stop crying because "if she uttered another sound he would cut her head off." As evidenced by these *published* remi-niscences, women had experienced the hardships of the guerrilla war and were seemingly in an excellent position to dictate what *male* elements of it would and would not become part of the Lost Cause narrative they man-aged.[19] (Although, as will be explored in chapter 5, the commemorative power of women in the guerrillafront was quite complicated.)

Published well before this volume or even the advent of the UDC, *The Life of Samuel Hildebrand* sporadically cast southern women in a positive light—mainly Hildebrand's wife and mother—but made no concerted effort to honor them as a collective group. And while Cole Younger also died before *Reminiscences of Women in Missouri* went to press, by 1903, when he published his own memoir, the UDC and other southern women had achieved new standards of public power. *The Story of Cole Younger as Told by Himself* acutely noted the newly prominent place of women in conservative space. Unlike Hildebrand's tale, which placed women in an auxiliary capacity, Younger bluntly stated, "I should like to say something of the ladies who have honored me with their presence. But as I have been a bachelor all of my life I scarcely know what to say. I do know, though, that they are the divine creatures of a divine creator; I do know that they are the high priestesses of this land; and, too, God could not be everywhere, so He made women." Later in the memoir, Younger included an anecdote telling of his desire to appease women in power:

> Perhaps you have heard of banquets "for gentlemen only." Well, it was upon one of these occasions that one of the guests was called upon to respond to a toast—"The Ladies." There being no ladies present, he felt safe in his remarks. "I do not believe," he said, "that there are any real, true women living any more." The guest opposite him sprang to his feet and shouted: "I hope that the speaker refers only to his own female relations." I never could understand, either, when a man goes wrong it is called "misfortune," while if a woman goes wrong it is called "shame." But I presume, being in prison twenty-five years, I am naturally dull, and should not question a world I have not lived in for a quarter of a century. I tell you, my friends, that I know very little of women, but of one thing I am morally certain: If the front seats of Paradise are not reserved for women, I am willing to take a back seat with them.[20]

Penned following his release from prison, Younger's tribute to the ladies of the New South immediately revealed that he understood their cultural prowess and that to ingratiate guerrilla memory with the mainstream Lost Cause, he needed to appease the female guardians of Confederate tradition.[21] Appropriately, then, as the first guerrilla to publish a major memoir after the turn of the century, Younger freely confessed his inability to set down adequately elegant prose in honor of women. At first glance, Younger's description of women as "divine" or "high priestesses" may call to mind terminology designed to constrain women to "the pedestal" and their duties to the domestic realm. But as proclaimed by C. Vann Woodward, the Lost Cause failed to operate in a "religious" capacity until the conservative women of the UDC ascended to lead it.[22] Thus, Younger's homage to women fit snugly within the context of powerful Daughters serving as the directors of a civic religion rooted in Confederate tradition. The nature of Younger's praise for women does, in some ways, still link them to traditional gender norms as embodiments of feminine virtue and purity—but the fact that Younger and all proceeding guerrilla memoirists paid their obligatory dues to women suggested that they were well aware of the role women would play in determining the fate of guerrilla memory.

William H. Gregg's 1906 memoir, titled *A Little Dab of History without Embellishment*, also included a section of text that specifically and explicitly targeted southern women. "Heaven bless the women," he wrote, for "they were friends in need and indeed. No braver than the southern ladies of Missouri, we owed our lives to them. So, to say again, heaven bless them." Unlike Younger's account, however, Gregg's manuscript was never published. During the war, Gregg had served as one of William C. Quantrill's most trusted and deadly lieutenants. After the war, financial woes influenced Gregg to sell his story (and full publication rights) to amateur historian William Elsey Connelley—a resident of Kansas and perhaps Quantrill's harshest biographer. Even still, the value of Gregg's memoir should not at all be discounted because it was penned with publication in mind.[23]

Gregg takes the importance of women a step farther than Younger through this explanation of the 1863 raid on Lawrence, Kansas, in which some two hundred men and boys were gunned down by Quantrill and his men. According to Gregg, "wholesale killing was repugnant to many of the men" at Lawrence, but they fought on in great part because "Anderson's sisters had been murdered, Crawford's sister's, [sic] had been murdered, and, any day, any of our sisters were liable to be murdered." Bloodlust notwithstanding, Gregg also reported that a Union man held hostage in the Eldridge Hotel during the massacre would honestly testify that "if there was a woman or child harmed by Quantrill's men, I never heard of it." Gregg offered southern women the best of both worlds: guerrillas had waged a savage campaign to protect them, but they had also respected womanhood and not harmed women during the most controversial battle of the entire guerrilla war.[24]

More than any of his predecessors, Hampton Watts wrote in his 1913 memoir, *The Babe of the Company,* as if he could literally feel the passage of time chipping away at guerrilla memory. He included a roster of all the men from William "Bloody Bill" Anderson's guerrilla company that he could remember (even if it was only a last name); took care to record when and where lesser-known guerrillas had fallen in battle; and, on more than one occasion, noted where "over a lapse of forty-eight years" some guerrillas had simply been forgotten once and for all. Watts ended his memoir with a poem that he hoped would remind his grandson of the glorious sacrifices that guerrillas—men such as Hildebrand, Younger, and himself—had made during the war:

> Rest on, embalmed and sainted dead!
> Dear as the blood ye gave;
> No implous [*sic*] footstep here shall tred
> The herbage of your grave.

On the surface, very little of Watts's account has to do with women. In fact, they are virtually absent from his descriptions of battles fought by guerrillas in 1863 and 1864. But Watts's fear of being forgotten—a sentiment clearly verified by the subtitle of his book: *An Unfolded Leaf from the Forest of Never-to-Be-Forgotten Years*—suggests that securing a long-term place for guerrilla memory within the female-led Lost Cause was a serious concern. As had Younger and Gregg before him, Watts paid homage to the women of Missouri, but he also became the first guerrilla memoirist to specifically honor the UDC by name. On the very first page of his account, Watts wrote: "To the Ladies of Fayette Richmond Greys Chapter No. 148, United Daughters of the Confederacy, who will erect a monument to the memory of the 'Brave and Fallen Guerillas' in the Fayette battle, September 20, 1864. Over the graves it decorates, the brave comrades it ennobles, and the dear women who are made angelic by their deed, I give this truthful story." Watts clearly understood that while he could record his narrative in print, the Daughters could immortalize it publicly in marble.[25]

John McCorkle published *Three Years with Quantrill* a year later, in 1914. The memoir marked a significant break from the dedications to southern women by Younger, Gregg, Watts, and Dalton; rather than a stand-alone paragraph or even a chapter dedicated to women, McCorkle infused his personal story with strong female characters throughout. During the war, McCorkle's sister was among the women imprisoned in and then killed by the collapse of a Union prison in Kansas City. According to McCorkle, this incident, along with the threatened kidnapping of his cousin, Mollie, should he not join the Union militia, prompted McCorkle to become a guerrilla. He explained, "When we returned from the singing school, Mollie Wiggington told us that there had been a company of Federal soldiers there that evening, leaving an order for George and me to come to Independence the next Monday to join the State Militia, and that unless we did report, that they would come back and take Mollie and put her in prison and hold her until we did report."

Later in the book, McCorkle described how various women had aided the guerrilla cause and, unlike Younger, added an element of danger shared between the sexes in his narrative. His cousin Mollie, he maintained, risked severe punishment to help arm guerrillas in the bush. Using luggage designed specifically for smuggling, she traveled to Illinois and revealed a bounty of 35,000 percussion caps on her return. Importantly, for McCorkle women do not replace men as the primary figures of combat, but he implies that Mollie, as a quartermaster of the guerrilla war, helped make that combat possible in the first place.[26]

Toward the end of his account, McCorkle recounted the story of a woman who had been "outraged" by two men. After authorities tried for several days to apprehend the culprits, Frank James told the captain in charge "that he could take six of his men and capture these two fiends." James and his posse supposedly caught the two men—and executed them both. By coupling these events with the bravery of his cousin Mollie, McCorkle exhibited a conflicted understanding of how to portray women in the New South. On one hand, strong women such as Mollie had taken on important roles during the war and were, in more ways than not, steering the Lost Cause ship in 1914. On the other hand, though, McCorkle was still compelled to include an example that would, at least theoretically, serve as an example of the protection that "pure, innocent" women needed from men to avoid imprisonment in a "Northern Dungeon" where they could have met a fate "more terrible than death itself." The conundrum, then, amounted to including women adequately enough in his memoir to curry favor with the Daughters while not destroying the hypermasculine component of guerrilla memory in the process. If McCorkle's treatment was to be representative or in any way universal, the southern damsel in distress would not disappear completely from guerrilla memory, but with powerful women helping shape the development of the New South, she would no longer be nearly so helpless.[27]

Also published in 1914, Kit Dalton's brief memoir, *Under the Black Flag*, included a pair of separate encounters with women—one pro-Confederate, one pro-Union—that again connected female characters directly to the dangers of irregular warfare. Following a fierce skirmish with Federal troops, Dalton, then an enlisted soldier in the regular war, was forced to hide under the eaves of a nearby house. As night fell, Dalton made contact with the residents of the home—a woman and her infant. The woman asked Dalton to identify himself. "A stranger, madam," he answered, "who wants to get into the Conniersville road, if you will be kind enough to direct me." When the young woman asked where Dalton hailed from, he confessed that he was a "Confederate soldier in distress." With that, the woman identified herself as Mrs. Stone, invited Dalton into her home, tended to his wounds, provided him with a new shirt, and fixed him something to eat. She also provided Dalton with information: the rest of his Confederate companions had been killed in "cold blooded murder" after surrendering. Before leaving her home, Dalton remembered Mrs. Stone saying, "I hope you will live to even up matters with those brutes, Mr. Dalton," thus strongly implying that he resort to the sort of activity that would *enable* him to even his vendetta with the Federals. So began, Dalton recounted, his career as a guerrilla shortly thereafter.[28]

Later in the memoir, while commanding his own band of Confederate guerrillas, Dalton wrote about capturing a vessel on the Cumberland River. Initially, the captain of the ship refused to surrender himself or his passengers to Dalton's men. After an exchange of gunfire and promises from Dalton that the captain's passengers would not be taken hostage or murdered, the crew and cargo were captured. Then, Dalton wrote, "One of our lady prisoners, having a pretty keen sense of the ridiculous, approached me and said: 'And you don't eat 'em alive, captain?'" The rest of Dalton's flirtatious exchange with the young lady (an avowed Unionist) went as follows:

> *Dalton:* No, they are too tough, but if I were a cannibal chieftain, your fate would certainly be an unhappy one.

Female Prisoner (after uttering a "merry chuckle"): Aren't you Captain Dalton, of those terrible guerillas [*sic*]?

Dalton: Guerillas eat 'em alive, don't they?

Female Prisoner: We read all sorts of things about the guerillas but I don't believe they are as bloodthirsty as they are represented.

Dalton: No, they are not savages or cannibals. Look around you and see if there's a man in my command who impresses you as a demon.

Female Prisoner: No, they seem to be pretty genteel fellows, but you are Captain Dalton, now, aren't you?

Dalton: I am his friend, madam, and am a guerilla—as terrible as the word may sound to you. You have seen a band of guerillas in action. They have treated you and your companions as rudely as they ever treated captives in their whole career. You can judge better now what a guerilla is.

Female Prisoner: I think better of them, captain, and as a souvenir, I want a cutting of that drake's tail on your forehead. I will cherish it as a souvenir.

Dalton's use of the two major female encounters in his memoir cleverly communicated two main ideas to readers: first, that a woman, Mrs. Stone, had seemingly encouraged his transition from regular soldier to guerrilla out of wartime necessity, and second, that another woman, this time an unnamed Unionist, had vouched for his honorable behavior and the way he treated women after he had become a guerrilla. So at the same time Dalton included female characters in his story who shared the risks of war with men, he also conveyed how those women had both supported and approved of his résumé of bushwhacking. This underlying message alluded to the hope that women in the twentieth century should continue the support of Mrs. Stone and the unnamed prisoner in the form of their joint efforts.[29]

The prominence of women in narratives penned by Younger and McCorkle (and to a lesser extent, Dalton) notwithstanding, Joseph Bailey's *Confederate Guerrilla: The Civil War Memoir of Joseph Bailey* (1920) arguably sheds the greatest light on the relationship between an evolving guerrilla memory and the rise of female Lost Cause leadership. Bailey, the husband of a prominent officer in the UDC, actually gave a copy of the memoir to his wife's local chapter as a gift. Like McCorkle before him, Bailey included memories of the guerrilla war that displayed an element of shared danger and risk between men and women. In one case, he described how a company of Union soldiers approached him and a female companion. "Amid a shower of bullets," he recalled, "the danger from which was shared equally by my sweetheart and me, I mounted my horse and began the race for my life." Elsewhere in the book, Bailey reported how southern women such as his wife had trekked miles to procure food and supplies during the war. They "walked that distance crossing mountains and wading swiftly flowing mountain streams; bought half a bushel of corn each and carried it home on their shoulders to make bread for hungry children," he wrote.

After expounding the virtues of Confederate women throughout his memoir, Bailey still included an entire dedication titled "Heroism of Southern Women." In it, he remembered the story of a young southern maiden that carried a wounded Confederate boy to a "secluded place in dense woods over a mile distant" and then braved foul weather and fear to wait all night with the boy until he died. He added, "Miss Baines volunteered to keep a lone vigil over his lifeless form" while two other women went to find help. Despite being alone in the dark with the boy's corpse, "her courage never faltered." Bailey concluded the dedication with the affirmation that "this incident, one of many heroic acts of southern women, will portray in some measure the fortitude and courage of women in the War Between the States." In many ways, Bailey's account metaphorically conceded the leadership role taken by women after the war to watch over and commemorate the Confederate dead.[30] In short, Joseph Bailey fully understood that updating his legacy in a manner that might allow for its acceptance into the mainstream Lost Cause meant not just injecting women into his wartime narrative—it meant paying the commemorative piper.

Commemorating the "Other" Wars

In the late nineteenth and early twentieth centuries, a man's physicality—that is, his ability to impose his will physically, to exhibit forceful prowess over other men, women, animals, or even nature itself—played an essential role in determining how society would gauge his masculinity. In other words, to be a "real" man in America, one had to do the things that historically seemed manly.[31] But as a direct consequence of assertive women such as the Daughters venturing out of the domestic realm and into the public affairs of southern society and culture, many turn-of-the-century

Americans lamented a perceived decline in male chivalry. So much so, in fact, that historian Kristin Hoganson contends: "Many of those who fretted about a decline in chivalry regarded the assertive new woman as evidence of that decline, for at the heart of chivalry was the juxtaposition of feminine vulnerability and masculine power."[32]

What better way to replenish the collective chivalry of American men and to restore their mastery over women than to stage a war? The short-lived Spanish-American War provided just such an attractive remedy for these deficiencies of manliness. In the Cuban revolutionaries struggling to break free of Spanish imperial power, American war hawks found a viable underdog in need of heroic assistance—an underdog for whom martial aid might equal a restored sense of American civil valor and chivalry. So as southerners rushed to claim their share of this newly rehabilitated American masculinity, ex-guerrillas took care not be left out of the mix.

Following the conclusion of the war against Spain's failing empire—a contest that lasted for all of five months—temporarily satisfied Americans forgot all about the needs of their Cuban allies and used the quick, total victory as a catalyst for revamped notions of manhood, commemoration, and chivalry. One man by the name of Roosevelt even used it to help land himself in the White House. In any event, the sight of ex-Union and ex-Confederate soldiers fighting under the same flag spurred positive feelings on both sides of the Mason-Dixon Line. To former Union vets, ex-Rebels carrying the American flag reiterated their victory in the Civil War. To former Confederates, the Spanish-American War was an invaluable opportunity to renew their status as citizens of the United States once and for all. But as Hoganson cleverly points out, the war also initiated a shift in the commemoration of American veterans as a new crop of returning heroes started to replace the aging Civil War generation. And, perhaps more critically, the service of these new men in Cuba altered the fundamental criteria for remembrance. Rather than noble causes, honorable intentions, and mutual sacrifice, this shift in commemorative attitudes centered much more explicitly on physical abilities and feats of martial power.[33]

In his autobiography, Younger included this tract on Cuba and the Spanish-American War:

I am not exactly a lead man, but it may surprise you to know that I have been shot between twenty and thirty times and am now carrying over a dozen bullets which have never been extracted. How proud I should have been had I been scarred battling for the honor and glory of my country. Those wounds I received while wearing the gray, I've ever been proud of, and my regret is that I did not receive the rest of them during the war with Spain, for the freedom of Cuba and the honor and glory of this great and glorious republic. But, alas, they were not, and it is a memory embalmed that nails a man to the cross. I was in prison when the war with Cuba was inaugurated, a war that will never pass from memory while hearts beat responsive to the glory of battle in the cause of humanity. How men turned from the path of peace, and seizing the sword, followed the flag! As the blue ranks of American soldiery scaled the heights of heroism, and the smoke rose from the hot altars of the battle gods and freedom's wrongs avenged, so the memory of Cuba's independence will go down in history, glorious as our own revolution—'76 and '98—twin jewels set in the crown of sister centuries. Spain and the world have learned that beneath the folds of our nation's flag there lurks a power as irresistible as the wrath of God. Sleep on, side by side in the dim vaults of eternity, Manila Bay and Bunker Hill, Lexington and Santiago, Ticonderoga and San Juan, glorious rounds in Columbia's ladder of fame, growing colossal as the ages roll. Yes, I was in prison than [*sic*], and let me tell you, dear friends, I do not hesitate to say that God permits few men to suffer as I did, when I awoke to the full realization that I was wearing the stripes instead of a uniform of my country. Remember, friends, I do not uphold war for commercial pillage. War is a terrible thing, and leads men sometimes out of the common avenues of life. Without reference to myself, men of this land, let me tell you emphatically, dispassionately, and absolutely that war makes savages of men, and dethrones them from reason. It is too often sugarcoated with the word "patriotism" to make it bearable and men call it "National honor."

In his tribute to the war's victorious servicemen, Younger sought to resituate himself within the newly drawn boundaries of twentieth-century commemoration. While he remained proud of wearing "the gray," he focused extensively on the physical merits of his service—the startling number of wounds he survived—rather than the nobleness of the Confederate cause that had prompted him to accumulate them. At fifty-four years old, Younger's regret that he could not participate in the conflict underlines two key points. First, ex-Confederates, even former guerrillas, viewed the Spanish-American War as an excellent means of reestablishing their personal claims to not only citizenship but also chivalry. Second, Younger under-

stood that Civil War service no longer held a monopoly on commemorative activities. Therefore, while he could not fight in Cuba, Younger
could at least reframe his Civil War record and recast memories of the
guerrilla theater in a way that would help preserve his story against a tide
of newer, younger, and stronger veterans seeking to displace it (and him
along with it).[34]

The conclusion of Younger's thoughts on the war in Cuba revealed that
while he might have wanted for youth or physical prowess, he had a craft-
iness that came only with age and experience. Many Americans disapproved of intervention in Cuba; they protested jingoism and fought to
impede the industrialists and politicians who stood to profit handsomely
from the conflict and production of its materials. Younger understood the
complexity of the politics that surrounded the war with Spain and took
measures to ensure that both sides—the hawks *and* the objectors—would
find something to like in his narrative. With this in mind, his assertion that
he did not "uphold war for commercial pillage" and his subsequent explanation of war and its terrors only show that he was trying to compose his
narrative (as a representation of himself) to be accepted by as broad an
audience as possible.

Much like Younger, Harrison Trow devoted a section of his memoir to
foreign wars and commemoration. Unlike Younger, however, he refused
to acknowledge that other, subsequent wars (such as World War I) had
unseated the memory monopoly once enjoyed by the Civil War generation; rather, he made a full-on attempt to reframe the bushwhacker experience as service worthy of remembrance even when pitted against the
horrors of modern, mechanized warfare. Ironically, then, Trow essentially
attempted to update his legacy for the New South by contending vehemently that it did not actually need to be updated. On the very last page
of his memoir, Trow opined:

> During the World War, in conversation with friends, I told them to take away
> from Germany her airplanes, gases and machine guns, and if it were possible
> to call Quantrell's old band together, of which at no time were there over
> three hundred and fifty men, all told, under Todd, Poole, Yager, Anderson,
> Younger, Jarrett, Haller, Quantrell, and myself, I could take these three hun-
> dred and fifty men and go to Berlin in a gallop, for history does not now and
> never will know the power there was in the Quantrell band. It has been given

up long ago that they were the most frightening devils the world has ever known or ever will know.

Because he was writing several years after Younger, Trow had to grapple with two new waves of veterans—opponents for commemorative attention—as opposed to just the Spanish-American War generation, a decent portion of whom were ex-Confederates anyway. Brazen to the point of absurdity, Trow's declaration that Quantrill's "old band" could have conquered the German Empire with Civil War–era weaponry broadcasted a pair of critical ideas. First, the fact that he felt obligated to include this antitribute to the soldiers of World War I illustrated that shifts in commemoration took a real toll on ex-guerrillas in the New South—none of whom wanted to become forgotten relics of the Old South. Second, and perhaps most important, Trow was clearly not interested in renegotiating the requirements or criteria for veneration and commemoration. While Younger understood that newer waves of veterans would eventually replace the Civil War generation and that ex-bushwhackers needed to preserve what they could, Trow not only scoffed at resetting himself or his comrades within the context of "new commemoration" but also bluntly countered those models by stating that older meant better and that the South would "never know" another group of veterans as worthy of remembrance as Quantrill's guerrilla band.[35]

Evolve or Die?

In 1870, with Reconstruction ongoing and the war still fresh on southern minds, Sam Hildebrand concluded his autobiography on a presumptuous note. "If the strange hallucination should ever enter the mind of a man that I could be captured," he boasted, "let him immediately send for a physician, have his head emptied and filled up with clabber to give him a better set of brains."[36] Five years had passed since Appomattox and Hildebrand still imagined himself as invincible—uncatchable and unbeatable; an entity more at home with the other "supernatural" beings that would prowl the pages of *Noted Guerrillas* than the ranks of mortal men. Most of all, Hildebrand wrote as a prisoner of the moment, with the foolish confidence of a man who believed he would *always* be famous.

As we already know, Hildebrand could be caught—though, in an ironic twist, it was his own head that ended up hollow, made so by a bullet rather than a physician. In still another twist, that same bullet saved Hildebrand from his own shortsightedness: he did not live long enough to realize just how wrong he had been about the endurance of his outlandish notoriety. But other guerrillas did live long enough. So they had two choices: become irrelevant and forgotten (a fate many proud ex-bushwhackers, still defining their identities by their parts in the war, would have understood as identical to death) or find new relevance—in short, evolve before it was too late. Collectively, they chose the latter. These former guerrillas consciously attempted to reequip their legacy for survival by breaking free from the established literary standards of nineteenth-century guerrilla memory. On paper, they adapted to shifts in gender, commemorative attitudes, and race relations; they refashioned themselves as upstanding citizens of the New South; they repositioned themselves safely under the umbrella of the Lost Cause.

As we will soon discover, these efforts could not, and did not, exist in a textual vacuum. Aging bushwhackers would also go to great lengths to physically and publically influence their prospects for long-term remembrance. But rebooting guerrilla memory in print was one thing; acting out these new devotions to the Lost Cause and the New South before a live audience was quite another.

FOUR

Getting the Band Back Together

> We kept monotonously falling back upon one camp or another, and
> eating up the farmers and their families. They ought to have shot us;
> on the contrary, they were as hospitably kind and courteous to us
> as if we had deserved it.
> —Mark Twain, "The Private History of a Campaign That Failed"

> Dinner will be served in the Christian church yard here next Friday
> during the re-union of Up Hays camp of ex-Confederates and
> Quantrell's men. Everybody is invited to bring a basket of eatables
> as the old soldiers deserve to be fed.
> —*Oak Grove Banner*, 1900

On May 12, 1888, the Saturday edition of the *Kansas City Journal* reported that a "small but select gathering," the likes of which "had not been seen since the days when civil war reigned," had assembled in the neighboring town of Blue Springs, Missouri. For many residents of Blue Springs, the occasion that prompted the meeting must have been as novel as the characters it attracted: Mrs. Caroline C. Quantrill, mother of the famed guerrilla commander with whom she shared a surname, had trekked all the way from her native Ohio to hold court.

Several of William C. Quantrill's former "men-at-arms" received official invitations to appear at the City Hotel in Blue Springs. There, for the first time ever, they could meet the mother of their deceased chieftain and architect of the notorious Lawrence Massacre. According to the paper, fourteen ex-bushwhackers, now sporting clear signs of middle age, "recounted in a friendly way their exploits while with Quantrill"; they spent most of the day talking "with her [Mrs. Quantrill] about her son" and "the parts in the great internecine strife that they had enacted while with him." Mrs. Quantrill, it seems, knew surprisingly little about her son's sordid military résumé and wanted to hear the "facts"—graphic as they may have been—from his old comrades.

Those who wondered whether or not Quantrill's men would return to their marauding ways on reassembly were met with relief or disappointment, depending on their lingering partisan allegiances. Because despite their reputations for wartime savagery, the *Journal* noted that the guerrillas, whose roster that day in Blue Springs included notables such as A. J. Walker, Warren Welch, J. Hicks George, and John Koger, "were an intelligent and well behaved lot of men." And more important, with the war now two decades in rearview, they "did not seem possessed of any of the bloodthirsty characteristics ascribed to them." Whether on the prowl or now as apparently reformed citizens, the old guerrillas could still command attention from the public. In fact, their reuniting "was regarded as such a rare occurrence in this piping time of peace that it was deemed of interest to the public to chronicle what was said and done there."[1]

The meeting also came to the attention of Union veterans of the regular war—and they were less than thrilled with the prospect that Quantrill's men might hold such reunions and besmirch the integrity of their own commemorative activities. One response from the *Grand Army Advocate* of Des Moines, Iowa, sneered that the festivities in Blue Springs gave the former guerrillas ample opportunities to discuss "their bloody murders and fiendish crimes without the slightest hesitancy." Another reaction, in the form of a letter to the editor penned by a former Union soldier in Kentucky, labeled the event the "most extraordinary reunion of any of the men who took part in the attempt to destroy the country" because it involved "these shriveled up old demons" glorifying "the days when they murdered prisoners, ravished women, and pillaged towns, with as much delight and seeming honor as any of the brave confederate soldiers who recognized the rules of war, would speak of their battles and service." "That not one man in the bloody group should have escaped the gallows," the editorial concluded, "has been overlooked."[2]

Rather unintentionally (and perhaps quite controversially), then, Mrs. Quantrill's reception in Blue Springs struck a chord among the ex-bushwhackers and their onlookers, both curious and outraged. Her visit set plans in motion for more formalized reunions—but it would take a decade for veterans of her son's command to get Quantrill's band back together.

In recent years, scholarly attention paid to commemorative ceremonies and other Decoration Day–like events staged by veterans of the regular war has increased dramatically. A host of scholars have explored the various ways in which northern and southern veterans' organizations employed reunions to welcome or ward off sectional reconciliation, to implement (or reimplement) racial controls on white society, or even to make a statement concerning the war's broadest meanings and legacies for posterity. Given this academic fascination with the Civil War genera-tion's physical rituals of memory, surprisingly few historians have grap-pled with the larger implications and significance of guerrilla reunions.[3]

When these guerrilla reunions *are* addressed, it is typically in one of two ways. On one side, Quantrill's raiders are depicted as having craved the sort of attention conferred on their Confederate contemporaries—but also as having turned to the literary construct of the "noble guerrilla" to achieve that status. Within this line of reasoning, around the beginning of the twentieth century, ex-guerrillas did not break from the Edwardsian tradition but actually doubled down on the commemorative merits of his irregular Lost Cause as conceived in the 1870s.[4] On the other side, annual reunions of Quantrill's men are employed to show "the complex ways that memories of the border war served at once to unify and to divide people along the Missouri-Kansas line well into the twentieth century."[5] In other words, guerrilla reunions in Missouri served as a comparative lens to two simultaneous and conflicting developments: gradual reconciliation and diehard sectional loyalty (that is, Union vs. Confederate, North vs. South).

When Quantrill's men did organize and begin to host official reunions in 1898, they admittedly had much more in mind than a revalidation of *Noted Guerrillas* or assuaging wartime grudges. As evidenced by chapter 3, guerrilla memoirists from Cole Younger in 1903 to George Cruzen in 1930 sought to update and replace the memory narrative popularized by John Newman Edwards. While the political usefulness of Edwards's work (and its construct of the "noble guerrilla") dwindled, so too did its value as social and cultural currency to Quantrill's surviving men. In response, ex-bushwhackers turned to the medium of print not to strengthen their ties to Edwards but to discard them. Bearing these issues in mind, this chapter offers a new consideration of guerrilla reunions: that they should be recognized as both a party to and an extension of the work performed by guerrilla memoirs—that they should be understood as commemorative events designed to mirror the activities of regular veterans' organizations with the ultimate goal of assimilation into conventional circles of southern remembrance and social hierarchy. And unlike the fainéant, would-be bushwhackers of Twain's account, *these* guerrillas wholeheartedly believed that they *did* deserve it.

Not coincidentally, then, reunions of Quantrill's men, which occurred each summer in Missouri from 1898 to 1929, paralleled this thirty-year window of memoir writing almost exactly, and many of the memoirists featured in the previous chapter attended reunions at one time or another— often frequently.[6] The activities involved in these gatherings revolved around many of the same thematic categories explored in guerrilla memoirs: the roles of women in commemoration, the proper racial attitudes and place of African Americans in southern society, and homage paid to veterans of subsequent military conflicts. But while memoirs allowed ex-guerrillas to reimagine or reboot their identities on paper, from the privacy of writing desks and print houses, reunion activities afforded them the opportunity to *physically* act out those scenarios before the news media, and to interact much more directly with the regular veterans with whom they desperately sought to "fit in."

The Encampment Model

Before exploring the formative elements of a guerrilla reunion, we must first examine the events they were designed to mimic. Reunions of regular army veterans—also called encampments—were commonplace throughout the South into the 1930s and 1940s. Encampments could revolve around different organizational factors: the reunion of a particular army, the coming together of veterans from a particular battle or campaign, the regional or national meeting of a specific organization (such as the United Confederate Veterans or its Unionist counterpart, the Grand Army of the Republic), or even the reconciliation of formerly opposed forces at special Blue-Gray reunions.[7] The location, date, and time of these meetings would be broadcast months—if not years—in advance; hotels, restaurants, train companies, photographers, caterers, and taxi services were all contracted to serve the special needs and wants of attending veterans and guests. In this way, reunions also functioned as economic stimuli for their chosen destinations, much like the modern-day Olympic Games, albeit on a relative (that is, much smaller) scale.

As illustrated by the official program of the October 1919 reunion of

the United Confederate Veterans in Atlanta, Georgia, the variety of activities planned for attendees over the course of three days was staggering. They included musical performances, choral concerts, invocations,
numerous welcome speeches, organized luncheons, battlefield tours, committee meetings, announcements of the reports of committees, officers' reports, commanders' reports, political speeches, historical presentations,
memorial ceremonies, readings of the Honor Roll, dinners, presentations
of "Official Ladies," benedictions, grand balls, grand parades, and private
receptions at various hotels, mansions, and eateries. Amid all of these activities, while male commanders and officers were technically "in charge"
of their various camps and committees, women played a major role as
organizers, official escorts, chaperones, handlers, fund-raisers, maids of
honor, and speakers.[8]

Political campaigning represented a core component of most regular
encampments. Few and far between were the politicians who could resist
the chance to stump before a ready-made audience of thousands—not to
mention an audience who so clearly wore their allegiances and sympathies on their (sometimes empty) sleeves. While speeches were common,
printed ads were also popular. William D. Upshaw, newly elected to the
Fifth Congressional District in Georgia—but perpetually campaigning—
chose the latter option to ingratiate himself with the visiting ex-Rebels at
the 1919 meeting.[9] "You are comrades to the immortals," he wrote, wel-
coming the old men in gray "not only as Congressman from the fortunate
district where you are our honored guests, but as the Son of a Confederate
Soldier whose 'vocal dust' breathes again upon me under the sacred inspiration of your presence." "I join with all Atlanta," Upshaw continued, "in
extending to you that measureless measure of welcome that we cannot
measure in words." "God bless you every one," Upshaw concluded dramatically, "the one time knightly soldiers of the STARS AND BARS—
and you, the gallant sons and soldiers of the STARS AND STRIPES,
blend your heroic efforts for the glory of our COMMON FLAG and the
vital victories of our CHRISTIAN civilization." Congressman Upshaw
adroitly played to his audience and likely helped solidify the support that
kept him in office until 1927.[10]

Like political pitches, presentations concerning the history of the Civil
War were also a mainstay at reunions; these speeches often focused on the
war's causes and made specific efforts to exclude the presence of slavery

from that list. The official souvenir book of the 1895 United Confederate Veterans reunion in Houston, Texas, decreed the important role of (re)-writing history through annual gatherings:

> The prime objects of the United Confederate Veterans' Association are the meeting and intermingling of friends and comrades of the war time and the preservation and promulgation of the true history of the causes leading up to the strife, the manner in which it was carried on through four bloody years, and the salient features of the succeeding period of Reconstruction. The historical part, to the end that succeeding generations of Southrons may know the reasons that animated their ancestors; that they may appreciate their courage upon the tented field, their patriotic devotion in accepting the stern decree of war, and in the face of mountainous obstacles, carrying the commonwealths of their section once again to the front rank of the sisterhood of states.[11]

The grandiose rhetoric of N. E. Harris at a June 1905 reunion of Confederate veterans in Louisville, Kentucky, typified these history-defining speeches:

> For four long years the red tide rolled from sea to mountain, and from mountain to sea again; every soldier became a hero, and every hero of the nation became a soldier in that strife. The struggle dignified the Anglo-Saxon race, and dwarfed every other conflict known to modern history. No such titanic contest was ever waged between peoples or nations of the same blood and interest. It was a war, on the one hand, for civil liberty and national independence, for home and fireside; on the other, for the restoration of the integrity of the Union, for the flag and the Government. The freedom of the slave was a mere incident that grew up from the necessities of the conflict. In the forum of history the great Confederate war will always be regarded and treated as one which involved and settled greater and more far-reaching issues for humanity than any other that was ever waged on this earth.[12]

At their most fundamental level, talks such as Harris's were geared toward maintaining the underlying righteousness of the failed Confederacy, thereby breathing continuous life into the Lost Cause Movement.

To the extent that their means and abilities allowed, this basic organizational scheme, the "encampment model," is what Quantrill's men sought to mirror at their own reunions in Missouri. As we will soon see, the familiar-looking roster of festivities at a guerrilla reunion—filled with officer elections, business meetings, picnics, political speeches, dances, and female participants—was aimed at achieving more or less the same ends outlined by the UCV at their aforementioned Houston meeting. The main difference in the case of the guerrillas, however, was that preserving and promulgating *their own* "true history" of the war required them to simultaneously convince other "Southrons" that it—along with the guerrillas themselves—was worthy of lasting, wide-scale remembrance.

Irregular Encampments

When Quantrill's command finally organized a reunion in 1898, they pulled out all the stops. According to the *Kansas City Star*, the only downside to the meeting in Blue Springs, Missouri, was the weather. Despite the cold, a wide array of political candidates, both Republican and Democrat, courted the guerrillas' support; the *Star* reported that "there were many among the old soldiers who will vote a mixed ticket this fall unless they change their minds between now and the election." Local candidates debated, and U.S. senator F. M. Cockrell spoke on the "free coinage of silver and gold at the ratio of 16 to 1 and the east wind was not colder than his reception." Rebuffed, Cockrell "said he favored independence for the Philippine Islands and sat down."[13]

The *Kansas City World* estimated that at least five hundred spectators had come out to see the old bushwhackers—and the *Jackson Examiner* reported that a "large number of ex-Confederates" who had "served near the Quantrell men but did not belong to them" were also present.[14] A large picnic dinner was served to guests and the *Saint Louis Republic* described how Frank James "rapped on the fence with a light cane" amid the festivities and "briefly announced that it was his desire to have reunions of the once notorious band at least once a year." "It is the intention of the men," the *Republic* continued, "to make a permanent organization"—a group that "will be unique in the history of social bodies."[15] Thus the guerrillas had adapted the encampment model for their own purposes and the logistical paradigm of the Quantrill Men reunions was established: a fairlike atmosphere with large crowds, political speakers, swapping yarns, regular veterans, a basket dinner coordinated by women, and organizational meetings.

At the next gathering, in 1899 at Lee's Summit, Warren Welch (who had been elected captain of the Quantrill Men Survivor's Association at the 1898 meeting) "gave the word to march," the "oldtimers grew light-hearted" and "up the racetrack they swept." When the guerrillas came within reach of the crowd, the band "struck up 'Dixie'" and "the men who rode with Quantrill took off their hats and one or two gave the old familiar yell." The playing of "John Brown's Body" "was received coldly." The *Kansas City Journal* made clear that the second annual reunion of Quantrill's guerrillas was a success—and that 1898 had not been an anomaly. "The Quantrell reunion drew a large crowd to the fair grounds," the paper stated, as "the rings were excellent, and some of the finest Herefords in the country were on exhibition." Overall, it was a "happy crowd" of roughly three thousand people—large enough, it seems, "that the stores of the town closed during the afternoon."[16]

The success of the second reunion signified that meetings of the Quantrill men would indeed be annual. As such, members of the Quantrill Men Survivor's Association at each subsequent reunion elected a new committee of officers—a captain (sometimes labeled "commander"), a secretary, and two lieutenants—to select a meeting site and preside over the next year's festivities. From 1898 to 1911, locations rotated among Oak Grove, Sni-A-Bar, Wallace Grove, Independence, and Blue Springs, Missouri. Beginning with the 1912 encampment, however, all reunions were hosted by the family of J. D. Wallace and his sister, Elizabeth C. Wallace, at their homestead called Wallace Grove. The Wallace family had historical connection to the Quantrill command, and their property included several acres of greenery, perfect for parades, picnics, and gatherings. Regardless of the meeting venue, the basket dinner always represented the social highpoint of the reunion. "Dinner was served under the trees and there were heaps and heaps of fried chicken, and homemade bread cut in big, thick slices and jelly and big fat cakes," the *Kansas City Post* observed in 1914. The "daughters of the old raiders set the table and watched over the old people to see that all were served." Old age apparently was not an issue, as the ex-guerrillas could "'put away' the 'grub' in a way that might betoken another raid."[17]

Ex-Confederates continued to participate in the Quantrill reunions until the final meeting in 1929. It is virtually impossible to recover what many of these men, who had left home to join the rank and file of the Confederate army, truly thought about the guerrillas' savage reputations or their brand of warfare—but on the whole, it appears that relations between the two groups were quite cordial. Frequently the guerrilla reunions were even scheduled to coincide with or run very closely to reunions of the Up Hays Camp of the United Confederate Veterans; some of Quantrill's men also attended these meetings. Beginning around 1900, because of the intermixing, the ex-bushwhackers began sporting ribbons to distinguish themselves from regular Confederate veterans in attendance. Quantrill's command wore red souvenir badges emblazoned with the date and location of the reunion, while other Confederates sported white badges.[18]

Regular vets, typically officers, were invited to address the crowd as official speakers on many occasions. One such presentation given by Captain Tom Todd contended that "we were not rebels, we never were rebels, and we are not now." Todd concluded by remarking that "[Francis] Marion's men of Revolutionary days" compared closely "to the Quantrell band."[19] Another vet, Colonel John T. Crisp, "spoke on the war fought against domestic slavery of the Negro." News outlets failed to note how the crowd reacted to Crisp's remarks on slavery—a topic not usually broached at reunions—but he did preface the speech by confessing that he was not "brave enough to be a bushwhacker."[20] In 1910 Colonel Hopkins Hardin represented a very special guest. Hardin was a survivor of Pickett's Charge at Gettysburg and represented the increasing reach and prominence of the Quantrill Men and their meetings. (On a similar note, local history articles even allege that future commander in chief Harry S. Truman made his political debut on the "front porch of the weathered old J. D. Wallace home" but fail to note whether or not the speech took place during a Quantrill reunion.)[21]

Political speeches and historical presentations did not always go according to plan at Quantrill reunions. Prosecutor Roland Hughes, invited to give the "Speech of the Day" at the 1903 meeting, found this out the hard way. As reported by the *Kansas City Journal*, Hughes spoke before a crowd of nearly fifty ex-guerrillas. He began on a high note. His opening remark, "I do not hesitate to say that you fought for what was right," garnered great applause from the audience. But it was all downhill from there. Shortly thereafter, Hughes "launched into a discussion of the recent criticisms of the supreme court" and "scored the newspapers for criticizing the supreme court." This segment of the speech "touched a keg of powder," and William H. Gregg, then captain of the association, interrupted him rudely. Hughes continued his speech but was again halted by Gregg.

"After this interruption," the paper chronicled, "Prosecutor Hughes drew his speech to an abrupt halt and left the court room . . . and the whole room seemed to be in contempt of the supreme court." In the wake of the speaker's retreat, A. J. Liddil came to the rescue and gave a well-received talk on "the troublous times of the 60s, and declared that for the outrages committed on Missourians he would have been glad if Lawrence had suffered more."[22]

As Frank James found out a year later at the 1904 encampment, Quantrill's old command would censor anyone speaking out of line at their reunions–even one of their own. Detailed by the *Sarcoxie Record*, the guerrilla-turned-bandit was invited to address the group and in the process of doing so, "exploded a political bombshell, which all but disrupted the meeting." James had made no secret of his displeasure with the Missouri state legislature; roughly four years before, in 1900, it had chosen not to elect James as doorman of the Lower House. James's grudge finally boiled over at the reunion: "I have been in Ohio, Pennsylvania, and other states we had learned to hate because they gave birth to the federal troops we hated so well and their people have treated me like a man. But here in Missouri, among my own people, I am unhonored and unsung." These outbursts, according to the paper, "were considered by the grizzled, warscarred veterans as little less than treason." Some of James's more levelheaded comrades "forcibly pushed him from the crowd in the courthouse yard" as tensions rose. Had they not, the paper opined, "it might have been the scene of a conflict recalling border days."[23]

In the arena of memory politics, the Frank James incident was a serious issue for the ex-guerrillas and had to be handled with the care of a full-on scandal. James had publicly called out the Democratic Party and risked estranging the rest of Quantrill's command from the South's dominant political machine and the mainstream southerners who supported it. At the 1905 reunion (to which it is clear James was not welcome) it was made known that "there will be no speech-making and no particular effort will be made to enlist public interest in the meeting."[24] The *Kansas City Star* reported that "quite a breeze was created at the reunion in Independence a year ago when Frank James announced to his old comrades in arms that he had become tired of the Democratic Party and in the future would vote with the Republicans." A. J. Liddil, who had come to the rescue after Roland Hughes's unpopular speech in 1903, was now captain and stated that "we [the association] are not going to have any politics or politicians this year. We have been bothered too much with them already. We simply want to get together, talk over old times, and have a good time among ourselves."[25] In reality, Liddil astutely recognized that the ex-guerrillas could not risk another misstep like James's in back-to-back years; he wisely let the smoke clear and politicians returned to their craft at later meetings.[26]

Frank James did not attend another Quantrill reunion for several years—but occasional incidents unfolded without the old bandit. These events, however raucous, were generally met with apathy and even amusement so long as they did not endanger the ex-guerrillas' political standing or commemorative credibility. Case in point: the Dave Edwards–Jim Cummins feud of 1907. The *Kansas City Post* recalled that in 1863, Edwards and Cummins had "fought side by side under the leadership of the famous Confederate Charles Quantrell." But according to eyewitnesses at the 1907 encampment, when Edwards caught sight of Cummins, he produced a revolver from his hip pocket and "shot deliberately" with a distance of "only about three feet between them." Time had apparently eroded Edwards's fighting prowess as the bullet tore a hole in Cummins's coat before onlookers and a local marshal seized the gun.

The previous October, as the story went, Edwards and Cummins had lived together at Higginsville, a home for Confederate veterans: "While there Dave Edwards owned a pet coon and also some tools. One day the tools and the coon were stolen. Edwards, according to his own statement, accused Jim Cummings [sic] of having stolen them." According to Edwards, "Cummings grew very angry at the accusation and threatened to beat him to death." The raccoon was apparently never recovered, Edwards was taken to jail for the shooting, and Cummins chose not to press charges.[27]

Attempted homicide would certainly seem to outweigh the political miscue committed by Frank James, but the other ex-guerrillas and their guests did not think so. "Oh, it's nothing! I turned to see who was fighting then went on about my business," announced one female witness. Another woman flatly declared that "it didn't amount to anything. . . . The old men just had a quarrel." Even the newspaper noted nonchalantly that the shooting "would have broken up almost any other picnic. But the veterans of the Quantrell raids, their wives and daughters, forgot all about it in fifteen minutes and resumed their merrymaking."[28]

The 1911 reunion of the Quantrill Men Survivor's Association. This reunion of Quantrill's raiders was among the best attended—and following it, attendance of genuine Quantrill men would never again exceed forty. Courtesy of the State Historical Society of Missouri.

Most media coverage of the Quantrill Men Survivor's Association lacked the excitement of the Frank James outburst or the Edwards-Cummins feud. In fact, the most recurrent theme in the twentieth century was news of members passing away. In 1915 the *Independence Examiner* announced that "six men have died since the last reunion." The fallen included Frank James, who had returned to grace among the former bushwhackers before his death. The following year, the *Examiner* ran a similar article. "Death has dealt very severely with the Quantrill Association since its last meeting a year ago," the paper noted, as "both leading officers of the Organization have died since the last reunion." Longtime captain Ben Morrow and longtime secretary Warren Welch both died, as did notables Cole Younger and William H. Gregg. In 1917 the *Examiner* again reported sad news: Fletcher Taylor, Dave Hilton, and John Koger were all dead.[29]

The 1920 reunion of the Quantrill Men Survivor's Association. By this time the
vast majority of Quantrill men had died; of those still living, few were healthy
enough to travel for reunions. Courtesy of the State Historical Society of Missouri.

Even as their ranks thinned rapidly after 1915, the Quantrill Men tried
to make the most of their time—however much remained. "In the program
yesterday," the *Independence Examiner* reported in 1922, "some men 80
years old joined the square dances with enthusiasm."[30] But while the holdouts could still dance, the association started losing its ability to function in
the 1920s. When Warren Welch—who had served as secretary and de facto
group historian for decades—died, much of his vital records went missing. According to his son, Harrison, Welch kept his roster of the Quantrill
command hidden until his death. The problem, then, came after he died:
no one could find the hiding spot. Without Welch's meticulously managed
roster of the ex-guerrillas still living and their most recent addresses, letters and other communications concerning the reunions tapered off sig-

nificantly. Plus, that the group had been much smaller than most other such organizations only amplified the absence of longtime reunion-goers. The elected officers had trouble contacting survivors, and "those who have attended the Quantrill reunions [after Welch's death in 1920] have done so on their own initiative."[31]

Between 1898 and 1917, the average attendance of ex-guerrillas at the Quantrill reunions was in the range of thirty to thirty-five. After 1917 that figure never exceeded fifteen; after 1922 it never rose above single digits. The final five meetings, 1925 to 1929, averaged less than three former bushwhackers per year. The Wallace family, longtime hosts of the old men at their home in Wallace Grove, called off the 1930 meeting due to a death in their family. The next year, only one surviving guerrilla, Frank Smith of Blue Springs, could be verified, and the Wallace family again cancelled the reunion. Without the duty of planning encampments and too few members living to field even a card game, the Quantrill Men Survivor's Association ceased to exist.

Myth of the Black Guerrilla?

Reunions of men who once hailed from prominent, slaveholding families—and had burned large swaths of Lawrence to the ground to help retain their human property—might seem like a strange place to find African American visitors. That did not stop John Noland, William Hunter, Sam Jackson, or Henry Wilson. Though background information is admittedly harder to come by for these men, especially Hunter, Jackson, and Wilson, they all shared a common bond: all three men were born slaves, had a wartime connection to Quantrill's guerrillas, and attended annual meetings of the Quantrill Men Survivor's Association.

In their memoirs, ex-guerrillas constructed an unmistakable dichotomy that differentiated between "good" and "bad" African American characters during and after the Civil War. This "either/or" relationship tapped elements of both the Lost Cause movement and the New South movement. In conjunction with the former, guerrilla memoirs used the notion of the happy, loyal slave who had enjoyed enslavement and pined for yesteryear on the plantation; by way of the latter, guerrilla writers borrowed the idea that southerners needed to paint a rosy picture of postwar race relations for the sake of economic recovery and saving social face.

Thus, in the image of "Rapist versus Remus," the likes of Jack Mann, the lustful black rapist, was pitted against a cast of loyal and lovable slaves such as Rube and Aunt Suse. As mentioned in the previous chapter, the fact that memoirists cherry-picked core concepts from both movements—movements sometimes at odds with each other—points directly to the extent to which they were attempting to fit themselves, by whatever means necessary, within mainstream southern society in the twentieth century.

Encampments constituted the ideal situation for Quantrill men to put this literary construct on public display for spectators and the media. Naturally, the ex-guerrillas did not invite any African Americans who fit the mold of Jack Mann, but they did welcome and pay tribute to former slaves who typified the Uncle Remus paradigm. The first mention of a black man attending a reunion actually came a year after the meeting, in December 1903, when the *Oak Grove Banner* marked the passing of Sam Jackson. According to the *Banner*, Jackson "was born a slave in this [Jackson] county 65 years ago" and was "quite a character." He had attended the 1902 reunion in Independence, where the paper noted that he "shook hands with all the old soldiers and was able to call nearly every one by name." While enjoying his visit with the guerrillas—and potentially even with relatives of his former owners—Jackson allegedly claimed that "these were his people and many a time he had carried provisions to them from the old home when they were hidden in the woods."[32]

Three years after Sam Jackson greeted the Quantrill men in Independence, John Noland appeared at the 1905 encampment there. Contradictory reports of Noland's role within Quantrill's command have abounded since 1863, but none among the reunion-goers questioned his irregular credentials. The *Kansas City Times* made a special note about him: "Another man who received much attention from his old comrades because of his unique position was John Noland." "John is," the paper continued, "the only negro who ever had any connection with Quantrell's band. He is said to have been with the guerrilla chieftain during much of his career, though rather in the position of a servant than as a fighter." The *Times*'s hesitancy to state emphatically that Noland was not just a servant—he was a slave—may point to the unique nature of his relationship to the bushwhackers.[33]

Before the war, John Noland (sometimes referred to as John Henry Noland) was the property of Francis Asbury Noland. The slave census of 1860 for Jackson County, Missouri, notes that Francis Asbury Noland owned two slaves: both boys, ages 23 and 16, the former listed as mulatto and the latter as black. (Francis Asbury Noland likely went by Asbury among friends and family to avoid confusion with his father, Francis Marion Noland, who was still alive in the 1860s.) Francis M. Noland also owned at least one mulatto slave (age 11) in 1860, along with two female slaves roughly old enough to be the boy's mother (ages 46 and 45). Eli Glascock, a member of the Nolands' extended family, also owned at least one mulatto slave in 1860. Given the family's penchant for sleeping with their female slaves, it is quite possible—and seems likely—that John Noland was the son of Asbury Noland. If this were the case, John Noland shared the status of third cousin with noted bushwhackers George M. Noland and George W. Noland, both of whom partook in the Lawrence Massacre. Additionally, John Noland would also have been blood kin to Edward, James, Henry, and William Noland, all of whom rode with Quantrill during the war and accompanied him to Kentucky in 1865 (where James, Henry, and William were killed in action).[34] Thus in a war fought almost entirely on the homefront and within the confines of local communities and neighborhoods, self-preservation may have prompted Noland (that is, out of mortal necessity, *not* ideological unity or support of slavery) to side with his pro-Confederate kin.[35] As such, the article concluded that "his [Noland] comrades declare, however, that John could fight as hard as any of them when occasion required."[36]

John Noland attended the group's reunion again in 1907, though far fewer details exist following his 1905 debut. A short obituary published by the *Independence Examiner* in August 1908 stated that Noland had not attended the meeting that year because "he died several weeks ago."[37] In 1907 the *Kansas City Post* only noted his presence as "one of old Asbury Noland's slaves, who went across Missouri with Quantrell." William Hunter, also in attendance at the 1907 meeting in Independence, was reportedly "the bodyservant of General Joe Shelby during the war." Given the closeness between Shelby's Iron Brigade (which included John Newman Edwards as adjutant) and many of Quantrill's men—some of whom also served under Shelby or even journeyed with him into Mexican exile after the war—Hunter probably found himself a welcome addition to the mix and yet another African American man whose participation helped the guerrillas propagate the Remus model employed in their memoirs.[38]

From 1907 to 1923, rosters kept by the Quantrill Association and newspaper coverage indicate that no African American men attended reunions—or at least none with historical connections to the group or that the papers thought worthy of mention. This changed in 1924 with the arrival of Henry Wilson. Despite what the *Kansas City Times* had published in 1905 about John Noland having been the only black man with any connection to Quantrill, the *Pleasant Hill Times* now declared that Wilson, "an aged negro" from Lawrence, Kansas, had "served as body guard of Quantrell and cook for the bushwhackers when they were on raids." The paper also noted that in 1924, only eight of the "original gang of 300" still lived, but Wilson was counted as separate from the eight white guerrillas.[39]

By 1929, the year of the final Quantrill men reunion, Wilson's presence was a more valuable commodity. A report by the *Independence Examiner* claimed that now only four former bushwhackers remained alive, along with Wilson, who was the life of the party. "At today's gathering," the story continued, "Henry Wilson was exceedingly loquacious and insists upon telling a good one on George Noland, who he said was captured near Independence during the war and was made to chop down a Confederate flag there with a broadaxe." The veracity of Wilson's story is unknown, but George Noland (a white relation of the late John Noland) "seemed to derive little pleasure from the story."[40] So, in a near-perfect dose of irony, it appears as though an African American man—the last survivor from an enslaved group that guerrillas had exploited for their own commemorative gain—got the last laugh on one of the last guerrillas at the very last of the guerrilla reunions.

Honoring "Other" Veterans

Even in the twentieth century, ex-bushwhackers were quite picky regarding who might draw their praise or qualify as worthy of remembrance. In some instances, Quantrill's command would shun one of its own for failing to meet the obligations or criteria of public commemoration. Case in point: "The Kansas City survivors, says Gregg, are Wm. H. Gregg, John C. Hope, George Noland, Tom Maxwell, Ran Venable, Jim Pool, and 'another feller don't want known.'" This "other feller," according to Gregg (by way of the *Kansas City Times* in 1902), "was with us but if he is ashamed or afraid to admit it, we don't want anything to do with him."[41]

Picky as they were, members of the Quantrill Men Survivor's Association often invited veterans of the regular Confederate army to attend their annual reunions. In fact, it is likely that at more than one of the later meetings held in the 1920s, regular veterans actually outnumbered the guerrillas, whose ranks were devastated by age. In theory, public interaction with ex-Confederates helped whitewash some of the "irregularities" from the reputations of guerrillas, something that could not be witnessed physically and broadcast in public via the printed page.

In their memoirs, Quantrill's men paid tribute to the soldiers of the Spanish-American War and World War I for two reasons: first, because more than three decades after the Civil War doing so constituted a convention of mainstream southern society and helped cement the long-term endurance of guerrilla memory; and second, because even though these newer generations of combat soldiers threatened to crowd Civil War veterans out of the singular spotlight they had enjoyed for years, these veterans of Cuba, the Philippines, and the European trenches were often their sons and grandsons—and most importantly, they granted the aging guerrillas a vehicle through which to re-relate and connect their own wartime experiences to their present surroundings.[42]

In this context, we might read the article of the *Kansas City Journal* published in September 1918 under the headline "Quantrell's Raiders Would Fight Huns" as having been both a patriotic statement and a clever hand of memory politics. It reported that "a Confederate flag swayed here and there in the breeze while American flags were everywhere. The old warriors showed little traces of bitterness over Civil War days." Rather, the reunion-goers "gathered in groups and chatted of old times, but most of them talked of their grandsons and other relatives now serving in France or shortly to go there." According to the *Journal,* "prosperity has come to most of the former fighters and they have Liberty Bonds and contributed to all the Red Cross and other war funds." Not to be outdone, "many of the women present wore service pins," and "Miss E. Wallace, one of the hostesses has six nephews in the army." As Missouri and the rest of the South mobilized to help restrain the hostilities of Kaiser Wilhelm II, so too would ex-bushwhackers donate money and sport their pins partially in an effort to show, that by 1918, they behaved—and thereby should be remembered—just like everyone else.[43]

Notwithstanding that "none of the veterans in attendance [at the same meeting in 1918] was less than 73," the former bushwhackers harbored no paucity of fighting spirit. As Harrison Trow similarly pronounced in his published memoir, the guerrillas were ready for the trenches. "We only wish we were able to go over with the boys and take a few shots at the Germans," they claimed as a collective. Of course, recalling the ethnic tensions of chapter 1, it did not hurt that the Germans were German, either: "Of all the troops that did things to cause bitter memories in western Missouri during the Civil War, none left so many monuments of hate as the Germans. We are not surprised at the stories of their depredations, when we remember what happened here in the '60s. We'd like to take a crack at the Germans for that reason. This is our country and we are all willing to do everything we can for it." All at once, then, the former bushwhacker cleverly co-opted their lingering wartime hatred of "the Dutch" into a point of patriotism that, in turn, fueled their own agenda of remembrance.[44]

Hostesses of the Border War

Guerrillas paid special attention to women in their memoirs, recognizing them as the gatekeepers and guardians of southern memory—and so it was much the same at guerrilla reunions. Speaking at the 1901 meeting in Oak Grove before twenty-five former bushwhackers and a healthy crowd of spectators, Rev. Mark Rider eulogized "the good women of the war times and of the present day." "Glory be to God," he praised, "for the good women of our great country." Soon after, Frank James also ascended the podium to make a short speech. According to the *Kansas City Journal,* James "offered a resolution asking that a monument be erected to the noble women who stood by them [Quantrill's guerrillas] in the dark days of the war." And, the paper also noted, James generously began the fundraising effort for such a monument himself by a donation of fifty dollars.[45]

Ten years later, William Gregg penned a letter to Hiram George honoring the crucial role women had played on the front lines of Missouri's guerrilla war. "The time is growing short with us all[–]we are on the shady side of life," he lamented in 1911. But Gregg had no intention of fading away quietly or of being forgotten—and he paid women their commemorative due in his open letter (which was printed in the *Oak Grove Banner*) like he had in his published memoir. "We must not forget the good women who with their heroism," Gregg commanded, "made it possible for us to live in the midst of so brutal an enemy as that with which we had to contend." More than a generic "shout out," he went a step further and named names: "Such for instance your wife and sisters and sister-in-law, etc. Then there was aunt Betty Bowman and her daughters, God bless them all. The Austins, Webbs, Philpots, Corn, Barnetts, Clarks, Hudsons, and thousands of others too tedious to mention." "O that I were in a position financially," Gregg concluded, "I would build to the memory of these glorious women (heroines) the finest monument ever erected."[46]

Guerrillas such as Frank James and William Gregg were well aware that the hostess work of women made the Quantrill reunions possible. They also would have recognized a clear link to the past: just as women had operated as irregular quartermasters during the guerrilla war, they resumed many of these duties to make the annual encampments logistically feasible, especially as the guerrillas themselves aged. Women aided their husbands, fathers, and eventually grandfathers with traveling to meetings; women prepared and served the renowned basket dinners; women served as escorts, dance partners, and willing listeners; and prominent female relations were invited to make official speeches.

Such was the case of Feta Parmer—the daughter of noted bushwhacker Allen Parmer. At the 1907 meeting of the Quantrill Association a collection of forty ex-guerrillas and nearly one hundred participants was treated to a basket dinner served by the "ladies who were the wives and daughters." As reported by the *Independence Examiner*, Parmer addressed the sizable crowd after dinner and proclaimed that "if it were in her power she would raise a monument to the skies for Quantrell."[47] Eight years later in 1915, the *Kansas City Post* saw fit to remark on the prominence of female commemoration at the annual encampment. "Woman, lovely woman, played her part in the border warfare that is being commemorated today by veteran members of Quantrell's band at St. Clair on the Independence electric line." According to the *Post*, "an unusually large number of women are in attendance at the twentieth annual reunion," and far from simply supervising the serving of dinner, they "are as busy repeating old time incidents as the former guerrillas themselves."[48] Thus, the feeling of affection between guerrillas and their female relations was a mutual one both during *and* after the war.

On other occasions, members of the Quantrill Association did more than simply recognize the role, however important, women had played on the homefront in the 1860s; as would be the case in multiple published memoirs, ex-guerrillas made distinctions for women who had experienced irregular warfare from the saddle. In 1910, while encamped at Wallace Grove, a crew of thirty-five ex-bushwhackers bent over backwards to honor two women of this variety. The *Kansas City Post* chronicled that the pair "who received unusual attention were Mrs. W. S. Gregg and Mrs. H. V. Kabrick." "Both of these women," the *Post* declared, "had ridden with their husbands upon forays with Quantrell." Women such as Gregg and Kabrick were not simply honored for their work behind the scenes of irregular warfare; they received additional praise for sharing the dangers of the trail and brush with their husbands and Quantrill. In other words, they were—at least temporarily—recognized as guerrillas in the sense that their husbands had been.[49]

Any doubt that attention paid to women at Quantrill Men reunions reflected in great part their powerful stake in determining how the guerrillas would and could be commemorated and remembered by southern society is directly countered by the failed "Coup of 1912." As reported by the *Kansas City Journal* that year, "action was taken which marked the passing of the famous Quantrill band" when "24 Confederate officers and soldiers met at the same place and organized as veterans of the 2nd Missouri Confederate Cavalry." This new organization, the *Journal* read, "will meet for the first time at the annual Lone Jack picnic next September and the name of Quantrill's band will pass into history and they will be known as members of the 2nd Missouri Confederate Cavalry." Put another way, guerrillas William Gregg and Cole Younger had struck a deal with regular Confederate veterans to fold Quantrill's old command into the rank and file. Unfortunately, Gregg and Younger, neither of whom was an elected officer at that point, had failed to run their scheme past the rest of the Quantrill Association before going to the press.[50]

Ben Morrow, the rightfully elected captain of the organization, responded via an open letter in the *Independence Daily News* in which he castigated Gregg for attempting to hijack the group without at least hearing from the men themselves. "I have given Captain Gregg two weeks to deny that he is commander of the Quantrill men," Morrow's letter continued. "Bill, you know as well as I do that it is impossible for you to fill that place unless you get the majority vote of this company." After finishing off his public emasculation of Gregg, Morrow's letter took a different—and on the surface very surprising—course: "The Quantrill men have been meeting for 17 years. Now do you think we would sit quietly and be taken with [out] having one word to say in the arrangements they [regular veterans] make for us. They ignored our company, also our committee. We were not taken in during the war and we will not be taken in after the war is over."[51] As the leader of a group that strove to mimic the reunions of regular veterans and to integrate itself into the mainstream Lost Cause, Morrow's rebuttal of the opportunity to be counted officially, albeit retroactively, among the rank and file of the Confederacy seems peculiar, if not backward. Then again, Morrow's move may have belied the shrewdness of memory politics in postwar Missouri. Quantrill's old command needed to be accepted in the manner and fashion of regular veterans—but to give up their identity as Quantrill's command altogether would be giving up a significant portion of the commemorative limelight. In short, the Quantrill Men Survivor's Association wanted to have its cake and eat it, too—because this arrangement allowed for the best odds of being remembered long-term. Also important, though, is the extent to which Morrow's and the organization's refusal to join a regular cavalry company exposed the way the ex-guerrillas used regular veterans as stage props: men they needed to glad-hand and appear with publicly for the sake of remembrance, but not men for whom they would give up their wartime identities completely.

Most important of all, however, the rift between Morrow and Gregg and the failed Coup of 1912 revealed the influence women held over the Quantrill reunions and is symbolic of the power women held over southern memory more broadly. When Ben Morrow, elected captain of the group, required crucial support to suppress Gregg's mutiny, he did not turn first to the other members of the command nor to his elected committee members. Instead, Morrow looked to the "Wives and Daughters of the Quantrill men." "You," he explained, "and you alone are the whole cause of our meeting. Also Miss Wallace. She is always in the game. She has been a good sister to the Quantrill men and I am sure she will remain the same. She has the good will and good wishes of every man in the command." As we decode Morrow's tribute to the Quantrill women, the message is quite clear: the command can and will only be absorbed by the Second Missouri (and thereby destroyed) if the womenfolk allow it. And as Morrow surmised correctly, they did not, it was not, and the upstart Gregg was put back in his place. The Quantrill reunion of 1913 at Wallace Grove went off without a hitch—the hostesses of the border war had spoken.[52]

Heated Reactions from Lawrence

Given the front-page coverage of early guerrilla reunions, it was not long before tempers from across the border ran hot. Many of the "old time" residents of Lawrence, Kansas, wore their survival of the 1863 massacre like a badge of honor—not unlike survivors of the Third Reich's "final solution" several decades later. As such, these Kansans were never particularly pleased that annual Quantrill reunions were unfolding less than fifty miles away (from Lawrence) in Independence or Wallace Grove, and they attempted, whenever possible, to undermine the festivities. With schemes ranging from political propaganda to legal action, results were generally unsuccessful; however, they highlighted that Kansans, and especially those in Lawrence, would not be taken by surprise again—they would not sit idly by while their former tormentors tried to rehabilitate their collective image for posterity.

The first reported incident occurred at the 1902 meeting held in Independence. As noted by the *Saint Louis Post-Dispatch*, it was then and there that Jim Cummins—whose "unique distinction" was "that he is the only member of the outlawed band of Missourians who was not killed or captured and who has not surrendered"—made his first appearance at a Quantrill reunion. (It should be noted that Cummins did, in fact, *attempt* to surrender himself to authorities at least once with regard to his criminal activities as a postwar member of the James-Younger Gang, but law enforcement officials believed him an imposter.) While Cummins and other ex-guerrillas mingled in the courthouse yard, "a man came up" and "began complaining about having been robbed during the Lawrence raid." The paper quoted Cummins's response: "If you are not satisfied just step out here on the grass and I'll fight it out with you. There is some fight left in me yet, I reckon." The man wisely declined Cummins's invitation to fisticuffs—but this retreat only marked the opening salvo in an ongoing clash between the Quantrill Men and Kansans to settle the Lawrence Massacre's proper place in guerrilla memory.[53]

Just a few years later, in 1905, the *Jackson Examiner* declared that the "sensational reports about the reunion of the Quantrell men" had "aroused the old Kansas feelings." The people of Lawrence, according to the paper, had recently discovered that murder indictments levied against William C. Quantrill and his men in the wake of the Lawrence Massacre had never been cancelled or "outlawed." This being the case, a congress-man from Kansas wanted "the reunions of the Quantrell men . . . sup-pressed by law." The *Examiner* labeled these demands as "sensational and foolish" but also reported that enraged Kansans would likely peti-tion Missouri's governor, Democrat Joseph W. Folk, to extradite surviv-ing veterans of the raid to Kansas to stand trial. In all, the documents filed on November 18, 1863, with the Fourth Judicial District Court (Douglas County) of the State of Kansas included first-degree murder charges for thirty-four men, Quantrill, Bill Anderson, Dick Yeager, and George Todd among them. Multiple surviving witnesses had offered testimony before a grand jury that Quantrill and his men had "unlawfully, feloniously, will-fully, deliberately and of their premeditated malice did make an assault" in Lawrence on August 21, 1863.[54] Folk, who was a native Tennessean and an attorney himself, never made any effort to forcibly return the ex-guerrillas to Kansas (nor is there conclusive proof that he was ever even asked to do so). In any event, it is clear that wounds left over from the raid remained raw in Lawrence.

Along with coverage of the potential legal proceedings against the Quantrill reunion attendees, the same article from the *Examiner* also quoted selections of a letter received in 1905 by Judge A. J. Liddil, then chief officer of the Quantrill Men Survivor's Association. The author of the letter, one "W. Jones, Co. C., Seventh Kansas Vol. Cavalry (Jenni-son's men!)," essentially challenged Liddil and the Quantrill men to open combat:

> I would suggest that you hold your next annual reunion at Lawrence, Kan-
> sas, and join with members of the Seventh Kansas Cavalry in celebrat-
> ing Quantrell's last raid across the Kansas border. I assure you that Jenni-
> son's Jayhawkers would be exceedingly glad to meet Quantrell's men over
> in Kansas and talk over old times with them. If you still have any fight left in
> you, and desire to settle old scores, we will be perfectly willing to bring our
> trusty old carbines along and join you in a little match, just to let the natives
> see how we whipped thunder out of you away back in the sixties. A little

scrap of this would be a mighty big drawing card for the reunion and would add considerable ginger to the occasion. The grand-children of those whom Quantrell murdered at Lawrence, would be present, and would no doubt enjoy the fun hugely.

The newspapers ran no reply from Liddil, and no violence of note ever stemmed from the invitation. Even if the remnant of Quantrill's old command had been ready and willing to swap lead with whoever had penned the inflammatory letter—and with men such as Jim Cummins still spry, virtually anything was possible—crossing the border into Kansas would have constituted a serious legal misstep for anyone associated with Quantrill or the Lawrence Massacre. Exactly who wrote the letter remains a mystery; whether or not the author in question had designs on taunting wanted men back into the jurisdiction of the Fourth Judicial District Court was a pragmatic possibility.[55]

On October 17, 1906, little more than a year after the dust settled from the Jones letter, the *Kansas City Journal* headline read: "As in Days of '63 — Quantrell's Men Plan Descent upon Lawrence; Wait for Harris' Election." Considering the aforementioned murder indictments and invitations to shed blood, this would seem to have been a strange plan indeed. Nonetheless, the *Journal* contended that members of the "Quantrill organization in this section of Missouri" were keeping anxious track of the gubernatorial race in Kansas. "All of them are hoping that Colonel W. A. Harris will be elected," the paper declared. "For forty years they have dreamed of holding one of their annual reunions in the city of Lawrence, Kas., and they believe that the candidacy of Colonel Harris offers them their only hope of the realization of their dream." Technically, as the article noted, the Quantrill men did not need the governor's permission to encamp in Lawrence—but their unpopular meeting would require protection offered by the Kansas state militia, which they would request from the Democratic governor. The thigh bones of William C. Quantrill himself, then held by the Kansas Historical Society, the *Journal* even exclaimed, would be borrowed for the pro-Missouri festivities if Harris won the election.[56]

The reply from pro-Democrat (white) Missourians was swift and condemnatory. The *Oak Grove Banner* reprinted the *Journal*'s article under the heading "Fake Quantrell Story" and shot back that the "article which we publish below originated in the brain of some Journal reporter and there is not a word of truth in it. Frank Gregg, who the *Journal* says is one of the movers in the scheme, has been dead several months."[57] Under yet another caption, "The Journal's Peanut Politics," the *Banner* excoriated the Republican-leaning Kansas City paper for resorting to "fake methods" and "mighty poor politics" in attempts to "frighten the voters of the Sunflower State into voting for Hoch." Quantrill's men, the article stated for the record, "do not nor did have the remotest idea of holding a reunion in Lawrence . . . but the Kansas Republicans are becoming desperate over the way the voters are flocking to the Democratic nominee."[58] Even so, Edward W. Hoch, the Republican candidate in question (who was ironically—and then again, perhaps not—a former newspaper editor himself), won the gubernatorial election of 1907.

From a historical perspective, no evidence, then or now, suggests that any truth laid beneath the *Kansas City Journal*'s story about a Quantrill men reunion in Lawrence. As mentioned above, many of Quantrill's former command were still fugitives from justice in Kansas, and any event celebrating the 1863 raid would have, in all likelihood, required more protection than even a *willing* Kansas state militia could have mustered. But the print spat over the 1907 Hoch/Harris race and its electoral ramifications is particularly interesting because it represented the virtual highwater mark of Lawrence's resistance to guerrilla reunions in Missouri. Citizens of Lawrence were never able to effectively halt—or really even hinder—the annual Quantrill meetings. Therefore, using the reunions' own popularity in the press to help ensure the victory of a Republican sympathetic to the Kansans' own side of the story amounted to a significant victory, albeit a secondary one.

Following the sparring of 1907, direct interaction between the Quantrill reunions and residents of Lawrence tapered off. None of the thirty-four indicted men ever saw the inside of a Kansas courtroom, and no ex-guerrillas ever set foot on Kansas soil in attendance of a reunion. For years, however, the annual gatherings served as launching pads for the Missouri side of the Lawrence saga. In 1913 the *Kansas City Post* described one such scene: "Under a tree in front of the Wallace home on Blue Ridge where forty veterans of Quantrell's guerrillas gathered yesterday and Friday for their annual reunion, sat a wiry little man chewing on a cigar stub. His hands rested on a hickory cane and with it he poked the nudged out little pieces of sod." "It was this little old man," the *Post* continued, "who commanded Quantrell's rear guard of sixty men and held back 1,200 federal soldiers on the retreat from Lawrence." The referenced man was Captain William H. Gregg, who, the paper claimed, desired to "tell our side [just] once."[59]

For starters, Gregg asserted that a neglectful band of Federal troops could have stopped the raid before it ever began; Captain Pike, he alleged, saw Quantrill and his men crossing the border and chose not to intervene. And this decision to attack Kansas, Gregg assured his audience, came only after "the boys" had doggedly pestered a reluctant Quantrill into leading the assault. In the midst of the fighting, Gregg argued that no Missourian had shown as much cruelty as had the townsfolk of Lawrence on capturing, killing, and dismembering Larkin Skaggs (much more on him in chapter 6); plus, according to Gregg's version of events, the only woman shot down during the raid had died accidentally and of her own fault at that.

Most telling, though, was the motive element for the raid: revenge. Here Gregg's abstract explanation diverged sharply from the outmoded justifications provided by John Newman Edwards in 1877. In *Noted Guerrillas*, Edwards offered that in addition to personal revenge, Lawrence had been a hotbed of abolitionism and a safe haven for African Americans. By redacting the racial component, Gregg continued the trend (detailed in chapter 3) of ex-guerrillas reshaping their racial attitudes publicly to aid the process of reintegrating themselves into mainstream society. "That's the story of the Quantrell raid on Lawrence made by the farmer boys of Missouri in revenge," Gregg concluded, "and not one of us has ever regretted that we were in it. We are proud that we were able to revenge our fathers and mothers and sisters."[60]

In 1925, when asked to discuss the Lawrence Massacre, a few aged guerrillas continued to justify their actions without evoking harsh racial sentiments and now even took exception to the notion that the assault had even been "irregular" in the first place. Much like guerrilla memoirists seeking to "regularize" their wartime records, the *Kansas City Journal* chronicled how "every member of the party took exception to certain references to the Quantrill expedition as a 'raid.'" In fact, as the *Journal* relayed, "some even hinted the damage done in Kansas by the small band was negligible when compared to the havoc wrought by Sherman in Georgia." In other words, now in their mid- to late eighties, the few remaining members of the Quantrill Men Survivor's Association took great pride in their service records—but also took the opportunity, despite the howls of protest from Lawrence, to extend a final plea for their case. Their service, like that of Sherman's men and the Confederates who opposed the Army of the Tennessee in 1863–1864, the guerrillas argued, should be deemed worthy of inclusion among the annals of legitimate southern history and therefore as part of the collective memory movement designed to commemorate legitimate Confederate soldiers.[61]

Forgetting Caroline Quantrill

On August 30, 1942, the Sunday edition of the *Kansas City Star* ran a feature marking the fifty-fourth anniversary of Caroline Quantrill's visit to Blue Springs. "There has always been a lingering question in the minds of a few citizens of this Missouri town," the story alleged, "as to whether or not it really was Mrs. Caroline Clarke Quantrill, mother of William Clarke Quantrill, the guerrilla leader who visited here in 1888. But to one person in Blue Springs there is no question about it." That person, Miss Narra Lewis, was by 1942 the only female resident of Blue Springs living with firsthand memories of the occasion that began this chapter.

"She [Caroline Quantrill] was dressed in a cheap calico dress," Lewis recalled, "and wore a splint calico sunbonnet, the garments of poverty. At that time a woman considered herself hardly dressed for decent appearance on the public street unless she had at least three starched muslin petticoats. Clothes in those days were definitely to conceal the figure, instead of as now, to reveal it." Accordingly, "feminine backs stiffened" and "feminine noses went up." As for the ex-guerrillas, they were quite upset that the women of Blue Springs dared to snub the mother of William C. Quantrill and immediately took to raising funds on her behalf; as penance, their snooty wives and sisters were forced to take Mrs. Quantrill on a shopping spree in Independence. Then clad in her new wardrobe, Mrs. Quantrill was the guest of honor at an ice cream social.[62]

When the *Star* article appeared in 1942, Missouri, the United States, and even the world were in very different places than they had been in 1929—the year of the final Quantrill reunion. America had suffered through a decade-long economic depression and, along with much of the globe, found itself drawn into another war to end all wars. But even with these powerful excuses in hand, the fact that the Caroline Quantrill affair stood ready to pass into myth after hardly more than a half century's time pointed to the inherent weaknesses of physical ceremonies as producers of long-term remembrance in the realm of guerrilla memory. As Narra Lewis made evident, eventually attendees of the Quantrill reunions, and thereby most of their recollections, would also disappear.[63] And while the regular military reunions the guerrillas mimicked might involve thousands upon thousands of men and spectators, thus improving their odds of establishing a lasting memorial impact, Quantrill's command had never numbered more than a few hundred, several of whom failed to even survive the war.

The fate of the Wallace homestead at Wallace Grove—the site of so many guerrilla reunions—also pointed to gloomy prospects for long-term remembrance. The Wallace family and local lore told that the Wallaces hosted Quantrill's men because the guerrillas had saved Wallace's father from the hangman's rope during the war. But in 1938 Elizabeth Wallace, by then invalid and blind, died at the home. In 1967 the *Kansas City Times* recollected that "fifty years ago," Wallace's niece, Nell Wallace, "was a brown-haired young belle and the darling of the old warriors who rode with Quantrill." Back in the present, however, Wallace cited a leaking roof and frequent vandalism as the reasons for putting Wallace Grove—the house and eight surrounding acres—up for auction.[64] (The house was torn down in the 1970s.) And by 1980, a column in the *Independence Examiner* stated solemnly that "the tall oak and elm trees that once shaded William Quantrill's band of Confederate guerrillas will soon turn their leaves to shade a school bus parking lot if a rezoning request for Wallace Grove is approved by the Independence City Council." Perhaps most telling of all, the owner of the B. and J. School Bus Company stated that he was totally "unaware of the history that lay in the land."[65] In the East, battlefields have served as reunion destinations and lasting sites of Civil War memory until the present day. But owing to the nature of irregular warfare, Quantrill's men had no formally preserved military parks—and Wallace Grove, where more of their memories had been shared than anywhere else in the state, had been demolished, paved over, and largely forgotten.

So considering that the ex-guerrillas had formed the Quantrill Men Survivor's Association and organized annual meetings from 1898 to 1929 with the purpose of rehabilitating—and thus preserving via "regularization"—their wartime memories, this lack of endurance constituted a sig-

nificant problem. Many of the same tropes presented effectively in guerrilla memoirs for this same purpose were staged for display at reunions:
deference paid to women as gatekeepers of the Lost Cause, protocol concerning southern race relations and African American behavioral standards, and homage paid to veterans of subsequent wars. New strategies
also emerged; gathering in the flesh allowed the former bushwhackers to
commingle openly with veterans of the regular Confederate Army and
style themselves as both similar and equal. But unlike the printed word,
such real-time encounters required constant planning, organization, main-
tenance, and, above all else, attendance to keep the cogs of the memory
machine turning. For these reasons, guerrilla reunions lacked the longevity and geographic reach of a published memoir and must ultimately be
deemed far less effective instruments of long-horizon memory shaping—
though, in truth, *neither* medium was wonderfully effective to begin with.

To end the Quantrill reunion story on this timbre, however, would
be selling rather short their broader importance to the story of guerrilla
memory in the first thirty years of the twentieth century. Even as the
meetings alone likely failed to sway much nonlocal opinion regarding the
proper place of Quantrill and his command in the annals of Civil War
history and memory, it would be a severe misstep to overlook the direct,
dialectic relationship between guerrilla reunions and the guerrilla memoirs of the previous chapter. The point here is simple but vitally important: if the major themes of the memoirs were on physical display at reunions, so too must the reunion activities have influenced and informed
the printed page—wherein neither would be the same without the other,
and the post-Edwards "caretakers" of guerrilla memory (guerrillas themselves) might have taken an altogether different approach to its evolution
and preservation.[66]

Then again, the fact that ex-guerrillas even *believed* that such lengths
were necessary to ensure their acceptance in postwar society should raise
serious red flags about orthodox understandings of postwar racial attitudes and politics. Eminent accounts of Civil War memory have essentially conceded that to whatever extent sectional reconciliation occurred,
it happened at the expense of Emancipation-centric legacies of the war;
in effect, the white side of the "color line," especially in the South, resolidified after Reconstruction ended and uniformly vested itself in a memorial
platform of mutual valor and shared sacrifice. But the motive and intent

behind guerrilla memoirs and reunions—however heavily they might have leaned on standard racial tropes of the day, such as Uncle Remus and his predatory counterparts—shed light on a vastly more complicated and *divided* scenario.

The Quantrill Men and their efforts show that "whiteness" and Confederate sympathies simply were not enough to guarantee remembrance at a time when one's role in the war—the defining event of a generation—still meant everything. Such was a lesson that women in the guerrilla theater would learn all too well themselves.

FIVE

The Gatekeepers' Conundrum

> The women were busy and out of our sight; there was no sound but
> the plaintive wailing of a spinning-wheel, forever moaning out from
> some distant room.
> —Mark Twain, "The Private History of a Campaign That Failed"

From the vantage of Martha F. Horne, life in the borderlands had been
good before the outbreak of civil war. As late as 1861 she shared a sizable
and fertile plot of land with her husband, Richard, in Cass County, Missouri, just fifteen miles from the Kansas line. There the Hornes prospered
as farmers and, as an indication of their good fortune, owned twelve
slaves—a diversified assemblage of men and women, adults and children.
But by February 1862 the good times were swiftly drawing to a close; idyllic memories of Horne's antebellum life culminated in the arrival of men
on horseback. They were not friendly callers.[1]

It was then, Horne recalled, that "the Jayhawkers came." These raiders—essentially the Kansas equivalent of the Missouri bushwhacker—com-
mandeered the family's horses, hitched up their remaining wagons, and
used them to plunder vital winter supplies. The Kansans, she reported,
"stole everything that was movable." And when Horne said everything,
she really did mean *everything*. Her story described the Jayhawkers mount-
ing entire houses "on wheels" and "hauling them over into Kansas" and
even recounted them digging up whole orchards and resetting them in
Kansas.[2]

She also remembered a particular encounter with the raiders in 1865—
perhaps the most trying, but also the most historically telling, of her entire
wartime experience. "Mr. H," she began, "had just unloaded a few loads
of high-priced corn which he had hauled five miles from out of town."
When she spied Union men "helping themselves" to the precious cargo,
Horne did not flee from the marauders, nor did she spur her husband to

action. Instead she "grabbed an ax and a few nails" and sped down to the crib. Horne initially intended to nail the door shut (and did), but then one of the men ordered her to reopen it. At this, she "took a step toward him" and "drew back the ax over [her] shoulder." Having made up her mind to save the family's food supply or perish trying, Horne told the raider that if he attempted to open the corn crib door, she would "brain him." The man pondered the prospect of having an ax embedded in his skull, gave the enraged women standing before him "one full look in the eyes," decided she was deadly serious, and then "the whole party left." Overcome with emotion, Horne broke down trembling and sobbing after the raiders had bolted from the scene empty-handed.[3]

As this account and others like it make evident, the main battlefields of the guerrilla theater were not battlefields, traditionally conceived, at all. Instead, irregular sites of conflict were corn cribs, front porches, orchards, and individual homes; they were, collectively, the homefront. In turn, homefront violence was local, personal, and more often than not unable to distinguish between the sexes. Within this matrix of domestic battlefields, neighbors and friends became mortal enemies, and children, along with their grandparents, found themselves in the line of fire. Terror assumed the power to dismantle entire communities—it yanked families up by their roots and put scores of refugees on the hunt for safer ground in Arkansas, Texas, and the East. Such violence ultimately transformed the domestic realm; it came with long-lasting social and emotional consequences for women, producing a unique texture of trauma wherein they became fundamental variables of the guerrilla equation.

Half a century after the war, Horne and several other members of the Missouri Division of the United Daughters of the Confederacy researched, compiled, and published *Reminiscences of the Women of Missouri during the Sixties*. The book was put together by a Reminiscences Committee (with chairwomen from chapters in Kansas City and Lexington) and a Publication Committee (with a chairwoman from a chapter in Jefferson City). They did this work because despite the unquestioned success of the UDC in fund-raising, policing school curricula, and constructing monuments across the South, they felt that the wartime experiences of Missouri women had been disregarded. "For many years after the close of the war the whole South," the book's introduction announced, "our dear old state,

Missouri, included, was intent upon rehabilitating itself as it were; upon accepting the new order of things, and trying to bring a new life out of the ashes of desolation; a desolation appreciated only by the brave who had cast their all in a righteous cause and lost." Gradually, however, "order came out of chaos" and "there arose a mighty gathering of the Daughters of the Southland, to band themselves together for the purpose of caring for the helpless veterans who had worn the gray, for the rearing of monuments to the memory of the 'Lost Cause,' and for the gathering of and preserving all the matter of historical nature." In sum, when the war ended the Daughters had spent years—in some cases their entire adult lives—helping transform a cause lost, by way of much ink and marble, into *the* Lost Cause. But that movement as most know it was not, then as now, designed to accommodate and commemorate the experiences of women such as Martha Horne. "All these things have been and are being done," they noted, "but for years the heroines of this most disastrous period have been forgotten."[4]

Instead, the Lost Cause trended explicitly toward a male pantheon of Confederate heroes capped off by Robert E. Lee; it honored the valor and sacrifice of the men who had gone to war not to preserve the institution of slavery but to defend states' rights against northern agitators; and it lamented—albeit proudly—that the Confederacy had succumbed only to overwhelming manpower and material resources on well-known eastern battlefields. These narratives left little room for burning homes, for women and children fighting and dying as irregular combatants while their men hid in the bush. The mainstream Lost Cause had little use for the aforementioned texture of the borderland's guerrilla experience, and as a result, the record of the Missouri Daughters' own participation in it had been incomplete.

Domestic violation set the female guerrilla experience apart—it was the cornerstone of irregular violence and had constituted the "regular war" as many women in the guerrilla theater knew and understood it. Unlike the homes of southerners caught in the crossfire in the Eastern Theater, Missouri dwellings had been the command centers, communication hubs, and supply depots in this conflict. Thereby, in keeping with the nature of guerrilla war, they had also become the primary sites of violent collision. Women had been in charge at home while husbands, fathers, and brothers were off fighting in the brush; their households were targeted and destroyed while still occupied, effectively creating the ruins of irregular fortresses. Women morphed into soldiers, messengers, and spies as their homes militarized around them.[5]

Thus, while the men of William Clarke Quantrill's command employed their published memoirs and annual reunion celebrations to venerate women as the gatekeepers of the mainstream Lost Cause—the branch of southern commemoration to which the ex-guerrillas desperately sought admission in the twentieth century—those same women had a different narrative in mind. In addition to profiling the various capacities in which women fought as guerrillas, this chapter demonstrates that, as a result of their service, these Daughters were not content to stand by only as the referees of male memory any longer. In publishing *Reminiscences* in 1913, they were attempting to catalog a new class of memorial tropes that could better convey the themes of domestic violation that had defined *their own* irregular experiences in Missouri in the 1860s.

On the surface, writing themselves in as more important wartime actors appears harmless enough. After all, it is not surprising that the women who had survived the hardships of war would desire to be remembered just as their men had. In reality, though, the Daughters' efforts placed themselves, and by extension their male kin, in something of a commemorative conundrum. As the literature of the mainstream Lost Cause had argued for decades by 1913, southern men marched off to war to protect not the institution of slavery but their homes from Yankee invasion. In the plainest terms, it had been a war fought on behalf of southern women by their chivalrous guardians in gray. By marking women as brave but ultimately dependent on men, ex-Confederates could be remembered honorably, even in defeat. *Reminiscences* threatened to throw this arrangement hopelessly out of sync.

On one side, for women to have fought and survived as guerrillas, they required attackers. Throughout the book, those attackers were invariably male. Young wives and mothers wielding axes to fend off male combatants no longer had the appearance of a war fought on behalf of women; rather, it looked like one specifically waged against them on the homefront. This was a potentially damaging blow to the claims made by southern men concerning their abilities to protect white women from predacious black men in the postbellum period. On another side, that numerous accounts in *Reminiscences* depicted strong female characters successfully managing households at war without their men present raised fundamental questions about whether or not women actually needed—or had *ever* needed—such protection in the first place. On yet another side, and perhaps most horrifying of all for former Confederates, images in which women became the guardians of hearth and home also had the potential to raise questions about whether southern men actually required female protection.

So while the appearance of *Reminiscences* constitutes a critical moment in our story of guerrilla memory—a moment in which the "gatekeepers" of Confederate memory made a stand to be remembered of their own—the changes it might have imposed on guerrilla memory also had the potential to germinate and influence much broader patterns of southern Civil War commemoration. If the Missouri Daughters could have successfully interjected themselves into the Lost Cause narrative as primary military figures not in need of male protection or sacrifice, they would not only have retooled the guerrilla theater's pro-Confederate memory machine but also severely undermined the gender-based scaffolding on which the mainstream Lost Cause—the movement that *they themselves* had worked tirelessly to construct and used to collect immense social and political power—clearly rested. A commemorative conundrum indeed.

Setting the Stage: Homefront as Battlefront

In any war in which soldiers' mobility is their primary asset, adversaries will often attack immobile targets—homes foremost among them. Guerrilla warfare in the borderlands fit this strategic archetype precisely; with men lurking in the bush, their households, support networks, and the female relations in charge of such operations became primary military objectives. Thereby, for Missouri women, the Civil War came to their doorsteps with full force, and it was this experience they hoped to highlight in Civil War memory and memorialization.

According to Mrs. C. C. Rainwater, when Confederate troops evacuated, her community was "ever after left to the mercies of home-guard rule." Of the men who remained, those suspected of harboring southern sympathies were under "constant surveillance" and were routinely "called to the door at night and shot down without warning or provocation." On a single afternoon, she recalled, these "[homeguard] fiends started out and by Monday morning had murdered three innocent men in their homes surrounded by their families." Before the homeguard committed these acts, Rainwater concluded, "drinking was always resorted to."[6] Similarly, Mrs. S. E. Ulstick recollected when Jayhawkers "swooped down on us day and night, searching our homes for money or contraband goods." These raiders "frequently ran their bayonets through all the clothing in the wardrobe or through the mattress to see if there was any one concealed there." She alleged that her home had been searched seven times by "drunken Jayhawkers"; the armed invaders interrogated Ulstick and her terrified daughters and blew "their drunken breath in my face cursing the most bitter oaths until I was so frightened I could not tell my name."[7]

In her own contribution to *Reminiscences*, the wife of guerrilla William H. Gregg asserted that "the battles of Carthage, Wilson's Creek and Lexington were fought, General Price being successful in each of these battles, but it was not until 1862"—when the guerrilla war blossomed in full—"that the horrors of war were realized." "Our homes," she remembered, "were ransacked and jewelry, money, in fact, everything they could carry away was taken." Mrs. Gregg's mother-in-law attempted to conceal a watch in the breast of her clothing, but on discovering her deception, Union guerrillas "tore her dress open" and "robbed her, almost choking her to death in trying to release the chain."[8] Mrs. Maggie Stonestreet English opined that the brutality of the guerrilla theater "was almost unprecedented in the annals of American history." "My most painful childhood memories," she offered, "were of officers searching the house for my father, who was secreted there." But while English's father may have survived the recurring raids, the family's household did not. "Our home was raided and robbed," she stated, and "the house was burned and the plantation devastated." Amid the plunder and chaos, even "a locket containing a dead child's hair" was usurped from her mother.[9]

Clearly women did not have to stray far from home for the irregular conflict to find them. In reality, staying put may have actually been more dangerous than the itinerant life of a male bushwhacker. But home or abroad, one tactic existed in the guerrilla theater designed specifically for use against women: sexual assault. Mrs. J. M. Thatcher wrote in her addition to *Reminiscences* that her husband had been forced to swear an oath of allegiance to Union authorities but, even so, was "detained in their camp for two weeks" before "he was taken out and deliberately shot." "We dared not murmur," she remembered, as Jayhawkers "invaded my house and

"Jemison's [*sic*] Jayhawkers." This etching, produced in 1864, shows a pro-Confederate heroine being assaulted by a pro-Union Jayhawker under the command of Charles Jennison; it illustrates the dangers faced by women on the Missouri-Kansas homefront. Courtesy of Prints and Photographs Collection, Library of Congress, http://www.loc.gov /pictures/item/90709991/.

terrified us, even throwing their loaded guns across my baby's cradle." More trying still, according to Thatcher, was that "these marauders almost forced themselves upon us borders" and that "we dared not refuse." "A young girl," she continued, "dared not refuse to take a ride with officers." Rebuffing—or at least attempting to rebuff—such advances was unquestionably a dangerous business as "one lovely girl died three days afterward with a dread secret untold."[10] And if the meaning of Thatcher's statement was lost on readers, Mrs. H. F. Hereford analogously recalled when Jayhawkers burst into her home with guns drawn and more than jewelry or dinner on their minds. "I bared my breast," she concluded, "and told them to do their worst, but to kill the little children at the same time."[11]

Contemporary historians debate whether the Civil War was the first modern war or the last of the Napoleonic breed. But to Daughters writing in 1913, the distinction could not have mattered less. Their homes—from households invaded and children terrorized to men shot down and women assaulted—had been the constitutive element of the conflict. As a result, domestic violation left permanent scars on the homes and families of women in the guerrilla theater. These scars served as an equally permanent reminder of the wartime environment and the experiences the Daughters sought to commemorate in *Reminiscences.*

The ruination of individual homes and family units was simultaneously both a cause and effect of women becoming guerrillas—in many cases, by refusing to stand by as victims or noncombatants, they brought further destruction down on themselves. Like women in Virginia or Georgia or Tennessee, those in Missouri watched over homes and farms of various worth and size. They fed and clothed themselves and their children and occasionally managed slaves. But the wartime service of these borderland women was also quite different. Guerrilla warfare prompted these women to stand in for men in ways they hardly could have imagined before the war; they became household commanders, real-time diplomats, hostage negotiators, quartermasters, smugglers, spies, triage nurses, morticians, pallbearers, and even outright combatants—all roles they refused to forget when the war was over.

The Diplomacy of Survival

Women transformed homes situated in the guerrilla theater into irregular command centers, supply depots, and fortresses. Time and again, like male-dominated forts and logistical centers of the regular war, these hives of guerrilla activity could be raided, breeched, sacked, and even surrendered. When this last scenario unfolded, women, as commanders of their households, became responsible for its occupants, be they children, other female guerrillas, or male relations. The decisions they made as negotiators and diplomats carried the weight of life and death—and sometimes, as with all things in the guerrilla theater, even the best-devised strategy or the most polished tongue could not *guarantee* a successful outcome.[12]

Mrs. N. M. Harris remembered a banker from Kansas City forced to abandon his home when his southern sympathies became public knowledge. One night in his absence, she began, "while the family was asleep, the door of Mrs. McC.'s room on the first floor was broken in and a squad of noisy soldiers rushed into the apartment." Mrs. McC. (whose full name is redacted throughout the account) begged for time to put on her clothes, to which they "told her to get up pretty d−n quick or they would prod her with their sabers." Moving from room to room, the men systematically ransacked the house. When the woman's youngest daughter started crying, one of the raiders held a saber to her face and "told her if she uttered another sound he would cut off her head." Next the invaders turned their attention to a pair of older daughters who had been sleeping upstairs and, amid a stream of "ribald songs" and "obscene jokes," the men roughly− and likely unnecessarily−searched the girls for valuables. Finally, according to Harris's rendition, the men took the three daughters "by force" into the yard and "marched back and forth in the moonlight" while making "most vicious threats and insinuations." Throughout the ordeal, the banker's outnumbered and outgunned family had effectively become POWs within their own home; his wife, as chief diplomat, was able to both keep charge of her children and placate the plunderers enough so that none of her daughters were captured or killed *and* the house was left standing.[13]

Another Daughter also reminisced about a visit from moonlight raiders− though in this case, the difficulty of negotiations in the guerrilla theater and the ubiquitous possibility of diplomatic failure became more readily apparent. Mrs. Kate S. Doneghy wrote that a company of Union men "had been told that my husband had returned from the South," so they came to capture him and burn the house. Rather than resisting with force−a strategy that might have unnecessarily increased the odds of her young children being injured−Doneghy informed the men that her husband was not presently at home, but that she would open the door to confer if the soldiers agreed to hold their fire. Moments later, the house was filled with "much excited" and "enraged" men; despite her cooperation and attempt to parley with the invaders, Doneghy was abruptly told that the home would still be torched. So unlike the heroine of Harris's story, Doneghy had been too trusting of her opponents and erred badly as a negotiator. Consequently, had her toddler-aged son not influenced the Union commander to spare them, these mistakes would have severely undercut the prospects of survival for her family.[14]

Quartermasters, Smugglers, Spies

In addition to household diplomacy, many women in the guerrilla theater were also in the business of smuggling and espionage. Multiple scholars, Joseph Beilein most notably among them, have recently underscored a

"Formation of Guerilla [*sic*] Bands." This etching from 1863 reflects the role of the household—including women and children—in the creation of guerrilla companies, which included female quartermasters and intelligence gatherers. Courtesy of Prints and Photographs Collection, Library of Congress, http://www.loc.gov /pictures/item/90709989/.

fundamental reality of guerrilla warfare in the borderlands: that it could not have operated in any prolonged or effective capacity without women willing to act as quartermasters and turn their homes into irregular supply depots.[15] Even so, maintaining these stockpiles was really just the tip of the proverbial iceberg as far as the Missouri Daughters were concerned. Whether their shadowy activities entailed serving as quartermasters for bushwhackers in the field, procuring vital supplies and moving them across occupied lines, transporting people through enemy territory, or passing along crucial intelligence, they had done it all—and were not about to let such vital, dashing contributions go unheralded.

According to Mrs. S. E. Ulstick, she and other women took on "the responsibility of getting supplies for their families"—a function that un- doubtedly allowed their men and boys to survive in the bush. This meant not only keeping children alive at home but also keeping irregular com- batants stocked with the necessities of war. This wartime actuality of the guerrilla theater made smuggling people, supplies, and information a very dangerous enterprise. In some sense, the Jayhawkers who cracked down on this activity were applying military pressure where they knew it would be most effective. They were, in some sense, Sherman's troops before Sherman's troops ever lit a match or marched to the sea, making war on political will by making households howl.[16]

The tale of Mrs. Tyler Floyd was perhaps a case in point of all three forms of risky business tied together: spying, smuggling, and supplying men in the bush. "At the beginning of the Civil War," she recounted, "we had an underground road of communication" by which messages and people "would go from one point to another" and, if they so wished, could be linked directly with the army of Confederate general Sterling Price. Floyd's own home was an important way station along the secret route: "They would come from Dr. Lewis's house to our house," she wrote, and then "we would direct them on out to Versailles" and the next stop at the home of a Doctor James.[17]

Women working on this underground transportation and information network would often receive reports that men in the field had run out of vital supplies such as quinine or morphine. The Daughters were quick to describe how they responded when such requests for help came in. Floyd recalled one such mission to Boonville, Missouri. There, despite the fact that the town was occupied by Union forces, she gathered up nearly all of the quinine and morphine left in Boonville's only drugstore and then secured a large quantity of gray flannel and black velvet from the dry goods emporium. "Mrs. Ellis and I cut the flannel into shirt lengths and made a skirt out of the whole two pieces," Floyd remembered. Next, the two women fashioned containers and head rolls from the cloth strips and used them to hide the medicines under their dresses and atop their heads. When stopped at a Federal checkpoint, Floyd informed the soldiers that she had an ill aunt twenty-five miles away and that she needed to arrive there before the poor woman died. The story was a complete fabrication, but it convinced the men to allow Floyd and her companion through their lines without searching their bodies. The flannel was later transformed into shirts for southern men. Suspicion of her quartermaster's operation eventually landed Floyd in a Saint Louis prison. Much to the chagrin of Union authorities, she refused to reveal anything about her accomplices, their underground railroad, or their smuggling operations. Proudly, Floyd concluded, "I never opened my mouth" when interrogated about her activities or the stolen drugs.[18]

Triage to Burial: The Work of Life and (More Often) Death

The stories of women such as Clara Barton and Louisa May Alcott serving as nurses in the Eastern Theater of the Civil War are well known; they run the gamut from scholarly sources such as published diaries to pop culture representations as seen in *Gone with the Wind* (1939). In the East, however, most women were not asked to collect and dispose of corpses; nor, for that matter, were they typically asked to provide emergency medical care in individual homes that simultaneously served as hospitals and battlefields. This work of life and death—that is, medical care on an active battle-front and corresponding burial duties—frequently fell to women in the borderlands with men either absent or unwilling, due to exorbitant risk, to perform it. As was the case with their roles as guerrilla diplomats, smugglers, and quartermasters, the Missouri Daughters believed that their distinction warranted commemoration.[19]

One such contributor to *Reminiscences* remembered being awakened early one morning in Independence, Missouri, by "a furious fusillade of guns." Chaos then ensued in the boardinghouse occupied by Mrs. R. T. Bass and several other girls as "they began to bring in the wounded men and lay them around on the beds and floors until the place was filled with the poor fellows wounded and bleeding, moaning in their agony." With no healthy men in sight, Bass was sent to fetch a doctor and recalled that "bullets cut leaves from the trees above my head and fell thick all around me." On returning to the residence-turned-hospital, she and the other girls spent the rest of the day tending to wounded guerrillas from William C. Quantrill's command while the sounds of firefights and skirmishes still echoed around them. "It required strong nerves for young girls to assist in dressing wounds, nursing and soothing the suffering," Bass reckoned, also sharing the praise with her fellow Daughters by suggesting that she "never heard of a southern woman, old or young, that was not equal to such an emergency when it came to her, and we did our duty as best we could."[20]

Sometimes—many times, in fact—the stories of women involved both nursing *and* subsequently attending to the bodies of men who could not be saved. In this light, Mrs. Ann C. Everett's account began when she, along with her young children, were visiting at a nearby neighbor's home. Suddenly, the group "heard the firing of guns and the whooping and yelling of men." When she looked toward her own house, Everett "soon saw that it was surrounded by a company of Federal soldiers." Unaware of the situation around her home, she collected her children and ran to investigate. According to Everett's account, the soldiers had discovered three young southern sympathizers asleep on her property, and an officer informed her that they "had sent them where they would cause no more trouble"; two of the boys had already been executed and the third lay gravely wounded. As the company prepared to leave, she inquired about their plans for both the living boy and the corpses. "We are going to leave them right where they are," one of the Union men replied. "They will make good food for the hogs." The man also warned Everett that he did not believe "it will be very safe for anyone to interfere with them."[21]

Horrified by this response, the young mother dared to ask the Union captain in charge for a pass that would allow her to care for the injured boy and to safely remove and bury the other bodies, to which the captain consented. Acting as the boy's nurse was very dangerous but straightforward; he was eventually regenerated to full health. Entombment, however, was another matter as Everett soon found that "it was almost impossible to get a man to help me care for the dead and wounded" because "the few men left at home felt it would be risking their own lives to give any assistance in a case of that kind." She would have to dispose of the corpses herself; with her two children, she "spent the night alone with the dead" and "washed the blood from their faces and hands" before wrapping each "in a clean sheet and blanket." Everett did virtually all of the work; the most help she could garner from local men was the placement of a few planks in each grave. Later, in August 1863, likely in retaliation for her interfering with the bodies, Everett's own brother was shot down in the front yard of her home. Not surprisingly, "there was not a man we could get to help in our great need," so "the women in the neighborhood came to my assistance and brought his body to the house and washed and dressed him for burial."[22]

In other instances, women simply could not save a guerrilla's life. Whether they arrived on the scene too late to provide medical attention or the injuries sustained were simply too severe (as multiple gunshot wounds had a habit of being), other Daughters such as Mrs. Larima Crow Reilley worked solely as morticians and undertakers. In May 1863, as her story went, a southern man was "shot three times and stabbed four times with a bayonet" by German homeguardsmen. In the face of these wounds, he died more or less instantly. "The next morning," Reilley continued, "he was found dead in the road by his family." Local authorities—the exact same men who had carried out the killing—refused to allow the dead man's wife and daughters to procure a coffin for his burial, nor would they allow any men in the area to touch his corpse or aid in the interment. As a result, four women, including the victim's own daughter, collected the body, wrapped it in a quilt, and eventually convinced a few local men to help them bury it, but only then in the middle of the night.[23]

No Fury Like a Female Guerrilla . . .

Historians have been quick to point out that many women were directly touched by the irregular conflict—or even that they "participated" or "served" in it as household commanders, quartermasters, and pallbearers. Few scholars, if any, though, have suggested that these roles made women "true" guerrillas in the sense of their male counterparts. (Here it may be helpful to note that while all bushwhackers were guerrillas, not all guerrillas were bushwhackers—nor was bushwhacking the only legitimate or authentic means of irregular combat.) The logistical or seemingly "noncombative" roles taken by women in the borderlands should not, however, exclude them from the distinction of having been guerrillas. Inasmuch as men from the regular army who served in logistical or command capacities have been counted as soldiers, these women hinted that they should be categorized as guerrillas without disclaimer or qualification. Furthermore, even with this new equivalency established, several of the Missouri Daughters (like the ax-wielding Martha Horne) hoped to make clear via their contributions to *Reminiscences* that they had, in fact, sought out and engaged in irregular combat on the homefront. Mrs. William H. Gregg seemed quite confident of this when she wrote, "my dear sisters, I had bullets whiz all about my head. . . . Do you wonder at me being a United Daughter of the Confederacy?"[24]

Mary Harrison Clagett detailed the story of the late Mrs. America M. Maddox. According to an account dictated by the latter, "families suspected of having money on the premises or valuables concealed were in peculiar danger of being raided upon." One night, in search of such treasures, a squad of Federal soldiers "swooped down" on Maddox and demanded entry into her Callaway County home. She informed the raiders that they were not welcome and could not come in, and when they refused to leave, "she stood with ax in hand ready to fell the first one that entered" and "advised them of her intention" to defend herself with deadly force. The ax, Clagett wrote, had been hidden away by the "farsighted" Maddox for use on just such an occasion. And so "a very determined woman, straight as an Indian, of slender build, ladylike, too, and not affected with nerves, was ready for battle inside, armed not with a broom but a dangerous ax." Realizing this, the would-be invaders attempted to parley with Maddox, but "she would not yield nor would she capitulate." Eventually, after several unsuccessful attempts to burn down the home around her, Maddox only opened the door when threats were made against the life of her young son, Irvin, who was not capable of fighting alongside his mother.[25]

While Maddox's responsibility for the life of her son—a charge of the household she commanded—had necessitated that she lay down her weapon, the contribution of Mrs. R. T. Bass to *Reminiscences* did not end so peacefully for its cast of Union invaders. As previously mentioned, Bass remembered visiting Independence, Missouri, and coincidentally being in town when Quantrill's band of bushwhackers clashed with Jayhawkers. As wounded guerrillas streamed into the house owned by her host, Bass became a triage nurse, and when Quantrill's command was forced to leave behind its injured, she became a prisoner with them when a group of Jayhawkers arrived and took control of the home.[26]

During her captivity in the makeshift hospital-turned-prison, one of these Jayhawkers began trying to flirt with Bass and, in the course of their conversation, asked for a drink of water. Bass happily recalled giving him the drink—dryly noting that it had possibly come from "a glass in which medicine had been mixed." "Shortly after returning to their quarters uptown," she mocked, "my gallant officer was seized with violent suffering." Almost immediately, the Jayhawker proclaimed that the drink "had a peculiar taste" and that Bass had poisoned him. For her own part, she added rather smugly that the man thought of poison so quickly due to "probably feeling he deserved it." Soon after being arrested for homicide, Bass was exonerated by a physician who happened to be a close friend.

The doctor "pronounced it a case of bad whiskey" and cleared her name, she concluded—after the tone of her writing had virtually (and proudly, at that) made clear to posterity that the assassination had not been an accident but an act of war.[27]

The Consequences of Irregular Activity

From smuggling supplies and gathering corpses to physically defending their homes and poisoning enemy officers, the Missouri Daughters presented themselves engaged in a host of irregular activities throughout the guerrilla theater. This much is made perfectly clear by the accounts referenced above. But the contributors to *Reminiscences* did not shy away from the consequences of such activity, either. Just like that of their male counterparts, all forms of female guerrilla activity came with a potential price ranging from physical injury and imprisonment to shattered families, exile, and death. To be sure, extant circumstances frequently forced the hands of many women into taking action; most important to recognize, however, was the ever-looming possibility that explicit resistance or an act of retribution would only attract greater hardship to the family or household. So in much the same way that the Missouri Daughters touted their having waged war like men of the borderlands, they were equally satisfied with how they had faced the consequences.

As described by several contributors to *Reminiscences*, the destruction of homes and property—which often resulted in broken families and exile—was the most common form of backlash for aiding and abetting southern men in the field. Mrs. J. A. B. Adcock remembered that "Quantrill was a frequent visitor at my father's home." In turn, her father "was taken out twice to be killed at night" by Jayhawkers but managed to escape both times. Following these close calls, he took to sleeping in the woods until the winter weather would no longer permit. At this point, the family had to abandon their homestead and relocate. In September 1865, on returning home, they found the surrounding countryside "a desolate waste, with now and then a lone chimney to tell the story of a fire." But the saddest feature of all, she concluded, was the disintegration of families the scorched chimneys represented. "Not all members of families ever returned," Adcock wrote. "Fathers and brothers and sweethearts and husbands yet sleep in far-off graves."[28] In similar fashion, Mrs. J. W. Holmes recounted her own family's experience with dissolution and exile. Raiders had twice attempted to kill her father in plain view of the family; he escaped, after receiving a bullet wound and then crawling off into the woods. While Holmes and her mother had no idea if her father had been killed, "the marauders returned and stripped the house of everything that night and made their camps comfortable with our belongings." The family eventually went to Kentucky until the war closed.[29]

The loss of a home or family member was indeed terrible, but other stories illustrated that women were not always just left alone to grieve or pick up the pieces. Mrs. Mary Jackman Mullins wrote about a southern soldier's sick wife who was forced by Jayhawkers to flee her home, young children and all. After taking refuge with her mother-in-law in neighboring Howard County, Union authorities cracked down on the family. The soldier's wife, his mother, and two sisters "were placed under military arrest and taken to St. Louis, where they were detained some time."[30] Another woman, Mrs. Judge Graves, remembered when "forty or fifty women and children were torn from their homes" and "cooped up in an old building as prisoners because they were accused of harboring and feeding bushwhackers." That building, she continued, eventually collapsed, leaving more than a few of the female inmates dead or crippled. "The scene," Graves finished somberly, "beggared description."[31]

According to the account of Mrs. R. K. Jones, even cooperation with enemy forces was no guarantee of safety in the guerrilla theater. She recalled an uncle who was blind in one eye being ordered by Union soldiers to provide directions. The uncle in question apparently helped the soldiers reach their destination—at which point they shot him, gouged out his good eye, and left him for dead. But Jones also understood the consequences of failing to cooperate, which most often meant harboring a southern sympathizer or bushwhacker. She wrote that if a southern soldier was discovered and caught visiting home, "death was instantaneous." "One young man," she noted, "was found secreted in his mother's house, taken out in the yard and hanged before her eyes." Not content just to have killed the man, the Union forces let loose a group of hogs to "devour his body."[32]

Gender in no way garnered the Missouri Daughters immunity from the grimmest possible after-effects of their wartime activities. In whatever capacity women served as guerrillas, they put the lives of their male relations and households at risk—just as men put their female relations and households at risk by bushwhacking and raiding. But in the process of equipping men, spying, smuggling, and fighting, women also faced mortal danger and risked their own lives. To make this point abundantly clear, Mrs. N. M. Harris told the story of a woman who attempted to protect her sick husband from raiding Jayhawkers in Jackson County, Missouri. The woman, Harris reported, was personally shot by Charles Jennison for her effort; although she survived, she never again walked without the aid of crutches. It is unclear from Harris's account whether or not the victim's husband survived the encounter, but the odds would usually indicate that he did not.[33]

The Orphaned Daughters of Guerrilla Memory?

Throughout the pages of *Reminiscences*, the Missouri Daughters painted the portrait of a war largely unrecognizable to their eastern counterparts. They outlined a conflict in which homefront violence involving women and children as primary combatants and causalities was both expected and commonplace. Missourians' households were epicenters of unimaginable traumas that most families—even in the days of Bleeding Kansas and John Brown—had never before experienced. Residents of the guerrilla theater fought and (sometimes) survived a different kind of war—one that set them apart from other southerners.

By publishing their accounts, the Daughters were not simply trying to insert their own personal remembrances of the Civil War into the Lost Cause; rather, they produced new kinds of memorial narratives that sorted and categorized and laid bare their unique wartime experiences. And when critics questioned their intentions, contributor Mrs. N. M. Harris responded with a simple question of her own: "Why? Isn't this part of the history of the Civil War?"[34]

Harris was correct. It was part of the history of the Civil War, but it would not become part of Civil War history—because despite their very compelling case, the sort of memorial shift that the Daughters envisioned in *Reminiscences*—one that might reckon their own experiences with the mainstream Lost Cause in a way that could provide some sort of commemorative closure—never really materialized in the South. Indeed, it never really even materialized in the borderlands. The idea of a war fought without heroic generals and major pitched battles, involving women and children and the unpleasant realities of bushwhacking, never gained institutional traction.

This is not to insinuate that the Daughters lacked commemorative authority. To be sure, in the 1910s and 1920s (and beyond), members of the Missouri Division of the UDC remained prominent as local historians and brokers of Confederate tradition. They helped manage the Confederate Veterans' Home at Higginsville, Missouri; spearheaded educational programs for children; maintained Confederate graves; and even sent birthday cards to elderly former Rebels. But they were never able to successfully integrate their own experiences into the Lost Cause narratives they helped administrate and disseminate because, in those accounts, women are not damsels in distress or stoic army wives. Instead, they are full-fledged partisans of the guerrilla theater. These women, along with the trauma they endured and the "other" war they represented, were commemorative competitors with Confederate veterans. Thus, *Reminiscences* threatened the mainstream versions of the war that best suited rank-and-file Confederates everywhere.

Perhaps most problematic of all, while the book provided a model for other southern women to express their wartime experiences, it also represented a danger to their own cultural power. To be remembered as the equals of Confederate soldiers on a wider scale would have meant women were no longer holding up their end of the gendered bargain through which the Lost Cause functioned so effectively. Therein, the cost of being remembered alongside their male Confederate counterparts would have meant giving up rule of the commemorative kingdom. Other chapters outside of the borderlands did not follow the example of the Missouri Daughters—this was a price they simply were not willing to pay.

Even as the editors of *Reminiscences* essentially failed in their mission, their simultaneous support of and conflict with the mainstream Lost Cause created a precarious scenario for Cole Younger, William H. Gregg, A. J. Liddil, and the rest of the Quantrill Men Survivor's Association. These guerrilla memoirists and reunion-goers looked to women as the gatekeepers of the commemorative tradition into which they strove to integrate guerrilla memory. And as guerrilla memory went before posterity, so too would their personal legacies. On one hand, then, former guerrillas actually stood to benefit greatly from women publishing their experiences in *Reminiscences*, in many ways the themes and experiences described by the Daughters closely resembled male memories of the guerrilla war—perhaps an important link in the quest for mainstream recognition. On the other hand, though, the process of forging that link with women—which entailed them pushing narratives clearly at odds with the standard Lost Cause paradigm—risked the Missouri Daughters alienating themselves from the rest of the Cause itself. In other words, in a purely commemorative context, ex-bushwhackers needed the Daughters on their side, but only if women still held the power to help reboot guerrilla memory.

In the short term, ex-guerrillas probably came out ahead of where they had started. The Daughters published their wartime experiences and, because their ideas did not fundamentally alter the thematic landscape of the Lost Cause, retained their status as powerful memory brokers. At the same time, regardless of *Reminiscences*' broader failure to introduce a lasting degree of gender equality into the Confederate memory establishment, veterans of the guerrilla theater could still adjust their rhetorical tactics accordingly in memoirs and at reunions to better court the commemorative aid of women. Thus it should not come as a surprise that guerrilla memoirs published after 1913 highlighted female participation in the guerrilla war and elements of danger shared between the sexes more so than their predecessors had. So in a rather ironic twist, it appears that the Missouri Daughters largely lacked the ability to breach the outer shell of the Lost Cause with *their own* irregular recollections but—at least according to ex-guerrillas in chapters 3 and 4—still had the power to shepherd men through that very same process of "mainstreaming."

Assessing the situation along a more sweeping chronological horizon reveals that the true long-term consequences triggered by the Missouri Daughters was not what their success altered but what their failure allowed to remain in place. Today, the most familiar of Missouri's guerrilla-based memory narratives revolve around large-scale raids and massacres at Osceola (September 1861), Lawrence (August 1863), and Centralia (September 1864). These wartime events involved larger-than-life guerrilla chiefs, abnormally high casualty counts, and a bevy of witnesses who spread fantastic—and often erroneous—descriptions of the violence. Popular narratives also focus attention on Union general Thomas Ewing's General Order #11, which forcibly evicted civilian residents of Jackson,

Cass, Bates, and Vernon Counties in an effort to stamp out support for Confederate guerrillas in August 1863. The assaults and Order #11 are the best-remembered scenes from the guerrilla theater of the borderlands because they offer a quick, easily processed glimpse of irregular warfare. Through them, the major figures and functions of bushwhacking and Jay-hawking are on display, but in a form that conveys many of the traits that make the public comfortable with the Civil War: political orders, official hierarchy, larger battles, and famous (or infamous, viewpoint depending) commanders.

Not unlike other collective remembrances of the war framed around Robert E. Lee, Thomas "Stonewall" Jackson, and Ulysses S. Grant, conventional accounts of Missouri's Civil War history are male-dominated.[35] The usual suspects include William Clarke Quantrill, "Bloody Bill" Anderson, Senator James Lane, Charles "Doc" Jennison, the Younger brothers, and the James boys, among others. These men are undoubtedly the borderland's most prominent Civil War exports—and most Missourians and Kansans have latched onto them and the narrative they represent. Even in the few cases where women of the Civil War generation have received memorial attention in the form of specified, permanent monuments, such recognition has typically come up well short of commemorating the roles played by women in guerrilla warfare. Consider a monument erected in 2009 in Cass County, Missouri, remembering the "Burnt District" created by Ewing's General Order #11. The structure—a lone, stone chimney—and corresponding placards hint at the domestic nature of irregular warfare in Missouri. But the memorial commemorates Order #11 itself and does not highlight women as actual combatants.

As should by now be clear, such emphasis on massacres, orders, and leaders actually misrepresents much of the guerrilla war in the borderlands, whether pro-Union or pro-Confederate. Quantrill, Anderson, and company were all very active players on the guerrillafront, no doubt, but isolating the flashiest exploits of a handful of notorious men cannot illustrate the guerrilla experience in its entirety; they cannot reveal multiple perspectives of the daily traumas suffered. Many contemporary Missourians and Kansans with an interest in the Civil War legacy of their respective states do have a basic understanding of guerrilla warfare as a "different" type of wartime experience. The same can generally be said of Civil War buffs outside of the borderlands. More often than not, however, even a cursory conception of just how hard the guerrilla experience hit the individual homes remains buried in the state's postwar commemorative strata.

As a result, most modern-day Missourians and Kansans, and Americans, it seems fair to say, are curiously content to recognize the irregular features of the guerrilla war and then continue to approach its memory and commemoration from a conventional (eastern, male) perspective. This is a serious misinterpretation. While the women of Twain's account might have been "busy and out of our sight," the "plaintive wailing of a spinning-wheel" was one of the sounds—literally—of them waging war in the guerrilla theater. But the Missouri Daughters were not the only party looking to shift the balance of commemorative power in the borderlands. Just as Martha Horne remembered the Jayhawkers bringing the fight to her farm in 1862, so too did those Kansans make plays for control of guerrilla memory in the postwar era—and not all of their tactics would be as peaceful as the printing of a book.

SIX

The Unionists Strike Back

It soon came out that mine was not the only shot fired; there were
five others—and division of the guilt which was a grateful relief to me,
since it in some degree lightened and diminished the burden I was
carrying.
–Mark Twain, "The Private History of a Campaign That Failed"

There's been so much written about the Lawrence raid from the
standpoint of the Kansans that I would just like to tell our side once . . .
–Capt. William H. Gregg, QMSA Reunion, 1912

The Sunday following Quantrill's infamous 1863 raid on Lawrence, Kansas, "had been a trying one to the people of Lawrence," noted Isadora
Allison in an account written several years later. Not surprisingly—it was
August, after all—the weather was exceedingly hot. "But," she added,
the "heat had been increased by the fires which still smoldered from the
burned buildings all over the town." In this postapocalyptic cityscape,
"the odor of fire and smoke filled the air" as Reverend Richard Cordley
conducted a mass funeral service at the Congregational church for those
killed two days earlier.[1]

"Weeping friends, widows and orphans, fathers and mothers, brothers
and sisters," Allison reported, "had gathered for the only funeral service
that was held for the 185 murdered men and boys, whose remains—many
of them burned beyond recognition—had been hastily buried in boxes
or roughly made coffins two days before." Among the dead was Duncan Allison, Isadora's thirty-year-old husband and the father of her infant
daughter, Clara Belle. As Allison and Clara Belle retired to the home of
a family friend for the evening, they, like the rest of Lawrence's shell-
shocked survivors, had not an inkling of "the night of terror and excitement" that would soon begin.[2]

At the home of a couple referred to only as "Mr. and Mrs. L," Allison
had finally coaxed Clara Belle to sleep when she noticed an eerie quiet
had fallen on the town—so quiet that she could "hear the soft breathing of

the children on the bed." Then, in an instant, she made out "the clattering of hoofs in the distance." In the early hours of August 21, just two days prior, the echoes of equine feet had been the first signal that death and destruction approached Lawrence. Now, as the distant rumbling drew nigh, Allison and her hosts began to fear the worst. An unidentified man on horseback streaked past the home and all within heard him shouting: "Fly, fly for your lives, Quantrill is coming, killing and burning everything as he goes!"[3]

"All was confusion in a moment," recalled Allison. Following a brief conference, all decided to take refuge in a nearby cornfield. So Isadora Allison scooped up her sleeping child and fled into the night wearing only a light dress and slippers. Mr. L grabbed his own child while his wife gathered a bundle of clothing and his mother-in-law collected valuables. The group had trekked only a few paces toward their "place of safety" when Mrs. L's mother exclaimed that she had forgotten her mother's silver teaspoons—much to the frustration of her companions, she refused to leave without them and soon returned. Theirs was not the only group preparing to flee; all around her Allison "could see in the starlight men, women, and children flitting in every direction carrying bundles of clothing and valuables."[4]

Eventually, Allison and company arrived at their destination: a cornfield of nearly one hundred acres located on Mississippi Street. "The corn," Allison wrote, "was of the tallest of Kansas growth and was tall above the head of the tallest man and, once within its border, one was safe from the enemy." The group made a crude bed from the bundle of clothing and sat down in "trembling silence to wait for the morning." Low whispers and hushed voices floated from every angle of the cornfield. Occasionally, a child would cry out and be quickly silenced by a terror-stricken mother. For the refugees of Lawrence, hundreds of them strewn amongst the corn, the dawn's light could not arrive soon enough.[5]

The home Isadora Allison had shared with her late husband, Duncan, also bordered the cornfield and, in search of warmth for their infants, the group made what they thought was a risky journey. On the way, Allison lost her slippers to the rough plowed ground and, on gaining sight of the house, left Clara Belle with her companions and crawled—on hands and knees—through the yard to the front door. Once inside the house, Allison shuttered the windows and lit a lamp. The rest of the night came and went—but no bushwhackers came with it. Cheered by the news that what little remained of Lawrence had not been destroyed completely, Allison prepared breakfast and watched as group after group hesitantly came to the edge of the cornfield to survey the situation. She noted that it was nearly noon before the last of the refugees had given up the safety of the corn.[6]

As it turned out, the entire ordeal was a false alarm. A farmer living on the outskirts of Lawrence had spotted a large fire in the nearby town of Eudora. Convinced that Quantrill had returned to "complete his murderous work," the man took it on himself to warn his neighbors.[7]

Considering the bloody sequence of events that had transpired less than forty-eight hours beforehand, it is difficult to fault the farmer for his would-be heroics. More significantly, though, Isadora Allison's account of that night—like those of Wilhelm Kroll, Louis Meyer, and William Brown from chapter 1—provides a clear glimpse into the sort of traumatic recollections that borderland Unionists brought with them to the commemorative table. Like those of their Missouri counterparts, these Unionist memories could not—and would not—simply be buried, forgotten, or artificially amended; nor would they be steamrolled by pro-Confederate narratives without a fight. Thus as the other half of the equation that produced irregular violence in the guerrilla theater, these Unionists understandably had their own preferred blueprint for guerrilla memory and how many of its best-known characters, arch-nemesis Quantrill chief among them, ought to have been remembered.

But laying claim to the dominant rendition of guerrilla memory proved much more difficult for Unionists than the likes of John Newman Edwards and his Missouri-based following. For starters, Edwards's political agenda necessitated that he convince only *other conservative southerners*—virtually all already sympathetic former Confederates—that his noted guerrillas had been legitimate and honorable warriors for their cause. With this in mind, Edwards cared little, if at all, what Kansans like Isadora Allison and her neighbors thought of his narrative. These Unionists who already despised the Missouri bushwhacker were not Edwards's target audience and would exert little influence over the achievement of his partisan goals.

For borderland Unionists, the impediments to establishing an influential (and lasting) collective memory narrative in the anti-Edwards tradition stood much taller. Their task required not only constructing an account of the guerrilla theater designed to tell their side of the story (in which Quantrill and Missourians were to blame for almost everything) but also finding a way to make anyone *outside* of the borderlands care about it. While Edwards knew exactly whom he needed to draw over to his side of the debate and could afford to ignore the North wholesale, Unionists had to make a tougher choice. On one side, most northerners likely agreed that "border ruffians" in Missouri had been the spark of wartime troubles out West—but the difficulty lay in prompting any public acknowledgment of that point on a regular or otherwise substantial basis. On the other side, most southerners, as evidenced by Edwards's work in chapter 2, did not and would never favor the Unionist position. Thus, from their headquarters in Kansas, they had to decide on which side to focus their efforts: the rock or the hard place. At the same time, they had to determine what form those efforts should entail in the first place.

Accordingly, this chapter surveys the broad and creative array of responses concocted and employed by Unionists as counterattacks against the likes of John Newman Edwards, his version of the guerrilla memory narrative, and its Missouri-centric, southern-based constituency. Spanning the 1870s to the 1930s, these reactions emanated from different sources, both military and civilian, and frequently took different forms: scholarly historical texts, published reminiscences, survivors' reunion addresses, poetry, newspaper editorials, commemorative contests, and even a theatrical production staged by university students. These pro-Unionist accounts often varied in terms of the geographical and generational demographics whose particular visions they represented and toward whom specifically they directed their propaganda. All, however, were devised with one common aim: to achieve the utter ruination of William C. Quantrill's reputation and legacy.

In this regard, Unionists, somewhat ironically, took their cue from Edwards. Throughout his campaign to glorify the Missouri bushwhacker, Edwards had operated with Quantrill as the unquestioned center of his commemorative universe. Anderson, Todd, James, Thrailkill, and Younger had all been fearsome guerrilla warriors—but only Quantrill would serve as the anchor of Edwards's "irregular" Lost Cause. As a case in point, in *Noted Guerrillas*, Edwards described Quantrill as "a living, breathing, aggressive, all-powerful reality—riding through the midnight laying ambuscades by lonesome roadsides, catching marching columns by the throat, breaking in upon the flanks and tearing a suddenly surprised rear to pieces; vigilant, merciless, a terror by day and a superhuman if not supernatural thing when there was upon the earth blackness and darkness."[8]

So essentially taking Edwards at his word—that is, believing Confederate Missourian's side of the debate over the guerrilla war's legacy would go as did Quantrill's "superhuman" pedigree—borderland Unionists concentrated their fire on the architect of the Lawrence Massacre. They wanted to behead the snake, so to speak, and in turn, everything about Quantrill became fair game. In addition to his bloodstained wartime résumé, bits of information either disputed or ignored by Edwards, such as Quantrill's childhood years in Ohio, his moral character, his shadowy dealings during the sectional crisis, and even his apparently genetic predisposition for murderousness and villainy were all much scrutinized and often accepted as fact.

A narrow, ad hominem focus on William Clarke Quantrill also afforded Unionists an extra benefit: the opportunity to gloss over the darker aspects of their own side's wartime record—most notably, the unseemly execution-turned-death pageant of Larkin Milton Skaggs, the only one of Quantrill's command killed during the Lawrence Massacre. So in the process of making their own case for memorial dominance—a case that revolved around a litany of damning evidence thrown against Quantrill—borderland Unionists had to work around elements of the story with the greatest potential to undermine it; they had to "explain away" the things that most made them look or seem like Quantrill.

Ultimately, this chapter suggests that paring the Kansas-versus-Missouri memory debate down to a discussion of Quantrill played right into the posthumous hands of John Newman Edwards. This singular strategy pitted Unionists against the heart of Edwards's well-rooted mythology while simultaneously lacking a suitable outside audience for consumption and support. At the same time, for many pro-Confederates the strategy only seemed to verify the larger-than-life persona Edwards had rendered of Quantrill. (If Quantrill had not been so important, they wondered, why were Unionists trying so hard to discredit the dead chieftain?) Borderland Unionists had decided to pick a fight they could not win because, as it turned out, most in the guerrilla theater had already made up their minds, and no one outside of it really cared one way or the other. These easterners had their own commemorative crusades to wage.

W. E. Connelley and the "Historical Approach"

In July 1909 William Elsey Connelley penned the preface to *Quantrill and the Border Wars* from his home at 816 Lincoln Street in Topeka, Kansas. He asserts that his was the first effort "to make any serious study of the condition prevailing on the border." In fact, he suggests that "little of the story has ever been told"; moreover, all the rest "has been myth, doubt, assertion, beautiful generalization, conjecture." But William Connelley was an avid chronicler of the Missouri-Kansas border war; he knew the work of John Newman Edwards well. Thereby the promise to "*serious* study" [my emphasis] represented the first shot in a campaign to discredit the legitimacy of Edwards's "irregular" Lost Cause as factual or historical. In the process, Connelley sought to achieve the opposite end of *Noted Guerrillas*: rather than deify William C. Quantrill (the linchpin of the Edwards narrative), *Quantrill and the Border Wars* demonized him.[9]

In order to tear away the Christlike aura Edwards had created for Quantrill, Connelley first seeks to distinguish himself as a proper historian compared to Edwards's roles as propagandist and mythmaker. Connelley's work pulls from an impressive archive of manuscripts, correspondence, and military records—and he employed extensive citations in the form of footnotes for his readers. "Nothing," he claims, "has been written in a sensational way." (For what it's worth, he broke this promise early and often.) According to Connelley, whose historical approach required him to appear as an objective scholar, the "simple statement of what occurred is sensational enough" and "the old idea that truth is stranger than fiction is demonstrated."[10] Next, he sets out to establish an interconnected trio of claims: (1) that Quantrill had inherited his penchant for vice from his family—a sinister legacy passed through the cells of an accursed bloodline; (2) as a result of his maladjusted genetics, Quantrill had lied about being a real southerner and had never, at any time, genuinely cared for the interests of the South or the Confederacy; and (3) because Quantrill had lacked a genuine Confederate ideology or southern identity, his heinous activities along the border, epitomized by the Lawrence Massacre, had been perfectly illegitimate. All together, instead of a martyred war hero, these ideas transformed William Clarke Quantrill into the "bloodiest man known to the annals of America."[11]

From the beginning of *Quantrill and the Border Wars*, Connelley determines to show that Quantrill, as a child, had been a serial killer in the making—and that such qualities were in the blood. To such an end, he offers that "the Quantrills exhibit the usual characteristics of a family deficient in sound moral fiber." In William Clarke Quantrill, then, "was exemplified the terrible and immutable law of heredity." As a result,

> He grew into the gory monster whose baleful shadow falls upon all who share the kindred blood. He made his name a Cain's mark and a curse to those condemned to bear it. The blight of it must fall upon remote generations, those yet unborn and innocent, so inexorable are the decrees of fate and nature. Because of him widows wailed, orphans cried, maidens wept, as they lifted the lifeless forms of loved ones from bloody fields and bore them reeking to untimely graves.

How did William Connelley arrive at such a conclusion? According to his research, the seat of the Quantrill family was Hagerstown, Maryland. The grandfather of William Clarke Quantrill was Captain Thomas Quantrill. As Connelley tells it, the captain's record was a mixed one: he was a blacksmith who had served valiantly in the War of 1812 *and* he was a prolific gambler. (Connelley also notes persistent rumors that one of Thomas Quantrill's brothers "became a pirate on the high seas, operating many years on the Gulf of Mexico between Galveston Island and the mouth of the Sabine.") Despite his fondness for laying the odds, Thomas Quantrill married Judith Heiser—the daughter of a very respectable family—and their union produced several sons. Among these children were William Quantrill's uncle, Jesse Duncan Quantrill, and his father, Thomas Henry Quantrill.[12] Within the bounds of Connelley's theory, Thomas Quantrill bestowed genetics predisposed for vice on his sons, and they would soon raise the ante well above gambling or fleeting rumors of piracy.

Jesse Duncan Quantrill was not the ideal oldest son for a war hero—even one with a gambling problem. "He was a sort of fop or dandy," Connelley argues, "with criminal instincts and tendencies, a dashing, handsome man wholly devoid of character." Jesse Quantrill wed Mary Lane of Hagerstown "clandestinely." At the time of the wedding, Lane was a year too young to receive access to a substantial financial trust. Her new husband talked the bank into releasing the funds to him early. Then, when Lane came of age to claim her fortune, Jesse Quantrill sued the very same bank for the very same funds on the basis that they should never have released the money to him the first time. This incident was, Connelley claims, only the beginning of a long career as a vagabond and confidence man.[13]

Jesse roved from New York to Virginia to Baltimore to New Orleans to Cincinnati to Saint Louis engaging in various financial frauds, counterfeiting schemes, and forgeries as he went. As a grifter, Jesse was frequently arrested and often imprisoned for months at a time. While his criminal career blossomed, he frequently took to the bottle and abused his wife. Eventually, Mary Lane divorced her husband while he sat in a Pennsylvania prison serving three years for forgery; in response, he threatened to kill her. On his release, Jesse Quantrill tracked Mary to her new home in Cumberland, Maryland, and attempted to murder her (after the divorce Lane had remarried to a Mr. A. Cowton). Quantrill entered the home, locked the door, threw Mary to the ground, and snapped a pistol in her face. When the gun misfired, he pulled a knife, but he was stopped by men responding to Mary's shrieks for help. Quantrill went back to prison and was eventually released on promise that he leave the state and never return. All told, Connelley contends that Jesse Duncan Quantrill "married and deserted six women."[14]

William Quantrill's father, Thomas Henry Quantrill, was a tinker and tinner by trade—a very bright man in Connelley's estimation. While visiting the Heiser family in Chambersburg, Pennsylvania, he met Caroline Cornelia Clarke. The couple was shortly thereafter engaged and married in 1836. Once married, Thomas and Caroline Quantrill moved to Canal Dover, Ohio. Like his own father, Thomas Quantrill had a mixed record so far as Connelley is concerned—but it is important to note that his transgressions had evolved beyond the sins of his predecessor (gambling) to include outright fraud and physical violence.[15]

In Canal Dover, Thomas was a trustee of the local school fund and an aspiring author. To finance the publication of a book on tinning, he embezzled the school's money. A man named H. V. Beeson discovered the scheme and Quantrill, caught red-handed, threatened to kill him. "One evening, late in autumn," writes Connelley, Quantrill "entered Beeson's house with a cocked derringer in his hand." Beeson was sitting before the fire heating an iron rod to treat his cider. "When Quantrill entered," he continues, "Beeson rose suddenly and struck him on the head with the poker before he could shoot." The blow left Quantrill "unconscious on the floor with a long gash in his scalp" before neighbors arrived to carry the would-be murderer home. At about the same time as his failed attempt on Beeson's life, Quantrill also had a run-in with a Mrs. Roscoe—a "bright, vivacious woman" who gave painting lessons in Canal Dover. All around the village, he "made remarks derogatory about her character" until Mrs. Roscoe "armed herself with an 'old-style' cowhide," found Quantrill on a public street, and beat him senseless in front of several local men.[16]

In just a single generation, Connelley purports that the debauchery of the Quantrill bloodline had germinated from the seed of gambling to financial fraud, embezzlement, counterfeiting, forgery, slander, domestic abuse, bigamy, and attempted murder. The future did not bode well for William Clarke Quantrill; even of his childhood, Connelley paints a startling portrait of cruelty and sociopathic tendencies. "He had few friends" because "there was little in common between him and other boys his age." While normal children ran and played and occasionally roughhoused, Quantrill "was solitary, wandering in the woods with firearms." Alone, "he shot small game and maimed domestic animals for amusement." Connelley, however, does not stop there. The young Quantrill, he reports, "would often nail a snake to a tree and let it remain there in torture until it died"; "he carried small snakes in his pockets, and these he would throw on his sister and other girls at school and laugh heartily at their terror"; and "he would stick a knife in a cow by the roadside, or stab a horse. He often tortured dogs and cats to enjoy their cries of distress." In the end, Connelley adds that "pain in any other person or in any animal gave him pleasure, delight."[17]

As Quantrill grew into a teenager and then a young adult, his disposition did not improve by Connelley's reckoning. "He was obstinate" and "often defiant"; Quantrill's "chief characteristic was treachery." Like his father and his uncle before him, William Quantrill's intelligence made him all the more dangerous. "Mentally," Connelley points out, "he was above the average." Correspondingly, Quantrill "was calculating and farseeing; he had patience and he did not forget."[18] As the first phase of Connelley's strategy concluded, the eponymous subject of *Quantrill and the Border Wars* was the product of a natural, and thereby inescapable, evolutionary process. Simply put, he was the evil scion of an evil family tradition—and the borderlands would pay the price for his family's collected sins.[19]

Having proven historically—at least to himself and other borderland Unionists—that William Quantrill had been a deranged murderer-in-waiting from the time of his childhood, Connelley proceeds to the second stage of his three-pronged attack; he endeavors to stamp out, definitively, once and for all, the notions that Quantrill had been a southerner and that he had cared about the Confederate cause. To accomplish this, Connelley focuses on Quantrill's brief but tumultuous stint in Kansas—during which he posed as both an extreme abolitionist and a proslavery ruffian—and on the manner through which he later endeared himself to Missourians across the border.

Connelley asserts that in the late 1850s, when Quantrill migrated from Ohio to Kansas, the negative moral characteristics that had pervaded his childhood "were still latent." "From the first," he notes, Quantrill "was ambitious to acquire property and have money. But he was lazy. He abhorred labor." Quantrill was "incapable of exertion in any particular direction," according to Connelley. In the beginning, he argues that Quantrill was an open proponent of abolition and the Free-State cause who said that "every Missourian should have been shot and that all Democrats were rascals." But among the Kansans, Quantrill was "a wolf in sheep's clothing, a hypocrite, a spy, a traitor."[20]

By spring 1860, as Connelley tells it, Quantrill had arrived in Lawrence, Kansas, and taken to loafing around the local ferry with "a very disreputable gang of border-ruffians." These men were alleged to be "thieves, murderers, kidnappers" and even "negro-stealers." From Lawrence, Quantrill—who was known there by the alias "Charley Hart"—played both sides of the slavery issue to suit his own purposes and line his own pockets. On one hand, Quantrill played the part of abolitionist, helping guide escaped slaves from Missouri to freedom via the Underground Railroad. On the other hand, he often used that façade, in conjunction with other border ruffians, to lure unsuspecting slaves into his company, kidnap them, and then resell the slaves back to their original owners for a reward. In one case, Connelley reports that Quantrill and his associates took in $500 from the ransom of a single slave.[21]

For a time, in Connelley's rendition of the story, Quantrill made a precarious living through his double life. Eventually, though, things began to unravel. He had "played out the game" with the proslavery crowd and needed an exit strategy. So he took up again, albeit temporarily, with the Jayhawkers and engineered his escape to Missouri—again as a proslavery advocate. Chapters 9 and 10 of *Quantrill and the Border Wars* are dedicated to a detailed treatment of Quantrill's entry to Missouri society via the Morgan Walker Raid. To make a long story short, he went with abolitionists to steal slaves from the farm of Morgan Walker just over the border in

western Missouri. Unbeknownst to his accomplices, however, Quantrill
had turned double agent. In advance of the raid, which was intended to
release slaves to freedom, he approached and warned the Walker family.
So when his group arrived at the Walker farm after dark, the family was
ready, armed, and waiting.[22]

Quantrill helped the Walkers gun down the other Kansans and then
attempted to use his newly found credibility in Missouri as a "pro-slavery
man" to take up residence there. For their part, Missourians wanted to
know what Quantrill had been doing with the Kansans to begin with,
so "it was necessary that Quantrill should give to the people of Missouri
some excuse for his treachery." To cover his tracks, he told two lies: that
he was a native southerner from slave-holding Maryland and that, while
trekking to California, Jayhawkers under the command of James Montgomery had murdered his elder brother in cold blood. In the wake of his
brother's murder—the brother in question, as related in chapter 2, was
wholly fictitious—Quantrill claimed to have joined the Jayhawker band
and then spent months waylaying the guilty men one at a time. The men
he double-crossed at the Walker farm were allegedly the last of the guilty
men and *that* was why he had been in such poor company on arrival in
Missouri.[23]

The story, Connelley quickly points out, was a total farce. And from a
historical perspective, he was more or less correct on all counts. But truthful or not, "Quantrill's holy life of hardship and devotion to the South
(as told by him) grew in Missouri with the lapse of time" and, "together
with his guerrilla outrages and inhuman massacres, became a deification."
At this point, Connelley resets his sights on John Newman Edwards—the
man most responsible for perpetuating Quantrill's false southern credentials and for spearheading the "deification" process. Edwards, Connelley
asserts, "believed what he wrote, for he was an honest man." That said, he
continues that Edwards "had no correct information upon the subject of
the life of Quantrill in Kansas" before labeling *Noted Guerrillas* the "most
pretentious on the subject." That book, which helped produce Quantrill's
"fame as a martyr and saint in Missouri," contained many "ridiculous
statements and bald untruths."[24]

In a footnote, Connelley suggests that Edwards, in his efforts to deify the
guerrilla, in "splendid rhetoric" had shed "many tears and wastes much
genuine sympathy for a Quantrill who never lived—a poor, honest, injured,

imposed-upon, outraged, innocent, guileless Maryland boy who fell victim to the rough mercies of the leading Free-state men!" For Edwards, though, Connelley offers that "excuse can be made"; the Major, as he calls him, "did not know the truth about Quantrill—none of the Missourians knew it." That truth—of which *Quantrill and the Border Wars* had been designed to expose—was that "Quantrill had no convictions, stood for no principles, was in favor of no State or party, had no choice of communities, could not comprehend honesty, was an utter stranger to loyalty, and did not know such a thing as friendship." In other words, Quantrill had not been a southerner, and he had not been capable of genuinely supporting the Confederate cause; cast as such, his behavior was no longer the stuff of glory and apotheosis, but of a bloodthirsty, self-serving maniac.[25]

Believing he had, beyond any reasonable doubt, successfully revealed Quantrill's true motivations in Kansas and Missouri, Connelley next turns to the third and final point of his anti-Edwards, anti-Quantrill campaign— a reinterpretation of the Lawrence Massacre, Quantrill's greatest triumph, in this new, unflattering context. For this purpose, *Quantrill and the Border Wars* features a whopping eight chapters on the Lawrence Massacre alone.

Connelley begins with Quantrill and his guerrillas' motivations for raiding the town. "Lawrence was founded in the spirit of human liberty," Connelley pronounces proudly, and "it had its inception in the idea that slavery should not be one of the institutions of Kansas." Thus the slave owners of Missouri viewed the city as the headquarters of their enemies. "The Missourian," he argues, "believed that in fighting Lawrence he was battling national abolitionism, and that in her destruction the evil day for his favorite institution might be postponed, if even complete victory should not be attained." But to Connelley, Quantrill's motive and intent for going there were another matter altogether: "And it remained for Quantrill, a man who cared nothing for slavery as an institution, nothing for the abolition of slavery, nothing for the North, nothing for the South, to seize upon his feeling and make it a means to gratify his thirst for blood and greed for spoil and plunder." In short, Quantrill went to Lawrence because he was a sociopath, and the men he led "had no sufficient cause" for the massacre because it "had its origin in the hatred slavery bore the town and in the depravity and desperation of Quantrill himself."[26]

Connelley tells readers that Quantrill "cared nothing for Missouri" and that "Missouri and Missourians were to him a means to an end—to harass,

murder, burn, rob, destroy, lay waste in Kansas." Moreover, he also suggests that by spring 1863, Quantrill had started to lose a power struggle
among his top subordinates, mainly George Todd and William "Bloody
Bill" Anderson. As such, Quantrill planned to hit Lawrence while he still
had the clout to command the majority of his men. (Following the massacre, Quantrill's band traveled to Texas for the winter and, as Connelley
and several other historians note, splintered into multiple guerrilla out-
fits.) With his version of Quantrill's motive and intent established, Connelley again looks to undercut the competing claim of John Newman Edwards. He contends that Edwards, "in attempting to justify the Massacre
recites all the murders and outrages that had occurred in Missouri to that
date and charges them upon Kansas." But what Edwards and other pro-
guerrilla authors (such as Captain William H. Gregg) failed to note, Connelley continues, was that very few "Kansas trips were in Missouri after
1861." "In writing history," he chides Edwards posthumously, "some regard ought to be paid to the facts."[27]

Connelley fills many pages with individual accounts of Quantrill's victims at Lawrence, based frequently on interviews he conducted personally; digested collectively, these snippets of pain and suffering and death
present a very ugly picture—exactly what Connelley needs to bolster his
arguments. John and Robert Speer, the sons of a printer in Lawrence,
serve as a case in point. As the raid ensued, John Speer had fled from the
back door of his father's office and made it roughly one block. At that
point, "he met a guerrilla who demanded his money." Valuing his life,
Speer conceded his wallet and apologized to the guerrilla for its lack of
volume. The guerrilla, a man named Larkin Skaggs, took the boy's money
and then shot him. Skaggs left Speer for dead next to a burning home,
but Speer clung to life next to the blaze. "When the heat became unbear-
able," Connelley writes, "he implored them [another group of guerrillas]
to move him and not let him burn alive." The guerrillas answered Speer's
pleas for help with a fatal bullet and rode off. Little did John Speer know
as he lay dying next to the burning building that his younger brother,
Robert, had been burned alive inside.[28]

Thus, when all was said and done, as far as Connelley is concerned his
accounting of the August 21 massacre comprises "only some of the experiences of the people of Lawrence on that terrible day . . . but enough has
been given to show conclusively that the actions of the guerrillas—that

John and Robert Speer Memorial,
Lawrence, Kansas. This marble
structure stands in Lawrence's Oak
Hill Cemetery to commemorate John
and Robert Speer, both of whom died
gruesomely during Quantrill's raid on
the city. Author's private collection.

there was nothing soldierly in their course." When stripped of its political
and military mythologies–something he believed his history could and
would do–the Lawrence Massacre simply became "atrocious murder,
arson, robbery, pillage–inexcusable savagery."[29]

And even in death, Quantrill could not escape the wrath of Connelley's
pen. "In the long days that Quantrill stood gazing into the Valley of the
Shadow of Death," he opines, "let us hope that remorse racked him, that
repentance seized him, and that the ministrations of the church invoked
by him were effective." But if what Connelley reports to his readers is all
true–that Quantrill "gave fair cities to torch and pillage, and reveled in the
groans and cries of the helpless and innocent victims of his ruthless and
inhuman cries"–such salvation seems unlikely.[30] More importantly, Connelley's audience receives one final dose of the message he had intended
them to be absorbing all along: Quantrill had been evil; Quantrill had not
been a true Confederate soldier in any sense of the label; Quantrill's triumph at Lawrence had been an abomination before God; and, finally, the
narrative of John Newman Edwards, stripped of its gravitational center,
must fall before Connelley's historical approach.[31]

Burlesque, Counterfactualism, and "Quantrell the Queer"

For borderland Unionists, William E. Connelley's *Quantrill and the Border Wars* endured for decades as the historical account that best undergirded their preferred narrative of the guerrilla theater. (The book served as the "authoritative" basis for many subsequent forms of remembrance and venues for commemoration.) But Connelley had not actually been the first to single out Quantrill as a specific strategy for combatting the "irregular" Lost Cause of John Newman Edwards. Nor was Connelley's book the first to publicly recognize Edwards as the main conductor of Missouri's pro-Confederate memory machine. The first documented jab directed specifically at the Edwards narrative was thrown in 1875 by a rather unlikely cast of characters, both real *and* fictitious.

That year, in late February, at Frazier's Hall at the University of Kansas in Lawrence, a playbill announced that audiences could enjoy "Quantrell the Queer, or, The Busted Bonanza"—four scenes' worth of "local burlesque absurdity." Produced and performed by a troupe of university students for two nights, the show's title roles included Quantrell [*sic*], as "the hero of the piece" and "a henpecked husband"; Jesse James, as a "spiritualist who manifests no desire to pay internal revenue"; Mr. Scoville, the "Editor of the Nowhereparticular Evening Thunderbolt"; and, perhaps most notable of all in the annals of guerrilla memory, Hallie Ray, a black, sword-carrying, pro-Confederate, hunchbacked dwarf.[32]

Despite its comical title and eccentric cast, the plot of "Quantrell the Queer" revolved wholly around the Lawrence Massacre of August 1863. But unlike Connelley's explanations for the raid—and unlike what virtually all subsequent observers would have to say about Quantrill's shining achievement—the writers of the play had an entirely different message in mind to achieve the same end. Rather than a scholarly or historical approach, the writers, producers, and performers of "Quantrell the Queer" intentionally avoided wading into semantic, partisan debates over motive, intent, and morality. Their strategy: to take the kingpins of Missouri's guerrilla-centric memory industry personally, head on, and all at once. Instead of suggesting a "true" or "authentic" rendition of the atrocities at Lawrence in print, the play harnessed the power of live performance and satire to not only lampoon but also *excoriate* William C. Quantrill, his men at Lawrence, and John Newman Edwards. So while their parents' generation took a more standard approach to the guerrilla memory debate—

printed accounts, speeches, published reminiscences—these college students tried to eschew a largely unwinnable argument with conservative Missourians. If they could not change the minds of their borderland rivals to the east, performers could, at the very least, attack them publicly with vicious, biting humor.

In this way, the show represented the crossing of two interesting developments. The first was a serious bid by a younger generation to push back against increasingly dominant collective memory narratives of the Lawrence Massacre. The second was an attempt by those same students to place their own stamp on how borderland Unionists might re-remember the Missouri-Kansas guerrilla war as a whole—an attempt to deal with the debate on their own terms and in their own way.[33] And for any who might doubt the political potency of a burlesque such as "Quantrell the Queer," it is worth noting the potential consequences of producing it. The James-Younger Gang, composed of several former guerrillas from Quantrill's command, was still quite operational in 1875. In fact, just a few days before the show debuted, word had spread as far as New York that the outlaws, led by Jesse James himself, had relieved a Wells Fargo Express traveling in western Missouri of $30,000 at gunpoint.[34] Lawrence was a relatively short ride from the scene of the crime.

In the first scene, audiences found a newspaper editor named Scoville nervously moving piles of unpaid bills around his desk; Quantrell enters the office (with the actor wearing red hair, spectacles, and a fat suit). Scoville apparently owes Quantrell's wife for a laundry bill but cannot pay it. In response, Quantrell launches a flurry of schoolyard taunts at Scoville: "You pencil pusher of the meanest class.... Who'd steal the nails from a pauper's coffin ... and to spite the children, [would] squash their mud pies." The insulted Scoville will not stand for such abuse, and the two men fight a hastily arranged duel in the middle of the office. Quantrell guns Scoville down. Audiences then meet Hallie Ray, a black, hunchbacked dwarf who secretly witnessed the killing. He blackmails Quantrell. Hallie Ray has already raised an army of guerrillas, but they lack a leader. So in exchange for silence, Hallie Ray convinces Quantrell to lead a raid against the people of Lawrence. For his part, Quantrell hesitates; he owns several pieces of property in Lawrence. But to avoid a date with the hangman, Quantrell agrees to lead the raid. As they exit the office, Hallie Ray addresses Scoville's corpse: "Now, like all true editors, he lies."[35]

The second act opens with Quantrell's wife doing laundry, and the couple's daughter, Clareen, is thumbing through several newspapers. (In the stage note Clareen is described as "an olive branch; an oily customer with a tendency to journalism, and matrimony.") Clareen is startled to read that, due to delinquent taxes, the people of Lawrence have placed her father's property on the auction block. The article calls Quantrell a "Red-leg," a "Rebel," a "traitor," and a "horse thief." When Quantrell returns home after his encounter with Hallie Ray, he fully expects his domineering wife to cancel their agreement. But Mrs. Quantrell asks her husband a question: "If a man dared call you a horse thief, what would you do?" "Oh, nothing," Quantrell starts to stammer. "That is—I'd, I'd refer them to you!" Following a brief scolding for his gutlessness, Quantrell is pleased to learn that his wife seeks revenge against Lawrence. Now in the clear, Quantrell reveals the details of his meeting with Hallie Ray, whom he calls a "regular Arabian Night-er," and sets off to meet his band of raiders.[36]

As the curtain opens for scene 3, Hallie Ray introduces Quantrell to his new band of marauders—also known as "the Gang" ("everybody with an old coat on"). In preparation for their assault on Lawrence, Quantrell, Hallie Ray, and the Gang have a meeting with Jesse James and Bill Younger. James and Younger are well-known distillers who live together in a nearby cave. But before arriving at the bootleggers' hideout, Quantrell and company stumble across a pair of convicts; the two men have just escaped from the Lawrence jail and decide to join the Gang. As they exit the stage it begins to rain, and Quantrell's men put on a display of marshal discipline for the audience. Hallie Ray orders them to "Present arms!" All of the men raise their umbrellas. He orders them "Ready!" Each man shoulders his umbrella. Hallie Ray shouts "Fire!" All of them open their umbrellas—but Quantrell, perhaps as a signal of impotency, fumbles and drops his umbrella. With the Gang now gone, Clareen and the family slave, Esau, appear on stage. They overhear a sheriff from Lawrence on the hunt for his escaped prisoners and a woman, Mrs. Barker, telling him the whereabouts of Jesse James's hideout. Clareen and Esau rush to warn her father.[37]

As the fourth scene begins, the audience finally meets Jesse James and Bill Younger. Younger is a dimwit obsessed with killing rats; James physically and verbally abuses him throughout. (The actor who portrayed Younger wore "extremely short" and "profusely ventilated" pantaloons, along with pale makeup expressive of "tape worms.") The bootlegging duo discovers that their housekeeper, Mrs. Barker, has poured coal oil on their food and run away just as Hallie Ray, Quantrell, and the Gang show up; Quantrell and Jesse James are introduced. All of the men begin to drink—and then break into song. "We are a band of brothers," they chant, "opposed to work and toil, / we try to keep the Southern Folks, like kettles, on the boil."

As the song ends, Clareen and Esau enter the cave. Quantrell forgot his spectacles at home, so Clareen, fearing that he could not wreak havoc in Lawrence without them, has followed her father. She relays the story of the sheriff and Mrs. Barker to the Gang and notes that Mrs. Barker looked as though she *had* been physically abused. Despite the allegation, Jesse James falls instantly in love with Clareen. "I love her more and more, myself I cannot stop," James declares. "I'm like a root beer bottle—just about to pop." Clareen and James agree to marry—but Quantrell objects. James threatens to kill Quantrell, who eventually consents to the union. In the meantime, however, the cave has been infiltrated by the sheriff and his men. Hallie Ray is shot and killed by Mrs. Barker. He falls from the whiskey still and knocks it into the furnace. The still explodes in slow motion. The rest of the men try to fire their guns but they all mis-fire. Quantrell is killed in a sword fight by the sheriff; after seeing her father die, Clareen drinks Bill Younger's rat poison and dies in the arms of Jesse James. The sheriff proudly addresses the audience: "Ladies and Gentlemen, the great Bonanza's busted!" (The stage note reads: "a Union flag is hoisted. All of the sheriff's men stick miniature Union flags in their hats. The curtain falls.")[38]

The cast of "Quantrell the Queer" purposely avoided rehashing seman-tic debates over possible motivations or justifications for the Lawrence Massacre. Clearly, an emasculated Quantrill having been forced by a black Confederate dwarf to lead a thwarted assault on Lawrence had little to do with the "official" back-and-forth of pro-Confederate Missourians and bor-derland Unionists. It was something more than counterfactual: it was out-right mockery. But it was purposeful mockery. "Quantrell the Queer" took on the best-known architects and strategies of Missouri's memory indus-try: it took on John Newman Edwards, who had begun construction of his "irregular" Lost Cause; it took on William Clarke Quantrill as an appro-priate figure for southern deification; and, critically, it took on Missouri's ex-Confederate, pro-Democrat print media using satire and the stage.

As discussed in chapter 2, Edwards published editorials throughout the 1870s designed to crown Quantrill as the "king of guerrillas." These polemics, like "Quantrell the Queer," appeared prior to the release of *Noted Guerrillas* in 1877—but unquestionably constituted a prelude to what was coming (much of the material was in fact recycled in the book). There the editorials began the process of cementing Quantrill's status as *the* iconic Missouri guerrilla. There was "no good reason," Edwards wrote, "why the truth shall not be told of one who, brave and steadfast to the end, died as he had lived, a fearless Ishmaelite." Similarly, Edwards boasted that "if there is a race born without fear, Quantrell belonged to it." "He knew no law but the revolver" and "no flag but the black flag," he continued, "and having shaken hands with death, he [Quantrill] thought no more of the word 'surrender.'"[39]

These stylized representations of Quantrill, engineered by Edwards and popularized in print, are precisely what "Quantrell the Queer" was designed to diffuse and counteract with comedy. On one level, humor, especially of this acerbic quality, undoubtedly helped alleviate the trauma of an event as terrible as the Lawrence Massacre. But more important, the organizers of the show openly lampooned the literary source and subject of Missouri's dominant guerrilla narrative, the process through which it was derived and disseminated, and anyone who might have accepted that narrative as factual. According to the performance, Quantrill might still be the "king of the guerrillas," but he is also a cowardly murderer in a fat suit lorded over by his wife and disrespected by his raiders; the highwater mark of Quantrill's career as a guerrilla commander is actually planned by a black Confederate dwarf and unraveled by a simple town sheriff; Jesse James is not a politically useful Robin Hood but a common criminal who abuses women; and Bill Younger, who might have represented any of the Younger brothers—Cole, Jim, John, or Bob—is portrayed as a nitwit man-child.

Fundamentally, however, "Quantrell the Queer" failed to achieve its fullest potential and did not catch on as a long-term weapon against Edwards and Missouri's version of the guerrilla theater's story. (After all, it had probably only been performed once.) The play *had* raised stinging questions about Missouri's claim to a legitimate Confederate fighting past— the credential that Edwards himself considered the cultural key to postwar political and social linkages with the rest of the (ex-Confederate) South.

But in doing so, the show relied on a medium and a brand of humor that older generations of borderland Unionists were not willing or able to pull off or that even the younger generation could not produce with regularity. Furthermore, even as "Quantrell the Queer" undermined the past that Edwards had concocted for Missouri, it simply remained incapable of reaching a broad enough audience outside of the borderlands to do lasting damage. This factor ultimately helps explain why so many Unionists stuck to traditional communication mediums and why, as Connelley's *Quantrill and the Border Wars* became a staple of guerrilla memory after its release in 1909, the likes of Hallie Ray had already faded into obscurity.

Protesting Quantrill's "Fiendish Work"–Fifty Years Later

In July 1913 throngs of veterans and onlookers—thousands of them, all told—descended on Gettysburg, Pennsylvania, in recognition of the eponymous battle's silver anniversary. Members of the Quantrill Men Survivor's Association hosted their annual reunion in August at Wallace Grove, complete with yarns of the Lawrence Massacre spun and basket dinners happily devoured. But another lesser-known commemorative ceremony also unfolded that summer: residents of Lawrence, a great many of them survivors of the massacre, gathered to observe the fiftieth anniversary of Quantrill's raid.[40]

Somber subject matter duly noted, the activities of the "Quantrell Raid Victims Semi-Centennial Memorial Reunion" were no less organized or politically charged than those in Wallace Grove or Gettysburg. This was a major event—the first of its kind in more ways than not for Unionists in Kansas. In 1895 residents of Lawrence had dedicated a permanent monument to the massacre's dead, but the events of August 21, 1913, were, in fact, the only occasion since the raid itself that victims had been invited from abroad to attend a formal memorial service and reunion in one. (As noted by historian Richard Sheridan, roughly 364 raid survivors still resided in Kansas in 1913. Another 182 survivors lived in other states ranging from New York to California.[41]) According to the seventeen-person organizing committee, more than 546 survivors were still alive in 1913; and according to the varying estimates of local newspapers, between 200 and 500 of them attended. The official itinerary included decorating the graves of massacre victims, a cemetery service to honor their memory, and a slew of historical presentations to put those deaths in commemorative context. So far from a farrago of parades and pandering stump speeches, borderland Unionists took the opportunity to stage something of a protest rally against the continued eminence of William C. Quantrill's legacy and the "irregular" Lost Cause it pillared.[42]

Speeches delivered on the topic of the massacre naturally tried to place blame for the bloodshed squarely on the shoulders of Quantrill and to make clear that the people of Lawrence had done nothing to warrant such a dreadful assault on their homes and families. In pushing such themes and by concentrating on Quantrill as an individual target, speakers such as Charles S. Gleed—who delivered the keynote address of the event—had much in common with William E. Connelley and his book, *Quantrill and the Border Wars*, published four years prior. In fact, Gleed and his fellow orators openly cited Connelley as a historical source for gaps in their own recollections; in turn, it is not surprising that their accounts of August 21 appear to play out similarly. Even so, Gleed also employed his own strategies for poisoning the roots of Quantrill's southern identity and his legitimacy as a pro-Confederate icon of the guerrilla theater.[43]

As previously noted, Gleed's speech was the formal keynote of the commemorative ceremonies. (It was also, not coincidentally, very much representative of the rhetorical and thematic strategies employed against Quantrill and Edwards in the other papers delivered.[44]) Given this prestigious position, he was introduced by the former mayor of Lawrence, S. D. Bishop, who also offered a very brief tribute to the men killed, the women who survived, and the people of Leavenworth "who responded so promptly to the cries of the stricken city." This done, Gleed took to the rostrum and began his speech. He first set the scene in Lawrence, fifty years before to the day. It was a "glorious, sunlit morning but no joy came with it." "Instead," he continued, "there fell upon the town a blow so brutal, so unwarranted, so unpardonable, that the world has ever since remembered it with horror, and we have assembled a full half century later to commemorate and condemn it." Fifty years ago to the day, he pronounced, "the streets of the little city were baptized in blood."[45]

Gleed next took issue with the possibility that Kansans had invited the massacre on themselves. The settlers of Lawrence, he argued, "were not soldiers" but "men of people, who sought a place where their own vines and fig trees could be conjured from the virgin soil." The notion of war, to such peace-loving pilgrims, "was distasteful, almost incomprehensible to them." Unfortunately for Lawrence, it was precisely this quality of pacifism that Gleed suggested had left it so vulnerable to Quantrill's attack. After establishing the point that the massacre had been unwarranted in the context of wartime relations between Missouri and Kansas, he turned to a case for why the city's strong support of abolitionism did not justify the assault for southerners, either. And this is where his address got very interesting.[46]

In a very clever way, Gleed sought not to sever Quantrill from a southern identity directly but to force southerners to do the cutting for him—out of shame tied to the peculiar institution. Lawrence, he noted, had been named after Amos A. Lawrence, a well-known figure in the fight against the "institution of human slavery." Many Kansans agreed with Lawrence that slavery was "a crime against nature" and "an unmixed evil against which moralists have contended since moralists began." But Gleed did not axiomatically point to southerners for bringing this evil on the nation; he stated bluntly that slavery in America was *not* the invention of southerners. Rather, "it was the invention of the European slave trader." All of the South's most prominent statesmen—many of them great Americans, regardless of their regional affiliation—had decried the evils of slavery. He announced to his audience that George Washington had manumitted his slaves in protest of the institution; Thomas Jefferson had lamented slavery as a growing cancer among the southern states; Patrick Henry had pleaded that "we ought to lament and deplore the necessity of holding our fellow men in bondage"; and others, such as John Roanoke, James Madison, and George Mason, had all harbored like sentiments. In short, all the best and brightest the South had to offer throughout history would have agreed with the people of Lawrence on the issue of slavery.[47]

That being the case, at least so far as Gleed was concerned, he asserted that a "rank of violent orators," men such as the fire-eater Robert Toombs, had led the South astray by yoking the region's fortunes first to slavery and then to secession. With the war afoot, criminals such as William C. Quantrill, whom he dubbed a "great dry-land pirate with plunder his business and murder his pastime," took advantage of the chaos for their own nefarious purposes. As chief among the borderland's wartime terrors, Gleed concluded of the Lawrence Massacre that "every death in Lawrence that morning was murder" but not "every member of the Quantrell band" had behaved so evilly. Some of these men, he alleged, reformed, became "good citizens," and forever regretted their role in the slaughter. Thus the orator hammered a strategic wedge not just between Quantrill and the South's pantheon of great men; he also sought to cut the commander off from his own troops—and force contemporary southerners to make the same decision.[48]

As Gleed constructed the choice rhetorically, it is difficult to assess whether he believed it to be a pragmatic line of attack or entirely academic. No former marauders sat among his audience, but the speech *was* reprinted in full by the *Kansas City Journal*, a well-known newspaper in western Missouri, in the town that served as the postwar seat of Quantrill's command. But, even if just to affirm his own principles, Gleed was going to make southerners—however many did catch hold of his words—as uncomfortable as possible about rejecting his logic. For this, he deployed one final card to undercut the validity of the Lawrence Massacre, its architect Quantrill, and the "irregular" Lost Cause that glorified him: the highest deity of its mainstream counterpart, Robert E. Lee.

The Confederate general, Gleed proclaimed, "would have foresworn the cause he loved and for which he fought, rather than to have sanctioned what was done that day in Lawrence." In other words, the thrust of the keynote address—the most important element of its design—was intended to leave the deciding southerners with a "lose-lose" scenario. On one hand, they could admit that Quantrill had not been a true Confederate in the borderlands and renounce his legacy. This option would have leveled a major blow to the Edwards narrative. On the other hand, southerners could continue to support the "irregular" Lost Cause of Edwards knowing that Lee, the man who supposedly embodied the best of Confederate discipline, chivalry, honor, and Christian virtue, likely would have disapproved. Unfortunately for Gleed, most southerners, and especially Missourians, simply rejected his new memory-morality paradigm altogether.[49]

The Lawrence Massacre in Epic Verse

As credentials for debating the morality of the Lawrence Massacre went, those of the poet Minnie E. Blake were unassailable. As a child, not only had she witnessed—and lived to describe—Quantrill's great raid, but her

Mourning the Massacre. To commemorate the lives lost in the Lawrence Massacre, this marble monument was erected and dedicated in 1895. Author's private collection.

father had been counted among its victims. Moreover, as the granddaughter of Judge John Andrew Beam, a prominent member of the Free-State legislature of the 1850s, and as the niece of Major Leroy J. Beam, the commander whose unarmed troops were slaughtered in the opening moments of the attack, Blake hailed from a family steeped in borderland conflict and controversy. This in mind, it likely was not a surprise to many when she burst into the arena of guerrilla memory in the late 1920s with a stinging indictment of William Clarke Quantrill and his seminal moment as a guerrilla commander. The *form* of that indictment, however–a book of poetry titled *The Quantrill Raid*–proved unlike anything else Unionists had tried before.

The first of the volume's three poems, "Jim Lane," immediately begins the task of revising the noted Jayhawker's legacy. Lane, both a U.S. senator and a military officer during the war, had been responsible for the sacking of Osceola, Missouri, in 1861, as well as numerous other assaults executed by Unionist guerrillas from Kansas. After the war, with his

Gathering of survivors. Not unlike the reunions of Quantrill Men held in the early
twentieth century, survivors of the Lawrence Massacre gathered formally in 1913 to recall

political career on the rocks and his mental health rapidly deteriorating,
the one-time hero of the Kansas plains committed suicide. So in keeping with the moral binary of Connelley and Gleed—in which Quantrill
stood as the ultimate symbol of evil and Unionists held no culpability for
the Lawrence Massacre—Blake needed to recast Lane's narrative in a way
that differentiated his irregular activities from Quantrill's; Lane, despite
his obvious shortcomings, needed to be remembered as a heroic counterpart to the man who planned the assault on Lawrence, not as his tactical
contemporary. Thus the first stanza of the poem begins with a reassessment of Lane's character and the means through which it could be properly judged:

> Why did we love old Lane,
> Frenzied and half insane,
> Grim, vaunt, disheveled, vain,
> Cant politician?
> Stranger, the while you stare
> Hard at his portrait there,
> With its wild shock of hair
> Courting derision,—
> Think not to measure him,
> Lane, our stern chieftain grim,
> Mad old tempestuous Jim,

their experiences and mourn the dead. Courtesy of the Prints and Photographs Collection, Library of Congress, http://www.loc.gov/pictures/item/2007661777/.

> Giant, magician,
> With the puerile line,
> With your manhood, sir, or mine,
> In these dull days supine,
> Mind find sufficient.[50]

The answer to this rhetorical question came shortly thereafter. Lane, according to Blake, had been made heroic, his actions justified by the difficult circumstances of guerrilla warfare in the borderlands. With Missouri bushwhackers—the "sons of Cain"—bearing down on Unionists in Kansas, only Lane, as the poem reads, rose up to meet them head on.

> If in our day of doom
> You had but seen him loom
> Godlike from out the gloom
> To smite asunder
> Bolt, bar, and demon chain
> Wherewith the sons of Cain
> Cowed all the conquered plain,
> Though we should worship Lane,
> Small then your wonder. (11)

Dealing with the Lawrence Massacre specifically, Blake much exaggerated Lane's courage—in a portrait at odds with many other historical renditions of his behavior. In reality, on learning of Quantrill's arrival in Lawrence, Lane took refuge in a cornfield that adjoined the back portion of his yard and hid there until the guerrillas left town. (This was the same cornfield in which Isadora Allison and her companions also took refuge.) In the early stages of the raid, several guerrillas approached Lane's home with the intention of capturing the hated Jayhawker and forcing him back to Missouri to suffer the humiliation of a public execution. Fortunately for Lane, these men did not find his home until after he had found sanctuary amid the corn; guerrilla scouts in Lawrence just prior to the raid believed that he had returned to Washington, D.C., so not much of an effort was made to find him.

This version of events—rooted in historical fact—did not align with Blake's account. Rather than accepting Lane's behavior as the most logical course he could have taken to preserve his life against insurmountable odds, the poem instead perpetuated a popular myth among Kansans that Lane really had been in Washington, D.C., for a session of the U.S. Senate. This approach allowed Blake to put forth hypothetical assumptions concerning what Lane *would have* done had he been present to confront Quantrill's horde:

> (God! Had old Lane been there,
> Flouting our mute despair
> Till throbbed in heart of hare
> Half his heart oaken;
> Though all the fiends of hell,
> Swarming with demon yell,
> Up from the pit profound,
> Leagured the city round,
> that gun had spoken!) (12)

Perhaps even more problematic was that while Blake issued such counterfactual scenarios, she later states that Lane *had* actually been present in the immediate aftermath of the Lawrence Massacre by giving him credit for helping lead the pursuit of Quantrill's retreating guerrillas.

> Who sent them hurtling back,
> Reeling in utter rack,
> Rout and mad ruin,

> Howling across the line,
> Each in his den to whine,
> Like a whipped bruin?
>
> Who but the Lion-heart,
> He whom we set apart,
> There in his lion-mane,
> Freedom's own lion, Lane. (13)

Though seemingly at odds with her own narrative, then, the idea that Blake would deal selectively with historical events to present Lane in the best light possible was nothing new to the debates over guerrilla memory; as underscored in chapter 3, several bushwhackers-turned-memoirists had done the same in "cherry-picking" favorable components of the Lost Cause and the New South Creed—movements theoretically at odds with each other—when it suited their commemorative agendas.

The final stanza of "Jim Lane" most fully reveals Blake's partisan motives. On one hand, she makes the final pitch for Lane having deserved the legacy of a hero—a legacy that pitted him as the righteous opposite of William Clarke Quantrill. But on the other hand, the ending of the poem also illuminates the possibility that Lane and the perspective of guerrilla memory he represented for Unionists were being forgotten altogether. At once, then, Blake seeks to rehabilitate Lane's image, remind Kansans of their Civil War debt to him as the heaven-sent hero who clashed with Missouri demons, and iterate that the struggle to define right and wrong in the guerrilla theater had not yet ended.

> Lane forgot today?
> Sixty years ago you say?
> Thousands shall roll away;
> Regal beneath the play
> Of flashing streamer,
> While man shall bare his arm,
> Wife, child, to shield from harm,
> High on the scroll of Fame,
> Girt round with shafts of flame,
> Kansas shall write his name:
> "Lane, our redeemer." (15)

Keeping with the notion that Blake's poetry was designed in part to distinguish between William Quantrill, as an icon of the Missouri bushwhacker, and Jim Lane, as an icon of the Kansas Jayhawker, the second poem of the collection, titled "The Colour Guard (An Incident of 1861)," also depicts Lane as a biblical avenger sent by God to smite marauding Missourians. The poem first describes "the Sunset Land," the scene of a bushwhacker raid in Kansas, and holds little back in the way of partisanship or objectivity. The guerrillas, as portrayed by Blake, were illegitimate, evil, and even otherworldly:

> Raging with liquor more rank than wine
> Thundered exultant across the line,
> Black-browed, malignant, the ruffian band,
> To waste all the shimmering Sunset Land
> With fire and sword that day.
>
> Not merely once on History's page
> Black are written such scenes of rage;
> Twice and thrice and three times again
> Ruthless hordes of relentless men
> O'ersurge each defenseless spot.
> War at the best is waste and woe,
> But when the heartless guerrilla foe,
> Rending the night with demonic yell,
> Fall in their fury on sleeping dell,
> War outrivals the rack of hell,
> And hell heated seven times hot. (19)

Enter Jim Lane. As the poem continues, he and his men ride to Pleasant Hill, Missouri, the alleged source of the aforementioned guerrilla scourge. In the town square, Lane hoists a Union flag and directs an ultimatum to residents: he is well aware they side with the South and harbor bushwhackers, but if they fail to protect the newly installed ensign for any reason, the Jayhawkers would return that Lane might unleash his "terrible wrath." Yet again, Blake sets Lane apart from Quantrill, this time by highlighting how Unionists, despite their moral high ground, refused to behave like the dishonorable Missourians and would only make war against civilians, innocent or not, after first giving them the chance to avoid bloodshed.

As readers soon found in the final poem of the trilogy, "The Quantrill Raid," Lane's counterparts offered no such courtesy on the morning of August 21, 1863. But before undertaking a description of the raid, Blake again pauses to remind readers that guerrilla memory itself was still both relevant and worthy of contemporary consideration. Much like memoirists Cole Younger and Harrison Trow before her, Blake openly acknowledged the claims to commemoration of subsequent veterans, but she also employed the longest of her poems to draw a parallel between the horrors experienced by World War I soldiers and the survivors of the borderland's guerrilla theater. Moreover, knowing full well that veterans of the Great War would only cede so much commemorative attention to their martial forebears, Blake made sure that readers would understand specifically which faction of the Civil War generation deserved attention: not regular soldiers or their famous battles, but civilians of the guerrilla theater.

> Oh, the Great World War was an awful thing,
> The loss to the nations past reckoning!
> Our Civil War seems but as play beside
> When we reckon the hosts in the trenches that died.
> And yet we shudder and hold our breath
> When we think of the Carnival Camp of Death
> America saw in 'Sixty-three
> Had met in the final giant grip
> Where one or the other or both must slip
> And plunge in the tide beneath
> Nay, not on Gettysburg's gory field,
> Nor yet in Vicksburg's heights grim-steeled,
> Nor at Chickamauga nor mad Lookout,
> Nor at Chancellorsville with its bloody rout
> Lay that Carnival Camp of Death. (25)

And if borderland Unionists were most worthy of remembrance alongside veterans of other wars in the twentieth century, the survivors and victims of the Lawrence Massacre—witnesses to the "Carnival Camp of Death"—Blake reasons, stand out most among them. She paints the portrait of a conflict in which the violence had been so personal and so intense that time became incapable of healing emotional and psychological wounds, something many World War I servicemen, still reeling from the effects of trench warfare, mustard gas, and newly perfected machine guns might well understand. At the same time, Blake underlines that this sort of war had originated in Missouri and been forced on Kansas Unionists by "black-bowed" and "malignant" ruffian bands.

> This was the phase of the Civil War
> That left Missouri as deep with scar
> As the pitted face of the luckless man
> Who camped with a stricken New Mexican.
> But there lies in the West a deeper scar
> Not wholly healed, though the Civil War
> Is calendared now by decades past,
> Since the bugle sounded the final blast.
> For this scar of scars cut deep and wide,
> And drenched the land with crimson tide
> That we sometimes see in our dreams of fright
> When we waken ashiver at dead of night,
> And hold our breath for the demon yell,
> The fusillade and the glare of hell,
> That startled us sixty years agone,
> That wakened us thus in the August dawn,
> When Attila, Scourge of God, swept down,
> When Quantrill fell on old Lawrence town. (26–27)

Later the poem provides a blow-by-blow accounting of the massacre itself. Blake starts with the slaughter of the Fifteenth Kansas Infantry— the troops commanded by her uncle—and then reports how the guerrillas moved systematically through town and gunned down all the men and boys who crossed their paths. Women and young girls, wives and daughters, the poem suggests, had tried to shield their male relations from harm, or at least to hide them from the guerrillas. These attempts often proved unsuccessful, Blake reveals. And eventually, she recounts how her own father, despite the best efforts of her mother, had been shot down in plain view of the family.

> They shoot left and right at each man that they meet;
> And many fell thus in their route, for the roar
> Had called every citizen swift to his door.

Did he reel back in horror on seeing the horde,

Through gate and o'er fence a demon squad poured;

What avail that the householder hid for his life?

What avail the entreaties of children and wife?

From cellar or attic they routed him out,

And wild the exultance of ruffian shout

When he who assayed in his wife's skirts to hide,–

Her sheltering garments swept roughly aside,–

Ball-riddled, alas! at her very feet died!

Thus fell my father! But I–somehow–I

Was spared for the death that this moment I die,

And have died each August these sixty years gone

When the calendar-hand marks this shuddering day. (36–37)

Equal parts requiem and homiletic, Minnie Blake's poetry recounts the plight of innocent Unionists: loyal, good, and godly Kansans, she offers, beset upon by a horde of unholy terrors from across the Missouri border. All three poems, "Jim Lane," "The Colour Guard," and "The Quantrill Raid," combined to depict William Clarke Quantrill as the most impor- tant—and thus the foulest—of all the Missouri bushwhackers. In turn, the Lawrence Massacre he planned and orchestrated became the ultimate showdown of good versus evil in the guerrilla theater. Therein Blake's verse shared much strategic ground with the work of William Connelley and Charles Gleed. Both men had wielded a pro-Unionist narrative of the Lawrence Massacre specifically for the purpose of establishing a moral dualism to topple Quantrill's legacy. With the ghost of Quantrill slain, they hoped, so too would go the strength of the "irregular" Lost Cause he represented.

But as much as Blake's poems, especially "The Quantrill Raid," func- tioned in the same way as books or speeches, they also introduced new rhetorical components. The attention paid to Jim Lane—the man pro- Confederates in Missouri viewed with the same disdain that pro-Unionists in Kansas eyed Quantrill—was particularly important. At least for outside eyes, Blake thought it necessary to reassure readers that Lane, a prolific raider in his own right, had not simply operated as a mirror of Quantrill. Through her verse and assignment of biblical symbolism to Lane, Blake sanitized all aspects of his life, from his controversial wartime record to

the shameful circumstances of his suicide. This "all out" effort to but-
tress the arguments wielded by Connelley and Gleed earlier in the twentieth century was likely prompted by the passage of time. In the fourteen
years since the 1909 publication of *Quantrill and the Border Wars* and the
1913 reunion of massacre survivors in Lawrence, the ranks of the Civil
War generation had been thinned dramatically. At the same time, what
remained of it came into conflict with waves of new veterans and their
corresponding memory movements. Therein, perhaps more than anything, Blake's poems reminded readers that even sixty years later, while
the likes of Quantrill and Lane were long dead and gone, the trauma of
the guerrilla experience they represented had not subsided for Unionists—
nor would it without commemorative closure.

The Execution of Rev. Larkin M. Skaggs

William E. Connelley, Charles S. Gleed, and Minnie E. Blake each extolled
the people of Lawrence, Kansas, as having been God-fearing, peace-
loving settlers who desired nothing more than to live in harmony with
African Americans and their neighbors across the border. Whatever linkages had existed between Lawrence and bands of Jayhawkers who carried
out violent raids in western Missouri—and those linkages appear to have
been quite strong—these authors propped the town and its residents up as
a collective foil to Quantrill's evil. If the Lawrence Massacre had not been
a justified military strike against a legitimate military target, their logic
entailed, then the pinnacle of Quantrill's career was an illegal atrocity and
his reputation ruined. But such a dualism of pure good against pure evil
required just that—that one side remains purely good and innocent of all
blame or role in precipitating the raid of August 21, 1863.

The death of Larkin M. Skaggs greatly complicated this arrangement
for pro-Union polemicists in the borderlands. The actual facts of Skaggs's
demise are few and far between. The first is that he was the only one of
Quantrill's command killed during the Lawrence Massacre. The second
is that he died within Lawrence proper (as opposed to the surrounding
countryside) after having attempted to retreat from the city on horseback.
This invariably means that Skaggs was brought back to Lawrence alive
and later killed. The third and perhaps most notable of these facts is that
after Skaggs's death, his corpse was brutally mutilated, paraded through

the streets of the town, and then left to decay, unburied, for several months. Even by guerrilla standards, the postmortem abuses were excessive. According to ex-guerrilla William H. Gregg in 1912, no Kansan killed in Lawrence had been "treated with the cruelty of Jim Skaggs was subjected to [when he] was captured by the 'red legs.'"[51]

The most pertinent detail of all, however—the true identity of Skaggs's executioner—remains an unsolved mystery. Three different accounts of the incident are relayed below, each with its own version of events and theory as to who launched the projectile (bullet or arrow) that killed Larkin Skaggs. But while these reminiscences cannot prove who or what ultimately dealt Skaggs's fatal blow, the manners in which each presents the story of his slaying reveals a great deal about what borderland Unionists stood to lose in the memory debate if their behavior too closely resembled that of the guerrillas they denounced so fervently. Put another way, these accounts form a case study concerning the ways in which the anti-Edwards, anti-Quantrill camp tried to "explain away" the seediest elements of *their own* wartime experiences for sake of broader public perception and remembrance.

The first widely disseminated account comes from William E. Connelley's *Quantrill and the Border Wars* in 1909. According to Connelley, as Quantrill and his command exited Lawrence, Skaggs, alone with two other unnamed guerrillas, "rode back to the City Hotel, called out the landlord Mr. Stone, and shot him dead." After murdering Stone, the trio attempted to catch up with the main body of guerrillas—but again they detoured. This time, they stopped at the home of a prominent citizen named John Speer and "brutally treated his wife, holding her by the wrists while they fired the house." When the smoke prevented breathing inside the home, the guerrillas dragged Mrs. Speer outside to make sure she could not put out the fire. Next, Connelley asserts, Skaggs and his companions "robbed her of a pair of little gold armlets belonging to her dead babe." (As mentioned previously in this chapter, Connelley details the killing of the two Speer boys, John and Robert, in full during his description of the massacre.)[52]

After robbing Mrs. Speer, Skaggs and company again looked to reconnect with Quantrill and the command. This time, however, they ran into a group of farmers in the nearby countryside. During the course of this encounter, the third Speer boy, William, "appeared upon the scene with a loaded rifle he had found." William shared the tragic news of John and

Robert with his mother and, on hearing this, she replied: "There is one of them—go and shoot him." On his mother's orders, William Speer fired at Skaggs, who then fled from the group of pursuing farmers that had cut short his escape route. Connelley alleges, based on personal interviews and the testimony of witnesses to the scene, that Speer's shot had been true and "the dust flew out from where the ball struck Skaggs on the shoulder-blade." Even so, he ascribes the actual death of Skaggs to another man—a Delaware Indian named White Turkey. As Connelley's version of the story concludes, immediately after Speer fired his rifle, White Turkey exclaimed, "Oh! He kill everybody! Me kill him!" and then shot Skaggs fatally through the heart with a bow and arrow.[53]

Connelley's rendering of events is problematic to say the least. For one, Skaggs's two companions vanish without a word, calling into question whether or not Skaggs had been by himself all along. This possibility— which is actually quite likely correct—recasts his capture and execution significantly; rather than a shootout or standoff between dangerous parties, it appears more like a separate massacre. Moreover, the usually detail-oriented, adjective-loving Connelley's description of the kill shot was uncharacteristically brief and fails to list even the precise location of the ground where Skaggs fell. Most interesting of all, however, is that as part of this inexplicable ambiguity on the matter, he also allowed—perhaps just a little too conveniently—a Native American, instead of the white William Speer, to take final responsibility for killing Skaggs and not turning him over to military authorities.

Furthermore, Connelley relegates what the people of Lawrence did to the slain guerrilla's body postmortem to a footnote—hardly an indicator that it constituted an important element of the story. In that citation, well before he begins to reveal the ceremonial mutilation of Skaggs's corpse, he first pauses to affirm for readers that the guerrilla had been a man of ill repute—a ne'er-do-well even among his own kin. "The author," he offers, "knew many of the relatives of Skaggs in Kentucky" and "knows that the family was a good one." Thus, while the details to follow would likely be horrific to some readers, Skaggs's character and treatment somehow went hand in hand. Even then, Connelley avoids trying to justify the "indignities to which his body was subjected" outright. He calls the treatment "barbarous and wholly inexcusable"—before immediately offering the excuse that such behavior "never would have been permitted in Lawrence at any other time" than right after the massacre. "Resentment," he states in a conclusion on the matter akin to a modern-day plea of temporary insanity, "should have stopped at death and would have done so but for the excitement under which the people labored after that bloody and terrible day."[54]

Granted, all of this text appears in the footnote *before* Connelley actually tells his readers what was done to the corpse—at which point he employs the published testimony of a third party and refuses to verify the story with his own authorial voice. Thus, by way of C. M. Chase, who claimed to have witnessed everything, he reports that African American residents of Lawrence had outfitted the corpse with a noose, attached the rope to a saddle hitch, and then rushed through town, dragging and mutilating the body for all to see while a crowd gave chase and hurled stones at it. "There was an attempt," Chase's account continues, "by the negroes to burn the body, which was not successful." As such, "the bones lay naked all winter in a ravine in the town" where "negroes and boys sawed finger rings from some of them." "No part of the body," he concludes, "was ever given burial." For his part, Connelley adds or retracts nothing to or from Chase's description.[55]

The next version of the story was penned by Andrew Williams in the early 1900s—a semiliterate former slave who had taken up residence in Lawrence by the time of the massacre and who, as a result, claimed to have witnessed the execution of Skaggs firsthand. It is worth noting here that Williams's story is one of the few—if not the *only*—surviving account of an African American witness at Lawrence. Also worthy of mention is the fact that he worked as Connelley's gardener in Topeka for three years, from 1908 to 1910, before his death in 1913. As a result, it is virtually impossible to presume that Connelley, working full-time on his book, would not have been aware of Williams's tale (or perhaps even influenced it). In fact, odds are quite good that his connection to Connelley is the only reason Williams wrote down his experiences in the first place. The closeness of their relationship, however, did not translate into their accounts emphasizing the same details—not by a long shot, in fact.

According to Williams's handwritten log, he had been living in Lawrence for roughly five months when "Quantrell done his murdering." When the raid began, "a bout 400 men he [Quantrill] came right by our house it was a little after day light [they] had on all sorts of uniforms some in their Reed Shirt Sleeves." Like some of his neighbors, he thought Quantrill's men were actually Union soldiers until "one in the crowd broke ranks then they scattered in all directions." Williams reports that as the guerrillas swarmed the town, "we seen one Bushwacker call out one man and talking a minut to him they shot him downe."[56]

Then Williams turns his attention to Larkin Skaggs. "Thir was one of them that got so drunk he could not get a way," he writes. The guerrilla "was shoot in the Back of the head and the Ball come out through his mouth knocking all of his teeth out." Williams states definitively, "it was William Sphear that shoot him" and delivered the death blow. With Skaggs dead, "they takn him and hitched a Rope around his neck and atached a horse and drug him all over town." Next, Skaggs's corpse was taken "down to a Revene" where the unnamed men in question "burned him up." Williams also discloses another violent incident that played out in the wake of the raid. "The faew men that was lucky a nugh to a scape and save thir lives," he asserts, "found a man that was living in Lawrence at the time of the Rade" who had been seen helping bushwhackers locate the hiding places of men in Lawrence. In retribution, this man was apprehended, taken to a barn, and strung up. His captors "made him up on a dry box and taken it out from under him and be four he was dead shot him half dozen times while hanging."[57]

Examined alongside Connelley's story, Williams's presents striking differences. Chief among them, rather than claiming that a Delaware Indian dispatched Skaggs, the former slave states that William Speer had shot and killed the guerrilla. White Turkey fails to even appear in his narrative. Additionally, while Connelley provides a footnote that relates another man's account of the mutilation of Skaggs's body—an account that claimed those responsible for the depredations were African American—Williams makes no secret of the treatment unleashed on the corpse, nor does his testimony conclusively state, one way or the other, that the men responsible were black. These points concerning race are intriguing on their own; they become much more so when combined with the fact that Connelley neglects altogether to inform his readers that white men in Lawrence had apparently lynched *another* man, this time *not* one of Quantrill's guerrillas, in the aftermath of the raid. Such an allegation not only damaged the peace-loving image of Lawrence that Connelley had constructed; it also undercut the "one-time only" excuse he had provided for the abuse of Skaggs. With all of this in mind, the explanation as to why Connelley chose to cite the account of C. M. Chase rather than his own employee seems quite clear.

In September 1913 a survivor of the Lawrence Massacre named J. M. Henry provided his own version of Skaggs's execution to a local newspaper because, according to him, so many others contained incorrect information. He opens by stating that Skaggs had become separated from the "main body" of Quantrill's command when they evacuated Lawrence, and he lingered for nearly half an hour on his own. The guerrillas rode due south out of town, he continues, but when it finally dawned on a "bewildered" Skaggs to make his own retreat, he chose his direction poorly and "started east on the Eudora road."[58]

Along the Eudora road, Skaggs "discovered his mistake" after stumbling into a large group of men gathered near the farm of H. L. Enos. Recognizing that the guerrilla was lost and alone, "the farmers gave chase on their horses" and managed to wound Skaggs's mount. Unable to escape on a lame animal, he fell into the custody of the men, whose party included Miles Walters, Thomas McFarland, Robert Peebles, and several others. It was Walters, Henry contends, that "had personal charge of Skaggs, having disarmed him." Either way, the farmers now led the captured guerrilla back to the smoking ruins of Lawrence.[59]

In town, the group holding Skaggs prisoner merged with another crowd of townsfolk on horseback. Then a man described as "a volunteer soldier" allegedly rode up to Skaggs, struck him violently in the face, ordered him off of his horse, and commanded him to make a run for it. "Skaggs immediately sprang from the horse and ran east toward the brush half a mile away," but the escape attempt had been doomed from the start. The soldier chased closely behind Skaggs and attempted to shoot him in the back of the head, but missed. The powder from the shot, Henry notes, set fire to Skaggs's shirt, "which was still burning when he fell." At this, the rest of the group opened fire on the scrambling bushwhacker; several found their mark, but Skaggs remained afoot and continued to flee for his life. Slowed by his wounds, Skaggs made an easy target for White Turkey, a Delaware Indian, who shot an arrow through his midsection. With the shaft protruding from his ribs, Skaggs regained his feet yet again, but another Indian named Little Beaver, also a Delaware, "then shot with his big buffalo rifle and at the crack of the gun Skaggs fell forward on his face." The last guerrilla left in Lawrence was dead before he hit the ground.[60]

Little Beaver approached the body of the fallen bushwhacker and re-moved his boots, which had supposedly been stolen during the raid hours earlier. The Indian also "turned Skaggs' pockets inside out but found nothing." Before leaving the scene, Little Beaver "caught Skaggs by the hair of the head" and before the assembled crowd "made a motion pre-tending to scalp him." As for himself, Henry claims that he had had no desire to shoot at Skaggs personally because so many others did and would not have allowed the guerrilla to escape. He also confesses that, at the time of his capture and execution, Skaggs had been drunk. In addi-tion, he "had no cartridges or ammunition to load his revolver and was completely without means of defense." Perhaps this is why the man in charge of Skaggs (Miles Walters), as Henry reveals toward the end of his story, "made a desperate effort to protect him, intending to turn him over to the sheriff of Douglas County." In any event, he was certain that Little Beaver had fired the fatal shot.[61]

While factually out of line with both Connelley and Williams, Henry's story is equally revealing; in more ways than one, it seems to expose damning details about the Kansans in spite of itself. First, Henry asserts that he had been a firsthand witness to the whole event; however, his testimony completely ignores the mutilation of the corpse. Next, Henry openly admits that Skaggs had been both drunk and unarmed when cap-tured and then forced to run for his life. Perhaps ashamed of the spectacle-style manner in which the townspeople gunned the guerrilla down, Henry rather weakly pins the blame on a stranger: the unknown "volunteer sol-dier" who ordered Skaggs to run and started the whole execution. Third, this rendition not only placed the responsibility for killing Skaggs on a nonwhite character but actually introduced a second, Little Beaver, that had been completely absent in *Quantrill and the Border Wars* and Williams's account. In very suspicious fashion, Henry replaces William Speer, the rifleman reported by Williams to have shot Skaggs to death, with a Native American while simultaneously revealing that Miles Walters, the man in personal charge of the guerrilla, desperately wanted to turn Skaggs over to the law. Therein J. M. Henry inadvertently lets slip that, raid or no raid, gunning down the raider in the street had been extralegal—a lynch mob, essentially—and that guilt needed to reside with an Indian, not a respected member of the white Speer family or other white men possibly involved in the shooting.

After examinations of each account in turn and then collectively, little more in the way of objective facts has become clear concerning the death of Larkin Skaggs. That said, the variances that exist between each story— especially between those of William Connelley and J. M. Henry versus that of Andrew Williams—seem to expose the degree to which the commemorative strategies of borderland Unionists depended on a certain accounting or narrative of the Lawrence Massacre. In order to attack the morality and character of William Clarke Quantrill, these Unionists needed to present a glaring contrast between good and evil—a contrast that both pro-Confederates and Unionists abroad could not help but recognize. Within this context, Larkin Skaggs was not a dead guerrilla or a mutilated corpse. He was a commemorative problem that required an explanation—and like John Newman Edwards before them, Connelley and Henry explained.[62]

As spring turned to summer in 1907, John Sharp was little more than an aging night watchman for the West Vancouver Coal Company in Coal Harbor, Canada. But in August he dropped a bombshell on local media and sparked a continent-wide controversy: Sharp confessed to being the notorious William Clarke Quantrill.[63]

It had been previously accepted by virtually everyone involved that Quantrill had died in 1865, paralyzed by his wounds, in a Louisville, Kentucky, prison hospital. But as Sharp's version of events went, he had managed to escape from the hospital, rode some seventy miles (despite multiple, seemingly mortal wounds), and eventually came upon a woman with Confederate sympathies who nursed him back to full health. Following this miraculous recovery, Sharp then allegedly moved to Chile, back to Texas, and then to Oregon, before finally settling in Canada in 1897. Local residents and tourists alike agreed that Sharp bore a striking resemblance to the man who had masterminded the bloodiest guerrilla massacre in American history.[64]

Sharp's admission stemmed from a chance encounter with an American named J. E. Duffy. According to local testimony, Duffy traveled to Coal Harbor on business and, having clashed with Quantrill's company during the war (while serving with a Michigan cavalry outfit), claimed to immediately recognize the ex-guerrilla on spotting John Sharp. After an extensive conversation, Sharp confirmed to Duffy that he was Quantrill, and Duffy left the meeting utterly convinced. Soon after, Vancouver papers went public with the news; by taking the identity of such a polarizing figure, even as more than four decades had passed since war's end, John Sharp had interjected himself into a debate for guerrilla memory much more serious—and dangerous—than he realized.[65]

As word of Quantrill's apparent survival spread southward to the United States, it reportedly crossed the ears of two Kansans that had dealt with the guerrilla in the 1860s. Borderland Unionists—especially from Kansas—had long believed the architect of the Lawrence Massacre dead and gone. Word of John Sharp's revelation changed that immediately. Taking the story at face value, the men traveled to Sharp's home in Quatsino Sound, tracked down the would-be guerrilla chieftain, and delivered a savage beating with iron pokers. Sharp barely survived the assault and strangely refused to comment on the motives or identities of his assailants. Approximately one year later, when Sharp died as a result of alcoholism, investigators found a pair of Colt Navy revolvers engraved with the initials "W. C. Q." and a stash of letters addressed to Quantrill.[66]

Despite these material findings and Sharp's own ability to convince those around him, all available evidence concerning the veracity of his story leads to one conclusion: the real William Quantrill *did* die in a Kentucky hospital in 1865. In turn, Sharp's true identity will likely never be known, but odds are exceedingly good that he had served as a Missouri bushwhacker during the war—hence his knowledge of guerrilla activities and possibly even access to a dying Quantrill's personal effects. Much more important, though, were the broader consequences of his charade and what they illustrated about the ongoing struggle to control guerrilla memory in the borderlands.[67]

There can be little doubt that this was a commemorative conflict with intellectual as well as physical ramifications. Sharp was assaulted and left for dead by men believing they had righteously assassinated their greatest enemy. And Unionists had good reason to want Quantrill dead. Even before the publication of Connelley's *Quantrill and the Border Wars* in 1909 or remarks delivered at the Lawrence reunion in 1913, Unionists had collectively attempted to undermine their opposition by way of blasting its primary icon. To systematically destroy the honorable legacy first established by Edwards for the most powerful of guerrilla deities, they surmised, would cause irrevocable damage to the foundations of pro-Confederate memory in the guerrilla theater.

But before Sharp's rapid, albeit brief, ascension to fame in the summer of 1907, borderland Unionists had generally failed to attract the necessary attention outside of Kansas and small segments of Missouri to achieve their goals on a meaningful scale; to date the commemorative battle had been one in which Edwards and other pro-Confederate pundits held too many logistical advantages. Even so, Unionists refused to stop fighting.

With this in mind, three key observations crystallize from the tale of the "mystery man of Quatsino Sound": (1) Unionists could not live with the notion that the man who had brought wholesale destruction to their doorsteps might still be alive and, moreover, basking in a resurgence of international celebrity; (2) as Confederate borderlanders had spent decades transforming Quantrill into a deity of their own "irregular" Lost Cause, Unionists could ill afford now for a living, breathing "guerrilla god" to turn up and wade into the memorial struggle; (3) perhaps most important, the attempt on a Quantrill impostor's life foreshadowed a bitter, decades-long struggle still to come over which version of guerrilla memory would ultimately be victorious. It revealed that Unionists, as a means of striking back, were willing to do just about *anything* to swing the odds in their favor.

SEVEN

Guerrillas Gone Wild in the West

> The look and style of his comrades suggested that they had not come
> into the war to play, and their deeds made good the conjecture later.
> They were fine horsemen and good revolver shots; but their favorite
> arm was the lasso. Each had one at his pommel, and could snatch
> a man out of the saddle with it every time, on a full gallop, at any
> reasonable distance.
> —Mark Twain, "The Private History of a Campaign That Failed"

On the night of July 14, 1881, a man stumbled through the moonlit streets of Fort Sumner, New Mexico, toward the home of the Maxwell family. On entering the house, which he found pitch black, the slightest hints of motion caught his eye. Someone or something, it seemed, was skulking in the shadows. Now alarmed and brandishing a revolver, he called out nervously: "*Quien es?*" The answer to his question ("Who's there?") came as a sudden burst of light and a thud—the muzzle flare and subsequent impact of a .44-caliber bullet plowing deep into his chest. At just twenty-one years of age, Henry McCarty, aliases William Bonney and "Billy the Kid," had been shot dead by Sheriff Pat Garrett.

Less than a year later, another such fatal encounter played out roughly six hundred miles to the east of Fort Sumner in Saint Joseph, Missouri. There, on April 3, 1882, a secretive man known to local businessmen as "Mr. Thomas Howard" rose from a parlor couch, collected a wooden chair, and climbed atop it to straighten a picture hanging crookedly on the wall. As Howard tinkered with the frame, another man stood up. This second figure produced a revolver and aligned its open sights with the back of Howard's head. The bullet, a .45-caliber slug, shattered Howard's skull before burrowing into the plaster wall. The man who had fired it, a would-be bandit named Robert Ford—forever derided as "the dirty little coward that shot Mr. Howard"—had just assassinated none other than Jesse Woodson James.

In the annals of American frontier mythology, no two figures have become more synonymous with generic notions of the "Wild West" than Billy the

Kid and Jesse James. According to film, fiction, and popular memory, these six-shooting, renegade cowboys occupied the same abstracted geographic space (the "West") during an equally abstracted period of time (when that ambiguous western locale was particularly "Wild"). Even their violent ends, eerily similar at first glance in both date and circumstance, appear to justify overlapping status as western icons.[1] But from a historical perspective, the seminal components of their lives tell a different story; significant differences emerge and reveal that one was, in many more ways than not, an intruder in the cultural realm of high-noon showdowns, Rio Grande cattle drives, and Indian powwows.

This chapter, then, is designed to address the beginnings of the process by which Missouri's bushwhackers were culled from the Civil War borderlands, stripped of their Confederate context, and conflated with other western figures. Put another way, it will explore how guerrillas were commemoratively excommunicated to the Wild West in the late nineteenth and early twentieth centuries. Key to this process were a series of "outlaw histories" (aimed at adults) and dime novels (aimed at a younger demographic), penned in the 1880s, 1890s, and 1900s, that recast—sometimes inadvertently—a core group of former guerrillas as "western" rather than Confederate or otherwise southern. Ultimately, these materials illuminate the beginning of the demise of guerrillas as Civil War soldiers and the advent of guerrillas as gunslingers and cowboys in American popular culture and historical consciousness.[2]

As the catalyst for, and most conspicuous commemorative casualty of, guerrilla memory's westernization, Jesse James is employed here as both guide and case study. James did not participate consciously in his transmogrification from guerrilla to gunslinger, but he served as the template many others would follow. It helped that most of the best-known guerrilla leaders failed to survive the war (contributing to their legend but also making impossible their memorial migration west). This left James as one of the few who could step into a representative void of the Missouri bushwhacker with a postwar "career," and in virtually every way—from kinship, age, and political persuasion to social standing and economic status—he achieved "distinction" in that career.

As an outlaw, Jesse James represented the small minority of outlaws who hailed from the ex-guerrilla ranks. This cohort included his brother Frank, as well as Cole Younger and his brothers, Oliver Shepherd, Jim Cummins, Clell Miller, and John Jarrette—all of whom, like James himself, became behavioral anomalies by turning to crime in the postwar period. His figurehead standing with both elements of Quantrill's command left James with a complicated double identity: half standard veteran (as it was understood in Missouri) and half outlaw. So beginning in the 1880s, with the rise of popular outlaw histories—titles such as *The Border Bandits: An Authentic and Thrilling History of the Noted Outlaws, Frank and Jesse James and Their Band of Highwaymen*, and *Train and Bank Robbers of the West: A Romantic but Faithful Story of Bloodshed and Plunder Perpetrated by Missouri's Daring Outlaws*—James and his extralegal associates made the easiest candidates for a western makeover. And, as a result of their widespread criminal celebrity, their own exportation to the Wild West opened the proverbial door for other ex-guerrillas to be dragged along with them.

For the most part, academics have failed to identify James's iconic role in the westernization of guerrilla memory or, for that matter, that guerrilla memory existed to be westernized in the first place. Popular historian and Pulitzer Prize–winning biographer T. J. Stiles came closest to capturing the process in *Jesse James: Last Rebel of the Civil War* (2002), where he contended that Jesse James had not only turned to crime as a result of circumstances stemming directly from the Civil War in Missouri but that the crime spree itself was a politically motivated act of pro-Confederate terrorism and an extension of the guerrilla war into the Reconstruction period. Thus, while Stiles does not deal specifically with the impact of the James Gang's outlawry on how other former bushwhackers would and could be remembered, his book does at least attempt to pull James the western brigand back into the ambit of the Civil War.[3]

To be clear, I do not contend that James was wholly unique. Dodge City, the Dalton Gang, and even Wild Bill Hickok himself reveal that Kansas, the crucial other half of the guerrilla theater, also had its fair share of western credentials and would undergo a similar process of exportation to the "wilds." But James's memorial transformation from guerrilla to gunslinger is unusually well documented and unusually complete.[4] Again, to be clear, I am not interested in the "real" Jesse James, and I do not seek to restore him to his "proper" historical context—Missouri's guerrilla theater. Rather, I seek to diagram the cultural process by which he, and through him others, came to exist symbolically, first in two places—Missouri and the Wild West—and then only in one: the West of the popular imagination.

Understanding this process is far more important than we might realize, for this is not merely a process of westernization but, through it, "Americanization." Bloodthirsty Confederates are being reincorporated (and "made safe") via a process that moves them west and buries them there— allowing them to become larger-than-life legends of American machismo. With them gone, the Civil War can safely remain the *civilized* test of American manhood, and the Wild West can become the *civilizing* test of American manhood. In the end, then, both "histories" become genres of American masculine self-congratulation.

"Dingus the Fingus" versus "Billy the Kid"

On September 5, 1847, Robert and Zerelda James (née Cole) of Clay County, Missouri, celebrated the successful delivery of their second son, Jesse Woodson James. Both of Jesse's parents hailed from Kentucky, where his father had studied at Georgetown College before taking up work in Missouri as a hemp farmer and Baptist minister. Before long, Robert James owned more than one thousand acres of farmland in the vicinity of Liberty, Missouri, and upwards of six slaves. In 1849, however, gold fever lured Robert to California; death befell him there just one year later. Zerelda quickly remarried an affluent farmer named Benjamin Simms in 1852, but he died abruptly after only two years of matrimony. Zerelda's third and final marriage, this time to Dr. Reuben Samuel in 1855, provided a stable stepfather for Jesse and also produced four additional half siblings: Sarah Louisa Samuel (b. 1858), John Thomas Samuel (b. 1861), Peyton Quantrill Samuel (b. 1863), and Archie Peyton Samuel (b. 1866).[5]

The Missouri-Kansas borderland of Jesse's childhood had been an incubator for outbursts of sectional strife; by his teenage years in the early 1860s, those divisions had matured into full-scale civil war. An 1863 incident involving his stepfather, Dr. Samuel, ultimately prompted Jesse to join the ranks of Missouri's most notorious band of Confederate bushwhackers. Two years prior, Jesse's older brother, Frank James, saw action as a Confederate volunteer at the Battle of Wilson's Creek on August 10, 1861. Roughly a year later, in May 1862, local Union authorities coerced Frank to swear an oath of allegiance that forbade him from further assisting the southern rebellion. But Frank ignored the terms of his parole and, along with several other young men from Clay County, joined William Quantrill's guerrilla outfit that very summer. This was why, in 1863,

Jesse James as Civil War guerrilla, circa 1863–1864. This photo taken during the war shows a teenaged Jesse James sporting the signature accoutrements of irregular war: a guerrilla shirt and revolver. Courtesy of the Prints and Photographs Collection, Library of Congress, http://www.loc.gov/pictures /item/2005682818/.

Union militiamen arrived at the James-Samuel home looking for Frank— and in an effort to discern his whereabouts, the militiamen tortured Dr. Samuel by repeatedly hanging him from a large tree. Some accounts also allege that the Federals tortured Jesse, then sixteen years old, for information as well. No longer believing it safe to remain at home, Jesse found his way to the irregular ranks soon after, in late 1863 or early 1864.[6]

The two seminal guerrilla engagements of Jesse's Civil War career were the ill-fated assault against Fayette, Missouri, led by "Bloody Bill" Anderson in September 1864 and the massacres at Centralia, also orchestrated by Anderson, later that same month. Among the bushwhackers, Jesse was particularly close to John Thrailkill, Dave Poole, and Archie Clements; various sources report that the group—especially when Jesse and Clements were together—was known for especially brutal killings and the mutilation of corpses. Some of them, along with his brother Frank, endearingly called Jesse "Dingus" (short for "Dingus the Fingus") after an accident in which he shot off the tip of his left middle finger. In 1865 Jesse attempted to surrender with a large group of guerrillas led by Fletcher Taylor, but he ended up in a gun battle with Federal soldiers. This botched attempt to put the Civil War behind him helped steer Jesse toward a postwar career as the most celebrated outlaw in American history.[7]

In February 1866 Clements headed a small group of former bushwhackers that robbed a bank in Liberty, Missouri—and managed to murder an innocent bystander in the process. Shortly thereafter, Clements's own bloody death in 1866 propelled Jesse into a leadership position; by the late 1860s he became chief of the fabled James-Younger Gang, which included his brother, Frank, along with former guerrillas Clell Miller, Oliver Shepherd, John Jarrette, Jim Cummins, and the Youngers, Cole and Jim. (John and Bob Younger also periodically rode with the gang, but they had been too young to join Quantrill's band during the war.) It was during this early, successful phase of Jesse's bandit career that Major John Newman Edwards lauded him as a social bandit and warped him into a beacon for Democratic politics in Missouri.[8]

At its peak, the James-Younger Gang robbed banks and trains within a geographic range that included Missouri, Kansas, Iowa, and Kentucky. But this incarnation of the gang came to a disastrous end in September 1876 when an attempt to raid the First National Bank of Northfield, Minnesota, went awry. The failed robbery, which prosouthern presses claimed as an attempt to steal from Benjamin Butler, the despised Union general of New Orleans fame, cost Clell Miller his life and landed the Younger brothers in a Minnesota prison. For the remaining six years of his post-Northfield life, Jesse remained on the run, but he never again assembled an effective gang; new recruits simply lacked the war-bred skills and combat experience of the former guerrillas. The rapidly deteriorating quality of his criminal associates brought Jesse into contact with a pair of second-rate purloiners named Charles and Robert Ford.[9]

On April 3, 1882, Jesse James was assassinated at his rented home in Saint Joseph, Missouri. To evade authorities, he had been posing as a horse trader under the alias surname "Howard." According to multiple accounts, the Ford brothers had conspired with Thomas T. Crittenden, the governor of Missouri, to eliminate James in exchange for legal immunity and a cash reward of $10,000. Robert—known to Jesse as Bob—fired the fatal shot from only a few paces. (Both of the Ford brothers met violent ends: Charley committed suicide in 1884 and a disgruntled gunman murdered Bob in his Colorado saloon in 1892.) Jesse was initially buried a few steps from the porch of his mother's home in Kearney, Missouri, but constant attention from onlookers and relic hunters forced relocation. On his reburial in Mount Olivet Cemetery, several ex-guerrillas, including William H. Gregg, Hiram George, Benjamin Morrow, and Warren Welch, served as pallbearers. A headstone at Mount Olivet lists Jesse as a former member of irregular companies led by Fletcher Taylor, George Todd, and William Quantrill.[10]

Far from the hemp works of western Missouri, the delivery of an infant named Henry McCarty played out in November 1859 amid the Irish hovels of Manhattan. Few definitive facts exist concerning Henry's genealogy. He was the second son of Catherine McCarty, an Irish immigrant, herself born in 1829; the identity of his father has never been verified. Extant records do not indicate whether "McCarty" was Catherine's maiden or matrimonial name. In turn, this lack of ancestral distinction has led some historians to believe the surname "Bonney"–later adopted as an alias by Henry–had actually belonged to his biological father. (Still others contend that Catherine's maiden name was "Bonney," which might also explain the alias as having been a family name.) Either way, Henry grew up without a reliable father figure. Sometime in the mid-1860s, Catherine took Henry and his older brother, Joseph, to live in Indiana. There, in 1865, the single mother of two began a relationship with William H. H. Antrim, and the group had moved to Wichita, Kansas, by 1870. A year later, Catherine came down with tuberculosis and the family again relocated, this time to Colorado, as it suited her failing lungs.[11]

By early 1873 the McCarty-Antrim clan had settled in New Mexico–first Santa Fe and then Silver City. Here William and Catherine finally married, while Henry learned to speak Spanish and, perhaps more importantly, to gamble. Following his mother's death in 1874 and William's lack of interest in raising two teenage stepsons, Henry took to crime. In 1875 he was arrested for a relatively minor act of theft, but he managed to escape from the Silver City jail and rather unnecessarily transformed himself into a fugitive from justice. Now on the lam, Henry bounced from place to place in the Arizona and New Mexico Territories. He wore many hats: drover, shootist, sharper, rustler, and horse thief. From his fellow stockmen, he acquired the nickname "the Kid" (or "El Chivato" to the Mexican gauchos), and while working for one particular rancher, an Englishman named John Tunstall, Henry–then posing as William H. Bonney–became involved in the conflict that made "Billy the Kid" a *nom de guerre* of national acclaim: the Lincoln County War of 1878.[12]

The maelstrom he encountered in Lincoln County boiled down to a bloody feud over beef and mercantile contracts. On one side was the aforementioned Tunstall, a Canadian-born lawyer-turned-entrepreneur named Alexander McSween, and Texas-bred John Chisum, a cattle magnate with one of the largest ranching operations in America. On the other was merchant L. G. Murphy, an Irish immigrant who had fled the potato famines of County Wexford, and James Dolan, another Irish immigrant ten years Murphy's junior—his heir apparent, as it were. When hostilities erupted, the Murphy-Dolan faction held a monopoly on both mercantile distribution and cattle deals with the army. For all intents and purposes, it also owned William Brady, the sheriff of Lincoln County. Furthermore, the Irishmen were undergirded by the clout of attorney Thomas Catron, a man whose personal power and fortune more than rivaled that of the formidable Chisum. Catron was chief of the economic and political machine known as the Santa Fe Ring. He was also a close associate of New Mexico's territorial governor, Samuel Axtell, and one of the largest landholders in the United States, let alone the Southwest.[13]

Waging the Lincoln County War involved bands of "regulators"—that is, men deputized to enforce the law as interpreted by their respective employers—striking at opposing homes, ranches, and cattle camps in Lincoln and the surrounding prairies. Ambush, backshooting, and the execution of prisoners became commonplace, as did collateral damage of the civilian variety. Before the war officially concluded, Murphy had succumbed to cancer, Dolan had taken sole control over their operations, and both Tunstall and McSween had been assassinated. Men loyal to the latter pairing—including Henry, then known as Billy the Kid—did manage to gun down Sheriff Brady and several other important members of the newly consolidated House of Dolan. Such well-publicized mayhem forced action on the part of President Rutherford B. Hayes: he appointed former Union general Lew Wallace, a man with a reputation for maintaining law and order, as the new territorial governor. Wallace quickly brokered a cease-fire in Lincoln; most of the regulators disbanded, but Billy continued fighting and refused to leave New Mexico Territory. These interconnected decisions ensured that he would be a hunted man for the remaining three years of his life.[14]

Even John Chisum turned against his one-time ally. With the war over, Billy's antics were simply bad for business. To help repair New Mexico's image on the national stage, Wallace posted a $500 reward for his capture. And with backing from both Chisum and Catron, Pat Garrett became the new sheriff of Lincoln County. His mandate was simple: capture Billy the Kid once and for all. In 1880 Garrett did apprehend Billy—though the victory was short-lived. Following a brief trial he was sentenced to death by hanging. Before the execution could be carried out, however, Billy escaped from his makeshift jail and murdered two guards in the process. With this in mind, in July 1881, when Garrett tracked "El Chivato" to the Maxwell house in Fort Sumner, he made no attempts to take the outlaw in alive. According to some historians, Billy had come to see Paulita Maxwell, a girlfriend with whom he might have been expecting a child. Instead, he found Garrett. Their encounter was fatal.[15]

Even in such abbreviated form, biographies of Jesse James and Billy the Kid appear to have much in common. Both had multiple father figures; both became involved in extremely violent, localized wars; both firmly believed that involvement in those conflicts had afterward necessitated lives of crime; and both met violent ends in the early 1880s. Moreover, the style of hit-and-run combat used by New Mexican regulators even seemed to mirror the tactics employed by Missouri's Confederate bushwhackers. In reality, though, these similarities existed only on the surface. Because despite their reputations for social banditry and their analogous death scenes, the lives of Jesse James and Billy the Kid ultimately unfolded on opposite sides of a mammoth historical—and cultural—chasm: the Civil War.

On one hand, Jesse James was a southerner. He was a character forged by the Civil War—an unprecedented event in American history that involved millions of men taking up arms and more than 750,000 of them failing to return home alive. This was a conflict fought over slavery and sectional differences, partisan issues that divided the North from the South and Democrat from Republican. As residents of a strategically crucial border state in which irregular violence flourished at the local level, the Jameses had little choice but to choose sides when the war arrived, largely uninvited, at their doorsteps. After 1865, when it was at least "officially" over, Jesse may not (as he contended) have had a legitimate opportunity to reenter normal society—we will never know for sure. But true or not, for the public, Jesse's criminal career had just deep enough political roots for perception to gradually become reality. So when Crittenden arranged for the ex-bushwhacker's assassination in 1882, the governor essentially placed the final period on Missouri's Civil War story. The war had created Jesse James, and his inability to deal with defeat made him a much-extended casualty of it.

On the other hand, the young man known at different times as Henry McCarty, William Bonney, the Kid, and Billy the Kid was the product of a western world alien to Jesse James. In the Kid's formative environ, irregular battles were not waged by white kinship networks to settle matters of slavery or states' rights. New Mexicans, both white *and* Hispanic, fought to determine access to pastures and water holes. Here barons of the Gilded Age such as Chisum and Catron—or aspiring captains of industry such as McSween—all clashed over land grants, beef sales, and mercantile supremacy. Many of the chief belligerents of the range wars that made Billy the Kid a household legend were not simply economic or political competitors, either; they were often immigrants such as Tunstall, Murphy, and Dolan—Englishmen and Irishmen—using the rugged sectors of the American West as a new arena for their Old World ethnic feuds. Simply put, Billy the Kid lived his short, violent life in a western frontier thrown open by the Civil War—but it was a stage with its own social baggage, political issues, systems of violence, and unique cast of characters.

In spite of these differences, Jesse James and Billy the Kid are stock-and-trade figures of the Wild West—cultural icons forever associated with quick-drawing gunfighters, cow towns, raiding Indians, and, above all else, a brief, mythical moment of the American experience in which a certain breed of men were free to battle the frontier and create new, independent lives from nothing. This was the time to win the West and complete construction of a nation that spanned from sea to shining sea. But the merging of worlds inhabited by James and the Kid helped wash away the former's connections with the Confederate South and the Civil War. It remade him as a gunslinger and a stickup man. One persistent myth involving the westernized James even involved him playing poker in a smoky, New Mexico saloon with none other than Billy the Kid. T. J. Stiles correctly calls the meeting "patently absurd"—but the cultural forces that would spawn such an encounter cannot, and should not, be ignored.[16]

This reassociation came at the expense of James's Civil War context—and that of guerrilla memory through him. As noted by military historian Don Bowen in the 1970s, the average age of a rank-and-file guerrilla in western Missouri was twenty—and the vast majority were unmarried when the war began. More than 75 percent of guerrillas were either born in Missouri or a permanent resident by 1850; moreover, 68 percent were the children of parents born in a Confederate state (not counting Kentucky), and nearly half had at least one active relation also involved in the irregular war. Finally, 41 percent of "guerrilla parents" owned slaves in 1860. In other words, the average guerrilla was around twenty years old, unmarried, born in Missouri, related to another guerrilla, and from a mildly affluent, slave-owning family.[17]

As a representative of the whole, James fit the bill almost perfectly. Born in Missouri, the product of a successful, slave-owning family, he was unmarried and seventeen years old when he joined his brother Frank in the irregular ranks. This status was only exacerbated by the fact that so many of the guerrillas who had been more prominent than James *during* the conflict had not survived it. For example, on October 22, 1864, George M. Todd was riding a few miles northeast of Independence, Missouri, when the bullet of a Federal sharpshooter knocked him from his mount and ended his life. Just a few days later, William "Bloody Bill" Anderson charged recklessly—and almost entirely alone—into a well-covered Federal line in Albany, Missouri. When the smoke had cleared, Anderson was dead on the ground with two lead balls buried in his brain. Finally, in May 1865 William Quantrill was shot in the back while camping on the outskirts of Louisville, Kentucky. Paralyzed below the arms by the wound, he died in a hospital several days later.[18]

Such a combination of circumstances caused other former bushwhackers whom James had closely represented socially, economically, and politically during the war to become entangled in the process of westernization. The overwhelming majority of these ex-guerrillas had abstained from postwar banditry, but as James became increasingly notorious for his criminal exploits, the group as a whole shared the guilt by association. Thus proponents of a Civil War legacy that did not include the uncouth details of guerrilla warfare could actually wield James against his old comrades; by westernizing the head of the snake through outlaw histories and dime novels, the body could effectively be forced to follow.

Of Outlawed History and Historical Outlaws

Outlaw histories flourished in the final decades of the nineteenth century. As part of a wider national interest in western lore, these books purported to catalog the lives and "careers" of America's greatest frontiers-men, shootists, Indian fighters, and bandits: characters such as "Wild Bill" Hickok, Sam Bass, Sitting Bull, Kit Carson, William "Buffalo Bill" Cody, and Jesse James. Just how historical these "histories" really were is—and always has been—a matter of interpretation. While sometimes grounded in fact, authors routinely took liberties and often stretched the truth quite thin for the sake of a more riveting narrative. These books were, at the end of the day, intended to sell. Hence outlaw histories generally employed the purplest of purple prose to describe the manliest of manly exploits for eastern, adult audiences.[19]

In any event, whether or not outlaw histories featuring Jesse James are technically accurate—in fact, they are often painfully inaccurate—matters much less than the extent to which the public gradually internalized their content and, in turn, how such a sweeping case of perception becoming reality affected the commemorative standing of guerrilla memory. Piecing together this relationship requires a deeper reading of titles, main themes, and content—one that takes stock of geographic settings and chronological balances, direct linkages to the Civil War, and connections to other iconic western figures. The patterns gleaned from this examination help explain James's gradual metamorphosis from average Confederate guerrilla to quintessential western desperado and, as a result, the corollary transition of the Missouri bushwhacker from Civil War soldier to banditti to the stuff of outlawed history.

While most outlaw histories purported to tell James's life story, their titles—*The Outlaws of the Border, The Border Bandits, Train and Bank Robbers of the West,* to name a few—left little to the imagination concerning which phase of his life would be featured most prominently. Subtitles were gen-erally even more explicit about which version of James, the Confeder-ate guerrilla or the western gunman, would take center stage: *An Authen-tic and Thrilling History of the Noted Outlaws, Frank and Jesse James, and Their Bands of Highwaymen; A Romantic but Faithful Story of Bloodshed and Plunder, Perpetrated by Missouri's Daring Outlaws;* and *The Noted Western Outlaws* are prime examples. These titles signaled to readers that their respective pages abounded with bank heists, stage holdups, cattle rustlers, knife-toting Mexican "greasers," and shootouts amid the wide-open frontier. Without fail, the books themselves delivered these western tropes in dispropor-tionate measure. In *The Illustrated Lives of Frank and Jesse James* (1882), for instance, author J. A. Dacus spent only about 70 pages out of more than 450 recounting the early life and Civil War experiences of the James boys. Jay Donald's *Outlaws of the Border* (1882) offered a similar ratio: at nearly 500 pages long, the book used few more than 70 pages to cover the ancestry, childhoods, and Civil War records of the Jameses. The rest focused entirely on postwar crimes spanning from Minnesota to Mexico.[20]

More telling, however, is that before sufficient incidents of western outlawry existed to overshadow James's wartime story, early authors simply created them from thin air—and later authors "borrowed" them for their own works. The most blatant of these "creations" first appeared in 1880 in R. T. Bradley's *The Outlaws of the Border*. According to Bradley, in the wake of the failed Northfield Raid of 1876, Frank and Jesse James made a dash for western Texas. "They were loiterers then," he explained, "for they were in absolute safety and near their southwestern refuge, where they had homes and extensive herds of cattle." When the James brothers were away from these successful ranching operations, Bradley added, "their property was cared for and defended by some of their trusty henchmen, who had no idea that their employers were anything else than liberal and enterprising traders and graziers." Coincidentally, just as Frank and Jesse arrived at their Texas spread, they found that it had been robbed the previous night by Bustenado, a local chieftain of Mexican bandits from across the Rio Grande.[21]

To make matters worse, Bradley noted, the "Mexican devils" had kidnapped the (white) daughter of a neighboring rancher, a girl named Alice Gordon, and carried her off along with the cattle. Luckily, he continued, "a negro boy who was devotedly attached to her had accompanied her and it was well known that he would use every exertion to make her situation as endurable as possible." A group of eight men under the command of Frank and Jesse James set out after Bustenado and his band of thirty raiders. "In fighting the Mexicans," Bradley reasoned, "the plainsman or scout never stops to count numbers" and "the chiefs of his pursuit [the James brothers] had been outnumbered so constantly in their conflicts, that they almost thought it a necessary part of the programme." The posse caught up with Bustenado's force but decided against a night attack because "they knew that darkness was inspiriting to the cowardly Greasers, and determined that the fight should take place in the broad sunlight."[22]

"Alice Gordon Rescued by Jesse James." As told by Appler and other "outlaw historians," Jesse and Frank James charged the Mexican kidnappers of Alice Gordon and led her safely back to (white) civilization. From Augustus C. Appler, *Train and Bank Robbers of the West: A Romantic but Faithful Story of Bloodshed and Plunder, Perpetrated by Missouri's Daring Outlaws.* Chicago: Belford & Clarke, 1882.

When morning came, the James brothers led a charge on the Mexican camp with reins firmly gripped in their teeth and Colt revolvers in hand. As the posse of white avengers swooped down on the Mexican camp, Bustenado, the bandit leader, attempted to murder Alice Gordon before retreating—but a bullet from Jesse's gun left him "lifeless as a bag of sand" and saved the young woman's life. With Bustenado dead and the Mexican camp ransacked, the Jameses retrieved their herd and took Gordon home to her father's ranch. Bradley closed his coverage of the incident by stating: "It is said that Mexican mothers when they wish to terrify children to obedience or silence have only to whisper the dreaded name which the brothers have made familiar and by which they are known on both sides of the border."[23]

There are several worthy points to consider as they relate to westernization in this segment of Bradley's narrative. On one side, the James brothers—with Jesse always in the lead—were depicted not only as wandering brigands taking refuge amid the rough-and-tumble western frontier but also as mysterious cattle barons who owned extensive property, oversaw bands of cowboy "henchmen," and dealt in copious heads of beef. More than temporary visitors from Missouri, this account turned the Jameses into something more resembling John Chisum. On another side, the Jameses battle not with white Union oppressors, meddling Pinkerton detectives, or even with African American predators such as Jack Mann; instead, they go head to head with Mexican "greasers" to rescue a white woman and her loyal black servant. In other words, while Jesse James's usefulness as a political terrorist had disappeared in pro-Confederate sectors of Missouri, traces of his previous purpose—in the form of a Remus-like body servant—lingered as his violent antics made for a viable *western* hero against a new, ethnically defined enemy.

Perhaps most important of all, though, is that *no* evidence exists to even begin suggesting that *any* of the events in Bradley's story *ever* actually happened. For years following the Northfield disaster, both Frank and Jesse James lived under assumed identities in Tennessee, with Frank often resorting to manual labor to make financial ends meet.[24] Far from owning sprawling cattle operations in Texas, the Jameses had to labor manually to feed their families between robberies; they did not win shootouts with the dastardly Bustenado, because no such shootouts ever occurred; and, it is safe to assume, Mexican mothers did not invoke the Jameses' names to terrify their children. These critiques notwithstanding, Bradley achieved two major feats with his Mexican romp: first, he created what appeared to be a time-honored case for James as an occupant of the Wild West, despite the fact that *The Outlaws of the Border* was only published a few years after the rescue of Alice Gordon had allegedly occurred; second, he established the precedent for nearly all subsequent outlaw histories featuring James, to include—and gradually expand—the ex-bushwhacker's exploits in the exotic, Mexican reaches of the Wild West.

With this in mind, several outlaw histories included similar—and sometimes even verbatim—renditions of the James brothers' encounter with Alice Gordon and Bustenado. These included Dacus's *Illustrated Lives of Frank and Jesse James*, Donald's *Outlaws of the Border*, and Appler's *Train and Bank Robbers of the West*.[25] But these authors also tilled new ground; they integrated ever more and wilder exploits into their narratives that continued to pull James down the path to western icon status. According to *The Border Bandits*, for instance, the Jameses had been in Mexico as early as 1870. Following a bank robbery in Gallatin, Missouri, J. W. Buel wrote, Frank and Jesse James rode into Matamoras, Mexico, and decided to attend a local fandango. "When the night shadows fell," he continued, "they paid the price of admission" and "entered the hall, which was rapidly filling up with swarthy senoritas and hidalgoes." "From the belts of the latter," Buel noted, "protruded the glimmering handles of bright, keen stilettos, in preparation of the affray which is always anticipated." It did not take long before the James boys found such trouble.[26]

While not particularly graceful, Frank and Jesse attempted to dance with some of the fiesta's female attendees. But this "only served to excite the ridicule of the Mexicans who, by gesture and speech, went so far in their sport and mimicry of the outlaws that at length Frank James knocked down one of the boldest." With Frank under assault, "Jesse saw where his aid was most needed and the next instant the powerful Mexican fell with a bullet in his brain." The fandango then devolved into a general melee; with Frank and Jesse greatly outnumbered and essentially trapped, "nothing remained for the boys except for clearing a way by shooting those who stood before them." As Jesse fought his way out of the building, he turned and saw another Mexican on the verge of stabbing Frank in the heart—"but ere the hand fell to its purpose a bullet from Jesse's pistol entered the Mexican's eye and he dropped dead at Frank's feet, striking the dagger deep into the floor as he fell." At this, "the place was swarming so rapidly with blood-craving hidalgoes and greasers that the only avenue of escape lay in the river." The Jameses made a break for the Rio Grande, plunged into its current, and crossed the border back into Texas.[27]

In addition to his own version of the cattle-rustler shootout (in which he renamed Bustenado as "Palacio") and the Matamoras fandango, J. A. Dacus also recounted two new adventures in *Illustrated Lives of Frank and Jesse James*. The first unfolded when the James boys and a few of their outlaw compatriots wandered into the village of Carmen, Mexico, an important trading post "in the northern part of the State of Chihuahua." On arrival, they began scheming to rob a stagecoach transporting large quantities of silver and gradually infiltrated the shipping operation. After lulling the coachmen into trust and friendship, the Jameses ambushed the guards and killed two instantly. According to Dacus, "two were dead and sixteen survivors were prisoners, and at the mercy of five of the most desperate men who ever played the part of free-booters on this continent." The Jameses took their treasure back across the Rio Grande and disappeared into the rugged mountains of Texas.[28]

The second involved yet another gun battle, though this time soldiers from the Mexican army replaced "swarthy hidalgoes" and cow-thieving "greasers." In Monclova, Mexico, the Jameses attended a party thrown in their honor by an old friend from Missouri. One of the guests, however, an officer in the Mexican military, recognized the outlaws and attempted to corner them with a squad of soldiers. "The boys rushed out of the house," Dacus offered, and "the soldiers in the street met them with a volley of balls." While agitated by the odds, Frank and Jesse "opened fire on the line of guards around the house." "Seized with consternation," the yarn concluded, "the soldiers fled from their deadly revolvers . . . [and] never had Monclava [sic] been so shaken."[29]

Published in 1882, Jay Donald's *Outlaws of the Border*—not to be confused with Bradley's *The Outlaws of the Border*—included all of the fabricated anecdotes that were quickly becoming standard components of James's life story: Donald placed Jesse in Carmen, Mexico, scene of the stagecoach robbery; in Matamoras for the fandango bloodbath; in Monclova for the second party gone awry; and in the head-to-head collision with Bustenado for the life of Alice Gordon. Donald's narrative also managed to find the James boys in a Nevada mining camp—where they engaged in a deadly shootout with several miners. Most illuminating, however, is that while Bradley and then Buel had thrilled readers with Bustenado and Dacus had reissued the same story with Palacio in charge of the Mexican bandits, Donald seized an opportunity to maximize the action: he related two *different* incidents involving both Palacio and Bustenado, respectively. Following the Jameses' sanguinary victory over the latter, Donald reported: "Frank and Jesse were the heroes of the hour. Their gallant exploits were trumpeted through all the quiet valley, and it was well understood for years after that in that region the country, 'No greasers need apply.'"[30]

In *Train and Bank Robbers of the West*, Augustus Appler continued the trend of differentiating between encounters with Palacio and Bustenado, along with the other fandangos, shootouts, and robberies. Appler likely overstepped the bounds of creative license, though, when he alleged that the James brothers had actually survived their first Mexican shootout in 1860—when Jesse would have only measured thirteen years of age.[31] Clearly, in an effort to stay fresh, outlaw histories had evolved quickly from fabrication to the outright ridiculous; that said, the notion of a prepubescent Jesse James on a killing spree south of the border actually revealed the extent to which he had been sheared from his roots in Civil War Missouri and remade as a man of the Wild West.

The construction of this false equivalency amounts to the real importance of outlaw histories. Because fictitious as these texts were, they systematically transformed Jesse James; they downplayed the formative Civil War elements of his biography; they placed him, with increasing frequency, in murderous showdowns along the frontiers of Mexico and Texas; and they simultaneously made him over as a six-gun-slinging desperado of the southwestern frontier *and* as the proprietor of a vast Texas ranching operation. With this last tactic, Buel and company prosaically blended images of the outlaw (à la William Bonney) and the cattle baron (à la John Chisum) to create the ultimate, hybrid westerner, one who could work his violent trade safely outside the bounds of civilized, white society. This society had waged the Civil War and now had a vested interest in preserving the "proper" version of it—one that did not include bushwhackers such as James.

Donald made this point about conflicting environments quite clear while concluding his rendition of the Jameses' time in Mexico and their return to the United States: "The scene changes. We leave behind the quiet valley of the Pecos, the land of the Pampas and the Aztecs, and come once more within range of busy, bustling *civilized* life."[32] And if the content of outlaw histories had not solidified which of these environments James and his brethren belonged in, Buel's preface to *The Border Bandits* left no room for doubt. "No one can afford to ignore the lesson which the lives of these outlaws teach, and therefore a correct history of their desperate deeds becomes necessary as part of the country's annals," he wrote, "in juxtaposition with the commendable heroism of *our* brightest characters."[33] In other words, *our* brightest characters (men such as Grant, Lee, and Chamberlain—the heroes of publications such as *Battles and Leaders*) belonged among the busy, bustling *civilized* life. Therein the real "lesson" here was that "correct histories" (read: entirely fabricated histories) of James's exploits in the West underscored that he was anything but one of ours; rather, he belonged in the land of the Aztecs—and so too did guerrilla memory.

The authors of outlaw histories simply had to connect the dots for readers. Dot one: robberies and murders reportedly committed by Jesse James in Missouri, Minnesota, Kentucky, Iowa, Kansas, Texas, and Mexico were extensions of his wartime guerrilla career. Dot two: that crime spree technically thrived on both sides of the Rio Grande but seemed to fit most naturally within a Far Western context, meaning Texas and Mexico. Third and final dot: if James's criminal résumé did not belong to civilized postwar society, neither did the bushwhacking days that had trained him for and led him to banditry in the first place. Thus the Jesse James of outlaw history fame essentially became a version of Billy the Kid with more "Kid-esque" qualities than Billy himself. As rapidly as these myths were created, they were also coated with a false patina of "old" wives' tales involving Mexican mothers and children's fables featuring Jesse James. These finishing touches insinuated that the westernized Jesse, however unseasoned he was in reality, had withstood the test of time prior to entering the pantheon of Wild West lore. With this work completed, outlaw histories set the stage for turn-of-the-century dime novels to begin indoctrinating a whole new, and decidedly younger, generation of readers.

Westernizing a New Generation

While outlaw histories purported to chronicle James's western exploits as matters of fact, the authors of dime novels, or "penny dreadfuls" as they were known in England, freely adopted themes and settings from their "scholarly" counterparts minus the pomp and circumstance. With vigorous plots and flashy illustrations, dime novels functioned as the comic books of their era—but it is crucial to remember that in the heyday of dime novels from the 1870s to the First World War, the printed word still ruled the kingdom of nonlive entertainment. The topical breadth of dime novels was, and remains, truly staggering. From sleuths, pirates, backwoodsmen, pioneers, cowboys, Indian fighters, and boy detectives to grizzled soldiers, hunting guides, sports stars, inventors, medieval knights, and even wizards, choices existed for all tastes. Thus every variety of hero or villain imaginable to late nineteenth- and early twentieth-century audiences—which consisted mostly of young children but included everyone up to middle-aged adults—rolled out of eastern publishing houses headquartered in New York, Philadelphia, Baltimore, and Chicago.[34]

On frontier and Wild West–oriented stories, Daryl Jones writes in *The Dime Novel Western* that heroes came in four different types: the backwoodsman, the plainsman, the outlaw, and the cowboy. To a certain degree, Jones suggests that these templates appeared and evolved as the perceived position of the American frontier gradually moved westward. In many ways, the version of Jesse James featured in turn-of-the-century dime novels was an amalgamation of plainsman, outlaw, and cowboy—a figure who survived and thrived in his own western world by utilizing various skills inherent to each contributing identity.[35]

In 1901 Street and Smith began publishing *The Jesse James Stories* (*TJJS*) from their offices on Williams Street in New York. Priced at five cents per copy—dime novels often did not actually cost ten cents—or $2.50 for a full subscription, issues of *TJJS* ran weekly, but typically not as serials (that is, with narratives that spanned multiple issues). Multiple authors composed the stories under the house name "W. B. Lawson," though Saint George Henry Rathbone and Colonel Prentiss Ingraham, each prodigious in his own right, contributed heavily. Other publishing firms, most notably Frank Tousey and Arthur Westbrook, produced their own lines of Jesse James material but frequently reprinted old content. For this reason, though it only ran for two years, *TJJS* arguably stands as the iconic portrayal of James's western adventures in dime novel format. (Street and Smith, it stands to mention, did not abandon the series due to lack of popularity; rather, political pressure took its toll when post offices came under fire for shipping children's literature that glorified banditry and murder.)[36]

While not every issue of *The Jesse James Stories* unfolded in the Far West, readers often found the guerrilla-turned-outlaw in scenarios both western and wild: he pulled off daring train and bank heists; he clashed with other outlaws, bounty hunters, and sheriffs; he shot and gambled his way through cattle and mining towns, sometimes south of the Rio Grande; he met up with exotic Indian tribes and braved harsh frontier conditions in Arizona, Texas, Wyoming, California, and Nevada; and, not coincidentally, he accomplished these feats with minimal allusion ever made to his Civil War past. Indeed, as J. Randolph Cox pointed out in his authoritative reference *The Dime Novel Companion*, the richly illustrated covers of *TJJS* even presented James in "what can be called a uniform: a white western hat, a dark blue coat, white trousers, and knee-length cavalry boots."[37]

Like outlaw histories, dime novel titles very frequently matched James's new western digs—from *The Miner of Madman's Mountain* and *The Siege of the Lost Ranch* to *The Robber Rangers of the Rio Grande* and *The Desperate Stand at Cutthroat Ranch*. Just as frequently, their content followed suit. In

issue #6, *Jesse James in Wyoming, or, The Den in the Black Hills,* James frat-
ernized with tribes of Utes and Apaches before saving an abducted damsel in distress from a half-breed renegade Indian known as "Apache Jim."
Another issue had James in a California mining town where men came
for gold and found the "wild spirit" of the West. There the outlaw met Ben
Arnold—a noted gunslinger himself—who is terrified of Jesse and Frank
James because they were "two of the boldest rascals the West ever knew."
As the plot developed, readers had to determine whether a look-alike
dared to use Jesse's name or if he led a secret double life with a second,
Mexican wife in California. Still another issue, simply titled *Jesse James's
Exploits,* featured James in the role of bounty hunter; after rescuing a
pretty young girl from a raging bull with crack pistol shooting, audiences
learned that he was cutting a wide swath across the West toward Nevada.
There James planned to serve a warrant on a man named Larson—a murderer wanted as part of the Wilcox Gang in a murder in none other than
Tombstone, Arizona. (Tombstone would have been well known to turn-
of-the-century western lore as the site of the infamous "Shootout at the
O.K. Corral" between the Earp brothers, John "Doc" Holliday, and a
gang of cattlemen known as "the Cowboys.")[38]

As Jones noted, a widely popular series—like *The Jesse James Stories*—could
have flown off presses by the tens of thousands; some even sold in the
hundreds of thousands and went through multiple editions. And according to Cox, the target demographic for most of these western dime novels
included boys between the ages of eight and sixteen. This was no coincidence: beginning in the 1870s, literacy rates among children slowly began
to rise. At the same time, savvy publishers catered to younger consum-
ers in the marketplace by offering "half-dime" novels—which were half as
expensive as full-priced competitors and intended to be affordable on an
allowance. As is generally the case in cultural history, quantifying the "impact" through sheer volume is difficult; precise sales or subscription figures from Street and Smith are not readily available. Then again, the rate
of publication and the presence of copycat competitors do hint at a vast
readership for *The Jesse James Stories.*[39]

Most revealing, though, are the results of competitions printed in the
dime novels themselves. "That was the sound of the bell! Time!" trumpeted an advertisement in the back of issue #100. "Now is the time for
you to get in your finest punches in the way of splendid stores of boxing

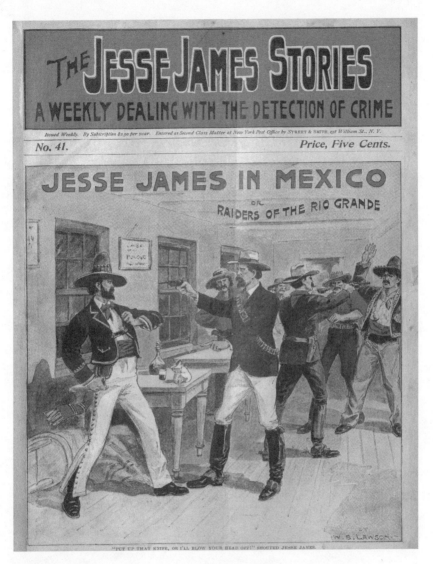

Jesse James in Mexico, or, Raiders of the Rio Grande. Placing James in Mexico allowed him to become not only an icon of the Wild West but also a valuable tool for implementing white civilization throughout the western frontier. Courtesy of Special Collections, University of South Florida Libraries.

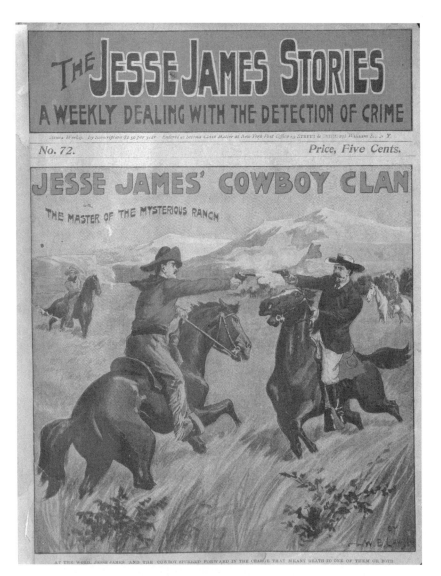

Jesse James' Cowboy Clan, or, The Master of the Mysterious Ranch. Despite the title of this dime novel, Jesse James was hardly a cowboy—a distinct, but often overlooked, dissimilarity between him and fellow outlaw Billy the Kid. Courtesy of Special Collections, University of South Florida Libraries.

bouts," the pitch continued. "You know it is very frequently the beginning of a fight that counts, so do your very best now." Children—presumably young boys—were invited to compose short narratives about boxing matches with their friends and submit them to the publisher for what must have seemed like a fantastic prize: two pair of genuine leather boxing gloves. The series held these contests weekly with entries pouring in from readers in Saint Paul, Brooklyn, Pittsburg, Erie, Chicago, Philadelphia, Boston, Washington, D.C., Denver, San Francisco, and more. Street and Smith had infiltrated the major urban centers of America's eastern half and even managed to extend a tentacle as far as California.[40]

Therein the series had an exceptionally long geographic reach and one that catered to what must have been a formidable sales demand. In short, *The Jesse James Stories* had the capability to put a westernized version of the outlaw—complete with illustrations—in the hands of an entire generation of boys in virtually every major city in the United States. This composite of James had little, if anything, to do with the Civil War, nor did this genera-tion of readers, save what came down to them from older relatives. Born in the 1880s and 1890s, the boys who wrote in for boxing gloves were tailor-made for a Wild West antihero because Indian wars, western boomtowns, and frontier spaces were the stuff of their collective childhood. Even Presi-dent Theodore Roosevelt, the scion of a patrician New York family, capi-talized on the cowboy mania; in office during the full run of *TJJS*, he had long ago tethered his public persona to the rugged badlands of the West and remade himself as a national political figure.[41]

With this in mind, it is not difficult to imagine how dime novels served to indoctrinate children with a specific understanding of Jesse James that neglected his wartime service or the broader role of guerrilla violence in the Civil War. Much like the United Daughters of the Confederacy strove to inculcate the generation of young southerners born in the aftermath of the war with the finer points of the Lost Cause to ensure its survival, dime novels functioned within the workings of a similar process. However, this process was not nearly as direct as the UDC; rather than Saint George Henry Rathbone or Colonel Prentiss Ingraham having carried out mis-sions to remove guerrilla memory from the war's legacy, the content of their dime novels mirrored broader cultural developments, such as outlaw histories and Wild West shows and, in doing so, simultaneously became a catalyst for them. Put another way, the owners of Street and Smith likely had no precise stake in determining whether or not Missouri guerrillas would be sanitized from mainstream memory narratives of the Civil War. Regardless, Street and Smith's products reflected contemporary changes in American society, culture, and literature that provided cover for parties that *were* interested in the excommunication of what James came to represent for the Civil War generation.

On July 10, 1901, Cole Younger strode through the gates of Stillwater Prison in Minnesota. After nearly fifteen years of captivity following the bungled Northfield Raid of 1876, he found himself a free man. Younger quickly gravitated back to old friends and even older haunts; before long, he returned to western Missouri, penned a memoir, and thrilled onlookers at Quantrill Men reunions. In this way, Younger directly participated in the movement of ex-bushwhackers detailed in chapters 3 and 4: the effort to reboot and integrate the "new" guerrilla memory into southern society as a way to ensure its memorial endurance. The relationship between this attempt at "self-southernization" and the process of westernization described above was inherently complicated. The formation of the short-lived Cole Younger and Frank James Wild West Company in 1903, however, unintentionally ratcheted up that complexity to an entirely new level.[42]

Wild West shows thrived in the late nineteenth- and early twentieth-century United States; they cashed in on Americans' interest in the rapidly vanishing frontier and stoked that interest by making their exhibitions as wild as possible. The best known of them belonged to William F. Cody—it traveled for several seasons, drew in large crowds, and generated a healthy revenue at its peak. Beneath the "big tops" of "Buffalo Bill's" traveling show, spectators could watch staged Indian raids and ghost dances, feats of daring horsemanship, reenactments of famous frontier battles, and feats of western-style marksmanship from no less than Annie Oakley. The combination proved so popular that Cody and company even toured Europe, delighting the Queen of England herself with hair-raising tales from the Far West of the former British colony.[43]

The Younger-James Wild West Show followed in this model; it toured the country during the 1903–1904 season. With stops from Maryland to Kentucky to Texas, one newspaper actually proclaimed it the biggest western act in the United States (with Buffalo Bill's renowned troupe of performers off wooing the crowns of Europe). A Chicago brewing magnate, Wally Hoffman, underwrote the operation. For $75,000, he purchased an extant exposition—props, performers, horseflesh, and some twenty-six railcars—formerly known as Buckskin Bill's Wild West Show and updated the marquee to reflect the involvement of Younger and James. From the beginning, all parties understood that James would participate as ringmaster and performer while Younger, still technically on parole, would take a far less public, managerial position.[44]

With that arrangement in mind, shows began with a street parade led by Frank James before entering a circuslike tent arena. There audiences witnessed "a series of episodic presentations of real life on the Western frontier." These scenes included "the perils of the pioneer, ever threatened by the merciless red men" and "the reckless sports of the roughest 'rough riders,' with the most vicious of all animals ridden." Better still, organizers touted the fact that such exploits were not performed "by a few trained actors" or "mere imitators of the deeds of others"; instead, paying customers could expect "hundreds of strong, forceful men who have gone through all those things in real life." According to the *Fort Worth Star-Telegram*, the exhibition boasted "cowboys and cowgirls," "Mexican vaqueros," and "Bands of Indians" who mimicked "attacks on stage coaches and settlers' cabins." Still another newspaper even declared that Younger and James held "great advantages" in managing such a show because they had so many "personal experiences in every phase of frontier life."[45]

In brief, the Younger-James Wild West Show embodied everything Americans had come to expect from a stylized version of the western frontier—as did its namesakes. Frank James, perhaps too enamored with his own press—by far the most attention he had received from the national media since his days in the James-Younger Gang—told one reporter that "the Wild West [Show] has done well this season and we are pleased with it. It has made a big success." In reality, problems beset the operation and its organizers at virtually every turn.[46]

During a May 6 performance in Chicago, an unidentified suspect absconded with Frank James's horse only moments before the mortified showmen needed to "sweep into the ring and announce that for the edification of the ladies and gentlemen his band of Indians would hold up the stage." In Louisville, Kentucky, "intense excitement reigned" as "a crowd of men and boys made an effort to take summary vengeance on William

Cook, an employee of the show." Apparently, Cook set off the would-be lynch mob by hurling a rock at a young boy attempting to sneak under the canvas; unfortunately, "the missile went wild" and struck an eleven-year-old girl named Lizzie Meyer, fracturing her skull. She reportedly fell on impact with a "ghastly wound in her head," and despite an emergency surgical procedure, the *Morning Herald* reported that the girl would "probably die." Two months later, when the show rolled into Fort Worth, Texas, to disperse for the winter, onlookers described it as "dilapidated." Rather deceptively, promoters had plastered the towns' walls with flashy play-bills and photographs of the show from a full year prior—before Younger, James, and their associates had run it into the ground. The show's financial ledger looked even worse—so bad, in fact, that the operation permanently disbanded in Texas. Performers claimed weeks' worth of back wages and the once-vaunted "red men" were summarily "returned to their reservation" per the terms of their release contract with the government.[47]

More problematic still for the pair of guerrillas-turned-showmen, the show's financial backers—the men who genuinely *owned* it—filed charges against Cole Younger for embezzlement. Younger's employers contended that he had secretly pilfered some $6,000 from the show's coffers, all while publicly claiming bankruptcy. These constituted very serious allegations for an ex-convict still bound by the terms of his parole. In his defense—one verified by Frank James—Younger fired back that the embezzlement charges amounted to nothing more than retaliation on the part of his old bosses. Younger, again with James in support, had previously brought suit against the show's owners for failing to properly equip the performers and for breach of contract. The issue really boiled down to a dispute concerning responsibility for driving away the packs of gamblers and conmen that constantly followed the show.[48]

Telegraph wires hummed. News outlets from Georgia to Boston to as far as South Dakota carried word of the allegations made against the former bandit. For readers old enough to remember Younger's outlaw days—that is, the reason why promoters had believed his name would attract crowds to begin with—this probably seemed like a trip back to the 1870s. Inaction on the part of prosecutors eventually cleared Younger's name of the embezzlement charges. The great irony of the scandal is that for once in his life, Younger, the internationally acclaimed highwayman, was almost certainly innocent on all counts and really *had* attempted to clean up the show by knocking the grafters from its tail. In any event, the damage was done.[49]

For guerrilla memory, the Younger-James Wild West Show served as an exclamation point for the sequence of westernization that outlaw histories and dime novels had already begun. Both ex-bushwhackers had involved themselves in the show because they needed money at a time when employment prospects for famous thieves and murderers did not rate well. So they turned to the one realm where their presence and "skills" still had value: a caricatured rendition of the Wild West. James himself told a reporter before the show started in 1903, "I think I see a chance to make some money with this show." "It made money last year," he continued, "and I see no reason why it will not do better this year." This brings two critical components of the story to light. First, the show itself—as a last means of sustenance—reveals the extent to which westernization had already taken hold of guerrilla memory. James, Younger, and their ilk had become geographical and cultural prisoners of a Wild West in which they had essentially no real-life experience. Second, in the process of capitalizing on this fabricated frontier identity, they actually reinforced the *collective* association of Missouri guerrillas with the West. Wild West shows afforded an audience the chance to see the action of their favorite books come alive—these people knew exactly what they wanted to watch and, more importantly, thanks to the conditioning of dime novels and outlaw histories, they knew what they *should* have seen in association with men such as Younger and James. Put another way, through Jesse James these literary mediums had constructed an allegorical "western bed" for guerrilla memory—one into which Younger and Jesse's own brother promptly and unassumingly jumped.[50]

Thus at precisely the same time the Quantrill Men had started making a concerted stand in their memoirs and at their reunions to reboot guerrilla memory and integrate themselves back into mainstream southern society, the advent of the Younger-James Wild West Show conceded—albeit based on false credentials—their proper placement in the West while the conditions of its abject failure only reinforced for turn-of-the-century Americans that these men were notorious for their associations with crime and corruption, *not* as veterans of the Civil War. This was a genuine turning point in the history of guerrilla memory; it signaled weakness to a broader conglomerate of eastern-based interests, north and south, with a commemorative agenda in mind that did not include the Quantrill Association or its checkered wartime record. Collectively, then, dime novels, outlaw histories, and Wild West shows allowed these interests to take advantage of current cultural developments to see ex-guerrillas ushered westward and out of what would become standard, traditional narratives of the war. The result of these ongoing efforts eventually led to a Missouri guerrilla sufficiently western to fill the role of cowboy-bandit on the silver screen and, as will be examined in full by chapter 8, initiated a whole new phase of commemorative sanitization for guerrilla memory in the twentieth century.

Even Mark Twain, writing during the apex of outlaw histories, appeared to have internalized a small dose of westernization. Indeed, the lasso-whirling horsemen encountered by his Marion Rangers strike one as being more at home under the Younger-James show's canvas than in the midst of a savage domestic conflict along the Kansas-Missouri border. This being the case, it is more than a little ironic that Twain himself was ultimately expelled from *Battles and Leaders* for failing to fit in with his more "regular" contemporaries.

EIGHT

Black Flags and Silver Screens

> Thousands entered the war, got just a taste of it, and then stepped out
> again permanently. These, by their very numbers, are respectable,
> and are therefore entitled to some sort of voice—not a loud one, but
> a modest one; not a boastful one, but an apologetic one. They ought
> not be allowed much space among better people—people who did
> something. I grant that; but they ought at least to be allowed to state
> why they didn't do anything, and also to explain the process by
> which they didn't do anything. Surely this kind of light must have a
> sort of value.
> —Mark Twain, "The Private History of a Campaign That Failed"

> I therefore claim to show, not how men think in myths, but how myths
> operate in men's minds without their being aware of the fact.
> —Claude Lévi-Strauss

A single scene from *Bandolero*—a 1968 film starring Jimmy Stewart, Dean
Martin, and Raquel Welch—offers an appropriate point of origin to begin
exploring the complicated relationship between guerrilla warfare, Civil
War memory, and motion pictures in the twentieth century. At this particular moment in the film, Stewart and Martin, who depict a pair of brothers, are attempting to explain why they had ended up on opposite sides
during the Civil War. Martin, whose character had favored the Confederacy, complains that his mother never understood or accepted his decision to ride with Quantrill. For his part, Stewart's character had stuck with
the Union and fought under Sherman during the infamous "March to the
Sea." And while Martin's character hints that both Sherman and Quantrill
had used total warfare to accomplish their equally destructive ends, Stewart replies that Sherman "was war" but Quantrill was "just mean."

Following the on-screen exchange, audiences are left with two conclusions. First, the two campaigns waged by the Williams—Quantrill and
Sherman—were inherently different. In many ways they seemed to represent different wars entirely. One was official, eastern, and thereby famil-

iar; the other was chaotic, western, and thus irregular. Second, in spite of this dichotomy (and in spite of Stewart's lecturing), Martin's role is a surprisingly sympathetic one. By comparison to his brother's service in the "regular" war, the integrity of which is never questioned or impugned, Martin's experience with Quantrill appears worthy in its own way when presented under the right set of wartime circumstances.

These takeaways notwithstanding, Hollywood has always found it difficult to determine just what constituted the proper blend of motive and intent to make irregular warfare culturally acceptable for moviegoers and the society they presumably represent. In fact, the merits of the Missouri bushwhacker and how to appropriately remember him were being debated on the silver screen as early as the 1920s, even before the arrival of "talkies." So the process of experimentation did not begin with *Bandolero*– far from it, as we shall see–and perhaps more importantly, it did not *end* in 1968, either.

Understanding the process through which guerrilla memory has and continues to evolve on the big screen is critical to understanding its place in Civil War memory and in American culture–because as mediums for communication go, film is in a class all its own. Like printed materials, movies have the ability to reach massive audiences. Unlike books, magazines, dime novels, and newspapers, however, movies are not typically constrained by matters of literacy or access. As such, they wield nearly unlimited power to share ideas and symbols; to praise and honor; to accuse and indict; to trumpet values; to endorse or attack ideologies; and to carve out legacies and regulate patterns of remembrance on a national scale. Even social media outlets such as Facebook and Twitter– each with millions upon millions of members at their metaphorical fingertips–can hardly begin to rival film's ability to tell a story and disseminate propaganda.

For example, in commemoration of the 150th anniversary of William C. Quantrill's 1863 raid on Lawrence, Kansas, a group of local enthusiasts in Missouri staged a digital reenactment via Twitter. Beginning on the morning of August 21, 2013 (from the hashtag "QR1863"), they spent hours portraying different characters involved on both sides of the massacre. They sent out hundreds of messages designed to re-create the massacre on a minute-by-minute basis. Thanks in no small part to entries such as "Cough, cough, BLAM! Blam! Blam! *wiping eyes* oh hell, I got one but they're getting away," the whole thing was well intended but largely fell flat. It lacked the ability to tell the story of the Lawrence Massacre—and thereby to alter how it could and should be remembered—in a coherent, stimulating, visually palatable, or timely manner. In short, the "tweet-enactment" could not overcome our limits of imagining. So despite a potential audience of millions, it failed to accomplish in several hours what a feature film might in just a few short moments.

But this communicative power does not exist in an intellectual vacuum. Even while films impart messages and influence how their viewers think about any range of topics or issues, dialectic exchange is ongoing. Movies are not conceived independently of their surroundings; they are shaped directly by the societies from whence they come. In plainer language, films perform two vital tasks at once on a continuous loop: (1) they influence how a society thinks, and (2) they reflect what a society—or at least a substantial segment of it—is actually thinking.

With this in mind, motion pictures become perhaps the best lens available for assessing the progress and impact of westernization, as discussed in chapter 7, on guerrilla memory. Here, much more so than outlaw histories or dime novels, the double-edged power of film is evident. At the same time films gradually began to absorb prior ideas about Missouri bushwhackers as icons of the Wild West (rather than significant players in the American Civil War), depictions of those bushwhackers as postwar western characters only amplified and spread the messages coming from those earlier sources. In this way, film has worked and continues to work not just as a mirror or mouthpiece for developments in Civil War remembrance but as a catalyst for it—a catalyst capable of reaching a widespread, previously untapped audience.[1]

So the story of the Missouri bushwhacker on film, as it pertains to our broader survey of guerrilla memory, has two entangled subplots. The first involves the gradual "writing out" of guerrillas from mainstream Civil War remembrance and commemoration. The second has to do with the themes and experiences actually portrayed in guerrilla pictures. As a result of their western setting, these characteristics have been, in many ways, unfairly discredited by many traditional Civil War historians. Because on the surface, when compared to Civil War standbys such as *Gone with the Wind* (1939), *The Horse Soldiers* (1959), or *Gettysburg* (1993), some of these movies do look like traditional westerns. But in reality, as should become clear throughout this chapter, they are simply vehicles for an unfamiliar rendition of the war and an unfamiliar debate over how to remember it—a rendition in which battle lines often fell across the homefront and in which the war itself did not always end in 1865.

The Origins of "Guerrilla Pictures": 1921–1940

Most moviegoers likely caught their first feature-length glimpses of a Missouri guerrilla on camera in *Jesse James under the Black Flag*, released by the Mesco Pictures Corporation in 1921.[2] Running a little more than an hour, the film itself was silent but supplemented with subtitles and accompanied by both a live orchestra and a live narrator. Despite his age (and having been woefully too old—decades so, at forty-six—for the part), Jesse James Jr., the only son of Jesse James, took on the role of his father during the Civil War and then as a postbellum social bandit.[3] The story begins when James's daughter (that is, the daughter of Jesse James Jr.'s character in the film) Lucille randomly encounters a man named Robert Standing and the couple falls hopelessly in love. Months later, Standing returns to ask for Lucille's hand in marriage—but her father will only consent to the union *after* Standing has learned the full, true version of the family's controversial history. Luckily for Robert Standing, Jesse James Jr. has just penned such a book.

As Standing begins to read, the audience is transported from James's home in the 1920s back to the 1860s. Missouri is described (in text) as a place where good men are forced to become guerrillas because of the outrages committed daily by Federal soldiers against innocent civilians. In response to such barbarism, Jesse James attempts to join William Quantrill's band of raiders; to prove his grievance against the Union government, James dramatically rips open his shirt for Quantrill and "Bloody Bill" Anderson to reveal a chest marked by several gruesome scars. James is made a guerrilla and swears allegiance to the black flag—a promise to seek no quarter and, more importantly, to give none. Quantrill, played by Harry Hall, equips James with a pair of revolvers and a gun belt, and sends him off with Cole Younger, portrayed by Harry Hoffman, to gather intelligence from a Union garrison.

What follows is a sequence in which James and Younger, with the help of daring southern women, sneak into the Federal headquarters, acquire information concerning the whereabouts of Union troops, and then report back to Quantrill. As a result of this espionage, Quantrill decides to lead a raid against the Union position in Plattsburg that very evening. The guerrillas—including James—mount an assault against Plattsburg; James is shown risking his own life to save a wounded comrade, yet another great victory for the guerrillas. Later, Cole Younger learns about General Order #11 while traveling home (the camera lingers on the full text of the order long enough for the audience to read it entirely) and is then forced to watch from a hilltop as a devilish-looking squad of Union soldiers set his mother's house ablaze. As the home is slowly incinerated, Wagner's "Flight of the Valkyries" echoes from the orchestra pit. Shortly thereafter, the plot jumps forward to 1865; Dave Poole and 129 other guerrillas have surrendered and sworn oaths of loyalty to the Union. Jesse James, who was at the time recovering from an injury, is pleased to think that he will now be able to live again as a normal, law-abiding citizen. As the rest of the film—which highlights James's rise to fame as leader of the James-Younger Gang, the disastrous Northfield Raid, and James's own demise at the hand of Robert Ford—makes clear, this was simply not to be. At the end of the story, the audience is returned to the present (the 1920s) just in time for Robert Standing to finish reading the book. He proclaims to see no reason why he should not marry Lucille and proposes to her on the spot as a grinning Jesse James Jr., again playing himself, looks on in approval.

From the outset, *Jesse James under the Black Flag* attempts to draw a clear distinction between the atrocities committed by Union forces in Missouri and the apparently legitimate reaction of pro-Confederate guerrillas such as Quantrill, Anderson, Younger, and eventually Jesse James. Throughout the film, then, guerrillas seem to have the full support of white Missourians—and especially women (such as two who help Jesse and Cole Younger spy on the Federal garrison, or Younger's own mother who is evicted by General Order #11 for supplying guerrillas in the field). But even as the domestic consequences of support for guerrilla warfare are revealed to the audience, rather than implicating guerrillas as the root cause of General Order #11, the film offers them as the only vehicle through which affected communities could fight back against abusive Federal forces. Moreover, the film is not shy about even highlighting African American support for

Quantrill's men. Servants, cooks, and mammies, who are presumably en-slaved, can frequently be seen rooting for, and in some cases aiding, the very guerrillas fighting to keep them in bondage. In this way, the film is unquestionably meant to justify guerrilla violence as a grassroots phenom-enon but also to establish the Missouri bushwhackers as having been—as a result of such justification—genuine Confederate characters and heroes.

With these ideas in mind, the scene in which Jesse James tears open his shirt is at once the most informative but perhaps also the most prob-lematic. Thanks in no small part to James's age, his flabby physique, and his thespian shortcomings (which abounded, unfortunately), the scene would almost certainly elicit laughter from a modern audience.[4] But in 1921, to rapidly aging veterans of the Civil War, it likely drew a more introspective response. The process of coming to terms with one's own physical scars—and how to justify one's own wartime activities, regular or guerrilla, Union or Confederate—was a serious affair, especially in an era that lacked any medical understanding of posttraumatic stress disorder. So however other veterans might answer this call to reflection, the film drives home here and whenever possible that James and his comrades had drawn blood for good reason and with clear conscience and that they should be remembered as such.

It is particularly problematic (though not surprising), then, that while the film does all it can to commemorate the Missouri bushwhacker as both legitimate and honorable, *Jesse James under the Black Flag* blatantly skips over several crucial, interconnected moments from James's life and the guerrilla war. The film does not depict—or even mention—the massa-cres at Lawrence (1863) or Centralia (1864). Nor does it portray the schism between William C. Quantrill and "Bloody Bill" Anderson or either of their violent deaths. More than any others, these two guerrilla chieftains had the greatest influence on James as an individual bushwhacker and on the guerrilla insurgency in Missouri as a whole. Put another way, it is impossible to walk away from the film unaware that it frequently glosses over the very wartime activities of guerrillas that are so fervently stamped with approval—the actions it uses to foster memories of the guerrilla as a champion of the Confederacy in Missouri.

Those who dissented from this notion of the noble bushwhacker would have to wait nearly twenty years for a rebuttal picture—but when one ar-rived, it had sound, a million-dollar budget, and star power.

In 1940, with Hollywood veteran Raoul Walsh at the helm and rising stars like John Wayne, Roy Rogers, and Claire Trevor, *Dark Command* was released by Republic Productions.[5] The film's decidedly antiguerrilla narrative is prefaced by an introduction that draws an immediate distinction between the versions of the Civil War experienced by residents of the East versus the Border West: "In those years, 1859 and on, in the dusk before the nation plunged into the dark night of civil warfare, the plains of Kansas were an earlier battleground. Down from the north, down to Kansas; up from the south, up to Kansas, came hordes—each bent on voting the territory into the Union as its own. The battle cry of the day was—"'On to Kansas.'" As the picture begins, viewers are introduced to Will Cantrell, played by Walter Pidgeon. Cantrell is a well-liked schoolmaster from Ohio vying for the affections of Miss Mary McCloud (portrayed by Claire Trevor), the daughter of a wealthy southern banker in Lawrence, Kansas. As the plot progresses, audiences learn that the woman Cantrell passes off as a housekeeper is actually his mother—more important still, the pair relocated to Kansas in an attempt to escape from their family's less-than-sterling reputation back in Ohio.[6] Without question, the character of Will Cantrell is based on guerrilla chieftain William C. Quantrill (who, in reality, did come from Canal Dover, Ohio, and, it was often reported, however erroneously, also hailed from a line of brigands and malefactors).

Soon after Cantrell's situation is revealed, Bob Seton, played by John Wayne, makes his first on-screen appearance; he is a former Texas cowpoke, wandering the West in search of both home and wife. In short order, Cantrell and Seton are competing for the job of town marshal in Lawrence and for the hand of Mary McCloud. Seton eventually wins both the job and the girl, while the losses push Cantrell to outlawry. Posing as an abolitionist, Cantrell begins forcibly freeing slaves in Kansas—and then driving them right across the Missouri border to resell into bondage. When word of John Brown's botched raid at Harpers Ferry reaches Lawrence, Cantrell decides that slave running is too risky and turns instead to illegal firearms.[7] As Cantrell changes his business, the war breaks out and regional divides are again emphasized: "While armies drew their battle lines in the east, like a swarm of locusts over Kansas, came hordes of Guerrillas, loyal to no flag . . . following but one lure—the promise of pillage. In Kansas these men found an Empire to loot . . . and few to defend it." With the war as a convenient backdrop, Cantrell forms a band of criminals to "live off the fat of the land." By sheer coincidence, they capture a shipment of Confederate uniforms and use them to pose as a "detachment" of the Confederate Army. His southern sympathies notwithstanding, Seton raises a militia to stop Cantrell and his men from raiding Lawrence and succeeds in gunning down Cantrell. Some of the town is torched, but the militia chases off most of Cantrell's men and Seton joyfully hints at going back to Texas with Mary McCloud, his new wife-to-be.

The implications concerning regionalism and wartime legitimacy underscored by *Dark Command* are as difficult to overlook now as they were in 1940. Both during the film's introduction and when the outbreak of civil war is announced, audiences are reassured of two things. First, Kansas— and by affiliation Missouri—are isolated from the rest of the Civil War. These are not the places where brave men line up to do battle. Instead, the Border West is where unsavory men, and hordes of guerrillas, come to plunder on the outskirts of civilization. Second, the guerrillas prowling these western outposts are at odds with broader, more familiar narratives of the war. From the moment they organize, Cantrell and his guerrillas are depicted as illegitimate and fraudulent; rather than grassroots heroes forced to take up arms in a desperate political struggle, they are presented as having lacked any true ideological devotion to the Confederacy. This accusation is reinforced twice over by the idea that a real southerner, Bob Seton, a native Texan and presumed southern sympathizer, not only proves himself to be more manly and honorable than Cantrell— but Seton also dispatched Cantrell on behalf of pro-Unionist Kansans. In short, Cantrell's motives and behavior are so despicable that the effort to halt them could create a bridge between Confederates and Unionists.

Guerrillas Raid "Ike's America": 1946–1965

December 25, 1946, marked both the Christmas holiday and the stateside release of *Renegade Girl* by Screen Guild Productions. Featuring noir starlet Ann Savage as Jean Shelby, the film centers on the tragic tale of the Shelby family—avowed Confederate sympathizers in war-torn Missouri, a place where, according to scrolling text shown to viewers as the film begins, "partisan and guerilla warfare" was "vicious and widespread." Jean Shelby is a scout for William C. Quantrill and his guerrilla band, which includes Jean's brother, Bob Shelby. Through the conversation of Union officers, audiences are informed that the intelligence Jean provides is what has allowed Quantrill (played by Ray Corrigan) to become so powerful; without her help, they contend, the guerrillas would be far less effective. That being the case, Jean Shelby is soon after captured by a Federal patrol and taken into custody while, simultaneously, a disgruntled Indian named White Cloud is helping the Union government track down her brother. Jean learns of the plot to arrest Bob, escapes from her Federal captors, and rushes to warn him and the rest of her family; her efforts are in vain and White Cloud kills Bob Shelby.

In retribution for Bob's death, Quantrill wants to kill Fred Raymond, a captain in the Union army and the man Jean Shelby secretly loves. She is able to stop Quantrill from hanging Raymond by pretending to take him prisoner. Soon after, she divulges to Raymond that she has done everything possible—from scouting and spying to seducing men—to help Quantrill and the guerrillas. In the meantime, White Cloud murders the rest of the Shelby family, and Jean receives a near-fatal knife wound trying to chase him off. Captain Raymond saves Jean and takes her to the home of another southern family to heal. During her recovery, a few guerrillas come to visit Jean; through them she learns that the war is over and Quantrill is dead. Rather than surrendering, though, Jean's visitors inform her of their plan to keep on fighting as guerrillas from the hill country and solicit her to start working again as a scout. "We got a lot of scores to settle," they offer, "with Yankees we've got a right to hate." Because of her wartime association with Quantrill, Jean is considered an outlaw by the government and decides to join the renegade guerrillas so long as they promise to help her hunt down White Cloud. Eventually, the band loses sight of its political motives, turns blatantly to crime, and slowly unravels as each man attempts—unsuccessfully—to seduce Jean. By the end of the film, Jean is reunited with Captain Raymond, and the audience is primed for a happy ending. But she refuses to quit her vendetta with White Cloud and, in the process of killing him, is mortally wounded. Jean Shelby dies in Captain Raymond's arms after admitting to him that choosing revenge over love had been the wrong decision.

While *Jesse James under the Black Flag* included women as secondary participants in guerrilla warfare, the character of Jean Shelby is undoubtedly a step toward a full-on female guerrilla. However, because so much of the plot takes place after the war and Jean is never directly involved in a guerrilla raid, the idea is never fully developed (and would not be until the late 1950s). Even so, two major, interconnected messages course through the plot of *Renegade Girl*. The first of these ideas is that the actions of Confederate guerrillas such as William Quantrill and the Shelbys—Bob and Jean—had been warranted by southern sympathizers. Throughout the film Union soldiers, with the exception of Captain Raymond, are presented as disruptive intruders; they are the sort of men who would gather intelligence from the devious White Cloud. On the other hand, Quantrill's men, with one or two notable exceptions, are portrayed as unsophisticated and even affable. Only once the war has ended and Quantrill has been slain does the plot begin to offer a critique of the guerrillas—but this only comes once they have stopped actually fighting as guerrillas and begun the transformation into common outlaws. Rephrased, the film offers up both a justification of the Missouri bushwhacker in wartime *and* a new set of limits on how long his behavior would remain justified afterward.

The second idea underlying the film's story is clearly an outgrowth of the first. At some point, as the plot makes abundantly clear through its calamitous ending, even guerrillas such as Jean Shelby and William Quantrill (though it was obviously too late for the deceased himself) had to see the benefits of postwar reconciliation and move on with their lives just like veterans of the regular war. This is an important turning point in guerrilla memory on film because it constituted a stark interpretive break from tropes and moral lessons found in *Jesse James under the Black Flag* and *Dark Command*. The former, which hints that Jesse James had been forced to violent means during and after the war by a tyrannical federal government, essentially sought to legitimize his service and simultaneously relieve him of culpability for the bloodshed it produced. The latter, coming just six years before *Renegade Girl*, reverses that assignment of blame by taking clear aim at the motives and reputation of William Quantrill (and by default his men). But the use of Jean Shelby's unnecessary death as a cautionary tale for both sides of Missouri's savage conflict and subsequent memorial debate—the lesson being that each needed to forgive and forget before it was too late—carves out a thoughtful, thematic middle ground that would become more and more prevalent in guerrilla movies as the twentieth century progressed.

A picture produced by Universal-International in 1950 called *Kansas Raiders* simultaneously fused and expanded on themes found in all three previous films. Starring Audie Murphy, Tony Curtis, and Brian Donlevy, the film chronicles how five young men from Missouri—Frank and Jesse James, Cole and Jim Younger, and Kit Dalton—fell in with guerrilla leader William C. Quantrill. The story begins with a montage of the regular war; viewers see men in blue and gray charging with muskets in hand, horses on the charge, cannons booming, and houses exploding. But then the narrator announces that the Civil War was not fought by the Union and Confederate armies alone. "There was a war-bred outlaw army of guerrillas masquerading under the flags of both sides," the voice explains. These men, unlike the regular troops of just moments prior, killed, burned, and pillaged for their own "private gain." And the very worst of these fraudulent, would-be soldiers, the narrator makes clear, are the men who fight under the "ominous black flag of William Clarke Quantrill."

The plot then shifts to Jesse James (played by Audie Murphy), Frank James, the Younger brothers, and Kit Dalton (portrayed by Tony Curtis) trying to ride through Lawrence, Kansas, in 1861–62 on their way to join up with Quantrill. In the process, they are captured by Unionist guerrillas called "Red Legs" and sentenced to be hanged. Just before the mob can execute them, a Union captain who disapproves of irregular violence and vigilante justice releases them and warns James not to join up with the guerrillas. The next day, as they search for Quantrill's headquarters, James and company rescue a woman on a runaway wagon—she asks if they are going to join Quantrill and his "Butcher Brigade." Eventually, they do find Quantrill (Brian Donlevy), who sports a full Confederate colonel's uniform, and are sworn into his company.

From the outset of their time with Quantrill, the woman from the wagon, who turns out to be Kate Quantrill, the guerrilla chieftain's wife, tries to warn Jesse James that her husband is a bloodthirsty murderer, not a real soldier. On his first raid, James is horrified to see unarmed men gunned down, men being shot in the back, and prisoners being murdered in cold blood. At this point, he realizes that Kate was right about her husband—these guerrilla raids are not *real* warfare. James refuses to ride on Quantrill's next raid because, as he tells Quantrill himself, the guerrillas are doing the same thing to other innocent families that had prompted himself, along with the Youngers and Kit Dalton, to join their ranks in the first place. When the rest of the bushwhackers are gone, Kate tells Jesse that all of this violence is just part of Quantrill's sick dream of "playing war."

Shortly thereafter, Quantrill's band—riding under a black flag donning his name—launch an assault against Lawrence, Kansas. James is again horrified to see that Quantrill has no interest in controlling his men or making them behave like real soldiers; he kills Quantrill's second-in-command, Bill Anderson, for mistreating a captured Union captain who had previously saved James's life.[8]

In the aftermath of the Lawrence Massacre, Quantrill's band is hunted by Union troops and gradually falls apart. The men announce that when Robert E. Lee turned against Quantrill, they decided it was time for them to quit, too. With only the Jameses, Youngers, and Dalton left under his command, Quantrill is blinded in a skirmish with Union cavalrymen at the very house where Jesse James first realized that Quantrill was not a genuine Confederate soldier. The guerrillas escape, but Frank James notes that Quantrill's blindness—the same injury that had befallen the Union captain in Lawrence—seemed like a judgment on him. As the Federals close in and try to capture Quantrill, the wounded guerrilla chief appears delusional to the end: he tells James and Kate that there are still glorious days and armies ahead of him. By the end of the film, however, Quantrill essentially confesses and apologizes to James for his evil deeds and sacrifices himself so that James and the others can escape. Before the credits appear, the narrator informs the audience that all five of the ex-guerrillas will turn to crime—and that their "warped lives" were "a heritage from their teacher, William Clarke Quantrill."

Throughout *Kansas Raiders*, an unmistakable dichotomy is established that differentiates Jesse James and his friends from Quantrill, Anderson, and the rest of the guerrillas. Quantrill and his men are clearly only using the war as an opportunity to murder innocent civilians and loot their burned-out homes. The guerrillas kill indiscriminately, they shoot men in the back, and worst of all, they seem to *enjoy* the pointless bloodshed. James and his companions, however, cite more personal, understandable grievances for their desire to take revenge against the Union. Their homes have been burned, their parents murdered, and their communities destroyed—so they understand almost immediately that a store-bought colonel's uniform and ceremonial salutes cannot make Quantrill and his men legitimate soldiers, nor can the war be used to justify the atrocities they commit in the name of the Confederate cause. As was the case with *Jesse James under the Black Flag* and *Renegade Girl*, the film implies that worthwhile motives for guerrillas did exist. These motives are represented by James's story in which his mother is assaulted, his father hanged, and their home burned by Unionist guerrillas. But also in keeping with *Dark Command*, *Kansas Raiders* presents Quantrill (and the majority of his men) as having no legitimate reason to raid. Instead, the guerrillas are cast as outsiders—as an element of the war that needed to be culled and isolated from accepted, mainstream narratives of the regular rank and file.

But while the divergent relationship between Jesse James and William Quantrill is informative, the relationship between Kate Quantrill and Jesse James is even more interesting. Over the course of the film, the pair does (rather predictably) fall in love, but Kate's warnings to Jesse concerning Quantrill's true motives and what will happen if Jesse and his friends do not escape from the guerrilla life are especially telling. By way of their conversations about Quantrill and through her own backstory, Kate communicates to Jesse that prolonged exposure to men such as Quantrill and Anderson will eventually result in his own corruption. She cautions James that there is a "point of no return," after which his life will be ruined and he will be just as bloodthirsty, delusional, and evil as Quantrill himself. In short, Kate Quantrill suggests that her own husband is an example of guerrilla warfare's power to make men defective.[9] Despite these warnings, Jesse James and Kate Quantrill cannot bring themselves to leave "Colonel" Quantrill once he is wounded—and Kate's prophecy is heralded as truth by the film's closing moment when the narrator describes the lives of James and his comrades as permanently "warped."

Kansas Raiders introduced filmgoers to two new components of guerrilla movies: Kate Quantrill and the notion that guerrilla warfare carried within it the ability to corrupt and destroy. It would not be long before this condemnation of Quantrill's company was echoed in another picture—or before audiences met up again with Kate Quantrill, albeit in a very different, much more masculine light.

Just a year after *Kansas Raiders*, filmgoers got another unpleasant portrait of William Quantrill and guerrilla warfare in *Red Mountain*—a picture released by Paramount in 1951 starring Hollywood heavyweights Alan Ladd, Lizabeth Scott, and Arthur Kennedy. The plot of *Red Mountain* picks up in 1865; audiences are informed that the Confederacy is dying in the South but that in "the vast no-man's land of the West," Confederate fortunes are still alive. In this ambiguous, clearly detached western space, the possibility of southern victory is buoyed by "General William Quantrell"– a "Confederate hero, fanatical soldier, and master of guerilla [*sic*] warfare." Over the course of the film, however, moviegoers learn that Quantrell's claim to Confederate hero status is fraudulent and unwarranted.

Much of the film's story revolves around the relationship between Confederate captain Brett Sherwood–played by Alan Ladd–and a former Confederate soldier named Lane Waldren–portrayed by Arthur Kennedy. Waldren is blamed for a killing in a Colorado Territory town actually committed by Sherwood. Nearly half of the movie involves Waldren trying to capture and turn in Sherwood to clear his own name and Sherwood eluding capture but then rescuing Waldren from various injuries and encounters. During this back-and-forth segment of the plot, audiences also meet Waldren's wife, Chris (Lizabeth Scott); she is not shy about sparring with Sherwood over his inability to admit that the Confederacy has been defeated. On one hand, Sherwood defends the Confederacy–and guerrillas such as Quantrell–because he is from Georgia and witnessed Sherman's destructive March to the Sea. On the other, Chris contends that she witnessed firsthand the raid made by Quantrell against Lawrence, Kansas, in 1863, and she is disgusted by Sherwood's comparison. She wins the argument by forcing Sherwood to admit that slavery was a problem–but in making the admission Sherwood adds that the North should have left the South to sort it out for themselves.

The plot turns dramatically when Sherwood finally meets up with William Quantrell and his men. Sherwood thinks Quantrell is "one of the few legends the Confederacy has left" and is intent on joining the guerrilla chieftain and his outfit. But almost immediately, Sherwood's expectations for Quantrell begin to crumble. The Confederate captain from Georgia is stunned to see Quantrell enlisting bands of untrained Indians among his raiders, and he is even more disturbed to learn that the so-called general allows these would-be soldiers to scalp their Union victims. As filmgoers watch Sherwood gradually realize that Quantrell is not dedicated to the Confederate cause, Chris erases any doubt by chastising Sherwood for ever having thought that a man such as Quantrell or his guerrillas had been fighting for the South. Quantrell, it is revealed, simply wants to establish a western empire for himself. Once the Union wins the war, he plans to employ thousands of Indians in a private army against a tired and depleted federal government.[10]

Sherwood decides that Quantrell must be stopped; he leaves the Wald-rens, Lane and Chris, in a cave with guns and ammunition on Red Moun-tain. Quantrell is determined to capture the Waldrens because he believes they know the location of a gold mine that he can use to fund his empire building. Back in a nearby town, Sherwood gathers men to stop Quantrell, and they, along with a late-arriving company of Union cavalrymen, res-cue Chris and run off Quantrell's Indian mercenaries. Lane Waldren is killed in the fighting and the guerrilla general attempts to flee. Sherwood tracks down Quantrell and kills him in a final, dramatic duel. As the film concludes, the symbolism of reunion presented to audiences is unmistak-able. Chris informs Sherwood that Lee has surrendered to Grant and that the war is finally over. Pleased by this, Sherwood tells Chris—whom he will presumably marry with Lane conveniently out of the way—that the North and the South are now "one country again." This dialogue only reinforces the partnership between an honorable Confederate soldier and Union forces that defeated Quantrell's personal bid for power in the West. Like *Kansas Raiders* and *Dark Command,* these points underscore the idea that William Quantrill was not a genuine Confederate soldier. Moreover, the intended correlation between Quantrill, guerrillas, and a western "no-man's land" bolsters the argument that irregular warfare was not part of the "real," eastern-based story of the Civil War. Reconciliation between North and South, it seems, included the ability of both sides to isolate and jettison their unwanted baggage to the western borderlands. And on this note, the film ends with Sherwood quoting Abraham Lincoln's 1858 "House Divided" speech to Chris as "our president" and the camera angle coming to rest on a waving American flag.

In 1953 Republic Pictures released *The Woman They Almost Lynched,* star-ring a host of familiar B-movie actors and actresses led by Audrey Totter, Joan Leslie, and John Lund. From the outset, posters for the film prom-ised moviegoers three things: excitement, female starlets, and guerrillas. To all three of those ends, one of the more prominent taglines read: "Kate Quantrill . . . rode like a man . . . fought like a man . . . killed like a man . . . and LOVED like the beautiful woman she was!" (As should be obvious, this version of Kate Quantrill would not be much like the wise and caring figure from *Kansas Raiders.*) The film unfolds in a fictional locale along the Missouri-Arkansas border with the rather uninspiring moniker, "Border Town." Border Town is unique, however, because residents—led by a surly female mayor—enforce a strict neutrality policy concerning support for the Union or the Confederacy. Because the town sits half in Confederate and half in Union territory, any attempt to rile up political unrest is halted quickly by a mob with rope in hand. Border Town is able to maintain this precarious position thanks to two lead mines, one on the Arkansas side of town, the other on the Missouri side, which are used to appease both armies and keep their soldiers at least five miles out of town at all times.

The vagueness of Border Town—much like the "no-man's land" of *Red Mountain*—is symbolic and worthy of immediate consideration. To be sure, the town is ambiguously named. But more important is how it falls along a fault line, or gray area of sorts, between the Union and the Confederacy. As such, it stands in appropriately for an untold number of small towns from the Border West that collectively formed the guerrilla theater. Because the town refuses to choose sides (and thereby shuns the regular war altogether), residents are faced with a complete breakdown of law and order that culminates with the invasion of irregulars such as William Quantrill, Cole Younger, and Jesse James. In other words, Border Town becomes a case study as to where guerrilla warfare could and should exist; rather than a primary feature of the Civil War in the East, it belonged in a poorly defined "western" space that conveniently quarantined it from mainstream renditions of the war.

The plot of the film revolves mainly around two female characters, Sally Maris and Kate Quantrill, portrayed by Totter and Leslie, respectively, as they arrive simultaneously in Border Town. Throughout the course of their interactions there with William Quantrill and his men, the film lays bare why the Missouri bushwhacker warranted such commemorative isolation. Two years prior, the audience is informed, Kate—then known as Kitty McCoy—had been engaged to Bill Maris, Sally's brother. Then one day Quantrill rode into town, kidnapped McCoy, and married her, and she gradually transformed into one of the worst, and certainly the most venomous, of his guerrilla outfit. By contrast, Sally Maris is an upstanding woman. As the story unfolds, she and Lance Horton, a resident of Border Town with a deadly secret, fall in love.

In reality, Horton is a Confederate captain using his position in Border Town to smuggle much-needed lead to his nearby troops. So while Sally Maris and Kate Quantrill feud over the latter's betrayal of Bill Maris, William Quantrill threatens to expose Horton as a violator of the draco-

nian neutrality policy unless he agrees to supply the guerrillas with lead
as well. Horton initially refuses; he cites his dedication to the Confederate
cause and accuses Quantrill of being a common hood. Some of the guerrillas take issue with Horton's claim and defend their Confederate credentials, but Horton rebukes them sharply. He insists that they are not, and
never were, real Confederates; even the venerable Robert E. Lee had dis-
owned them, according to Horton. The film eventually climaxes as Sally
Maris and Kate Quantrill fight a duel in the street, Lance Horton is forced
at gunpoint to take William Quantrill to the lead mines, and the mayor
of Border Town calls in Union troops to get rid of Quantrill once and for
all. When the regular soldiers arrive, the guerrillas scatter; Kate, still fum-
ing from her defeat in the aforementioned showdown, is abandoned by
her husband.

The guerrillas, through their own behavior—such as Quantrill's decision
to flee without his wife—are presented as corrupt, dishonorable, and self-
serving. And at no point in *The Woman They Almost Lynched* is guerrilla warfare considered legitimate by anyone other than the guerrillas themselves.
In this sense, the film follows heavily in the tradition of *Dark Command.*
Only Jesse James, as in most of *Kansas Raiders,* is made to seem the exception, the implication being that because of his tender age, he had not yet
been corrupted by the other members of Quantrill's band. Because of the
manner in which the film differentiates the positive and negative qualities
of William Quantrill and Lance Horton (much like Brett Sherwood in *Red
Mountain*), it can best be described as prosouthern for its depiction of Horton, a true Confederate, as an icon of honor and manly virtue. That said,
because Federal interference represented a better alternative for the residents of Border Town than further dealings with Quantrill, even regular
Union troops are looked on with more favor than the guerrillas.

In an act of kindness, Sally Maris helps Kate Quantrill hide from the
Union troops that burst into Border Town looking for William Quantrill
and company. It is revealed that Kate's connection with Quantrill and his
men gradually made her a defective woman. Exposure to guerrilla warfare twisted her once gentle, sweet, overly feminine disposition into a bitter, bloodthirsty, manly one. Kate herself admits to Sally once the pair begins to reconcile that her hatred for Quantrill slowly consumed her and
had eventually made her just like him; only then, with her transformation
from normal woman to would-be, outcast male complete, could she have

married and tolerated the one who had kidnapped her from Border Town in the first place. Once liberated from her husband, though, Kate Quantrill regains part of her former self and, as if to prove it, helps rescue both Sally Maris and Lance Horton from the Border Town hangman.

Aside from the obvious fact that one lives and one dies, the juxtaposition of Jean Shelby and Kate Quantrill is illuminating. In *Renegade Girl*, Jean Shelby's life is gradually ruined by hostilities *left over* from the guerrilla war. Her choice not to move on after the war ultimately spurs her demise, but the film and its message are far from an indictment of irregular warfare while the war was ongoing. In *The Woman They Almost Lynched*, spectators watch Kate Quantrill brood and brawl; they see her spearhead a guerrilla raid and gun down an injured Union officer. Thereby, rather ironically, at the very same moment the first true, full-on female bushwhacker gallops into the picture, her story is used to underline the inherent evil and corruptive power of guerrilla violence.

As the film draws to a close, Lance Horton rides proudly back into Border Town decked in full Confederate regalia. The mayor and townspeople are outraged that he would so blatantly trample the neutrality policy, and Horton, to avoid yet another lynch mob, happily informs all of them that the war is over. The whole town breaks into a rendition of Dixie, and Lance and Sally agree to move farther south (thus leaving Border Town for a destination more in keeping with his regular Confederate status) to presumably live happily ever after. But in addition to the storybook ending, audiences are left with the unmistakable notion that regular troops—from either side of the conflict—had been spurred to fight by understandable, credible motives, and that guerrilla warfare, as previously seen in *Kansas Raiders* and as now hammered home by the plight and metamorphosis of Kate Quantrill, harbored an inherently *unnatural*, uncommendable quality with the ability to *infect* and corrupt.

Released in 1958 by the Allied Artists Pictures Corporation, *Quantrill's Raiders* merged many of the anti-bushwhacker themes found in *Dark Command*, *Red Mountain*, *Kansas Raiders*, and *The Woman They Almost Lynched* into a single narrative. The film featured several industry veterans—Steve Cochran, Will Wright, Leo Gordon, and Diane Brewster—and revolves around the Lawrence Massacre of August 21, 1963. As had become typical of guerrilla pictures in the 1950s, it began with a narrated introduction meant to catch moviegoers up on the "other" Civil War that had played out in the Border West:

In the dark days of the Civil War, guerrilla raiders led by William Clark [*sic*] Quantrill terrorized the Kansas-Missouri border: looting, burning, killing. Quantrill fought for the South, with a savagery that shocked even his own allies. Many southern officers considered him little better than an outlaw, using the war as an excuse for pillage and murder. But in the desperate urgency of the conflict, Quantrill and his hard-riding band were useful to the Confederacy and he was often given missions of military importance. His fury reached its peak when he attacked the U.S. military arsenal at Lawrence, Kansas. This is the story of events leading up to that raid.[11]

As the plot goes, the film's protagonist, a man named Davis (played by Steve Cochran) posing as a Union veteran turned horse broker comes to Lawrence, Kansas, in 1863 to deliver orders from Confederate general Sterling Price to guerrilla commander William C. Quantrill (portrayed by Leo Gordon). In Lawrence, Judge Wood (played by Will Wright) is immediately suspicious of Davis, and the town's newly formed vigilance committee begins to track his whereabouts and business dealings. In the meantime, Davis—whose real name is Captain Alan Westcott, CSA—reaches Quantrill and delivers Price's orders: the guerrillas are to strike and destroy a Union arsenal in Lawrence as a prelude to Price himself leading a Confederate invasion of Kansas. Westcott bluntly informs Quantrill that this is a "legitimate military mission," which means that no looting or wanton killing will be tolerated. When Westcott exits the scene, Quantrill declares that he will loot whatever and kill whomever he wants, regardless of what Westcott or Price has to say about it.

In the process of contacting Quantrill, delivering orders, and then planning the raid, Westcott (who is still known as Davis to the people of Lawrence) gradually falls in love with Sue Walters, proprietor of the boardinghouse in Lawrence and foster mother to a young boy named Joel, whom Davis also befriends. As romance develops between Sue and Davis, Judge Wood warns Davis not to break Sue's heart—she had been previously engaged to a man in Lawrence named Charley Hart who turned out to be a criminal. (Audiences later learn that Charley Hart was none other than William C. Quantrill. These prewar events apparently had much to do with Quantrill's vendetta against the town.) As the time for the raid approaches, Westcott becomes increasingly worried that Quantrill will use the mission as an excuse to butcher innocent civilians and is especially concerned about what might happen to Sue and Joel. With that in mind, he orders Quantrill to stay out of Lawrence permanently and decides to oversee the raid himself.

Those plans all change when an unfortunate run-in with the Cheyenne outs Westcott to the authorities in Lawrence. In the process of being captured, he learns that the contents of the arsenal are being transported elsewhere. Westcott breaks out of jail to stop Quantrill from needlessly attacking the town, but the guerrilla leader vows to strike Lawrence anyway. To keep Westcott from interfering with the raid, the guerrillas hold him hostage, only to have Kate Clark (played by Gale Robbins) help Westcott escape in time to warn Judge Wood and the residents of Lawrence about Quantrill's plan. Westcott's intelligence report allows the town to prepare for the attack, and Quantrill's force—only about thirty or forty men—is easily repelled. While trying to make a second charge against the fortified defenders of Lawrence, Quantrill is gunned down and killed by Westcott.[12] Westcott, who is now known to everyone in town, including Sue, Joel, and Judge Wood, as a Confederate officer, is arrested and taken into custody by the Federal garrison. According to Judge Wood, however, Westcott will only be held prisoner until the war ends, at which time, it is made clear, he will return to Lawrence, marry Sue, and become Joel's surrogate father.

Like the other films before it, the driving force behind the plot of *Quantrill's Raiders* is the idea that William C. Quantrill and the guerrilla war he conducted required complete detachment from the rest of the "official" or "legitimate" Civil War. Quantrill is presented as a fraudulent Confederate soldier. Despite wearing a Confederate uniform (the only guerrilla to do so, in fact), he cares only about revenge, murder, and plunder, not the Confederate cause. This is made clear by Quantrill's motivations for raiding, by his disregard for official Confederate orders, by his unnecessarily violent methods, and by his decision to raid Lawrence for the sole purpose of butchery even after the contents of the arsenal (which did not exist in historical fact) had been moved. In contrast, Alan Westcott, even as a spy whom viewers never see in a Confederate uniform, is depicted as a genuine soldier. Westcott's concerns are for the Confederate cause, not plunder or revenge against civilians, and his concern for the well-being of innocent bystanders in Lawrence underscores the honorable nature of his character.

Perhaps even more informative than the comparison between Quantrill and Westcott is the relationship between Quantrill and his companion, Kate Clark. On meeting Westcott, it is immediately clear to the audience that Kate likes him more than Quantrill—and she underlines for Quantrill the differences between him and a real "gentleman" such as Westcott. Later in the film, Kate warns Westcott not to trust Quantrill and suggests that the guerrilla leader will kill Westcott the moment he stops being useful. Kate even attempts to seduce Westcott and asks him to help her escape from Quantrill. When Westcott tries to cancel the raid and is taken prisoner by the guerrillas, Kate tells Quantrill that both the Yankees *and* the Rebels will hunt him down and hang him; he responds to her claims that he is not a legitimate soldier with a fist to the face. When most of Quantrill's men have left to attack Lawrence, Kate helps free Westcott and is killed by a guerrilla in the process of aiding Westcott's escape.

As the film concludes, audiences are left with three lessons concerning the place of the Border West's guerrilla warfare in the Civil War. First, Quantrill was not a legitimate Confederate soldier and should be isolated from "true" narratives of the Civil War. Not only are his credentials undermined by the comparison to Westcott, but whatever justification remained with Quantrill is stricken from the record by the notion that Kate Clark was willing to die to stop him from carrying out another senseless atrocity against innocent civilians. Second, either side—the Union or the Confederacy—represented a better choice than the guerrillas. The plot of the film never really takes sides with either cause. On one hand, Westcott goes out of his way to save Unionists in Lawrence; on the other hand, Unionists in Lawrence go out of their way to welcome the Confederate captain back to live among them once the war is over. The symbolic union of Sue Walters and Westcott shows that the two warring sides could eventually be reconciled—but men such as Quantrill required extermination, both in life and in narratives of the war. Third, audiences are notified early in the film that Joel, the young boy who adopts Westcott as his role model, lost both of his real parents in a guerrilla raid. Thus, *Quantrill's Raiders* emphasizes more than any of its predecessors not only that proponents of irregular warfare lacked acceptable motives, but also that irregular violence belonged in the borderlands because it could not be contained and controlled like regular violence and therefore did not differentiate its victims by sex *or* age.

Arizona Raiders, released by Columbia Pictures in 1965, tells the sympathetic story of Clint and Willie, two young Missourians who join up with

William C. Quantrill *after* the Lawrence Massacre of August 1863. The men, played by Audie Murphy and Ben Cooper, respectively, join the guerrilla ranks in response to murdered family members and destroyed homes in Missouri (carnage appended by implication, but never explicitly attributed, to the aftermath of General Order #11). Following Quantrill's death early in the film, Clint and Willie are arrested by a Federal captain specifically assigned to track down and eliminate Confederate guerrillas. At trial, Captain Andrews (played by Buster Crabbe) speaks up on behalf of Clint and Willie; he understands that they had not taken part in the Lawrence Massacre and admits that the destruction of their homes and families had left the men with little choice but to become guerrillas. His help notwithstanding, Clint and Willie are sent to prison. Soon after, when former members of Quantrill's band turn to banditry in Arizona Territory, Captain Andrews—recently instated as head of the Arizona Rangers—recruits Clint and Willie to help stop the outlaws' spree. As the plot unfolds, audiences are treated to gunfights, Indian encounters, dancing saloon girls, and eventually a final showdown between Clint and the leader of the guerrillas-turned-outlaws, a man simply named Montana.

On the surface—despite its discourse regarding the Lawrence Massacre—the plot of *Arizona Raiders* does not seem designed to weigh in on the legitimacy or legacy of guerrillas as many of its predecessors in the 1940s and 1950s did. In fact, the guerrilla war itself or themes stemming directly from it constitute a negligible portion of the film's run time. That said, the film's opening narration is rather remarkable when compared to previous guerrilla pictures. Delivered by a newspaper editor (based on a real historical figure) alleging to have grown up around William C. Quantrill in Canal Dover, Ohio, the monologue is essentially a scripted, ten-minute crash course on the history of Quantrill and Missouri bushwhackers.[13] It is an interpretation in which Quantrill's personal character, his actions, his motivations, and the motivations of his men are presented and summarily condemned for filmgoers. Following his harangue of the guerrillas, viewers never see the newspaper editor again; as such, this opening section and its underlying message stand, in many ways, as a minidocumentary separate from the movie itself.

"At an early age," the narrator begins, "meanness and selfishness showed in his [Quantrill's] nature." According to the monologue, Quantrill had worked for a time as a teacher in Ohio, but "inside his cruel mind plans were already forming that would affect thousands of people before he came to a violent end." Next Quantrill went to Lawrence, Kansas, "where he found robbing for a living was easier than teaching." "Always a rabid anti-abolitionist," the statement continued, "he [Quantrill] formed a small band of men whose sworn job was to return runaway slaves to their owners. Only the slaves that Quantrill and his men picked up never seemed to get back to their rightful owners." Thus, "human misery became his livelihood at an early age."

The narrator's story continued as sectional tensions devolved into the Civil War. "When the break came between the North and the South . . . Quantrill formed what were to become Quantrill's border ruffians." With Quantrill in command, "these men sympathetic to the South fought actions against small Union forces or would catch a Union soldier in a dark alley and just kill him." "This," the narrator offered, "was Quantrill's idea of a true Southern patriot. Here was a desperate character steeped in crime." With the war now in full swing, "his murdering and robbing in his mind came under the articles of war"–"then he considered them a patriotic duty." At one point, "Quantrill decided to go to Richmond to seek a commission as a Colonel in the Confederate forces. Through his distorted vision, he saw promotions heaped upon him." In reality, the narration argued, "his reception in Richmond was cool" as "his background of robbery and murder were well-known to the Southern commanders." As a result, "they turned his commission down with a stern warning to disband his men and cease his border raids." Being denied a real command "worked on his already warped mind. Now only one thing interested him: revenge."

That vengeance, as the narration informed audiences, came at the expense of Lawrence, Kansas. In August 1863, "450 men rode toward a small, sleeping town of two-thousand people." At the head of this guerrilla column, Quantrill "looked at the small, doomed, defenseless city." "Now he was to become master, monster, avenger, of his own grievances. . . . A sense of gloating filled him as he signaled the charge." The narrator suggests that the guerrillas struck at dawn, following Quantrill's orders: "kill, kill, and you will make no mistake. Lawrence must be cleansed and the only way to cleanse it is to kill." And when the guerrillas rode out of town, "every man who could carry a gun in Lawrence was dead." Because of William C. Quantrill, "widows wailed, orphans cried, maidens wept, as they lifted the lifeless forms of their loved ones from the bloody fields and bore them to untimely graves."

These remarks are obviously meant to make Quantrill's military record—and the records of guerrillas, generally speaking—illegitimate. As in several of the earlier films, Quantrill's memory is disgraced and presented as unworthy of mainstream or regular commemoration. Unlike earlier films, however, the opening sequence of *Arizona Raiders* pulled quotations or paraphrased material directly from William Elsey Connelley's *Quantrill and the Border Wars* (1909)—easily the best-known biography (and indictment) of Quantrill penned in the twentieth century. In addition to showing that filmmakers had "done their homework," the mining of material from such a blatantly one-sided source underscores that filmmakers were not simply pushing melodramatics; they had also made a conscious decision to interject themselves *openly*, on a historical level, into the debate over Quantrill and how Border West guerrillas ought to be remembered.[14]

This is why Captain Andrews, during the trial scene, distinguishes Clint and Willie from other guerrillas who had fought at Lawrence: because they had joined post-massacre, there was a chance they had not yet been corrupted by the "warped mind" of such a "desperate character." In this way, the film continued to push for the exclusion of borderland guerrillas from mainstream narratives of the Civil War on the grounds that *Kansas Raiders*, *Red Mountain*, and *The Woman They Almost Lynched* had already established: it was unnatural, it was infectious, and it did not belong among the apparently more honorable stories of mutual valor and shared sacrifice of blue against gray.

Josey, Jake, and Rooster: 1976 to Present

In 1976 moviegoers were introduced to the most successful on-screen guerrilla of all time. Starring Clint Eastwood as the iconic farmer-turned-bushwhacker for whom the film is eponymously named, *The Outlaw Josey Wales* begins with a guerrilla raid in western Missouri. Kansas Red Legs torch the Wales homestead and murder the wife and young son of Josey Wales in the process. In short order, another group of irregulars approaches Wales—this time under the command of Missouri bushwhacker William "Bloody Bill" Anderson. Wales joins the group of raiders to help "set things aright." After a brief montage of successful raids and ambushes, the audience learns that "Bloody Bill" is dead and the future of his company is in jeopardy.

Without Anderson, the guerrillas determine to surrender to Union forces, who have promised pardons and a return to peace. Only Wales, with no home to return to after the war, decides to forego reunion with the "Blue Coats." Wales watches his former comrades gunned down by Federals while attempting to surrender, and after killing several of the two-timing troopers, Wales escapes with a wounded companion. From this point on, the film is framed around Wales's inability to put the war in Missouri behind him. Despite Lee's surrender to Grant and the cessation of hostilities, the unrepentant guerrilla is constantly hounded by Union troopers and bounty hunters—all of whom want to claim a reward placed on his head by Senator James Lane of Kansas.

Wales and a ragtag group of companions gradually make for Texas—supposedly a gathering place for other ex-Confederates trying to escape the grasp of the federal government. All along the way, however, Wales is forced into violent confrontations with Union soldiers. In one such show-down, he dispatches three men at once after asking if they would rather "pull those pistols or whistle Dixie?" In another, Wales finally claims revenge against the commander of the Red Legs—Captain Terrill (played by Bill McKinney), who butchered his family and burned his home—by forcing a saber into the disgruntled Kansan's chest cavity. By the end of the film, Wales has made peace with his past and established a new kin-ship network for himself. Having ended his blood feud with the Union, Wales can now start his life anew.

This is a very different portrait of guerrilla warfare than an entire gener-ation of film audiences had likely seen before. Near the conclusion of the film, Wales concedes to another ex-guerrilla named Fletcher (portrayed by John Vernon), "we all died a little in that damn war"; but, and it is critical to note, in expressing relief that his personal war was now over, Wales's motives for joining Anderson and for fighting as a Missouri bush-whacker are never questioned or deemed illegitimate. *The Outlaw Josey Wales* was the first film since the 1920s to buy completely into the idea that guerrillas had been involuntarily pulled into the service of the black flag by Union atrocities. As such, the film broke with nearly forty years of moral precedent; dating all the way back to *Dark Command* (1940), bush-whackers—especially the likes of Quantrill and Anderson—had been presented as "unofficial" combatants in a war disconnected from *the* Civil War that most Americans knew, revered, and remembered. In this rendition of the guerrilla war, Wales is not isolated and exiled to the West for legacy-building purposes; he exiles *himself* to Texas to escape from the oppressive postwar consequences of his alternative Civil War experience. In other words, through the sympathetic story of Josey Wales, Eastwood and company had discovered the elusive circumstances (to return ever so briefly to our introductory remarks concerning *Bandolero*) in which a Missouri guerrilla could be painted as wholly justified and legitimate in the eyes of a society trained for decades to view irregular warfare as unnatural, un-American, and deserving exclusion.

Despite the small thematic revolution *The Outlaw Josey Wales* constituted in the realm of guerrilla pictures, it was nearly another quarter century before a feature film again took up the subject. When *Ride with the Devil* debuted in theaters in 1999, it did not continue the trend of romanticizing and justifying the actions of Missouri bushwhackers wholesale. Directed by Ang Lee, the film represents a return to the more balanced approaches of *Renegade Girl* and *Arizona Bushwhackers* by offering both legitimate and illegitimate motives for Missouri men to become guerrillas but also by appending limits of conscience as to how much and what sorts of violence those motives could and should support.

The plot of the film follows a young German American man named Jake Roedel (portrayed by Tobey McGuire) as he is gradually pulled into the border conflict by his own beliefs and those of his friends—many of whom are not German and hail from more prominent, slave-owning families. Jake and his comrades form a small guerrilla band and patrol areas in and around their homes after Union troops begin to murder civilians; when necessary, they ambush or bushwhack Union soldiers and Union sympathizers alike. But more than any of its predecessors, *Ride with the Devil* infuses racial and ethnic tensions into the guerrilla debate. Gone is the simple, moral binary of whether men such as Quantrill, Anderson, or even Jake Roedel were "real" Civil War soldiers or whether their actions required extraction from popular narratives of the war. The protagonists of the movie do not gradually realize the folly or inherent evil of irregular warfare, and no overly masculine, honor-laden Confederate soldier (à la Lance Horton or Brett Sherwood) appears as a corrective alternative. Instead, the film offers a much more realistic accounting of guerrilla violence in which individuals experienced the war on more personalized, localized terms and seem to understand that the guerrilla war in Missouri *is* the regular war—not something that can simply be avoided, amended, or stopped. Therein, *Ride with the Devil* is the *only* guerrilla picture that does not resemble a traditional western, nor does it make any effort to "other" or westernize the combatants it portrays.

When Jake and his friends join with William C. Quantrill and take part in the Lawrence Raid of August 1863, Roedel and Holt (played by Jeffrey Wright)—a former slave turned black Confederate guerrilla who gradually becomes Jake's best friend—are disillusioned by the killing of women, children, and innocent civilians. They rescue a pair of civilians in a Lawrence restaurant, and for the rest of the film the duo are at odds with other bushwhackers who believe they have gone soft and strayed from the cause. Jake and Holt do not offer a sweeping moral code or statement concerning the behavior of other guerrillas. Rather, they find the personal limits concerning which elements of irregular warfare they can and cannot justify to themselves and choose not to exceed them. As a result of their individual choices, at the end of the war both protagonists are presented with promising new beginnings. Roedel sets out to start a family with the former sweetheart of a slain guerrilla, and Holt begins a quest to find his own family, now freed by the Thirteenth Amendment. In many ways, then, *Ride with the Devil* rebukes the ability of prior films to cast collective judgment, one way or the other, on Missouri bushwhackers and chips away at prior indictments of the guerrilla war cast by the film legacy of the 1940s and 1950s.

Compared to most of the guerrilla pictures produced in the 1940s, 1950s, and 1960s, *The Outlaw Josey Wales* and *Ride with the Devil* posited radically different assessments of how to remember and commemorate irregular warfare through film. The former saw Hollywood side with the Missouri bushwhacker wholeheartedly for the first time in more than fifty years, while the latter called out Hollywood's ability to collectively present the guerrilla experience with any measure of fairness in the first place. As the most recent film wading into the debate, *True Grit*, released by Paramount Pictures in 2010, builds on the message of *Ride with the Devil* and stands on almost neutral ground between the pro- and antibushwhacker pictures.

The plot of *True Grit*, which starred Jeff Bridges, Matt Damon, and

Hailee Steinfeld in a remake of the 1969 film of the same name, centers on a young girl named Mattie Ross who enlists the help of rough-and-tumble Federal marshal Rooster Cogburn and a prim Texas Ranger named Le Boeuf to track down the man who murdered her father. Over the course of their travels in Arkansas and the Indian Territory with Ross, Cogburn and Le Boeuf eventually track down their fugitive and avenge the death of Mattie's father. Two scenes in particular warrant consideration. In one, roughly halfway through the movie, Cogburn and Le Boeuf bicker about their respective service in the Civil War. The exchange proceeds as follows:

> *Cogburn:* Did you say hoorawed?
>
> *Le Boeuf:* That was the word.
>
> *Mattie:* There is no hoorawing in it. My agreement with the Marshall antedates yours. It has the force of law.
>
> *Le Boeuf:* The force of law! This man is a notorious thumper! He rode by the light of the moon with Quantrill and Bloody Bill Anderson!
>
> *Cogburn:* Them men was patriots, Texas trash!
>
> *Le Boeuf:* They murdered women and children in Lawrence, Kansas.
>
> *Cogburn:* That's a God damned lie! What army was you in, mister?
>
> *Le Boeuf:* I was at Shreveport first with Kirby Smith, then . . .
>
> *Cogburn:* Yeah? What side was you on?
>
> *Le Boeuf:* I was in the Army of Northern Virginia, Cogburn, and I don't have to hang my head when I say it!
>
> *Cogburn:* If you had served with Captain Quantrill . . .
>
> *Le Boeuf:* Captain? Captain Quantrill indeed!
>
> *Cogburn:* Best let this go, Le Boeuf!
>
> *Le Boeuf:* Captain of what?
>
> *Cogburn:* Good, then! There are not sufficient dollars in the state of Texas to make it worth my while to listen to your opinions. Our agreement is nullified.
>
> *Le Boeuf:* That suits me!

This discussion between Cogburn, an unapologetic ex-bushwhacker, and Le Boeuf, a proud veteran of the regular Confederate Army, is a far cry from the encounters of Bob Seton, Brett Sherwood, Lance Horton, or Alan Westcott with various—but always nefarious—incarnations of William C. Quantrill and his guerrilla band, in which the regular war *always* trumped the irregular. With this scene, audiences are left to decide for themselves which type of service had been legitimate and to what degree. On one hand, Cogburn insinuates that Quantrill's guerrillas were genuine patriots who fought on despite the surrender of Robert E. Lee's forces and the downfall of the Confederate state. On the other, Le Boeuf attempts to discredit Quantrill, and by extension Cogburn, with the Lawrence Massacre and the contention that Quantrill had never really been attached to the Confederacy in any official way (and was therefore not a genuine officer).

The content of this scene is particularly interesting when compared to its 1969 counterpart. In that exchange between Cogburn and Le Boeuf (then played by John Wayne and Glen Campbell, respectively), the subject matter is the same, but the conversation plays out quite differently:

> *Cogburn:* What outfit were you with during the war?
>
> *Le Boeuf:* Shreveport, with Kirby Smith.
>
> *Cogburn:* Oh, I mean what side were you on?
>
> *Le Boeuf:* I served with General Kirby Smith.
>
> *Cogburn:* (laughs at Le Boeuf)
>
> *Le Boeuf:* And I don't have to hang my head when I say it either. Go ahead and make another joke about it. You want to make me look foolish in the girl's eyes anyway.
>
> *Cogburn:* You don't need me for that.
>
> *Le Boeuf:* I don't like the way you make conversation.
>
> *Cogburn:* And I don't like your conversation about Captain Quantrill.
>
> *Le Boeuf:* Captain? Captain of what? Bunch of thieves?
>
> *Cogburn:* Young fella, if you're looking for trouble, I'll accommodate you. Otherwise, leave it alone.

The more in-depth discussion of guerrilla violence and the Lawrence Massacre found in the 2010 version of *True Grit* is pulled directly from the book on which the movie is based. It was available to filmmakers in 1969.[15] However, when other films weighing the merits of guerrilla service, such as *Arizona Raiders*, were still potentially matters of recent memory for moviegoers, the debate is cut short, likely because the decision between regular and irregular service was still quite clear. In this way, the sagas of Josey Wales and Jake Roedel helped pave the way for audiences to again choose how to remember and whether to commemorate guerrillas for themselves in 2010. In the concluding scene of the more recent version of *True Grit*, Mattie Ross tries to visit Rooster Cogburn twenty-five years after their adventures in the Indian Territory with Le Boeuf. Carrying the flyer for a Wild West Show, she meets Cole Younger and Frank James—both former bushwhackers under William C. Quantrill—and is informed by Younger that Cogburn had passed away just three days prior in Jonesboro, Arkansas. Most telling, however, for the evolution of guerrilla memory on film is the revelation that Younger and James had Cogburn, the former bushwhacker and veteran of the Lawrence Massacre, buried in a *Confederate* cemetery, almost certainly with veterans of the regular war.

Reassessing "Westernization" in History and Memory

Despite the variant interpretation of the Missouri bushwhacker offered by *The Outlaw Josey Wales*, the nuanced, complex understanding of the war in Missouri depicted by *Ride with the Devil*, or the broader implications associated with changes to the script of *True Grit*, most academic historians of social memory are reticent to respond. These scholars have shown scant interest in how the systematic westernization of the borderlands and the bushwhacker on film has altered our broadest understanding of Civil War memory and American culture in the twentieth and twenty-first centuries. Moreover, they are not particularly interested in deviating from standard interpretations of the West and the frontier to reassess how and why this process of cultural exportation to the Wild West occurred in the first place.

Richard Slotkin, perhaps the foremost historian of the American frontier as both a geographic space and a cultural idea, offers an alternative process of westernization altogether. According to *Gunfighter Nation*, Slotkin's seminal work on the subject, the likes of Jesse James and Cole Younger became icons of the Wild West because of their status as "Reconstruction bandits." He argues that the criminal activities of the James-Younger Gang made them viable symbols in a turn-of-the-century struggle between "labor" and "capital." Put another way, Slotkin suggests that the more recent status of James and Younger as social bandits who resisted industrial capitalism by stealing from railroads and sticking it to the federal government overpowered and then replaced their ties to the Civil War in the American imagination. Within this arrangement, then, Missouri's guerrilla war served as a training ground or springboard for social banditry, but it was not the reason, according to Slotkin, in any punitive sense or context, for their involuntary westernization in popular culture.[16]

On the surface, Slotkin's logic is sound. Postwar propaganda concocted by John Newman Edwards *was* intended to cast Jesse James as a Robin Hood figure, with the Younger brothers as his companions in a justified series of postwar crimes. But as outlined in chapter 2, Edwards's partisan motives and intent on this front had much more to do with the politics of Civil War memory, southern identity, and Democratic politics than with stoking agrarian or even proletarian discontent. As a result, this proposed transition from guerrilla to labor hero fails to compute when other ex-bushwhackers, such as William C. Quantrill or William "Bloody Bill" Anderson, are inserted as variables in the equation. These men—like the vast majority of their wartime peers—had nothing to do with postbellum banditry but, like James and Younger, *did* constitute fundamental components of Edwards's irregular Lost Cause narrative for Missouri. Therein, the common link that binds bushwhackers who are written out of mainstream accounts of the Civil War and exiled to the Wild West is not their retooled use as resistors of capitalism but the fact that they were spokesmen for a different, unfamiliar, and undesirable version of the war itself.

While this chapter is admittedly most interested in the effect guerrilla pictures had on American culture, an important factor must be borne in mind: the effectiveness of this cinematic propaganda relied a great deal on the ability of filmmakers to interweave issues of Civil War memory with contemporary matters of war-related remembrance, social and political trends, and cultural changes that audiences dealt with on a daily basis. So how were the qualities of this unfamiliar, undesirable rendition of the Civil War subconsciously linked to the real-life, real-time concerns of moviegoers in the 1940s, 1950s, 1960s, 1970s, and beyond when the process of westernization and cultural ostracism was operating at full power?

For one thing, films such as *Renegade Girl* and especially *The Woman They Almost Lynched* underscored the backwards nature of gender relations in the guerrilla wars of the Border West. In these pictures women such as Jean Shelby, Kate Quantrill, or the surly female mayor of Border Town take on political and oftentimes violent roles typically reserved for men. In the conservative, male-dominated Cold War environment of the late 1940s and 1950s, these gendered upheavals would have resonated strongly with men intent on preserving their place atop the sociopolitical hierarchy. The message here was clear: this sort of warfare and the people who would enable it as well as the geographic space where it might flourish must be avoided and shunned. A widespread lack of control over women endangered the traditional political primacy of men—and, according to conservatives and Cold Warriors during the Truman and Eisenhower administrations, this threat put the Union at risk yet again, albeit to an enemy in Soviet red, not Confederate gray. Additionally, films that featured the Lawrence Massacre prominently—and especially *Kansas Raiders*—also played on Cold War themes of domestic patriotism and "containment at home." They contend that guerrilla warfare erased traditional boundaries between homefront and battlefront and thereby put women and children directly in the line of fire. (This is made abundantly clear in *Quantrill's Raiders* when the honorable Alan Westcott agrees to serve as Joel's surrogate father and restore balance to a domestic environment shattered by irregular warfare.) Left unchecked, however, such developments pulled the traditional American family structure into danger and could potentially undermine the nation's ability to compete from within.[17] In other words, if the war at home could not be contained and controlled in this borderland environment, how could it possibly be contained and won abroad?

Moreover, as veterans returned home from World War II and then the Korean War, Americans were in the process of formulating legacies for these more recent conflicts. With that in mind, clear distinctions are made in films such as *Dark Command, Red Mountain, Kansas Raiders, The Woman They Almost Lynched, Quantrill's Raiders,* and *Arizona Raiders* about the differences between killing honorably and dishonorably in wartime. Honorable violence, according to the movies, plays out *soldier to soldier* on major battlefields for noble political causes. In other words, it was found on the beaches of Normandy or the plains of North Africa—not in German death camps or aboard Japanese suicide bombers. So by placing Quantrill and his guerrillas at odds with a heroic soldier from the regular army willing to do battle in the traditional sense, these pictures simultaneously made statements concerning the legitimacy and commemorative credentials of guerrillas and tapped the desires of American men to be remembered honorably for their own armed service in the 1940s and 1950s.[18]

Much more plausible, then, is the explanation that guerrilla pictures in the twentieth and twenty-first centuries were mirroring and sustaining extant patterns in American culture, remembrance, and historical scholarship. In attempting to present Missouri guerrillas and the borderlands as illegitimate and unworthy of commemoration, these films and their clear eastern biases were not actually deifying bushwhackers or turning them into national heroes in the context of an economic transition. Rather, guerrilla pictures continued the work of dime novels, theatrical productions, and other cultural outlets discussed in chapter 6; they outcast guerrillas to the most convenient geographic space and cultural place available: the western frontier. In this arrangement, the Wild West served as a dumping ground for the misfits of Civil War memory.[19] The aforementioned remnants of the war that did not mesh well with sectional reconciliation, those that failed to align with the Lost Cause agenda, or items that easterners felt tarnished their own wartime legacies could, in this way, be westernized, written off as uncivilized, and removed from mainstream consideration.[20]

Nowhere is this intent to write the guerrilla experience out of the national Civil War narratives more evident than in the materials produced for the celebration of the centennial in the 1950s and 1960s. For example, *The American Civil War: A Centennial Exhibition*, published in 1961 by the Library of Congress, was "presented as a part of the national commemoration." The volume itself catalogued hundreds of materials "taken exclusively from the collections of the Library of Congress." According to the exhibition's preface, it was intended to examine the "tragic struggle of 1861–1865 in as broad a scope as possible." Despite this seemingly inclusive manifesto, Missouri and irregular warfare are ignored wholesale.[21] On a similar note, James I. Robertson Jr.–himself an executive director on the Civil War Centennial Commission–published *The Civil War* in 1963. In all fairness, the booklet was not designed to stand as a comprehensive narrative of the war. Even so, the activities of more official raiders such as Nathan Bedford Forrest and John Hunt Morgan do appear in the text, while Robertson unapologetically notes in his foreword that Quantrill's raid against Lawrence had "import" to its "particular locale" but "of necessity had to be omitted."[22]

Another case in point is Bruce Catton's magisterial, three-volume *Centennial History of the Civil War*. As perhaps the best-known example of this anniversary-fueled literature–and possibly even the most popular account of the Civil War produced in the twentieth century–it is quite telling that in more than 1,300 pages of narrative, almost all of it focused on battles and military maneuverings, Catton mentions guerrilla warfare in the Border West less than six times.[23] This conflict, as Catton positions it, represented "a very ugly turn" in which the war "was brought down to isolated neighborhoods where people had divided minds and quick tempers." "Bushwhackers" in the Border West, as Catton describes them, were "Southern-minded residents who took to the woods with rifle and ammunition, sometimes organizing into bands that broke telegraph lines, tore up railway tracks, burned bridges, and ambushed supply wagons, sometimes operating alone, shooting straggling soldiers or Unionist civilians impartially and in general making life a burden for everyone." And according to an "indignant" and "somewhat biased" Union officer (whom Catton never actually disagrees with), the model bushwhacker "kills for the sake of killing and plunders for the love of gain"; "parties of these ferocious beasts, under cover of darkness, frequently steal into a neighborhood, burn the residences of loyal citizens, rob stores, tan yards, and farmhouses of everything they can put to use, especially arms, ammunition, leather, clothing, bedding, and salt." The activities of Kansas Jayhawkers and Senator James Lane are noted briefly, but neither William C. Quantrill nor the Lawrence Massacre is referenced a *single time* in *any* of the three volumes.[24]

Even in light of these movies' apparent success in pushing guerrillas out of Civil War metanarratives, to date historians of the war and film have not provided a systematic survey of films featuring the Missouri bushwhacker. On one side, scholars are quick to point out—sometimes without the greatest depth of evidence—that Quantrill and other Missouri guerrillas served a very specific role in films about the war: a bridge between North and South, Union and Confederate, that could link the former enemies through the mutual condemnation and exclusion of irregular warfare. On the other side, just as often, those same scholars cannot even agree on what to call or how to categorize these pictures. It is not surprising, then, that none have previously delved with any seriousness into the inner workings of the relationship between guerrilla memory and motion pictures in the formulation of American culture and identity.[25]

The approach of eminent Civil War historian Gary Gallagher to the Civil War on film has virtually become standard. He maintains that films depicting the war generally fit within one of our thematically arranged categories: the Lost Cause, Union victory, Emancipation, or Reconciliation.

Throughout *Causes Won, Lost, and Forgotten: How Hollywood and Popular Art Shape What We Know about the Civil War*, Gallagher argues that well-known films such as *The Birth of a Nation* (1915), *Gone with the Wind* (1939), *Shenandoah* (1965), and *Gettysburg* (1993) fit snugly into clearly demarcated categories. *Ride with the Devil*, despite its guerrilla-centric plot and alternative plot trajectory, can even be wedged into a preexisting thematic category using Gallagher's rubric—that is, it is a genuine Civil War film like *Gone with the Wind* or *Gettysburg*. Films such as *The Outlaw Josey Wales*, however, are where Gallagher draws the line. He contends that these films—which would likely include virtually all of the pictures discussed in this chapter (save for *Ride with the Devil*) and many of those referenced by Chadwick and Wills—are little more than dressed-up westerns that tried to capitalize on attention paid to the war by centennial celebrations. As noted by the author elsewhere in an essay about the historical origins of *The Outlaw Josey Wales*, Gallagher considers these films to be "posers in Blue and Gray—and poor ones at that."[26]

The main issue here is not that these films look like westerns. They do look like westerns; furthermore, based on their geographic settings, some of them technically *are* westerns. Nonetheless, they are valuable to our understanding of the Civil War in popular culture and memory for two reasons. First, as we now know, the reason for their western setting had much to do with controlling the legacy of the war by exporting unsavory components—irregular combatants—to the West. The plots of these films may not unfold in Virginia or Georgia or Pennsylvania, but the story of how and why they are situated in the West is, from the start, a direct linkage to the war and how it is commemorated today. Second, these pictures still chronicle, despite western makeup or costumes, an alternative wartime and postwar experience tied to guerrilla warfare in the western borderlands of Missouri, Kansas, and Arkansas. They do not simply use the Civil War as a convenient trope or publicity stunt to generate larger audiences and revenue; they depict an unfamiliar rendering of the Civil War—one that did not always end in 1865, one in which women and children were often combatants, and one in which the homefront typically *was* the battlefront. In other words, just as guerrilla memory does not fit comfortably within standard histories of battle, reconciliation, and remembrance, neither do the myriad ways in which the guerrilla experience has played out on film. The one cannot be properly studied minus the other.

In *Shooting the Civil War: Cinema, History, and American National Identity*

(2009), Jenny Barrett contends that Civil War narratives have been "present across multiple genres throughout the twentieth century." Even so, she asserts that these films cannot and should not be "labeled as a film genre in their own right." In Barrett's theorizing, there is "no such thing as the 'Civil War film,'" nor is there such a thing as the "Civil War genre" in the capacity that other films, such as westerns or science fiction pictures, are understood and categorized. What this leaves, according to Barrett, are Civil War films that *are* actually westerns, war pictures, and melodramas—though each one is still a perfectly legitimate window into how the Civil War has been remembered and used to shape American national identity.

Barrett pragmatically relaxes, to a refreshing degree, the parameters used by Gallagher to delineate between genuine and fraudulent Civil War films. But she also relies heavily on Slotkin's analysis of the frontier, and her own framework for organizing films seems ill equipped to make analytical distinctions between regular and irregular modes of warfare in the formulation of memory and identity. "The definition of the American is transformed," Barrett writes, "with his relocation to the frontier"; she describes "what he is, as well as what he is not" based on the litmus of frontier interaction and activity. In this regard, Barrett appears correct in echoing Slotkin, but she is actually ignoring alternative motives for transforming certain individuals and the distinct possibility that individuals were relocated to exclude them from a mainstream American identity all along.[27]

Outtakes and Conclusions

From the 1920s to the present, motion pictures have been the most powerful force driving the westernization of guerrilla memory and the most revealing lens to the motives and success of that cultural process. From *Jesse James under the Black Flag* to *True Grit*, movies featuring the likes of William C. Quantrill, "Bloody Bill" Anderson, Jesse James, Cole Younger, and a host of spin-off and outright fictitious bushwhackers have gradually exported to the Wild West the "nastiest bits and pieces" of the Civil War as described in chapter 1. This transition took place as part of a broader effort to define a legacy of the war based on eastern interests, North and South—a neatly arranged, sanitized legacy of heroic veterans, shared valor, and postwar sectional harmony. Working toward this end, western guerrillas and the borderlands they inhabited are routinely presented as uncivilized; irregulars such as Quantrill are fundamentally evil, and the brand of warfare they practice is unnatural and without honor; and, as a result, this irregular mode of war is presented as corrupting and infectious. It needed to be culled, isolated, and exiled from the bounds of respectable, mainstream Civil War memory narratives.

The ways in which the place of guerrilla memory has been blurred in American culture and remembrance is a critically important—and heretofore missing—link in the story of how the Civil War's legacy has been established and how it has evolved over time up to its present state. In the process of explaining how exiled guerrillas interacted differently with notions of the frontier than scholars had previously posited, this chapter reassesses what constitutes a legitimate "Civil War picture" and therefore offers an updated model for how historians should begin to reexamine the wider war and its aftermath on film. Traces of this whitewashed and westernized guerrilla conflict were always hidden in plain sight on the silver screen—historians were simply not looking for it. In many ways, like the rest of American society, they had no interest in allowing guerrillas to "explain" as Twain beseeched; like the rest of American society, these historians had simply been conditioned by Hollywood, just as Lévi-Strauss cautioned, not to like what they saw when it did appear.

Notes from the [Disappearing] Guerrilla Theater

In a recent interview with the Civil War Trust, award-winning historian Gary Gallagher was asked to discuss noteworthy developments in the field of Civil War scholarship. Before long, the conversation turned to where irregular violence fits within the broader calculus of how we can and, more importantly, should interpret the conflict. Gallagher began by stating that "a lot of attention, I think, is on the margins now," before surmising, "the argument that 'guerrilla war is the best way to understand the war' is another example of this phenomenon." "Well, it's the best way to understand the war if you don't really want to understand the war," he added. "There were millions of men under arms, and not very many of them were guerrillas. . . . The guerrillas did not decide the conflict, and the guerrillas did not decide whether there would be emancipation." "I mean they were there," Gallagher concluded, "they were interesting, and they are an important topic—they're not the main story."[1]

This perception of guerrillas, shared by many other Civil War historians, assumes that the regular war of the East was *the* war—with very little room left for the places in which guerrillas *did* play significant roles in deciding the course and outcome of the war or in which irregular violence *did* make up a significant part of the main story. This is of course not to say that either vein of war—regular or irregular—is inherently more important than its counterpart or that the study of one should flourish at the expense of the other; only that if and when we are willing to give both a line on the marquee, the bloodiest, farthest-reaching, most divisive, and arguably the most important war since the founding of the Union becomes even bloodier, even farther reaching, even more divisive, and even more important for its new boundaries of scope and depth.

This possibility raises a number of questions of public history and preservation in the Missouri-Kansas borderlands, namely, how have a century's worth of commemorative conflicts, re-remembering, memorial reboots, and cultural excommunication manifested themselves on the physical landscape of the guerrilla theater? In 2013 I decided to find out, and I jumped in my truck to take a tour through the heart of "guerrilla country." From graves and monuments to battlefields and homesteads, I visited, or at least attempted to visit, the most important sites of guerrilla memory. In doing so, I came face to face with what happens when the alchemists of memory finished their work and had no further use for the space—in this case, the borderlands—in which their ends were achieved.

In the late 1860s and early 1870s, Alexander Franklin James was arguably as famous as Robert E. Lee or Ulysses S. Grant—and perhaps even more so in the Border West. James had been one of William Quantrill's most trusted guerrillas during the war and co-leader of an internationally known Reconstruction-era crime ring with his brother, the bandit extraordinaire Jesse James. As a bushwhacker, Frank saw action in numerous irregular engagements, but particularly noteworthy were the Lawrence Massacre, Goslin's Lane, and the Centralia Massacre. His also happened to be the very first grave I attempted to visit during my self-guided guerrilla tour. Given the weighty place James and his compatriots occupy— or at least *should* occupy—in the state's Civil War history, I approached his gravesite in Independence, Missouri, expecting a monument, likely some sort of historical marker, or at the very least, a sign with an arrow to direct myself and other eager tourists toward the cemetery. Instead, what I found was a relatively puny parcel of land nestled in the corner of a large, grassy park; enclosed by a weathered stone wall, the cemetery bordered up against what appeared to be a blue-collar neighborhood.

Tucked away in the rear of the cemetery are the headstones of Alexander Franklin James (1843–1915) and his wife, Ann Ralston (1853–1944). His marker itself is unimpressive and does not, in any way, hint at Frank's role in making the guerrilla experience a frequently savage one. No unit or company is etched across the stone; no miniature battle flags festoon the surrounding turf; no corroded placard even attempts to explain James's broader historical significance. I snapped a few photos and left the gravesite with the distinct notion that no one in the surrounding homes knew just who was buried in their backyards.

Then again, that's exactly how Frank James wanted it.

When Robert Ford gunned down Jesse James in 1882 at the behest of state authorities in Jefferson City (better known as "Jeff City" to historians trying to pass for local), Frank convinced himself that scientists—who were never specifically identified—had performed a range of unholy experiments on his brother's corpse. The scalpel-wielding quacks, he insisted, had even extracted Jesse's brain to examine it for a visible criminal defect. This was an odd presumption at first glance, but given the disturbing conclusions of William Connelley three decades later concerning genetically inherited vice, perhaps Frank wasn't *totally* overreacting. In any event, he left very strict instructions for the care (read: protection) of his own remains.

As detailed by a local newspaper on James's death in 1915, the former guerrilla had no intentions of becoming a science experiment. Per his wishes, the corpse was to be sealed away in a secret vault and personally guarded by his nephew, Jesse James Jr., until it could be cremated. James's ashes were then to be buried in a discreet location far from the family homestead in Kearney, Missouri, where he would be safe from bodysnatching coroners, phrenologists, and overachieving souvenir hunters. The measures seem to have been quite successful. Trudging back to the car, I wondered what it meant about public history in the guerrilla theater that James is not remembered here as guerrilla *or* western badman. Could the two competing identities have cancelled each other out to nothing? Later an archivist informed me that the Hill Park area is nationally renowned for its production of methamphetamine; she advised against a return visit. Frank probably would have appreciated this added safeguard to his eternal privacy.[2]

I next called on the grave of a guerrilla around whom, in life, even the hard-nosed James brothers had tread lightly. The remains of Archibald "Little Arch" Clements rest in the far northwest corner of Arnold Cemetery in Wellington, Missouri. Clements achieved notoriety during the war thanks to his propensity for relieving Union dead of their scalps and by way of his own immoderate death. Rather than surrendering to federal authorities in 1866, Clements died in the streets of Lexington, Missouri,

The graves of Frank James and Little Arch Clements. While seemingly opposites of personality in life, in death, the boisterous Clements and the calculated James both ended up resting in relative obscurity. Author's private collection.

one arm shattered, his body riddled with lead, trying to cock a revolver with his teeth. (Did I mention that he even startled other guerrillas?) No placard or literature is available at the gravesite to explain his historical significance, nor even to detail his violent demise. But his rectangular marble stone (undoubtedly a recent upgrade provided by the Sons of Confederate Veterans or the United Daughters of the Confederacy) *does* at least allege that Clements had been a first lieutenant in William Anderson's company of Missouri partisan rangers.[3]

This explicit designation of guerrilla service is a clear departure from the anonymity of Frank James. Then again, the prospects of anyone reaching Arnold Cemetery to read it are daunting—a realization that left me curious about my own prospects for remembrance considering a larger-than-life character such as Clements could so easily be buried in a forgotten place. Access to Clements's gravesite requires would-be visitors to drive approximately 150 yards down an unpaved, unlit, and potentially washed-out farm road. The path runs adjacent to a private cornfield; for all intents and purposes, the cemetery itself is enclosed by private agricultural land. All of this is on top of the fact that its location near the junction of Highway 24 (which runs parallel to the original Santa Fe Trail) and Sni-a-Bar Road make Arnold Cemetery a venue that can safely be labeled well beyond the purview of even the most dedicated Civil War sightseers.

At one stage of my own trip to Wellington—after driving my rental vehicle down the wrong tractor path and into the middle of a cornfield—I was forced to enlist the aid of an elderly woman cruising down the otherwise empty highway in her Cadillac Deville. It's difficult to say what surprised her most: that a "historian" (in a rented, lime green Kia Soul, no less) had ventured so far out into rural Wellington, or that I asked for directions to Archie Clements's grave. Though clearly suspicious—my academic expertise didn't seem to instill much confidence in my tomb-hunting motives— she knew the place and sent me on my way before resuming her joyride. Even with Google Earth and what I *believed* were accurate directions, it turns out that I'd missed the correct "bunch of trees" that signal the turn-off by more than two full miles.

As I traveled more extensively throughout the guerrilla theater, a thought raised by the resting places of James and Clements continued to linger: how could it be that men so known, so notorious, are now virtually whispers on the land? Perhaps this was the final consequence of the borderland's westernization—that the occupants of the middle ground between abolition and empire could not be fully resolved to either conflict and, as a result, were simply ignored. Over time I came to understand that the headstones of many prominent ex-guerrillas—such as William H. Gregg, Jim Cummins, Dave Edwards (who you'll recall took a potshot at Cummins during a Quantrill Men reunion on account of a pet raccoon gone AWOL), George "Bud" Wiggington, Frank Harbaugh, and Henry Hockensmith—highlight military service during the Civil War but curiously lack *any* direct linkage to irregular violence. Cummins's marker, for example, eulogizes him only as "One of Shelby's men," while Gregg's counted him as one of "Shank's Regiment of Missouri Cavalry." Cummins and Gregg were among a number of guerrillas who served briefly with regular forces in the very beginning or near the very end of the war; the decision to prioritize this service, likely made by kin in the early twentieth century, is revealing to say the least.

George Spoonamore, Oliver Shepherd, and Cole and James Younger have quiet tombs, like Jesse James. Despite the fact that Cole Younger had been among the best known of Quantrill's bushwhackers during and especially after the war, his original headstone in Lee's Summit Cemetery only gives his name and lifespan before invoking a simple inscription: "Rest in Peace our Dear Beloved." In more recent years, a second marker was added to the plot—again most likely by local pro-Confederate organizations—that openly denotes Younger's guerrilla service.[4] They apparently haven't gotten around to claiming Shepherd; his marker, only a few paces from Younger's, simply says that "he was assassinated"—an attention grabber, no doubt, but not a particularly informative one as historians are concerned.

As efforts to educate the public go, Lee's Summit Cemetery is an interesting case unto itself. While stones for Younger and Shepherd don't publicize their irregular wartime status, the cemetery at least *attempts* to close the breach by providing a map of individual graves and a very short historical walking tour. Lee's Summit is located along a busy commercial highway that could be conducive to easy access—much easier, at least, than Arnold Cemetery. (Though, full disclosure: I was the only living soul present during my hour-long visit.) But while the two-page tour pamphlet notes that Younger, Shepherd, Wiggington, and Harbaugh rode with Quantrill's company, it is devoid of any other useful Civil War–related information. While driving back to my hotel from the cemetery, I wondered which scenario was more viable for public history and commemoration: Clements's explicit headstone exiled to a field in Wellington, or James, Younger, and company seemingly hidden in plain sight.

Still other graves commemorate irregular service *without* the great logistical hardships. The headless body of William Clarke Quantrill is buried in the Confederate Cemetery at Higginsville, Missouri; looming over his remains is a clean, marble headpiece that conferred on him the title of Captain of Partisan Rangers for the Confederacy in Missouri. His missing head, as discovered by Quantrill biographer Edward Leslie, is now buried in a "fiberglass child's coffin" at the Fourth Street Cemetery in Canal Dover, Ohio. Apparently some of Quantrill's bones were stolen from their original resting place in Louisville, Kentucky, by his own mother, Caroline, and a boyhood acquaintance-turned-entrepreneur named W. W. Scott. While the skull was initially taken to Ohio, Scott later attempted to sell it to the Kansas State Historical Society and even threw in various other bones as a gesture of goodwill. According to Leslie, the Society declined to purchase the skull, which was eventually repurposed: Scott's son, Walter, and his fraternity brothers nicknamed the artifact "Jake" and used it to initiate new members. Thankfully, by the late 1980s, it was finally agreed that the bones held by the Kansas State Historical Society and others in Ohio—including the skull—would be buried once and for all in Canal Dover. That was, at least, before members of the Missouri Sons of Confederate Veterans erupted in protest; they claimed that the internment ceremony wasn't up to par for a man of Quantrill's eminent stature. The Missouri SCV was eventually given the remains, with the exception of the skull, and these relics were interred with much pomp at Higginsville, where they still re-side today.[5]

From a memorial perspective, I initially thought Quantrill's situation ideal: his marker is easy to find along well-trodden roads, and his head-stone prioritizes involvement in the guerrilla war. In reality, though, it began to register that *all* of the gravesites, however large or small, acces-sible or foreboding, that I visited suffer from one universal problem: a complete lack of on-site interpretation. There are no placards, no pam-phlets, no literature; nothing in place to help the general public place bushwhackers and Jayhawkers back within the broader context of the war, to help them understand the guerrilla experience, or to make sense of how either has been remembered and re-remembered over time. I shuffled back to the car—past a locked and, from the look of things, little-visited Confederate chapel—trying to imagine what a spike in statewide historical awareness would mean to the future chapters of guerrilla memo-ry's story. I could not, however, work past the notion that men so vaunted (and feared) in their own time required such imaginings in the first place.

When examined in the proper context, irregular belligerents such as Quantrill, James, Clements, and Younger were the primary exports of their own theater of war. They were the chief spokesmen for the wartime experience that became standard for so many residents of the Missouri-Kansas borderlands. Like it or not, these men were—and are—the guerrilla theater's equivalents of Robert E. Lee, Joshua Chamberlain, "Stonewall" Jackson, and William T. Sherman. So while I still couldn't clearly envision what a well-publicized guerrilla memory would look like, as I continued my tour, I began to understand—or at least I began to feel like I under-stood—the triangular relationship between these men, remembrance, and the land. Certainly I don't mean to imply that bushwhackers or their Unionist counterparts *deserve* to be remembered because of the righteous-ness of their causes or the merits of their service; "deserved," as the saying goes, has not a damned thing to do with it. Rather, their absence from the landscape helps reproduce myths about the war, where it was fought, how it was fought, and by whom.

The Smith-Davis Cemetery in Jackson County, Missouri, constitutes a case in point of the lessons learned from such absences. Once just a small family cemetery, the Smith-Davis burial plot was eventually transformed into a communal space for Civil War dead. Noted bushwhackers such as Daniel Boone Scholl (the great-grandson of frontiersman Daniel Boone), Jabez McCorkle (brother of guerrilla memoirist John McCorkle), and Ferdinand Marion Scott are all interred there. Perhaps more importantly, and in keeping with the gendered nature of irregular warfare, Charity McCorkle Kerr, Armenia Crawford Selvey, and Susan Crawford Vandevere are also buried at Smith-Davis.[6]

Each of these women perished, crushed by bricks, splintered beams, dust, and other debris, when a Union prison building located at 1425 Grand Avenue in downtown Kansas City collapsed on them in August 1863. Along with several other women—including William Anderson's young sisters Mary, Martha, and Josephine—they had been incarcerated on suspicion of smuggling vital supplies to bushwhackers in the field, guerrillas who also happened to be their brothers, cousins, and husbands. Many pro-Confederate Missourians believed, and continue to believe, that the gruesome deaths of these women motivated the Lawrence Massacre or, at the very least, incited an extra degree of rage from Quantrill's men when they invaded Kansas.

But even with this many veterans of the irregular war, male or female, on site, and with events as notorious as the Lawrence Massacre and General Order #11 tied directly to them, the most telling feature of the cemetery is that it's one of the few I was unable to visit on my trek across the guerrilla theater. Literally—because *nothing* is left above ground. For decades, the land was held and maintained (albeit poorly) by private families. As the descendants of those interred gradually died or moved away, the area immediately surrounding the cemetery became increasingly urban and commercial. Year after year, headstones went unpreserved; in fact, many were intentionally moved, vandalized, and even repurposed by locals. As virtually all of the original markers are gone, little to no information survives concerning precisely where individual persons are buried throughout the quarter-acre plot. In 1987 the larger parcel of property to which the cemetery belongs was rezoned for commercial purposes, and as of 2011, it was in foreclosure. State laws in Missouri prevent the complete destruction of the cemetery, but little hope presently exists that anything official will be done to repair, re-mark, or preserve it. Adding insult to injury, while a roadside marker indicates the general vicinity of the prison building itself, the actual scene of the disaster is also gone. It now resides beneath the Sprint Arena.

In fairness, there are pitfalls to preserving sites of guerrilla memory and to effectively using them as tools for public history. In fact, many of the qualities that combined to make irregular warfare seem so "irregular" to outsiders *during* the war also make contemporary efforts at preservation difficult. The vast majority of guerrilla encounters took place on private property: in homes and fields, on front porches, among barns and corncribs, down dusty wagon trails, and along isolated creek bottoms. More often than not, these spaces were (and are) in very rural or otherwise secluded areas that are not easily accessible. Irregular melees often took place not in or around a town, such as Sharpsburg or Gettysburg, but on individual farms and/or between only handfuls of men. And in many cases, these homes have been subsequently razed—or just as likely, the incidents that took place in and around them were never recorded for posterity.

Take, for example, a monument erected in present-day Richmond, Missouri, in the 1980s to commemorate the Battle of Albany—an October 1864 skirmish between Union troops and bushwhackers in which William "Bloody Bill" Anderson was fatally wounded. Standing at roughly five feet tall, the stone memorial is surprisingly impressive: it marks the date of the battle, then lists Anderson and ten other guerrillas killed. The issue, however, is that the monument sits approximately 100 yards up a very steep, narrow, gravel path in a tiny meadow on private property. For lack of a better description, the monument is located in a stranger's front yard, roughly 40 to 50 yards from their doorstep. Because the meadow doubles as a defunct family cemetery, Missouri statutes allow access—but that makes the visit no less awkward or unnerving. And that's assuming you can even find the site in the first place. Complete directions are nearly impossible to procure through normal channels, and I was only able to find an approximate address through a combination of street maps, old newspaper articles about the monument's construction, and Google Earth. From there, I had to guess which driveway to invade, unaware of who or what might be waiting at the other end. Thankfully, this time at least, I was lucky on the first try.

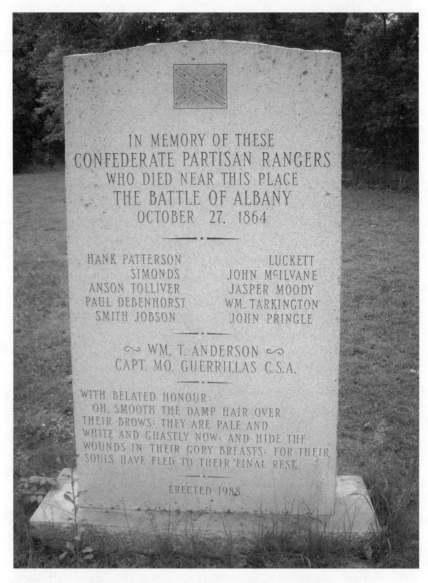

The Last Charge of Bloody Bill Anderson. In the so-called Battle of Albany, an enraged Anderson charged headlong (and virtually alone) into a fortified group of Union soldiers; he was quickly gunned down. Author's private collection.

At about one hour's drive on Route B and Route 124 from Columbia, Missouri, the site of the Centralia Massacre may not be as difficult to find as its commemorative cousin in Richmond, but its location in rural Boone County isn't exactly a beacon for historical tourism. (Once on Grassland School Road—which takes visitors directly to the massacre site—be ready to share the narrow access with tractors and other assorted farm vehicles.) In September 1864 William Anderson and his men stopped a train carrying furloughed Union soldiers at the station in Centralia; the guerrillas executed all but one of the abducted (and unarmed) Federal passengers. When Major A. V. E. Johnston heard of Anderson's butchery at the rail depot, he immediately set out in pursuit of the bushwhackers. The two sides clashed in an open field surrounded by dense greenery on three of its four sides. As Johnston's mounted infantrymen rode into the center of the field with their single-shot carbines, a wave of mounted guerrillas—likely between three and four hundred—burst from the tree line and slaughtered them. Numerous Federal corpses were scalped or otherwise mutilated in the aftermath of the battle.[7]

The first time I visited the field, good friend and fellow guerrilla historian Joseph (Joe) Beilein took me on a personal tour. We walked through the dense woods and along the deep ridges that drop down to Young's Creek—the same trenches that allowed the guerrillas to spring their deadly three-pronged ambush on Johnston's doomed men. In the middle of the field, which is no longer under cultivation, a large marble monument sits next to a wooden gazebo. The memorial was constructed in 1994 by the Boone County Historical Society. Its front gives a very brief account of the ambush while its back lists the names of the Union dead by company. As sites of guerrilla memory go, Centralia is unquestionably unique: it's one of the few known irregular battlefields to still exist in more or less the condition it had during the war. Exciting as this may seem, the other reason for Centralia's uniqueness makes it a historical outlier. Very rarely were so many guerrillas in the same place at the same time; with Lawrence being the other exception, irregular combat almost never played out this way. So while Centralia is accessible to sightseers willing to make the effort *and* looks almost exactly the way it did in September 1864, it represents the best-preserved instance of the way guerrillas almost *never* waged war.[8]

A straight shot across Interstate 70 from Kansas City, Lawrence—the best-known site of guerrilla warfare during the Civil War and likely in American history—is another site that's not too difficult to find. But once there, you may be surprised how difficult it can be to track down tangible artifacts of guerrilla memory. More than two years after our trip to Centralia, I spent an afternoon traversing the site of the Great Raid with Joe. Looking down on Lawrence from Mount Oread, we realized just how dramatically the University of Kansas had altered the local landscape since Quantrill had perched in the same spot 151 years earlier to watch the slaughter unfold. In town, we found that the site of the Old Eldridge Hotel—which plays a seminal part in the story of the massacre—is marked by little more than a brass placard, while the city arsenal, once another vaunted military target, is now occupied by the Free State Brewing Company. We pondered the state of remembrance in Lawrence over a few drinks (ironically, John Brown would likely not be pleased by his prominent place on the logo of a microbrew) and, as a reward for our thoughtfulness, received a parking citation. In the spirit of the guerrilla theater, we decided not to pay the $8.

On our way out of town, now ourselves fugitives from authorities in Lawrence, we stopped to explore the Oak Grove Cemetery. Oak Grove is home to the monument erected in 1895 by survivors of the Lawrence Massacre. The large marble block honors the victims who "defenseless fell" on August 21, 1863. Nearby is a slightly weathered but still legible obelisk with the names of John and Robert Speer etched across its beveled base. As noted in chapter 6, these boys, ages ten and thirteen when they died, were the sons of John Speer Sr., a newspaperman in Lawrence during the war. Robert was robbed and then fatally shot in the stomach by bushwhacker Larkin Skaggs, while John's badly charred remains were excavated from beneath a torched building. These memorials are isolated, not particularly easy to find within the cemetery itself, and come with no on-site interpretation or contextual information. In other words, they're there, and that's about it.

These half-forgotten but technically surviving and accessible traces of the guerrilla war illustrate that the nature of commemoration in Lawrence is double-edged. On one hand, the university has kept the town populated and relevant. So unlike Smith-Davis, all physical hints of memory have not been erased. But because the majority of the raid took place *in* the town rather than beside or near it on less commercially valuable land—à la Gettysburg or Antietam—prospects for wide-scale preservation or inter-pretation of these surviving artifacts aren't particularly good. On the other hand, the nature of these sites and of irregular violence don't often trans-late neatly into standard military museums, parks, or walkable battle-fields. So perhaps private homes—the logistical headquarters and most frequent venues for irregular violence—would be the most viable place to search out physical remnants of guerrilla memory?

At first glance, the answer seems to be yes. It's worth pointing out, how-ever, that few of these homes are still standing. Time, urban sprawl, and weather—the guerrilla theater also being nationally renowned for severe weather and tornadoes—have all exacted a heavy toll. (Recall, for ex-ample, that the home of Lizzie Wallace, the site of numerous Quantrill Men reunions, was torn down in the 1970s to make way for a school bus storage lot.) But more than anything, the day-to-day operations of war in the guerrilla theater made the survival of wooden, highly combustible homes difficult. If we might revisit the sentiments of chapter 5 for just a moment, what historians traditionally label the "homefront" offered little in the way of insulation from irregular warfare. In fact, it was the very incubator from which it most often sprang to life.

Due to the reliance of guerrillas on their female kin to accouter them with the materials necessary to fight from the bush, homes, as the phys-ical sites of quartermasters' operations, made for prime military targets. Untold homesteads in western Missouri and eastern Kansas were as-saulted, besieged, burned out, or sometimes simply abandoned to the wrath of nature. Then in August 1863, Union general Thomas Ewing's infamous General Order #11 dealt another severe blow to future pros-pects for preservation. In response to the Lawrence Massacre, Ewing vowed to stamp out bushwhacker activities from their wellspring; he forc-ibly evacuated residents of Cass, Bates, Vernon, and Jackson Counties. In the process these structures—once formidable domestic fortresses—were left unguarded and susceptible to the torch. (Even Sherman's men had had to contend with the presence of residents while pillaging and raz-ing homes in Georgia and the Carolinas—not so in western Missouri for much of the war.) As a result, the "lone chimney" became a hallmark of the guerrilla theater.

These caveats aside, the most obvious point of interest resides in Kear-ney, Missouri: the James family homestead, now run by the Friends of the James Farm. The house is situated in its original location—the same place where Union soldiers tortured Dr. Reuben Samuel and allegedly prompted Jesse, then sixteen years old, to join his older brother Frank among Quantrill's ranks. From a preservation standpoint, the James Farm is a phenomenal success story. Both the exterior and interior of the home are well preserved and authentic. The walls of the kitchen, once blown apart (along with a healthy portion of Zerelda James's arm) by overanxious Pinkerton detectives, has long since been restored; the countryside and brush immediately surrounding the structure mimic very much how the landscape appeared in the 1860s; and, perhaps most refreshingly, house tours are available and given by guides who are well versed in the home's Civil War significance. To interested researchers, the Milton Perry Library is even available on site with a large trove of related documents and artifacts.

The James Farm, however, is something of an anomaly. The same post-war notoriety that made Frank and Jesse the poster boys of guerrilla memory's sanitization from Civil War history is also what probably saved the home as a historic site. But the fate of the Younger house—the boyhood stomping grounds of Cole, Jim, and Robert Younger—tells a very different story—one that is, unfortunately, much more representative. Like the Jameses, the Younger brothers were first spurred to join Quantrill by the murder of their slave-owning, southern-sympathizing father, Henry Washington Younger. While fulfilling his duties as postmaster of Clay County, Henry was waylaid by Unionist partisans and killed. Also like the James family, the Youngers were related, through blood or marriage, to several other guerrilla families (including the McCorkles). This meant that their home was part of a major female-run supply network.

The home—which, much like the Smith-Davis Cemetery, cannot be visited today—started running into preservation-related red tape as early as the 1950s. In 1932 the home had been opened as a museum and tourist center by Mr. T. B. Miller, a transplant to the guerrilla theater from Pennsylvania. Despite the fact that the house represented the *only* trace of Younger property not destroyed in the aftermath of General Order #11, the preservation project was eventually abandoned in 1957 as a long-term lease could not be negotiated. In 1966 the *Kansas City Star* announced that the Younger homestead would again be restored and reopened to the public as a museum, this time by a pair of Pennsylvanians, Mr. and

Mrs. William Taylor. Returning the flooring alone to its original condition required the removal of eight layers of linoleum—but the article lauded the work, for Civil War–era homes in this sector of Missouri were extremely rare and those left were typically dilapidated.[9]

As did the efforts of T. B. Miller in the 1930s, however, the preservation push mounted by the Taylors stalled, and by the mid-1970s the property fell into the hands of local developers. According to the *Lee's Summit Examiner*, cobwebs abounded throughout the house, while wood floors had begun to rot, concrete cracked, and water-stained wallpaper slowly peeled and fell to the floor. Despite the additions of modern plumbing and electrical wiring, plans to develop the house as a tourist attraction and curio shop never came to fruition. Things had become so bad that in 1982 Marley Brant, an independent filmmaker from Los Angeles then producing a picture about the James and Younger brothers, had to save the condemned home from the wrecking ball. Before it could be demolished, Brant arranged to have it dismantled, piece by piece, and placed in storage until it could be reassembled in the future—possibly even on a different piece of ground. Prior to Brant's rescue, Lee's Summit officials had deemed the house unsafe and ordered its owners, Raintree Investors Ltd., to either completely renovate the structure or tear it down. Calls to local historical groups concerning possible efforts to move the house or preserve it went unanswered. With the house safely in storage, Brant was quoted as saying, "I think it's a part of Missouri history and would like to hear what the people of Missouri would like to do. . . . I'd like to restore it to a period house, and it could be a museum of Younger things." As of 2014, following multiple failed fund-raising attempts and the denial of public finds by the Lee's Summit Council of Aldermen, the Younger house remains in storage with virtually no hope of being reassembled.[10]

With the ramifications of Missouri's role as connective tissue between wars in the East and the West beginning to crystallize, I caught up with a local expert, Chris Edwards, to get his take. Chris is part historian, part reenactor, and part public educator. Along with his band, he produces and performs in a traveling musical show called "Bloody Bill Rides" that employs the life of William Anderson to examine the causes, nature, and fallout of guerrilla warfare in Missouri and Kansas.[11]

I started by asking Chris why he does the show, and his answer touched on a fundamental pattern that I'd seen again and again while observing the intersection of public history and guerrilla memory. "Most folks in Missouri," he replied, "are not even aware that Civil War events took place here, so that's number one. Most are not aware that a lot of the guerrilla battles and skirmishes are in their back yards and haven't been officially marked by the state." This was Frank James in a nutshell. As another case in point, during one of my early grave-hunting trips, a usually reliable GPS unit led me astray. Rather than the cemetery I was expecting, I ended up in the parking lot of a Church's Chicken. Fearing that the graves of John Noland and George Todd had been paved over, I went inside to confer with employees about the age of the restaurant. I was informed by a particularly disinterested cashier that a "grave thing" might be located down the street.

According to Chris, the biggest impediment to improving the situation on the ground in the guerrilla theater is "finding a way to present the material in an interesting fashion." "The subject matter," he suggested, "needs to be given in a way that motivates students to want to learn more"— which is precisely why he took to the stage in the first place. "Most folks are not willing to read tons of books in order to get educated about a subject. They'd rather be spoon-fed. If folks can be entertained while being educated—all the better. People like music and film," he concluded. With this in mind, I asked why more wasn't being done—traditionally, digitally, or even on the stage—to commemorate the sesquicentennial anniversaries of major irregular battles and events. The answer here wasn't a surprise: "It's [the war and slavery] still a sore topic. And, it's still a sensitive topic." But when I inquired if he thought Missourians and Kansans would rather just forget about this bloodstained segment of their history completely, Chris responded that he believes "those feelings [the Missouri-Kansas border rivalry] will exist for years to come." "But," he added, "I think most folks will not be aware of the origin of those feelings or even care." In short, the guerrilla theater's scattered memory narrative has produced a commemorative void in which people seem to know a legacy exists—but not why.[12]

This tour paints an admittedly gloomy portrait of things to come on the guerrilla theater's preservation front—because just like memories themselves, the sites and objects that trigger recollections are anything but permanent. To a historian of social memory studying something that is, by its very definition, "irregular," this presents a serious problem. Even a history of forgetting is only possible if just enough of something remains to calculate the sum of what's been lost. As we already know, the margins of anything are typically not well preserved, especially when funding for things believed to be the main story is already so cherished and difficult to come by. But if nothing else, I hope this story of guerrilla memory—and of the scars it left, and of those it failed to leave—on the physical landscape of the guerrilla theater illuminate that the margins of Civil War history, however unseemly their violence or irregular their recollections, are worth accounting for . . . because one never knows when the fringes of one narrative will become the centerpiece of another.

APPENDIX 1

QUANTRILL REUNION LOGISTICS

Attendance figures for each reunion are based on a comparison of newspaper coverage and official rosters kept by reunion organizers. Numbers vary slightly between these accounts, and a margin of error consisting of 1–3 men per reunion is probable.

Reunion year	Location	Guerrillas attended
1898	Sni-a-Bar	37
1899	Lee's Summit	81
1900	Oak Grove	47
1901	Oak Grove	25
1902	Independence	25
1903	Independence	53
1904	Independence	48
1905	Independence	36
1906	Independence	20
1907	Independence	40
1908	Blue Springs	34
1909	Independence	30
1910	Wallace Grove	35
1911	Blue Springs	43
1912	Wallace Grove	30
1913	Wallace Grove	34
1914	Wallace Grove	N/A
1915	Wallace Grove	28
1916	Wallace Grove	20
1917	Wallace Grove	33
1918	Wallace Grove	14
1919	Wallace Grove	15
1920	Wallace Grove	12
1921	Wallace Grove	11
1922	Wallace Grove	10
1923	Wallace Grove	9
1924	Wallace Grove	8
1925	Wallace Grove	2
1926	Wallace Grove	4
1927	Wallace Grove	3
1928	Wallace Grove	1
1929	Wallace Grove	3

APPENDIX 2

QUANTRILL FAMILY HEREDITARY VICE TREE

Based on William E. Connelley's *Quantrill and the Border Wars*, 1909.

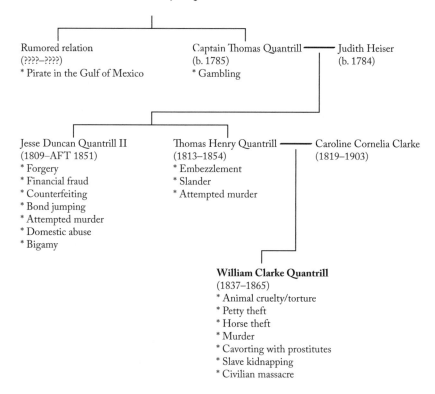

Rumored relation
(????–????)
* Pirate in the Gulf of Mexico

Captain Thomas Quantrill —— Judith Heiser
(b. 1785)   (b. 1784)
* Gambling

Jesse Duncan Quantrill II
(1809–AFT 1851)
* Forgery
* Financial fraud
* Counterfeiting
* Bond jumping
* Attempted murder
* Domestic abuse
* Bigamy

Thomas Henry Quantrill —— Caroline Cornelia Clarke
(1813–1854)   (1819–1903)
* Embezzlement
* Slander
* Attempted murder

William Clarke Quantrill
(1837–1865)
* Animal cruelty/torture
* Petty theft
* Horse theft
* Murder
* Cavorting with prostitutes
* Slave kidnapping
* Civilian massacre

NOTES

Introduction. The Borderlands of Memory

1. Mattson, "Mark Twain on War and Peace," 784.

2. Ibid., 785.

3. Twain, "The Private History of a Campaign That Failed," reprinted in Budd, *Mark Twain*, 863, 865, 867–868.

4. Ibid., 866–867, 869, 870, 871–872.

5. Ibid., 878–879.

6. Ibid., 879–880, 882.

7. Historians of memory frequently employ terms such as "social memory" or "collective memory." Just as frequently, they place the onus on readers to figure out precisely what they mean. These terms, along with others, however, are not universally employed—and definitions often fail to align from scholar to scholar. With this in mind, the following is a key to how such terminology will be employed throughout this project:

1. "Non-collective experience" refers directly to the fact that incidents within guerrilla warfare typically played out in domestic or otherwise isolated settings that did not facilitate the construction or development of state-, region-, or nationwide experiences to be shared easily among groups of people larger than the family unit or small community. For example, compare the non-collective experience of guerrillas raiding the home of a suspected Unionist and his family to the siege of Richmond as experienced collectively by thousands of people.

2. "Collective memory" refers to two interconnected scenarios: (a) an event that has been experienced by a mass of people and has, therefore, been remembered with similar enough detail by the majority of the group to represent a collective recollection of the event in question; (b) a case in which that mass of people is gradually influenced to accept memories of an event tailored for a specific purpose (such as achieving a political gain or prompting sectional reconciliation) as their own.

3. "Individualized memory" is the product of individuals or groups (such as those who experienced the guerrilla war) consciously determining not to concede or replace memories of their non-collective experiences with more common, and potentially more attractive, collective memory narratives (such as one that may serve to whitewash or glorify wartime behavior). For those to whom the guerrilla war constituted the "regular" war, the Civil War was experienced in a noncollective way, and, because the borderlands lacked an obvious collective memory narrative, many residents chose to forego attaching their specific memories to less familiar national reunification narratives.

8. See Fellman, *Inside War.*

9. See Sutherland, *Savage Conflict*; Beilein, "Guerrilla Shirt"; Whites, "Forty Shirts."

10. See Fellman, *Inside War;* Mackey, *Uncivil War.*

11. See Sutherland, *Savage Conflict.*

12. See Blight, *Race and Reunion.*

13. See Janney, *Remembering the Civil War.*

14. Also see Neff, *Honoring the Civil War Dead.*

15. Historians of irregular violence in Appalachia—especially Kentucky—will no doubt take issue with my placement of Missouri atop the guerrilla totem. Kentucky harbored its own pantheon of irregular badmen, from Edwin Terrill, M. Jerome Clarke, and Sam "One-Armed" Berry to Champ Ferguson, Henry Magruder, and Hercules Walker. That said, the scope, duration, and consistently high intensity of the irregular war along the Missouri-Kansas border is undeniable. For primary examples of guerrilla activity in Kentucky, see Charles Atkin, Civil War Letters, Huntington Library, San Marino, Calif.; Magruder, *Three Years in the Saddle*; Edwin Terrell to Thomas E. Bramlette, June 17, 1865, Kentucky Department for Libraries and Archives, accessed via *The Civil War Governors of Kentucky Digital Documentary Edition* (KYR-0001-004-1942).

16. On the "New War in the West," see Arenson and Graybill, *Civil War Wests*; Scharff, *Empire and Liberty*; Kelman, *Misplaced Massacre*; Nelson, "Indians Make the Best Guerrillas."

17. On white vs. white and home invasions, see Lepore, *Name of War.* On total war not having been designed by whites for use against other whites, see Mark Neely, *Civil War and the Limits of Destruction.*

Chapter 1. The Nastiest Bits

An earlier version of this chapter was published as "How to Remember This 'Damnable Guerrilla Warfare': Four Vignettes from Civil War Missouri," *Civil War History* 59, no. 2 (December 2013). Copyright 2013 by The Kent State University Press. Reprinted with permission.

1. G. W. Ballow to Mr. Frodsham, August 1862, G. W. Ballow, Letter, 1862 (C0223), State Historical Society of Missouri Manuscript Collection, Columbia (hereafter cited as SHSMMC).

2. On family matters specifically, note that each vignette is bookended by genealogical information for its main characters. This is not data for data's sake; instead, it is an effort to drive home the perspective—the hyperpersonal and hyperlocal—through which borderlanders experienced and first remembered the guerrilla war.

3. On the meaning of "individualized accounts," see introduction, n. 7.

4. On the circumstances and terms of the Louisiana Purchase, see Kukla, *Wilderness So Immense;* Kastor, *Nation's Crucible.*

5. See Forbes, *Missouri Compromise and Its Aftermath*; Childers, *Failure of Popular Sovereignty.*

6. On the state's various landmarks, landscapes, and ecosystems, see Chapman, *Archaeology of Missouri, I* and *II.*

7. See Burnett and Luebbering, *German Settlement in Missouri* and *Immigrant*

Women in the Settlement of Missouri; Rowan, *Germans for a Free Missouri;* Frizzell, *Independent Immigrants.*

8. See Arenson, *Great Heart of the Republic.*

9. For a concise narrative of the Missouri-Kansas border feud of the 1840s and 1850s, see the introduction of Castel's *William Clarke Quantrill.* Monograph-length treatments of "Bleeding Kansas" include Oertel, *Bleeding Borders,* and Etcheson, *Bleeding Kansas;* on the Marais des Cygnes Massacre specifically, see Cutler, *West Wind Rises.*

10. On Missouri's so-called Mormon Wars, see LeSueur, *The 1838 Mormon War in Missouri;* Moore, *Bones in the Well;* Spencer, *Missouri Mormon Experience.*

11. For various looks at Ozark culture, see Gerlach, *Immigrants in the Ozarks* and "Rural Ethnic and Religious Groups as Cultural Islands in the Ozarks of Missouri: Their Emergence and Persistence"; Vincent Anderson, *Bald Knobbers.* On William Wilson, see Hulbert, "Texas Bound and Down."

12. On the struggle for Missouri between Jackson and Lyon, see Adamson, *Rebellion in Missouri,* 186; for biographical treatments of each, see Phillips, *Missouri's Confederate* and *Damned Yankee.*

13. The Battle of Wilson's Creek, fought on August 10, 1861, is likely the main exception here, though the skirmish, in the course of which more than five hundred men fell dead, is greatly overshadowed by the First Battle of Bull Run, fought on July 21, 1861, in Virginia. See Piston, *Wilson's Creek.*

14. Letter from Soldier to Wife [Harriet], September 9, 1864, Francis Fairbank and Harriet Elizabeth Audsley, Papers, 1862–1912 (C2374), SHSMMC; Clifton Holtzclaw was a prominent guerrilla chieftain born in Missouri in 1833. For information on Holtzclaw, see Bowen, "Quantrill, James, Younger," 47; Fellman, *Inside War,* 137–38.

15. In *Mystic Chords of Memory,* Kammen argues convincingly for the existence of "a powerful tendency in the United States to depoliticize traditions for the sake of 'reconciliations'" and that "the politics of culture in this country has everything to do with the process of contestation and with the subsequent quest for reconciliation" (13–14). In other words, Kammen essentially offers that Americans, in the periods following major wars (the Civil War, World War I, World War II), have employed this sort of selective and collective remembrance in the process of reconstructing a more palatable past and corresponding national identity.

16. Inscoe, "Guerrilla War and Remembrance," 45–60.

17. William Brown, Quantrill Raid Account, 1909 (C2391), SHSMMC, 1.

18. 1870 and 1920 U.S. Federal Censuses, available at Ancestry.com.

19. Connelley, *Quantrill and the Border Wars,* 41. In the text, I refer to Connelley as a "pseudohistorian" for the same reason that John Newman Edwards should be categorized more as mythmaker and polemicist than scholar. Connelley, though Edwards's ideological opposite on the partisan spectrum, often relied on unacceptable methods of historical inquiry, such as theories of "inherited vice," that differentiate him from modern historians. For more information on Edwards, see chapter 2. For more information on Connelley, see chapter 6.

20. See Stiles, *Jesse James,* 94–96.

21. See Whites, "Forty Shirts," 56–78.

22. See chapters 23 and 29 in Connelley, *Quantrill and the Border Wars.*

23. Brown, Quantrill Raid Account, 1–2.

24. Ibid., 2–3, 5.

25. Ibid., 3, 4–5.

26. Ibid., 4–5.

27. 1870 U.S. Federal Census; Wilhelm Kroll Collection (KC1253), State Historical Society of Missouri, Kansas City, 1, 4.

28. Kroll Collection, 1–2, 4.

29. Kroll Collection, 2.

30. Kroll Collection, 2–3.

31. 1870 U.S. Federal Census; Kroll Collection, 4.

32. Louis A. Meyer, "The Battle at Emma, Missouri, as Seen by an Eye Witness," 1920s (C3982), SHSMMC, 1.

33. Ibid., 2.

34. 1880 U.S. Federal Census; Missouri Marriage Records, 1805–2002; 1860 U.S. Federal Census; New York, 1820–1850 Passenger and Immigration Lists, all available at Ancestry.com.

35. Meyer, "Battle at Emma," 2.

36. Ibid., 2–3. It is worth noting that the frequency with which white guerrillas raped white women is presently unknown and highly disputed. Many scholars seem content with the notion that guerrillas, whom they otherwise tag as nefarious or even sociopathic, behaved with notable sexual restraint in the presence of white women. The vast majority of postwar accounts that describe white female interaction with guerrillas do not mention rape, and historians have interpreted this source-based silence as proof of rareness. However, we should be cautious not to automatically discredit all allegations of white-on-white sexual violence simply because it may or may not have been rare. Guerrillas capable of scalping, decapitation, or burning men alive were almost certainly capable of using rape as a tool for terror—especially if a potential victim was the focus of an ethnic grudge. The instances of sexual violence described by Meyer are not intended to resolve this debate; rather, they shed light on the gruesome possibilities of ethnically charged guerrilla warfare and the atypical manner in which it has been remembered. For conflicting thoughts on rape during the Civil War, see Fellman, *Inside War*, 206–9; Barber and Ritter, "'Physical Abuse . . . and Rough Handling,'" 49–64.

37. Meyer, "Battle at Emma," 3; Missouri Death Records 1910–56, available at Ancestry.com.

38. James H. Rigg, memoir, 1877 (C3982), SHSMMC, 16.

39. 1860 U.S. Federal Census.

40. Rigg, 17–18; U.S. Civil War Draft Registration Records, 1863–65, available at Ancestry.com.

41. Rigg, 18–19.

42. Ibid., 20.

43. Ibid., 22–23.

44. Ibid., 28; 1920 U.S. Federal Census.

45. As mentioned in the text, exact figures for the dead at Centralia are difficult to calculate. Different accounts of both massacres typically provide a range of 20 to 30 killed on the train and a range of 120 to 200 in the field ambush. See *War of the Rebellion*, ser. 1, vol. 1, 3:419–423, 453, 455–456, 458, 488, 490.

46. 1910 U.S. Federal Census; Missouri Marriage Records, 1805–2002, both available at Ancestry.com.

47. 1850 and 1860 U.S. Federal Censuses, available on Ancestry.com.

48. Mary E. Lakenan, "The Bill Anderson Massacre," n.d. (C0995), SHSMMC, 2.

49. Ibid., 1.

50. Ibid., 2.

51. 1920 U.S. Federal Census; Social Security Death Index, available at Ancestry.com.

52. "A Romance of the War. Suicide of a Noted Jayhawker," *Leavenworth Bulletin*, February 25, 1871.

Chapter 2. An Irregular Lost Cause

An earlier version of this chapter was published as "Constructing Guerrilla Memory: John Newman Edwards and Missouri's Irregular Lost Cause," *Journal of the Civil War Era* 2, no. 1 (March 2012). Copyright 2012 by the University of North Carolina Press. Reprinted with permission.

1. Edwards, *Noted Guerrillas*, 20.

2. Ibid., 13.

3. Foster, *Ghosts of the Confederacy*, 48–50, 56, 60. On the Lost Cause, see Wilson, *Baptized in Blood*; Gallagher and Nolan, *Myth of the Lost Cause*. On Lee specifically, see Connelly, *Marble Man*; Alan T. Nolan, *Lee Considered*.

4. On Confederate nationalism, see Bernath, *Confederate Minds*; Thomas, *Confederate Nation*; Binnington, *Confederate Visions*.

5. For more on the possibility of western exclusion and postwar southern identity, see Phillips, "Chrysalis State," 158, 160.

6. For excellent treatment of a similar process of postwar realignment with the Confederacy, see Marshall, *Creating a Confederate Kentucky*.

7. Edwards, *Noted* Guerrillas, 21–22. This conceding of the "rights of civilized warfare" espoused by Edwards stood in stark contrast to the events of July 26, 1865, in Samuel's Depot, Kentucky. There, with the help of cousins T. W. Samuels (the high sheriff of Nelson County), Wilson Samuels (a prominent landowner and businessman), and W. T. Samuels (a prominent attorney and Kentucky's state auditor), Frank James and roughly a dozen others from Quantrill's command were granted official military paroles and allowed to return to Missouri of their own power. Frank James Parole Papers, July 26, 1865, and Frank James to Sarah Isabel (Samuels) Pence, January 18, 1909, both from the Private Collection of William T. Samuels Jr. and Family, Loretto, Kentucky.

8. Cobb, *Away Down South*, 63–64.

9. Edwards misspelled William Clarke Quantrill's surname as "Quantrell"—a very common mistake in the late nineteenth and early twentieth centuries (and one that persists in some histories even today). Please note that I have decided not to correct my sources' original spelling, but I employ the proper version of Quantrill when referring to the guerrilla chieftain myself.

10. Edwards, *Noted* Guerrillas, 31, 51.

11. Ibid., 54, 62, 326. In the Bible, Saul killed himself rather than be captured alive in battle. Aristophanes was a prolific satirist of life in ancient Athens. As for

Anderson's inability to be crushed by superior numbers: that ability apparently abandoned him in Richmond, Missouri, in 1864. He was shot dead while charging wildly (and virtually alone) into a line of Union troopers.

12. Ibid., 116, 390, 438, 31.

13. Foster, *Ghosts of the Confederacy*, 47, 59.

14. Edwards, *Noted* Guerrillas, 132–133.

15. Ibid., 193–194.

16. See Cushman, *Belligerent Muse*, chapter 4.

17. Blight, *Race and Reunion*, 142–143.

18. Edwards, *Noted* Guerrillas, 439–440, 14–15. The creation of novelist James Fenimore Cooper, "Leatherstocking" (also known as "Natty Bumpo" or "Hawk-eye") was an English frontiersman raised by Native Americans.

19. Ibid., 54–56.

20. Ibid., 15, 164–166, 439.

21. Ibid., 15–16.

22. Perhaps Turner Ashby, well known for his mounted exploits and long associated with cavalier chivalry, best paralleled the sort of equestrian image Edwards desired to superimpose on Quantrill, Anderson, and company–but with a Missouri-oriented, bushwhacking twist. For more on the memory of Turner Ashby, see Paul Anderson's *Blood Image*. For more on the roles of Ashby and his horse "Telegraph Tom" in Jackson's Valley Campaign, see Cozzens, *Shenandoah 1862.*

23. Edwards, *Noted* Guerrillas, 27, 164–166.

24. Ibid., 33–35. As chapter 6 will chronicle, Quantrill did have a brother, but not *this* brother–or any other who was slaughtered by bloodthirsty Jayhawkers in the years preceding the Civil War.

25. Foster, *Ghosts of the Confederacy*, 58.

26. Ibid., 57–60.

27. Ibid., 156–158.

28. Quantrill's "status" at this point in the war is mired in controversy. Many historians believe that Quantrill was made a captain under the Partisan Ranger Act of 1862 by Confederate general Sterling Price; others contend that Quantrill had no such authority. Official Confederate documents–including pay rosters and quartermaster's records–indicate that the former is correct, but that the commission was provided by Upton Hayes, a militia colonel. In any event, when Quantrill journeyed to Richmond, it was undoubtedly to acquire an official commission, not a promotion as a partisan ranger.

29. Dowdey and Manarin, *Wartime Papers of Robert E. Lee*, 688–689.

30. Mosby, *Take Sides with the Truth*, 32, 97, 134.

31. On postwar politics see Richardson, *West from Appomattox*; Foner, *Reconstruction*; and, Blight, *Race and Reunion.*

32. Phillips, "Chrysalis State," 150, 157.

33. Stiles, *Jesse James*, 246.

34. Edwards, *John N. Edwards*, 92–95; Stiles, *Last Rebel*, 210–211, 216–217, 224–225.

35. Phillips, "Chrysalis State," 150, 156.

36. See Hahn, *Nation under Our Feet*, 272, 282, 289.

37. See Edwards, "The Chivalry of Crime," *Kansas City Times*, September 29, 1872.

38. Edwards, "Robin Hood Letter," *Kansas City Times*, October 15, 1872.

39. Edwards, "Quantrell," as originally printed in the *Kansas City Times*, May 12, 1872, in Edwards, *John N. Edwards*, 69–70; Stiles, *Last Rebel*, 224–225, 241–242.

40. Edwards, *John N. Edwards*, 187–190.

41. Ibid., 206–207, 208, 210, 226.

42. Ibid., 88.

43. SOS, Missouri State Archives: Governors, www.sos.mo.gov/archives/history/historicallistings/governors.asp (accessed January 19, 2011).

44. The American Presidency Project, University of California at Santa Barbara, http://www.presidency.ucsb.edu/index.php (accessed January 19, 2011).

45. Edwards, *John N. Edwards*, 196–197.

Chapter 3. Rebooting Guerrilla Memory

1. See Hildebrand, *Autobiography of Samuel Hildebrand*, ed. Ross.

2. Introduction by Ross in ibid., xiv; "A Missouri Desperado–The Murderer of Seventy-Eight Men–Desperate Attempt to Capture Him," *New York Times*, June 18, 1869.

3. The memoirs of three men–all verified ex-guerrillas–have not been included as primary analytical components of this chapter. The recollections of Warren Welch (n.d.), titled *Warren Welch Remembers: A Guerrilla Fighter from Jackson County, Missouri*, are very brief, highly condensed, and devoid of virtually any social details or context. The account of Jim Cummins (1908), titled *Jim Cummins: The Guerilla*, also lacks social detail or context and focuses extensively on Cummins's career as a postwar criminal and fugitive. Finally, the little known, never published, and untitled manuscript of Frank Smith (written sometime after the turn of the twentieth century and before his death in 1932) also reads as a brief, condensed survey of military events; it lacks social details and, in many cases, appears to be the product of secondhand testimony to Smith from other guerrillas.

4. Nixon, *Henry W. Grady*, 340, 345, 346, 347–348.

5. The "New South" situation on the ground in Missouri mirrored much of what Grady espoused at the New England Club about the rest of the South. In *Paths of Resistance*, David Thelen argues quite convincingly that during the Civil War in Missouri, "no family or home was safe from a sudden visit by guerrillas or militiamen who demanded food, property, sex, lodging, and even lives." And in the postbellum period, Thelen continues, a resultant "popular crisis of law and authority" created by wartime chaos morphed into "new leaders" in Washington and Jefferson City "who were determined to use law to create a large-scale market economy." According to Thelen, the "old order"–marked by "family, work, leisure, friends, community, natural surroundings, and worship"–clashed fiercely with the "new order." This newer order would live and die by a set of economic imperatives rooted in market competition and rapid industrial growth. While the book notes stiff resistance from some traditional Missourians set on preserving folk memories and traditions, Thelen decries the changes as largely inevitable: railroads expanded competition and shipping, refrigeration battered down old

agricultural marketing impediments, women and children entered the workforce, and artisans "soon learned how cost had replaced skill as the guiding principle of labor." See Thelen, *Paths of Resistance,* 3, 5, 25, 32, 33, 48, 52, 60–61.

6. See Harris, *Uncle Remus: His Songs and Sayings* and *Uncle Remus and the Little Boy.*

7. On lynching in postbellum Missouri, see Harper, *White Man's Heaven.*

8. Hall, *Revolt against Chivalry,* 134, 149, 146.

9. On one hand, for the purposes of this chapter, the Lost Cause is generally de-fined as a regional (southern-bred) intellectual movement designed to help south-erners justify secession, to explain Confederate defeat in honorable terms, and to preserve alleged cultural features of the "Old South" (for example, a racial hier-archy previously pillared by the institution of slavery and the idea that African Americans were happy as slaves and loyal to their pro-Confederate masters). On the other hand, the New South (or the New South Creed) is defined broadly as a regional (again, southern-bred) economic movement that advocated modern-ization, industrialization, and a quick process of sectional reconciliation to allow for much-needed northern capital investment. Naturally, one movement seek-ing preservation and one movement seeking modernization would seem to be at odds, and their ideologies did often clash. That said, it is important to note that for guerrilla memoirists in the twentieth century, picking and choosing from the most attractive qualities of both sides—essentially, cherry-picking from each platform—actually represented the best way for ex-guerrillas to ingratiate themselves with the widest possible swaths of southern society.

10. Hildebrand, *Autobiography,* 110, 136, 148, 157.

11. Younger, *Story of Cole Younger,* 23, 57, 70.

12. Walker, *Recollections of Quantrill's Guerrillas,* 8, 11, 56, 57–58. Despite Walk-er's claim that no African American fought as a regular member of the band, the back of Noland's tombstone in Woodlawn Cemetery reads "A Man Among Men"—an inscription likely added years after his death by white, pro-Confederate commemorators.

13. McCorkle and Barton, *Three Years with Quantrill,* 99, 138–139, 141–142. Ac-cording to the memoir of Frank Smith, Jack Mann "had committed criminal acts in Jackson County" and "had been forced to flee when things became too hot." "He was made to dig his own grave," Smith recalled, before being "killed and dumped into it." See Frank Smith Manuscript (n.d.).

14. Trow, *William C. Quantrell,* 57–58, 119–120.

15. George Richardson Cruzen, "The Story of My Life" Reminiscences 1930, Missouri History Museum Archives, Saint Louis, 7, 15, 16, 21, 31.

16. For varying interpretations of the UDC's rise to power (and the extent of that power), see Foster, *Ghosts of the Confederacy,* 48–50, 52–55, 56–60, 61–62, 173, 174, 188; Karen Cox, *Dixie's Daughters,* 3–5, 9, 83, 84, 118–119, 121–122, 126, 158; Janney, *Burying the Dead,* 1–14, 55–58, 165, 167–169.

17. UDC *Scrapbook 1,* United Daughters of the Confederacy (John S. Mar-maduke Chapter #713), (C2296), SHSMMC, 1–6; *Scrapbook 1923–1936,* United Daughters of the Confederacy (Jefferson Davis Chapter) (KC20), SHSMMC; *Min-ute Booklet, 1954* (R1254), United Daughters of the Confederacy (Missouri Divi-sion), SHSMMC, 8, 45, 77–78; *Yearbook, 1916–1917,* United Daughters of the Con-federacy (Robert E. Lee Chapter) (KC152), SHSMMC.

18. *Reminiscences of Women in Missouri during the Sixties, Compiled and Published by the Missouri Division of the United Daughters of the Confederacy* (Jefferson City, Mo., 1913). See also Bynum, *Long Shadow of the Civil War*, Whites, "Forty Shirts"; Inscoe, *Race, War, and Remembrance*; Fellman, *Inside War*, Sutherland, *Savage Conflict*; McKnight, *Confederate Outlaw*; Myers, *Executing Daniel Bright*; Beilein, "Guerrilla Shirt."

19. *Reminiscences*, 26–30, 54–55, 91–93, 214–219.

20. Younger, *Story of Cole Younger*, 159–160.

21. In 1876 Cole Younger and two of his brothers, Bob and Jim, were captured in the aftermath of a botched robbery of the First National Bank of Northfield, Minnesota. Stories differ, but some accounts claim that the James-Younger Gang targeted the bank because members believed it held the savings of well-known Union general and Republican congressman Benjamin Butler.

22. Woodward, *Origins of the New South*, 156.

23. William H. Gregg, "A Little Dab of History without Embellishment," 1906 (C1113), SHSMMC, 10.

24. Ibid., 62–63.

25. Watts, *Babe of the Company*, 24, 27–28.

26. McCorkle and Barton, *Three Years with Quantrill*, 51, 157.

27. Ibid., 51–52, 212.

28. Dalton, *Under the Black Flag*, 19–20, 28.

29. Ibid., 33–34.

30. Joseph M. Bailey, *Confederate Guerrilla*, 39, 54, 69, 71.

31. See Rotundo, *American Manhood*; Bederman, *Manliness and Civilization*.

32. Hoganson, *Fighting for American Manhood*, 45, 54.

33. Ibid., 109–110.

34. Younger, *Story of Cole Younger*, 150–151.

35. Trow, *Charles W. Quantrell*, 266.

36. Hildebrand, *Autobiography*, 171.

Chapter 4. Getting the Band Back Together

1. "The Days of Civil Strife," *Kansas City Journal*, May 12, 1888, in Hale, *The William Clarke Quantrill Men Reunions* (hereafter cited as *WCQMR*); "Reunion of Quantrell's Band," *New York Herald*, May 12, 1888; "Not Ashamed of Their Bloody Record," *New York Tribune*, May 12, 1888.

Here a word on source material is in order. In addition to a few archival artifacts held by the State Historical Society of Missouri in Columbia (the J. B. George Collection) and the Jackson County Historical Society (the Warren Welch Collection), the vast majority of surviving primary information concerning Quantrill reunions comes from newspaper articles and print media. Naturally, a reporter stands as an intermediary—with his/her own agenda and perceptions—between us and the reunion participants, but the arrangement is simply unavoidable. Whenever possible, I have attempted to tip off readers concerning the biases of particular papers and present mainly the raw facts of articles unless the agenda of the reporter or paper is a point unto itself (i.e., propaganda).

2. "A Rebel Reunion," *Grand Army Advocate*, May 17, 1888; "Quantrell's Cutthroats," *Grand Army Advocate*, May 17, 1888.

3. On veterans' organizations, reunions, and Decoration Day ceremonies, see Blight, *Race and Reunion*; Gannon, *Won Cause*; Janney, *Remembering the Civil War*; Marten, *Sing Not War*; McConnell, *Glorious Contentment.*

4. Fellman, *Inside War*, 247–248, 249, 251, 253, 256.

5. Jeremy Neely, "The Quantrill-Men Reunions," 245–246, 248, 249.

6. Guerrilla memoirists who attended Quantrill survivors' reunions included Cole Younger, Harrison Trow, William H. Gregg, John McCorkle, and Andrew Walker.

7. The most famous of these Blue-Gray reunions took place in Gettysburg, Pennsylvania.

8. "Souvenir Book of the United Confederate Veterans Reunion, 1919," United Confederate Veterans, Hargrett Rare Book & Manuscript Library, University of Georgia.

9. William David Upshaw was a Democrat and fervent prohibitionist who won three successive terms to Congress between 1919 and 1927. Upshaw ran unsuccessfully against Franklin Roosevelt as the presidential candidate of the Prohibition Party in 1932 and died in 1952. See the *Biographical Directory of the United States Congress.*

10. "Souvenir Book of the United Confederate Veterans Reunion, 1919."

11. Philpott, *Sponsor Souvenir Album.*

12. Harris, *Civil War*, 3–4, 6.

13. "Quantrell's Men Together," *Kansas City Star*, September 11, 1898 (*WCQMR*).

14. "Quantrell's Men," *Kansas City World*, September 11, 1898 (*WCQMR*); "Quantrell's Men," *Jackson Examiner*, September 17, 1898 (*WCQMR*).

15. "Frank James and Other Men of Quantrell's Band Come Together for a Talk Over the Past," *Saint Louis Republic*, October 2, 1898 (*WCQMR*).

16. "Quantrell's Men," *Kansas City Journal*, September 14, 1899 (*WCQMR*); "Rough Riders of the 60s," *Fort Worth Morning Register*, September 17, 1899.

17. "Border Days Lived Over Again in Meet of Quantrell Band," *Kansas City Post*, August 22, 1914 (*WCQMR*); "Rough Riders of the 60's," *Fort Worth Morning Register*, September 17, 1899; "The Quantrell Reunion," *Kansas City Star*, August 17, 1906; "Survivors of Quantrell Band Hold Reunion," *Albuquerque Journal*, August 19, 1911; "Quantrell Survivors Hold a Reunion," *Columbus Daily Enquirer*, August 22, 1913; "Annual Quantrell Reunion," *Tulsa World*, August 27, 1921.

18. "Quantrell Men," *Independence Sentinel*, October 26, 1900 (*WCQMR*); *Kansas City Star*, August 22, 1902 (*WCQMR*); "To Have a Quantrell Parade," *Kansas City Star*, October 9, 1900.

19. "Quantrell's Men," *Kansas City Journal*, September 24, 1901 (*WCQMR*). Francis Marion (d. 1795) was an American military commander of the Revolutionary era well known–as the "Swamp Fox"–for his irregular tactics and penchant for guerrilla warfare. See Boddie, *Traditions of the Swamp Fox.*

20. *Kansas City Times*, August 22, 1902 (*WCQMR*).

21. "As They Raided in the '60's," *Kansas City Times*, August 20, 1910 (*WCQMR*); "Where Truman's Campaign Trail Began," *Kansas City Times*, May 7, 1970 (*WCQMR*).

22. "Made a Blunder," *Kansas City Sunday Journal*, August 23, 1903 (*WCQMR*).

23. *Sarcoxie Record*, August 25, 1904 (*WCQMR*); "Frank James an Apostate," *Kansas City Star*, August 21, 1904; "Frank James Is for Roosevelt," *Pawtucket Times*, August 22, 1904.

24. The headline of the *Kansas City Times* on August 26, 1905, read, "Frank James Was Missing," while the subheading stated, "Since the Reformed Bandit Renounced Democracy He Is in Bad Order with Quantrell's Old Band and Wouldn't Be a Welcome Guest." A report from the *Kansas City Star* the next day reported that James's old comrades had quickly forgiven him; this information, however, seems highly inaccurate. Much of the sentiment against James was anything but fleeting. An article from the *Kansas City Journal* of August 21, 1909, stated that "[Frank] James has not attended any of the reunions since his speech made in the Independence court house yard, in which he declared that his friends were in the North and that he was never turned down except by those of the Southland." Also see "The Forgiving Guerrillas," *Kansas City Star*, August 27, 1905; "Guerrillas at Their Reunion," *Duluth News-Tribune*, August 28, 1905.

25. "And Proud of Quantrell!" *Kansas City Star*, August 25, 1905; "Frank James Was Missing," *Kansas City Times*, August 26, 1905 (*WCQMR*).

26. By 1910, reunions had returned to business as usual concerning political orations. Congressman William P. Borland was listed as a headline speaker.

27. "Released 'Dave' Edwards," *Kansas City Star*, August 24, 1907.

28. "Army Friends," *Kansas City Post*, August 23, 1907 (*WCQMR*); "It Didn't Bother Them," *Kansas City Journal*, August 24, 1907 (*WCQMR*); "Shot at by Quantrell Man 'Jim' Cummings Attacked by 'Dave' Edwards at the Reunion," *Kansas City Star*, August 23, 1907. It is worth mentioning that in 1909 Jim Cummins *did* beat a different resident of Higginsville to death following yet another quarrel. See "James Boys' Friend Kills," *Kansas City Star*, March 23, 1909.

29. "Quantrill Reunion," *Independence Examiner*, September 23, 1915 (*WCQMR*); "Quantrill Men Meet," *Independence Examiner*, September 29, 1916 (*WCQMR*); "Quantrell Men Meet in Kansas City, Sept. 30," *Fort Worth Star-Telegram*, September 30, 1916; *Kansas City Star*, August 22, 1917 (*WCQMR*); "Taps Will Soon Sound for the Last of Quantrills," *Kansas City Star*, August 22, 1917; "Quantrill's Remnant," *Columbia State*, August 17, 1917.

30. "Quantrill Men in Reunion," *Independence Examiner*, September 9, 1922 (*WCQMR*); "Few Quantrell Veterans Left. Seven Who Attend Reunion All That Survive of Band of 300," *Kansas City Times*, August 13, 1922.

31. "Roster Lost," *Kansas City Journal Post*, August 21, 1927 (*WCQMR*). In the years leading up to World War I, Quantrill Men living in Texas and no longer able to travel to annual reunions in Missouri held much smaller meetings. See "Reunion Begins Today in Sherman," *Dallas Morning News*, August 12, 1913; "Quantrell's Men Gather for Another 'Attack'," *Fort Worth Star-Telegram*, May 9, 1914.

32. *Oak Grove Banner*, December 24, 1903.

33. Noland is undoubtedly the historical inspiration behind the character "Holt" in Ang Lee's film *Ride with the Devil* (1999).

34. See Slave Census Schedule 1860, Jackson County, Missouri, available at Ancestry.com.

35. On why John Noland may have chosen to fight as a black Confederate guerrilla, see Beilein, "Household War," 81–84.

36. "Frank James Was Missing," *Kansas City Times*, August 26, 1905.

37. *Independence Examiner*, August 22, 1908.

38. "Retelling Old Stories," *Kansas City Post*, August 24, 1907 (*WCQMR*).

39. "Quantrell Men Again," *Pleasant Hill Times*, September 5, 1924 (*WCQMR*).

40. "Quantrill Men Reunion," *Independence Examiner*, August 30, 1929 (*WCQMR*).

41. *Kansas City Times*, August 21, 1902; "Talked Old War and New," *Kansas City Star*, August 25, 1917.

42. Per chapter 3, see Hoganson, *Fighting for American Manhood*. Also see Keefer, *Conflicting Memories on the "River of Death."*

43. "Quantrell's Raiders Would Fight Huns," *Kansas City Journal*, September 1, 1918 (*WCQMR*); "Quantrell Men in Reunion," *Kansas City Star*, August 31, 1918.

44. Ibid.

45. "The Annual Reunion Brought Twenty-Five Survivors Together," *Kansas City Journal*, September 27, 1901 (*WCQMR*).

46. "Ex-Confederate Writes," *Oak Grove Banner*, April 28, 1911 (*WCQMR*).

47. "Quantrell Men Reunion," *Independence Examiner*, August 24, 1907 (*WCQMR*).

48. "Girl of Broken Heart, Quantrell's Fiancée, Grieved Self to Death," *Kansas City Post*, September 25, 1915 (*WCQMR*).

49. "Survivors of Raid on Lawrence Tell of Bloody Battle," *Kansas City Post*, August 20, 1910 (*WCQMR*).

50. *Kansas City Journal*, November 9, 1912; "Quantrell Band a Memory," *Fort Worth Star-Telegram*, August 11, 1912.

51. *Independence Daily News*, July 18, 1913 (*WCQMR*).

52. Ibid.

53. "Cummins Still an Outlaw," *Saint Louis Post-Dispatch*, August 24, 1902 (*WCQMR*).

54. "State of Kansas vs. William Quantrell, et al., Filed 18 November 1863," Quantrill (William Clarke) Research Collection, McCain Library and Archives, University of Southern Mississippi; "Would Try Guerrillas Yet," *Kansas City Star*, August 30, 1905; "To Locate the Survivors. Lawrence Indicted Forty-Three of the Quantrell Raiders," *Kansas City Star*, August 31, 1905; "Advocate Trial of Quantrell Raiders," *Tucson Daily Citizen*, September 2, 1905; "Quantrell Raiders May Yet Be Prosecuted," *Omaha World Herald*, August 31, 1905.

55. "Jayhawk vs. Quantrell," *Jackson Examiner*, September 1, 1905 (*WCQMR*).

56. "As in Days of '63," *Kansas City Journal*, October 17, 1906 (*WCQMR*).

57. "Fake Quantrell Story," *Oak Grove Banner*, October 19, 1906 (*WCQMR*).

58. "The Journal's Peanut Politics," *Oak Grove Banner*, October 19, 1906 (*WCQMR*); "The Campaign's Prize Fake," *Kansas City Star,* October 17, 1906; "The Quantrell Reunion. To Be Held at Judge Liddil's Home in Independence," *Kansas City Star*, August 17, 1906.

59. "Lawrence Raid for Revenge," *Kansas City Post*, October 4, 1913 (*WCQMR*).

60. Ibid. Additionally, Gregg recalled finding more than $250,000 worth of property stolen from Missourians on the road into Lawrence: "I went ahead with my five men and for a mile before we reached Lawrence we found little shacks built beside the road. They were filled with household goods that had been carried over into Kansas from Missouri."

61. "Raids Retold at Quantrell Meet," *Kansas City Journal*, August 29, 1925 (*WCQMR*).

62. "She Remembers When Quantrill's Mother Came to Blue Springs," *Kansas City Star*, August 30, 1942 (*WCQMR*); "Mrs. Quantrell in Neglect," *Sioux City Journal*, January 27, 1899; "Mother of the Celebrated Partisan Soldier," *Lexington*

Morning Herald, March 16, 1898; "Facts about Quantrill Brought to Light by His Old Mother Being Brought to Lexington," *Lexington Morning Herald,* March 27, 1898; "Mrs. Quantrill Arrives and Is Snugly Ensconced at St. Joseph's," *Lexington Morning Herald,* March 18, 1898.

63. Given their apparent fragility (in both a literal, physical sense and in the context of memory), it is striking to note how dependent historians have become on these oral and local newspaper accounts, without which almost nothing in the way of substantive archival materials would survive to lend context to the reunions. Minus these testimonies, a few scattered images and an incomplete attendance roster are all that would remain.

64. "Quantrill Men Reunion," *Kansas City Star,* August 20, 1931; "Elizabeth Wallace Obituary," *Independence Examiner,* December 7, 1938; "House with a History to Go on Block," *Kansas City Times,* September 20, 1967 (*WCQMR*).

65. "Column by Lola Butcher," *Independence Examiner,* August 29, 1980 (*WCQMR*).

66. A note here on the comparative importance and geographic reach of newspapers and memoirs is appropriate. On one hand, newspapers certainly kept guerrillas in the public eye at the local level more efficiently and on a much more regular basis than could a published memoir. On the other hand, memoirs at least had the *potential* to reach a much broader audience beyond the geographic circulation of a town paper–but *also* required a much greater degree of literacy to deploy their propaganda. We can state for the record, then, that newspaper coverage undoubtedly aided the endurance of the association's reunions and that those meetings ultimately helped propel and inform the production of guerrilla memoirs. As a result, while the reunions failed to draw national or even South-wide attention by way of the press, such interaction with the media still played an important role in the broader process of rebooting and mainstreaming guerrilla memory in the twentieth century.

Chapter 5. *The Gatekeepers' Conundrum*

Portions of this chapter were published in a special issue of *Common-Place* on Civil War memory and the sesquicentennial. See Hulbert, "Regularly Irregular War."

1. *Reminiscences of Women in Missouri during the Sixties,* 42. It is undoubtedly an understatement, but still one worth mentioning in the context of memory, that these twelve pieces of human chattel would themselves have remembered "life" in the antebellum period quite differently than their owner.

2. Ibid., 42.

3. Ibid., 43–44.

4. Ibid., 3.

5. On women and the Civil War experience more generally, see Whites and Long, *Occupied Women;* Clinton and Silber, *Divided Houses;* Rable, *Civil Wars;* Cashin, *War Was You and Me.*

6. *Reminiscences,* 19–20.

7. *Reminiscences,* 35–36.

8. *Reminiscences,* 26, 28–29.

9. *Reminiscences,* 124–125.

10. *Reminiscences,* 249–250.

11. *Reminiscences,* 252. For a more detailed analysis of the potential prevalence of sexual assault in the guerrilla theater, see chapter 1, n. 33.

12. Sherman's march through Georgia brought women into direct contact with soldiers and forced them to take on similar roles as family diplomats. See Campbell, *When Sherman Marched North from the Sea*; Rubin, *Through the Heart of Dixie*; Frank, *Civilian War.*

13. *Reminiscences,* 214–215. Providing protection for children came with the territory of commanding the family—but in some instances, when a child no longer felt that his or her situation was a safe one, the female-led, household-based structure of guerrilla warfare could implode from within. This appears so in the case of Robert Black, a man charged with fighting as a bushwhacker under the alias "Aaron Blackburn" in 1865. Though Black vehemently denied all of the provost marshal's accusations, his own son, Samuel Black, testified on behalf of the prosecution. Samuel's turn against his father was almost undoubtedly an act of self-preservation brought on by the inability of the Black household to function properly in the wake of General Order #11. See Reel F1138, Union Provost Marshal Records, Incidents Involving Individuals, Missouri State Archives, Jefferson City, Missouri.

14. *Reminiscences,* 186–187. Doneghy's son, on learning that the house would be burned, dashed inside to retrieve the family Bible. The officer in charge was apparently so moved by the boy's effort to rescue the treasured heirloom for his mother that the house was temporarily spared.

15. For specific treatments of women in Missouri's guerrilla theater, see Beilein, "Guerrilla Shirt"; Beilein, "Household War"; Whites, "Forty Shirts."

16. *Reminiscences,* 142.

17. *Reminiscences,* 106–107, 110.

18. Ibid.

19. See Oates, *Woman of Valor;* Alcott, *Civil War Hospital Sketches;* Jaquette, *Letters of a Civil War Nurse*; Brumgardt, *Civil War Nurse.*

20. *Reminiscences,* 234.

21. *Reminiscences,* 132–133.

22. *Reminiscences,*132–135. In the Eastern Theater, women working as nurses or laundresses outside of established hospitals sometimes did similar work with the dead and dying—a possible shared experience between women inside and outside on the guerrilla theater. See Schultz, *Women at the Front.*

23. *Reminiscences,* 292–293.

24. *Reminiscences,* 30.

25. *Reminiscences,* 126–127. While Horne and Maddox had threatened to wield axes against Unionist invaders, the circumstances of each situation eventually dictated that they not swing them. However, as a gruesome episode from the 1890 autobiography of Rev. James R. Ramsay reveals, it would be a major mistake to assume that such threats of physical violence from women were empty ones. Prior to the Civil War, Ramsay served as a missionary with the Seminole Indians and, when the fighting began, relocated to Rock Creek, Kansas, to find steadier employment as a schoolteacher. According to Ramsay, the community of Rock Creek resided just over the Kansas side of the border with Missouri, and "there was a certain class of men living in that part of Kansas" who "called themselves

Jayhawkers." "They presented to be friends of the Union," Ramsay continued, "but really they were robbers." The leader of this gang in particular was David Markram, who, along with his followers, "frequently made raids into the state of Missouri, and robbed people that they called 'Secesh.'" By Ramsay's math, Markram had made several very profitable raids into Missouri before "he made one raid too many." In winter 1862–1863, pro-Confederate Missourians "laid in wait" for Markram and wounded him "so that he could not get away." Then, Ramsay contended, "the women used axes and hatchets" and "hacked his [Markram's] skull open" after he had already been shot several times. At Markram's funeral, at which Ramsay led the prayer service, he recalled that the face of the corpse was "all chopped with axes and hatchets" and that it was "a terrible sight to behold." Ramsay concluded by stating that "with the death of Markram, Jayhawking ceased." In other words, these pro-Confederate women had carved a clear message into the body of David Markram that they, along with their men, would resort to whatever manner of violence became necessary to protect their homes from invasion. See "Autobiography of Rev. James Ross Ramsay," Western History Collections, University of Oklahoma, Norman, Oklahoma, 54–55.

26. *Reminiscences,* 235.

27. Ibid.

28. *Reminiscences,* 91–93.

29. *Reminiscences,* 253–254.

30. *Reminiscences,* 93–94.

31. *Reminiscences,* 256. The event described by Graves was the August 13, 1863, collapse of a makeshift Federal jail in Kansas City, Missouri. According to most accounts, ten female prisoners—including the sisters of "Bloody Bill" Anderson—were incarcerated in the building when its structural integrity failed. Four girls were crushed to death (including Josephine Anderson) and multiple others were maimed or crippled. Controversies exist to this day concerning whether Union authorities intentionally weakened the foundations of the building and to what direct extent the prison collapse spurred the Lawrence Massacre a few days later. See Harris, "Catalyst for Terror."

It is also worth noting that the women jailed by Union authorities in Kansas City were not particularly unique. Women faced a variety of legal consequences for the various roles they took in supporting guerrilla violence. For example, in 1863 Margaret Clifton was charged not only with treason as a result of her marriage to bushwhacker Samuel Clifton—she was also charged as an accessory to murders he allegedly committed while fighting in the bush. Another woman named Dozier was charged for simply saying that she supported Bill Anderson's right to kill Union soldiers at the Centralia Massacre. See Reels F1239 and F1305, Union Provost Marshal Records, Incidents Involving Individuals, Missouri State Archives, Jefferson City, Missouri.

32. *Reminiscences,* 248–249.

33. *Reminiscences,* 216.

34. *Reminiscences,* 214.

35. When an abbreviated adaptation of this chapter first appeared in a special issue of *Common-Place* (February 2014), it was met by the following reply (or rebuttal, perhaps): "But as was true of the Civil War at large, the course and outcome

in Missouri were determined by the respective fighting forces, their actions, tactics and policies. This is not a 'male-dominated' interpretation. It is how the war was fought and won." In other words, according to the author of the comment, the male-centric interpretation of the war in the borderlands described above is not actually biased in terms of gender; rather, it simply reflects historical facts and events—"*how the war was fought and won.*" In one respect, the comment is correct—the course and subsequent outcome of the war in Missouri *was* determined by the actions and tactics of its fighting forces. Unfortunately, in another respect, the comment also stands as a case in point that large segments of the interested public are still quite uncomfortable with the idea that women had both played an integral role in the waging of guerrilla warfare (i.e., as an integral part of the fighting force) and that they demanded to be remembered on equal footing with their irregular male counterparts.

Chapter 6. The Unionists Strike Back

1. Isadora August Allison (Johnson), "A Night of Terror," Kenneth Spencer Research Library, University of Kansas, 1–2.

2. Ibid., 2.

3. Ibid., 3–5.

4. Ibid., 5–6.

5. Ibid., 10–11.

6. Ibid., 11–14.

7. Ibid., 15.

8. Edwards, *Noted Guerrillas*, 31.

9. Connelley, *Quantrill and the Border Wars*, 5, 7.

10. Ibid., 6. For a detailed of analysis of Connelley's scholarly objectivity, see Beilein, "Nothing but Truth Is History."

11. Connelley, *Quantrill and the Border Wars*, 7.

12. Ibid., 41, 17–18.

13. Ibid., 18–19. For more on financial fraud and counterfeiting in antebellum America, see Mihm, *A Nation of Counterfeiters*; Kamensky, *Exchange Artist*.

14. Connelley, *Quantrill and the Border Wars*, 19–21.

15. Ibid., 23–24.

16. Ibid., 26–28.

17. Ibid., 42–43.

18. Ibid., 58–59.

19. For a complete breakdown of Quantrill's supposedly tainted genetics, see Appendix 2, "Quantrill Family Hereditary Vice Tree."

20. Ibid., 59, 91.

21. Ibid., 103–105, 111, 114–115, 119–121.

22. Ibid., 122–123, 131, 140–165. For an expert play-by-play of the Morgan Walker raid and analysis of how Quantrill entered Missouri society, see Beilein, "Household War," 163–178.

23. Connelley, *Quantrill and the Border Wars*, 166–167.

24. Ibid., 168–169.

25. Ibid., 162–163, 172–173. In another footnote, Connelley offered this com-

mentary on Edwards's description of the Morgan Walker raid in *Noted Guerrillas*: "It is a great pity that so beautiful a description as that written by major Edwards should have so little foundation in the facts as they occurred." See 164–165.

26. Ibid., 284–285, 297.

27. Ibid., 298–299, 311–312.

28. Ibid., 356, 391.

29. Ibid., 377.

30. Ibid., 482–483.

31. As the "Coup of 1912" (discussed in chapter 4) came three years after the publication of *Quantrill and the Border Wars*, Connelley believed that it was clear evidence that Missouri guerrillas had taken his message to heart. William Gregg, the historian believed, had attempted to fold the Quantrill men into the Upton Hayes camp of regular veterans—thus dropping the name of the guerrilla commander—because the message of *Quantrill and the Border Wars* had convinced him of Quantrill's nefarious character. See Sheridan, "Most Unusual Gathering," 188.

32. "Quantrell the Queer, or, The Busted Bonanza," 1875 (KC0025), State Historical Society of Missouri, Kansas City, 1, 27.

33. For more on how the Civil War caused generational rifts related to notions of honor, defeat, and the end of slavery, see Carmichael, *Last Generation*.

34. "The James Boys Again," *New York Herald*, February 18, 1875.

35. "Quantrell the Queer," 2–7.

36. Ibid., 7–12.

37. Ibid., 12–18.

38. Ibid., 18–26.

39. Edwards, *John N. Edwards*, 69–70; Edwards, "The Chivalry of Crime," *Kansas City Times*, September 29, 1872; Edwards, "The Fair Robbery," *Kansas City Times*, October 15, 1872 (C3896), State Historical Society of Missouri, Columbia (SHSMC); Edwards, "High Handed," *Kansas City Times*, September 27, 1872 (C3896), SHSMC; Edwards, "A Letter from Jesse James," *Liberty Tribune* (from *Kansas City Times*), June 24, 1870 (C3896), SHSMC.

40. "Fiftieth Anniversary of Raid by Quantrell," August 22, 1913, *Montgomery Advertiser*; "Survivors of the Raid Meet," August 22, 1913, *Idaho Statesman*; "50th Anniversary of Quantrell's Raid," August 22, 1913, *Daily Oklahoman*; "Quantrell Is Scored," August 22, 1913, *Tulsa Daily World*.

41. Sheridan, "A Most Unusual Gathering," 183. Survivors of the Lawrence raid who had relocated to Portland, Oregon, held their own memorial service to commemorate the fiftieth anniversary of the massacre. See "Survivor's Hold Meeting. Services Held in Portland on Anniversary of Quantrell Tragedy," August 31, 1913, *Morning Oregonian*.

42. Sheridan, "A Most Unusual Gathering," 180–182.

43. According to the Kansas State Historical Society, "Charles Sumner Gleed (1856–1920) was a Topeka Businessman involved in railroad, telephone, mining, land, banking and other businesses in Kansas and throughout the nation. He was also a lawyer, a newspaperman, and a member of the University of Kansas Board of Regents. He was active in the Republican Party and in various civic and cultural affairs." kshs.org/p/Charles-s-gleed-collection/14030 (accessed January 18, 2016). Perhaps not ironically, given his position as head of the Kansas Historical

Society, William Connelley delivered a historical address immediately following Gleed's talk. See Sheridan, "A Most Unusual Gathering," 188.

44. As noted in the text, Gleed's speech was the scheduled keynote address of the semicentennial reunion in Lawrence held on August 21, 1913. The address was published immediately thereafter by a local newspaper and was thus (thankfully) preserved for posterity. Other papers, such as the address of Samuel A. Riggs, were also prepared and delivered before the festival-goers—but Gleed's address is fundamentally representative of those transcripts (at least those that survive) in that it reflects well the thematic and rhetorical methods employed against William C. Quantrill and the Edwards narrative of the Lawrence Massacre for the occasion. See S. A. Riggs, "Paper for Centennial," part of (MC159) Recollections of Quantrill Raid: For Fiftieth Anniversary of Lawrence Massacre, 1913, Kansas Historical Society, Topeka, Kansas.

45. Charles S. Gleed, "Kansas City Journal, Memorial Address," part of (MC159) Recollections of Quantrill Raid: For Fiftieth Anniversary of Lawrence Massacre, 1913, Kansas Historical Society, Topeka, Kansas, 1–2.

46. Ibid., 3–4.

47. Ibid., 5–6.

48. Ibid., 6, 10, 11–12.

49. Ibid., 16–17.

50. Blake, *Quantrill Raid,* 11. Subsequent citations to this poem will be given parenthetically in the text.

51. "Proud of Their Campaigns," *Kansas City Post,* October 4, 1913. The term "Red Legs" referred to a specific group of Kansas guerrillas known to wear red leggings.

52. Connelley, *Quantrill and the Border* Wars, 391.

53. Ibid., 392.

54. Ibid., 382.

55. Ibid.

56. "Narrative of a Former Slave," Andrew Williams Collection, Kenneth Spencer Research Library, University of Kansas, Lawrence, Kansas, 8, 8–9.

57. Ibid., 9–10.

58. "Account of Eye Witness J. M. Henry," Mrs. A. W. Phillips Collection, Kenneth Spencer Research Library, University of Kansas, Lawrence, Kansas, 1.

59. Ibid., 1.

60. Ibid., 2.

61. Ibid., 2–3.

62. At first glance, it would seem most logical for Unionists to have written this episode out of the Lawrence Massacre narrative completely. However, because many pro-Confederate narratives reference the killing of Skaggs—including that of John Newman Edwards—the story was likely known well enough that it could not simply be ignored. For a more detailed account of Larkin Skaggs's death in Lawrence and its commemorative implications on the massacre, see Hulbert, "Memory in the Re-Making."

63. Patterson, "I Can Prove I Am Quantrill," 10–11, 54–56. Also see McDermott, "Mystery Man of Quatsino Sound," 12–16, 63.

64. Patterson, "I Can Prove I Am Quantrill," 10–11.

65. Ibid., 10–11.

66. Ibid., 11, 55–56.

67. In addition to John Newman Edwards and William Elsey Connelley, modern historians all agree that Quantrill was killed in June 1865 by men under the command of Union "guerrilla hunter" Edwin Terrill. See Monaghan, *Civil War on the Western Border;* Brownlee, *Gray Ghosts of the Confederacy;* Castel, *William Clarke Quantrill;* Fellman, *Inside War.*

Chapter 7. Guerrillas Gone Wild in the West

1. The sheer volume of films, popular history, fictional literature, and television shows attesting to this status is overwhelming. The 1999 fantasy film *Purgatory*, which features Jesse James and Billy the Kid living in a town for the spirits of misunderstood gunslingers of the Wild West, is a choice example. (Other residents of Purgatory include Bill Hickok, Jack Slade, and Doc Holliday.) Another interesting case is Garrett's *Famous Characters of the Wild West*. While useless as a serious biographical source, the book is representative of untold pop histories that tether the Kid and James—who is labeled "the ultimate outlaw"—together as western gunhands.

2. Past generations of scholarship have chronicled the Civil War in Missouri, Arkansas, Texas, and even the northern plains. In recent years, however, a new wave of historians has begun reimagining what the "Civil War in the West" might actually encompass. These histories document the conflict in the far-western territories of Colorado, Wyoming, Arizona, New Mexico, and beyond; they drastically expand the temporal, geographic, ethnic, and cultural makeup of the war by incorporating new belligerents—Hispanic and Native American populations—and new ideas, such as Confederate manifest destiny. This chapter in no way disputes the importance of wartime events that unfolded in the western territories or how they magnify the war's overall complexity for the better; like that of guerrilla memory, these are stories paramount to understanding the war as a truly *national* conflict. Therefore, my objective here is to delineate how and why the Missouri bushwhacker gradually became entangled with the environment of this Civil War West rather than the Border West of Missouri and Kansas and, in many ways, to document how the story of guerrilla memory (moving from East to West) illustrates just how connected the traditional war in the East and this newer war in the West really were, then and now. For cutting-edge treatments of the war in the West, see Kelman, *Misplaced Massacre*; Frazier, *Blood and Treasure*; Blyth, *Charicahua and Janos*; Scharff, *Empire and Liberty*; Nelson, "Death in the Distance"; Downs, "Three Faces of Sovereignty."

3. See Stiles, *Jesse James.*

4. The life of George Armstrong Custer—and his widow Elizabeth's decades-long battle to define his legacy—helps corroborate the existence of the process through which some Civil War figures were westernized. New status as westerners elevated both Custer and James to national prestige in ways the Civil War had not. The main difference between them, however, is that Custer not only invited but specifically helped foster his makeover as a hero of the western plains because he understood it as a net positive to his career. According to some historians of

the Battle of Little Big Horn, Custer recklessly engaged his men with a superior force because he believed that a victory over such formidable odds would restore his national reputation following a political scandal and potentially win him the Democratic presidential nomination in the election of 1876. For our purposes, Custer's example is especially important because it reveals two broader points about westernization: first, that James was not alone in undergoing such a transformation, and second, that it was not a uniform process, nor was it always enacted by the same forces or with similar motivations. Westernization did not inherently involve efforts to export or expel undesirable figures such as James; a geographic makeover could also be used to gather immense fame and power, as might have ultimately been the case for Custer had he been victorious at Little Big Horn. On Custer's reputation for methodically cultivating his public image, see Van De Water, *Glory-Hunter*, Sandoz, *Battle of Little Big Horn.*

5. Stiles, *Jesse James*, 16–19, 26, 30–31; Settle, *Jesse James*, 6–9.

6. Stiles, *Jesse James*, 88–91; Settle, *Jesse James*, 20–21, 26.

7. Stiles, *Jesse James*, 116–118, 119–122; Settle, *Jesse* James, 26–28, 29–31; Breihan, *Complete and Authentic Life*, 80–83, 86–89.

8. Stiles, *Jesse James*, 171–172; Settle, *Jesse* James, 33–35; on connection to Edwards, see chapter 2 in the present volume, and Hulbert, "Constructing Guerrilla Memory."

9. Stiles, *Jesse James*, 323–335, 357–359, 371–374; Settle, *Jesse* James, 92–94, 116–117, 119.

10. Stiles, *Jesse James*, 374–375; "Letter from Frank James to Warren Welch, 23 June 1902," and "Letter from Jesse James Jr. to Warren Welch, 23 June 1902," both from Warren W. Welch Collection (1860–1959), Jackson County Historical Society.

11. Wallis, *Billy the Kid*, 5–8; Utley, *Billy the Kid*, 2–6.

12. Wallis, *Billy the Kid*, 19–20, 38, 49, 52, 59–60, 66–68, 78, 88–89; Utley, *Billy the Kid*, 10–12, 14–16; Frederick Nolan, *Lincoln County War*, 3–9.

13. Frederick Nolan, *Lincoln County War*, 60–74, 99–119; Utley, *High Noon in Lincoln*, 10–23.

14. Frederick Nolan, *Lincoln County War*, 219–232, 322–331, 332–342; Utley, *High Noon in Lincoln*, 51–65.

15. Wallis, *Billy the Kid*, 246–247, 249–250; Utley, Billy the Kid, 186–196; Garrett, *Authentic Life of Billy the Kid*, 136–139.

16. Stiles, *Jesse James*, 352, 465.

17. Bowen, "Quantrill, James, Younger, et al.," 43–45; Bowen, "Guerrilla War in Western Missouri," 39–40, 43, 44, 46.

18. On Anderson's death, see Hulbert, "William 'Bloody Bill' Anderson"; on Todd's death, see Sutherland, *Savage Conflict*, 203–204; on Quantrill's death, see "Quantrell's Last Fight Story," August 30, 1873, *The Standard.*

19. This national fascination with all things western included not just outlaw histories but also autobiographies, dime novels, and Wild West shows. The latter two subjects are examined in subsequent sections of this chapter, but James did not live to produce or dictate a memoir (as did William "Buffalo Bill" Cody and Martha "Calamity Jane" Burk). Between these cultural mediums—all of which predated the films that will be explored in chapter 8—existed an unquestionably di-

alectic relationship. No single medium accounted for the entirety of the western fad, which was, predominantly at least, ascribed to eastern audiences, but each simultaneously gleaned and provided strength for the whole. On American perceptions, consumption, and early codification of the West, see Walle, *Cowboy Hero and Its Audience*; Bold, *Selling the Wild West*; Athearn, *Mythic West*; McVeigh, *American Western*.

While the full corpus of the genre cannot be cited here, other examples of outlaw histories and autobiographies include Burdett, *Life of Kit Carson*; Edward Sylvester, *Life of Kit Carson*; Buel, *Heroes of the Plains* and *Life and Marvelous Adventures of Wild Bill*; *Buffalo Bill and His Wild West Companions*; *Belle Starr, the Bandit Queen*; Burk, *Life and Adventures of Calamity Jane*; Fable, *Billy the Kid*; Garrett, *Authentic Life of Billy the Kid*; Daggett, *Billy LeRoy, the Colorado Bandit*; Cattermole, *Famous Frontiersmen, Pioneers, and Scouts*; *Life and Adventures of Sam Bass*.

20. For content ratios, see Dacus, *Illustrated Lives and Adventures*; Donald, *Outlaws of the Border*.

21. Bradley, *Outlaws of the Border*, 81–82.

22. Ibid., 82–83.

23. Ibid., 83–84.

24. Stiles, *Jesse James*, 339–341, 351–352.

25. Appler, *Train and Bank Robbers*, 260–263; Dacus, *Illustrated Lives and Adventures*, 316–322; Donald, *Outlaws of the Border*, 352–357.

26. Buel, *Border Bandits*, 47.

27. Ibid., 47–48.

28. Dacus, *Illustrated Lives and Adventures*, 292–297.

29. Ibid., 310–315.

30. Donald, *Outlaws of the Border*, 132–136, 345–351, 352–357.

31. Appler, *Train and Bank Robbers*, 239.

32. Donald, *Outlaws of the Border*, 358.

33. Buel, *Border Bandits*, 5–6.

34. For a general history of the dime novel and production logistics, see preface to J. Randolph Cox, *Dime Novel Companion*. On the dime novel as a genre related to western culture, industrialization, or adolescence, see Dinan, *Pulp Western*; Folsom, *American Western Novel*; Cook, *Dime Novel Roundup*; Vicki Anderson, *Dime Novel in Children's Literature*; Denning, *Mechanic Accents*.

35. See Jones, *Dime Novel Western*, specifically chapter 3, "The Hero in Transition."

36. J. Randolph Cox, *Dime Novel Companion*, 143–144, 154–155, 252–255.

37. Ibid., 144.

38. The dime novels referenced in this chapter (all published in New York City by Street and Smith) can be found in the Tampa Dime Novel Collection, Special Collections, University of South Florida. W. B. Lawson, *Jesse James' Red Rival; or, The Miner of Madman's Mountain*, Issue #60, June 28, 1902; *Jesse James' Strange Campaign; or, The Siege of the Lost Ranch*, Issue #89, January 17, 1903; *Jesse James' Death Vendetta; or, The Robber Rangers of the Rio Grande*, Issue #63, July 19, 1902; *Jesse James Surrounded; or, The Desperate Stand at Cutthroat Ranch*, Issue #43, March 1, 1902; *Jesse James in Wyoming; or, The Den in the Black Hills*, Issue #6, June 15, 1901; *Jesse James' Exploits*, Issue #25, October 26, 1901. For other examples see W. B.

Lawson, *Jesse James in Mexico; or, Raiders of the Rio Grande*, Issue #41, February 15, 1902; *Jesse James' Cowboy Clan; or, The Master of the Mysterious Ranch*, Issue #72, September 20, 1902; *Jesse James' Close Call; or, The Outlaw's Last Rally in Southern Wyoming*, Issue #12, July 27, 1901; *Jesse James' Desperate Dash; or, Raiding the Ranches*, Issue #79, November 8, 1902; *Jesse James Afloat; or, Holding up the Coast Towns*, Issue #78, November 1, 1902.

39. Jones, *Dime Novel Western*, 6–9, 79; J. Randolph Cox, Dime Novel Companion, xviii–xx, xx–xxi.

40. W. B. Lawson, *Jesse James on a Traitor's Trail; or, Fighting for Both Sides*, Issue #100, April 4, 1903. While this particular issue is cited here, nearly every issue of *TJJS* included a similar contest for boys.

41. On Roosevelt's time in the West in his own words, see Roosevelt, *Hunting Trips of a Ranchman*. For scholarly treatments of Roosevelt's life and western self-makeover, see DiSilvestro, *Theodore Roosevelt in the Badlands*; McCullough, *Mornings on Horseback*; Morris, *Rise of Theodore Roosevelt*.

42. "Cole Younger's Scheme," *Columbus Daily Enquirer*, February 19, 1903.

43. "Cody Tells of What the Wild West Show Is Doing," *Omaha World Herald*, November 29, 1905; *Buffalo Bill's Wild West and Congress of Rough Riders of the World*. On Wild West shows in general, see Moses, *Wild West Shows*; Reddin, *Wild West Shows*; Don Russell, *Wild West*. On Buffalo Bill's show specifically, see Sayers, *Annie Oakley and Buffalo Bill's Wild West*; Louis S. Warren, *Buffalo Bill's America*; Davidson, *Buffalo Bill, Wild West Showman*.

44. "Buy Wild West Show," *Aberdeen Daily News*, February 19, 1903; "Cole Younger and Frank James Here with Their Show Today," *Lexington Morning Herald*, August 15, 1903; "Younger-James Show Will Be Seen Here," *Lexington Morning Herald*, August 6, 1903.

45. "Big Show Coming Here," *Fort Worth Star-Telegram*, October 11, 1903; "Historical Wild West, the Great Cole Younger and Frank James Aggregation to Show Here Next," *Baltimore American*, June 30, 1903. For an in-depth account of the Younger-James Wild West Show's rise and fall, see Koblas, *Younger and James Wild West Show*.

46. "Wild West Business Good," *Colorado Springs Gazette*, September 28, 1903.

47. "Curses! Me Stead's Stole! R-Revenge!" *Salt Lake Telegram*, May 6, 1903; "Missile Thrown by James-Younger Wild West Showman Fractured Little Girl's Skull," *Lexington Morning Herald*, August 18, 1903; "Little Money for Employee Sadness, Therefore, Claims the Erstwhile Players in Wild West Show," *Fort Worth Star-Telegram*, October 15, 1903.

48. "Cole Younger Accused," *Idaho Daily Statesman*, September 22, 1903; "Cole Younger Arrested," *Aberdeen Daily News*, September 23, 1903. Younger and James habitually complained to the show's owners that a criminal element—conmen, grafters, pickpockets—had latched onto the show and steadily driven away customers. Each party involved in the business felt it was the other's ultimate responsibility to deal with the situation.

49. "Old Time Bandits Are in Trouble," *Macon Telegraph*, September 22, 1903; "Cole Younger Charged with Embezzling $6000," *Boston Journal*, September 22, 1903.

50. "Own a Wild West Show," *Kansas City Star*, February 18, 1903.

Chapter 8. Black Flags and Silver Screens

1. On the tumultuous relationship between history and filmmakers (and its ability to enact widespread shifts in public perception of the past), see Toplin, *History by Hollywood*.

2. I say "most moviegoers" here because at least two silent shorts predated *Jesse James under the Black Flag*. Released in 1914, *Quantrell's Son* featured a melodramatic plot involving the guerrilla chieftain's fictional son and grandchild. *Quantrell, or, The Cold, Cruel Wars of Northern Missouri* was probably also released in 1914, though no information concerning its plot or cast appear to have survived. (It is also possible that the latter was simply a creative retitling of the former.) According to the Library of Congress, a leader in the preservation of silent-era films, perhaps as many as 75 percent have been permanently lost or destroyed. http://www.loc.gov/today/pr/2013/13-209.html (accessed January 2, 2016). In any case, neither film left as lasting an impact or reached as wide an audience as *Jesse James under the Black Flag* did in 1921.

3. In this context, the term "social bandit"–typically interchangeable with "Rob Roy" or "Robin Hood"–refers to an individual criminal or a group of criminals (such as Jesse James or the James-Younger Gang) whose legal transgressions are sanctioned by a community or part of a community due to a broader perceived social or economic grievance with the victim(s) of the crime(s), often an oppressive government or financially elite demographic. For fundamental treatments of banditry and outlawry, see Hobsbawm, *Primitive Rebels*; Seal, *Outlaw Legend*; Slatta, *Bandidos*.

4. Jesse James Jr. (born 1875) played the role of his father in another film written and directed by Franklin B. Coates, *Jesse James as the Outlaw*, in 1921. As a native of Springfield, Massachusetts, Coates had no inherent connection to Missouri or the James family minus this second film. The extent to which Jesse James Jr. exerted pro-Confederate influence on Coates during the writing and preproduction phases of *Jesses James under the Black Flag* is largely unknown. Following his partnership with Jesse James Jr., it appears as though Coates never again wrote, directed, or acted in another feature film.

5. The film *Dark Command* was adapted from the W. R. Burnett novel *The Dark Command: A Kansas Iliad* (1938). For a more in-depth comparison of novel and film, see Tibbetts, "Riding with the Devil," specifically 188–189.

6. William C. Quantrill and his mother, Caroline, did in fact hail from Canal Dover, Ohio. Additionally, Quantrill was briefly employed as a schoolteacher before his involvement in the Civil War. However, Caroline Quantrill did not pose as a housekeeper in Lawrence, Kansas–nor did she even migrate to the Border West with her son in the first place. While some period correspondence from Quantrill to his mother has survived, these letters, along with Caroline Quantrill's attempts to learn about her son's wartime activities *after the fact*, suggest at best a distant relationship between mother and son in the early 1860s. See Castel, *William Clarke Quantrill*, 25–30.

7. In reality, William C. Quantrill was involved in slave smuggling prior to his career as a pro-Confederate guerrilla commander. Posing as abolitionists based in Lawrence, Quantrill and his associates would "rescue" slaves from bondage in

western Missouri—only to then re-enslave and sell them elsewhere for a profit. Quantrill's beginnings as a Confederate guerrilla arose from an occasion on which he alerted slaveholders (members of the Walker family of Jackson County, Missouri) in advance of the scheme to steal their slaves and then helped the slave owners gun down his former associates. See ibid., 30–40.

8. William T. "Bloody Bill" Anderson was actually killed by soldiers from the Thirty-Third Infantry (Enrolled Missouri Militia) in a running skirmish at Albany, Ray County, Missouri, on October 26, 1864. The Federals, led by Colonel Samuel P. Cox, had been specifically tasked with hunting down and eliminating Anderson following the Centralia Massacre of September 27, 1864. Anderson is buried in Pioneer Cemetery in Richmond, Missouri. For the complete story of Anderson's demise, see Hulbert, "Killing 'Bloody Bill' Anderson."

9. Determining a factual account or "control sample" concerning the life of Kate Quantrill is exceedingly difficult; as a result, so is determining what constitutes fact versus fiction when she is depicted on film. The historian LeeAnn Whites has deduced that a woman named Sarah Catherine King of Missouri met William C. Quantrill in 1861 (when she was just thirteen years old and he significantly older at twenty-five). When Kate's parents objected to her relationship with the guerrilla, according to Whites, Kate simply ran away with Quantrill and began using the alias Kate Clarke Quantrill. In the 1920s ex-guerrillas vouched for Kate's credibility when she claimed to have spent much time with Quantrill in camp, but stories remain conflicting as to how directly involved—if at all—Kate Quantrill became as a bushwhacker herself. Following Quantrill's death, she ran a successful brothel in Saint Louis under a different alias. For the full story (or at least the fullest story available to date), see Whites, "Tale of Three Kates."

10. No evidence exists to suggest that Quantrill ever imagined an Indian-based Confederate empire for himself or his men. In fact, the scale of such an imperial endeavor clashes directly with what likely motivated most of Quantrill's guerrillas to fight in the first place: the protection of homes and families at a very local level.

11. While the high command in Richmond often disapproved of Quantrill's methods, he and his band did occasionally cooperate with units from the regular Confederate army—most notably those under the commands of General Sterling Price and General Kirby Smith, who each found Quantrill's guerrillas useful in specific scenarios. See Brownlee, *Gray Ghosts of the Confederacy*, 128–137.

12. In fact, William C. Quantrill survived well after the Lawrence Massacre of August 1863. Following the splintering of his original band of bushwhackers (from which Anderson and Todd recruited their own units), Quantrill was wounded in an ambush staged by Union soldiers on the outskirts of Taylorsville, Kentucky, on May 10, 1865. Nearly a month later, he succumbed to his wounds in Louisville, Kentucky. For the complete story of Quantrill's death, see Castel, *William Clarke Quantrill*, 208–213.

13. Per the preface of Connelley's *Quantrill and the Border Wars*, the newspaper editor and boyhood acquaintance of William C. Quantrill featured in the film is based entirely on W. W. Scott. Scott, who was a historian of Quantrill himself, did actually know Quantrill as a child and later served as editor of the Iron Valley Reporter in Canal Dover, Ohio. Following Scott's death, Connelley purchased his papers. Connelley, *Quantrill and the Border Wars*, 6.

14. For specific passages of *Quantrill and the Border Wars* quoted in *Arizona Raiders*, see 41, 328, 343. On the veracity of ad hominem accounts such as Connelley's, which depict Quantrill as a "juvenile monster," the historian Albert Castel wisely writes: "Such accounts should be received with more than a little skepticism. As in the case of all men who achieve fame of any sort, the events of later life are reflected back upon their early years. In addition, deeds which on the part of any other youth would have been completely forgotten no doubt took on sinister quality in the case of Quantrill. Finally, one can readily imagine that the post–Civil War inhabitants of Canal Dover were not exactly bursting with pride over this particular home-town boy and how he had 'made good.'" Castel, *William Clarke Quantrill*, 24.

15. See Portis, *True Grit*.

16. Slotkin, *Gunfighter Nation*, 4–6, 8, 16, 127–130, 133–138, 151–153. For a more abstract interpretation of the structure of a myth and the roles of "dominant social institutions" in establishing the requirements for that structure, see Wright, *Sixguns and Society*.

17. The 1955 film *Rebel without a Cause* is a prime example of propaganda designed to strengthen America's "domestic core" as a means of bolstering its ability to combat and contain the spread of communism abroad. The film's plot chronicles the trials and tribulations of three families scarred by domineering women, absentee parents, and out-of-touch fathers to disseminate a strict code of proper "American" (that is, conservative) standards for nuclear families concerning gender roles, childrearing, and domestic life. At the same time, the film offers a preview of the possible widespread results–dysfunctional families undermining the moral fabric of entire communities, disillusioned children running wild in the streets, and a breakdown of traditional authority–of those lessons going unheeded.

18. As mentioned in the text, this chapter is imminently more concerned with how the intersection of guerrilla warfare and Civil War memory influenced the broader relationship Americans had with the Civil War (how they remembered it, its place in American culture, and its role in producing or rethinking American identity) than with how contemporary issues–the Great Depression, World War II, the Cold War, and so on–shaped or reshaped interpretations of the war's legacy. Even so, it is critical to note that the process through which films featuring borderland guerrillas were imbibed with conservative, Cold War tropes *is* a case in point of the dialectic exchange discussed earlier in this chapter. Thus, at the same time films produced in the 1940s, 1950s, and 1960s influenced the society that generated them, the movies were also unquestionably influenced by the social, political, and economic factors that undergirded the environment in which they were spawned. In this way, the medium of film truly serves as a broadcaster of cultural expression–that is, how a society thinks about and imagines its own reflection. On the influence of Cold War cultural mores and the legacy of World War II on film, see Doherty, *Cold War, Cool Medium*; Hoberman, *Army of Phantoms;* Sayre, *Running Time*; Hendershot, *I Was a Cold War Monster*; Bodnar, *Blue-Collar Hollywood*; Rose, *Myth and the Greatest Generation*.

19. In *The West in Early Cinema* Nanna Verhoeff argues that a series of short, silent films that depicted the James-Younger Gang positively as social bandits was banned in many cities around the turn of the twentieth century. Verhoeff suggests

that middle- and upper-class adherents of the Progressive movement disapproved of the pictures because they glorified criminal activity and distorted female gender roles. It seems very likely, however, that Civil War veterans from both sides who were struggling to retain a monopoly on commemorative attention (in the wake of the Spanish-American War and the slow buildup of hostilities that led to the First World War) would have disapproved strongly of ex-bushwhackers overshadowing them in the national spotlight and pushed for the censure of the earliest guerrilla pictures to preserve the purity of mainstream war narratives. See Verhoeff, *West in Early Cinema*, 42, 49, 137–139, 141–142. For more on western films in early cinema, see Fenin and Everson, *Western*; Smith, *Shooting Cowboys and Indians*.

20. As noted by Robert J. Cook in his history of the centennial efforts at the national, state, and local levels, Civil War films produced in the 1950s and 1960s took particular care not to alienate white audiences in the North or the South. Oftentimes this resulted in what Cook calls a "consensus culture": an exercise in reaffirming reunification between *regular* soldiers from both sides of the war on film—and one almost perfectly suited to outcast irregular combatants for this purpose. See Cook, *Troubled Commemoration*, 227–238.

21. Library of Congress, *American Civil War*, v.

22. Robertson, *Civil War*, 15, 21.

23. Shelby Foote's three-volume history *The Civil War* stands as Catton's most likely rival—but while Catton's work was popular on release, Foote's did not become well known until he appeared on Ken Burns's wildly popular documentary, *The Civil War*, in the early 1990s.

24. Catton, *Coming Fury*, 413; Catton, *Terrible Swift Sword*, 27–28, 54–56, 67, 384.

25. In *The Reel Civil War*, Bruce Chadwick establishes precedent for the notion that Americans have intentionally used film as a way to "revise their history in order to come together in the awful wake of the Civil War." In fact, the "mythmakers" behind these films, Chadwick contends, have given Americans a "glorious and honorable past that probably never was, but a past we would like to have had." In that context, it is not difficult to imagine the roles played by Quantrill and other Missouri guerrillas in the movies. They represented all that was negative and, by comparison, provided the characteristics and narrative of the Civil War that Americans needed and wanted for themselves: honorable regular veterans, heroic sacrifice, touching reconciliation, freedom earned at high cost and worth defending. As such, Chadwick asserts that Quantrill was used "in numerous movies over the years to show the seamy side of the Lost Cause" and that he "quickly became the exemplar of the bad reb who stained the honor of all the good and noble rebs" (16, 240–241). Brian Wills seconds the assertion that Quantrill served (and continues to serve) as a go-to bad man for filmmakers. In *Gone with the Glory* he suggests that "for an audience that can be unsettled through the labeling as evil of one side or the other in this, our American war, he [Quantrill] remains an accessible figure for common reproach, and thus for reconciliation." Together, Chadwick and Wills shed light on the ways in which film could disseminate propaganda and influence patterns of remembrance on a national scale; both understand that Quantrill's on-screen persona was often symbolic of a maligned, borderland wartime experience. Even so, both stop well short of tracing this cine-

matic construct and its broader cultural significance back to its roots in the story of guerrilla memory.

For an extensive catalog of Civil War films produced in the twentieth century, see Kinnard, *The Blue and the Gray on the Silver Screen.* For more on various aspects of Civil War films and American culture, see William B. Russell, *Civil War Films;* York, *Fiction as Fact;* Bosel, *Homogenizing History;* Cullen, *Civil War in Popular Culture;* Toplin, *Ken Burns's The Civil War.*

26. Gallagher, *Causes Won, Lost, and Forgotten,* 2–4, 54–55, 61–67, 70–72, 86; Hulbert, "Texas Bound and Down," 32.

27. For a different and admittedly much more radical method of categorizing (or uncategorizing) Civil War films, see Barrett, *Shooting the Civil War,* 4–5, 61, 90. In many ways, Barrett echoes Slotkin—but is actually ignoring alternative motives for transforming certain individuals and the distinct possibility that individuals were relocated to exclude them from a mainstream American identity all along.

Epilogue. Notes from the [Disappearing] Guerrilla Theater

1. Butler, "Understanding Our Past." For similar commentary in a peer-reviewed setting, also see Gallagher and Meier, "Coming to Terms with Civil War Military History," specifically 492–493.

2. "Pallbearers Few for Frank James," *Kansas City Journal,* February 20, 1915, in Donald Hale, *Jesse and Frank James Scrapbook Volume 1* (D. R. Hale, n.d.) [hereafter cited as *JFJSV1*]; "Frank James Asked Cremation to Prevent Autopsy on Brain," *Kansas City Post,* February 21, 1915 (*JFJSV1*); "Ashes of James Put in Safety Box," *Kansas City Post,* February 23, 1915 (*JFJSV1*); "Frank James Dead at 74," *Fort Worth Star-Telegram,* February 19, 1915.

3. I say "allege" because while Anderson did lead his own band of pro-Confederate bushwhackers, most notably at Centralia, there is no evidence that he ever received a formal partisan ranger's commission from the Confederacy proper.

4. Younger's more recent stone reads "Captain Cole Younger. Capt. Quantrill's Co. C.S.A."

5. See Leslie, "Quantrill's Bones."

6. See Petersen and Jackson, *Lost Souls of the Lost Township.*

7. See Hulbert, "The Business of Guerrilla Memory," in *The Civil War Guerrilla.*

8. On how the Lawrence Massacre fits within the broader paradigm of "Household War," see Hulbert, "Memory in the Re-Making."

9. "Owner Gets a Thrill in Exhibiting Former Home of Cole Younger," 1937, from Donald Hale, *Cole Younger Scrapbook* (D. R. Hale, n.d.) [hereafter cited as (*CYS*)]; "Absence of a Lease Closes Younger Home," December 7, 1957 (*CYS*); "Younger Home to Be a Museum," *Kansas City Star,* September 1, 1966 (*CYS*).

10. "Cobwebs Replace Outlaws in House," *The Examiner,* November 17, 1975 (*CYS*); "History in Storage," *Kansas City Star,* September 14, 1982 (*CYS*); "Film Maker Helps Arrange for Markers," *Kansas City Star,* September 8, 1983 (*CYS*); "Can Outlaw Draw Some Tourists?" *Kansas City Star,* May 4, 1995 (*CYS*); "Fund Raising for Younger Home Set to Get Under Way," *Lee's Summit Journal Advertiser,*

May 3, 1995 (*CYS*); "Area Resident Once Lived in Old Younger Home," *Cass-County Democrat-Missourian,* January 25, 2002 (*CYS*).

11. For details on Edwards's show, see www.bloodybillrides.com. Unfortunately, the site has not been updated since 2013.

12. Written interview with Chris Edwards (March 3, 2013).

BIBLIOGRAPHY

Archival Documents

Arkansas History Commission
   Smith, Anne Sanderson, Papers

Chicago History Museum Research Center
   Asbury, Henry, Papers

Hargrett Rare Book and Manuscript Library, University of Georgia
   Confederate Veterans / UDC Artifacts, 1898–1934
   Souvenir Book of the United Confederate Veterans Reunion, 1919
   Tuck, Judge Henry Carlton, Papers
   United Confederate Veterans Collection

Historical Society of Pennsylvania
   Cooke, Jay, Papers (Collection 148)

Huntington Library
   Atkin, Charles, Civil War Letters, 1863–1865

Jackson County Historical Society, Independence, Missouri
   Doerschuk, Albert N., Collection
   Hale, Donald R., Papers
   Welch, Warren, Collection

Kansas State Historical Society
   Babbitt, Benjamin Talbot, to Governor Thomas Carney, December 1863
   A Brief Sketch of Indian Tribes in Franklin County, Kansas in 1862–1906
   Brown, John Stillman, to John L. Rupur, September 1863
   Brown, William, to Sarah Brown, October 1863
   Case, Alex E., Collection
   Clark, Charles S., Papers
   Guerrilla War Claims, 1875
   Kansas Militia Broadside, September 1863
   List of Quantrill's Raid Survivors, Lawrence, Kansas
   Montgomery, James, Correspondence
   Newman, Harry, to Governor Thomas Carney, April 1863
   Recollections of the Quantrill Raid, 1913
   Rejected Quantrill Raid Claims
   Quantrell's Raiders Comic Book, 1952
   Quantrill Raid—Claims Paid, 1861–1875
   Savage, Mary, Correspondence
   Simpson, H. M., to Hiram Hill, September 1863
   Stewart, John E., Correspondence

Kentucky Department of Military Affairs, Frankfort, Kentucky
    Guerrilla Letters

Library of Congress
    Griffith, George W. E., "My Experiences in the Quantrill Raid," 1924

McCain Library and Archives, University of Southern Mississippi
    Quantrill (William Clarke) Research Collection, 1858–1964

Missouri History Museum Archives
    Cruzen, George Richardson, "The Story of My Life," Reminiscences

Missouri Valley Special Collections, Kansas City Public Library
    Beeson, Mary F., Autobiography
    Dee, Thomas F., Reminiscences
    Dix-Flintom, Mrs. R. C., "My Experience in the Quantrill," n.d.
    Edwards, John Newman (Vertical File)
    Williams, Mrs. J. O., Collection

Newberry Library
    Conroy, Jack, Papers
    Wiles, Robert Leslie, Journal, 1862–1865

Pickler Memorial Library, Truman State University, Kirksville, Missouri
    Connelley, William E., Interviews

Private Collection, Saint Louis
    Smith, Frank, Manuscript, n.d.

Rubenstein Rare Book and Manuscript Library, Duke University
    Knox Family Papers, 1837–1884

Samuels, William, Jr., and Family, Private Collection, Loretto, Kentucky
    Frank James Parole Papers, 1865
    Frank James to Sarah Isabel Pence, Letters

Southern Historical Collection, University of North Carolina
    Campbell, Given, Papers
    Folk, George N., Papers
    Red Clay Ramblers Papers
    Wallace, James T., Diary
    Wilkerson, Anne Golden, Family History

Special Collections, University of Chicago
    Barton, William E., Collection of Lincolniana
    Hitchcock Family Papers
    Robertson, Wyndham, Papers
    Walden, John Morgan, Papers

Special Collections, University of South Florida
    Tampa Dime Novel Collection

Kenneth Spencer Research Library, University of Kansas
  Allison, Isadora August (Johnson), Collection
  Asher, Kathleen, Collection
  Connelley, William Elsey, Collection
  Dark Command Premiere Collection
  Elliott Family Collection
  Fisher, Hugh Dunn, Collection
  Fitch, Edward, Collection
  Gunther, C. F., Collection
  Hamill, Thomas, Collection
  Johnson, W. M., Collection
  Killam, Mary Chelsey, Letter
  Manuscripts on Kansas History Collection
  Paddock, G. W., Diary Transcript
  Parker, Caroline Updegraff, Collection
  Phillips, Mrs. A. W., Collection
  Quantrill, William Clarke, Collection
  Randlett, Reuben A., Collection
  Scott, W. W., Collection
  Tappan, Samuel F., Collection
  Whitney, William H. H., Diary
  Williams, Andrew, Collection
  Young, George E., Collection

State Historical Society of Missouri, Columbia
  Alker, John H., James, and William, Papers
  Audsley, Francis Fairbank and Harriet Elizabeth, Papers
  Ballow, G. W., Letter, 1862
  Benecke Family Papers
  Breckenridge, William Clark, Papers
  Brown, William, "Quantrill Raid Account," 1909
  Burns, Dennis D., "William Wilson, A Missouri Guerrilla," 1936
  Civil War, Confederate Proclamation, n.d.
  Civil War Letter, 1862
  Crittenden, T. T., Papers
  Ex-Confederate Association of Missouri, Broadside, 1887
  Edwards, John Newman, Letters
  Evans, William H., and Floyd C. Shoemaker Papers
  Froman, C. V., "The James Boys," n.d.
  George, B. James, Collection
  Gregg, William H., Manuscript
  Hannibal, Missouri, Order of Provost Marshal, 1864
  Independence, Missouri, Notebook, 1961
  James, Frank, Letter, 1915
  Kingsville Massacre, Missouri, 1865
  Ladies of the G.A.R., Department of Missouri, Secretary's Book, 1898–1910

Lakenan, Mary E. "The Bill Anderson Massacre," n.d.
Leonard, Abiel, Papers
Meyer, Louis A., "The Battle at Emma, Missouri, as Seen by an Eye Witness," circa 1920s
The Missouri Collection
Rigg, James H., Memoir, 1877
Settle, William A., Jr., Papers
Spanish-American War Recruiting Poster, 1898
Wilson's Creek Battlefield National Park Commission, Deed, 1964
United Daughters of the Confederacy, John S. Marmaduke Chapter, Scrapbooks, 1927–1929
Younger, Cole, Papers

State Historical Society of Missouri, Kansas City
Brown, John, Collection
Connelley, William Elsey, Letters
Fletcher, Thomas Clement, 1866
James, Daniel L., Papers
Kroll, Wilhelm, Collection
Moore, Meredith Tarlton, Interviews
Quantrell the Queer, or, The Busted Bonanza (1875)
Schmitt, Vera G., Papers
Snyder, Robert M., Jr., Collection
Shalor Eldridge Winchell Letters
United Daughters of the Confederacy, Jefferson Davis Chapter, Scrapbook, 1923–1936
United Daughters of the Confederacy, Robert E. Lee Chapter, Yearbook, 1916–1917
Winchell, Shalor Eldridge, Letters

State Historical Society of Missouri, Rolla
Arthur, George Clinton, Papers
Bradford, Moses J., Letters
Grand Army of the Republic, Dan McCook Post No. 312, "Black List," 1887
United Daughters of the Confederacy, Kate K. Salmon Chapter No. 631, Registrar's Book, 1917
United Daughters of the Confederacy, Missouri Division, Booklet 1954

Western History Collection, University of Oklahoma
Autobiography of Rev. James Ross Ramsay, 1890

Government Documents

Missouri State Archives
Union Provost Marshal Records' File of Papers Relating to Individual Citizens, 1861–1867

Digital Databases

American Presidency Project (University of California at Santa Barbara)

Ancestry.com (Online Genealogical Database)
    Missouri Death Records, 1910–1956
    Missouri Marriage Records, 1805–2002
    New York, 1820–1850 Passenger and Immigration Lists
    Social Security Death Index
    United States Federal Census (1850, 1860, 1870, 1880, 1900, 1910, 1920)
    U.S. Civil War Draft Registration Records, 1863–1865

Archives.org (National Archives and Record Services)
    Population Schedules of the Eighth Census of the United States, 1860, Missouri
    Federal Population Census Schedules Slave: Adair to Lafayette (Reels 0661–0664)
    Federal Population Census Schedules: Butler, Caldwell, Callaway (Reel 0610)
    Federal Population Census Schedules: Clark, Clay (Reel 0615)
    Federal Population Census Schedules: Hickory, Holt, Howard (Reel 0623)
    Federal Population Census Schedules: Jackson County (Reel 0625)

Civil War Governors of Kentucky Digital Documentary Edition

Missouri Digital Heritage (Missouri State Library)

Union Provost Marshal Records' File of Papers Relating to Two or More Civilians: 1861–1867

GIS Databases

Minnesota Population Center, National Historical Geographic Information System, Version 2.0

Primary Interviews
Chris Edwards (March 3, 2013)

Secondary Interviews
Butler, Clayton. "Understanding Our Past: An Interview with Historian Gary Gallagher." http://www.civilwar.org/education/history/civil-war-history-and-scholarship/gary-gallagher-interview.html (accessed January 2, 2016).

Newspapers and Periodicals
Aberdeen (S.C.) Daily News
Albuquerque Journal
Baltimore American
Boston Journal
Colorado Springs Gazette
Columbia (S.C.) State
Columbus Daily Enquirer
Daily Evening Bulletin (Philadelphia, Pa.)

Daily Missouri Republican (Saint Louis, Mo.)
Daily Oklahoman (Oklahoma City, Okla.)
Dallas Morning News
Duluth (Minn.) News-Tribune
Fort Worth Morning Register
Fort Worth Star-Telegram
Gettysburg Star
Grand Army Advocate (Des Moines, Iowa)
Grand Forks (N.D.) Daily Herald
Huntingdon (Penn.) Globe
Idaho Statesman (Boise, Idaho)
Kansas City Journal
Kansas City Star
Kansas City Times
Kansas Semi-Weekly Capital (Topeka, Kans.)
Leavenworth Bulletin
Leavenworth Daily Times
Louisville Courier Journal
Macon Telegraph
Miami Herald
Missouri Democrat (Saint Louis, Mo.)
Montgomery Advertiser
Morning Herald (Lexington, Ky.)
Morning Republican (Little Rock, Ark.)
National Democrat (Little Rock, Ark.)
New York Herald
New York Times
New York Tribune
Omaha World Herald
Pawtucket Times
Philadelphia Press
Portland Oregonian
Salt Lake Telegram
Sioux City Journal
The Southern Magazine
The Standard (Clarksville, Tex.)
Tucson Daily Citizen
Tulsa World
Weekly Arkansas Gazette (Little Rock, Ark.)

Published Primary Sources and Memoirs

Alcott, Louisa M. *Hospital Sketches: and, Camp and Fireside Stories.* Boston: Roberts Brothers, 1869.

Anderson, Edward. *Campfire Stories: A Series of Sketches of the Union Army in the Southwest.* Chicago: Star, 1896.

Appler, Augustus C. *The Life, Character and Daring Exploits of the Younger Brothers.* Chicago: Laird & Lee, 1892.

———. *Train and Bank Robbers of the West: A Romantic but Faithful Story of Bloodshed and Plunder, Perpetrated by Missouri's Daring Outlaws, Frank and Jesse James.* New York: Bedford, Clarke, 1882.

Arthur, George Clinton. *Bushwhacker: A Story of Missouri's Most Famous Desperado.* Rolla, Mo.: Rolla Printing, 1938.

Bailey, Joseph M. *Confederate Guerrilla: The Civil War Memoir of Joseph Bailey,* ed. T. Lindsay Baker. Fayetteville: University of Arkansas Press, 2007.

Bailey, L. D. *Quantrill's Raid on Lawrence, with Names of Victims of the Raid.* Lyndon: Kansas State Historical Society, 1899.

Baughton, Joseph S. *The Lawrence Massacre by a Band of Missouri Ruffians under Quantrell, August 21, 1863.* Lawrence, Kans.: J. S. Baughton, 1885.

Beard, John S. *Address at the Unveiling of the Monument Erected by the United States Government to the Confederate Dead in the Pitville Federal Cemetery, Philadelphia.* 1911.

Bell, Ovid. *Short History of Callaway County.* Fulton, Mo.: Fulton Gazette, 1913.

Belle Starr, the Bandit Queen, or, the Female Jesse James: A Full and Authentic History of the Dashing Female Highwayman. New York: R. K. Fox, 1889.

Berneking, Carolyn. "A Look at Early Lawrence: Letters from Robert Gaston Elliott." *Kansas Historical Quarterly* 43, no. 3 (Autumn 1977): 282–296.

Blake, Minnie E. *The Quantrill Raid, with Introductory Poems.* Lawrence, Kans., 1929.

Booth, George W. *Illustrated Souvenir: Maryland Line Confederate Soldiers' Home, Pikeville, Maryland.* 1894.

Botsford, T. F. *Memories of the War of Secession.* Montgomery, Ala.: Paragon, 1911.

Bradford, Ned, ed. *Battles and Leaders of the Civil War.* New York: Hawthorn Books, 1956.

Bradley, R. T. *The Outlaws of the Border: or, The Lives of Frank and Jesse James.* Saint Louis: J. W. Marsh, 1880.

Brewster, S. W. *Incidents of Quantrell's Raid on Lawrence, August 21, 1863: Experiences of Hon. Henry S. Clark.* Lawrence, Kans.: Jeffersonian Print, 1898.

Brooks, Phillip. *An Address Delivered May 30, 1873, at the Dedication of the Memorial Hall, Andover, Massachusetts.* Andover, Mass.: Trustees of the Memorial Hall, 1873.

Browne, Francis F, ed. *Bugle-Echoes: A Collection of Poems of the Civil War, Northern and Southern.* New York: White, Stokes & Allen, 1886.

Bryan, William Smith, and Robert Rose. *Pioneer Families of Missouri: A History of the Pioneer Families of Missouri.* Saint Louis, Mo.: Bryan, Brand, 1876.

Budd, Louis J., ed. *Mark Twain: Collected Tales, Sketches, Speeches, & Essays, 1852–1890.* New York: Viking, 1992.

Buddington, William I. *A Memorial to Giles F. Ward, Jr.* New York: Anson D. F. Randolph, 1866.

Buel, J. W. *Heroes of the Plains, or, Lives and Wondrous Adventures of Wild Bill, Buffalo Bill, Kit Carson, Capt. Payne, "White Beaver," Capt. Jack, Texas Jack, California Joe, and Other Celebrated Indian Fighters, Scouts, Hunters and Guides.* Philadelphia: West Philadelphia, 1891.

———. *Life and Marvelous Adventures of Wild Bill, the Scout.* Chicago: Belford, Clarke, 1888.

——. *The Border Bandits: An Authentic and Thrilling History of the Noted Outlaws, Jesse and Frank James, and Their Bands of Highwaymen.* Saint Louis, Mo.: Historical Publishing, 1881.

——. *The Border Outlaws: An Authentic and Thrilling History of the Most Noted Bandits of Ancient or Modern Times, The Younger Brothers, Jesse and Frank James, and Their Comrades in Crime.* Saint Louis, Mo.: Historical Publishing, 1881.

Buffalo Bill and His Wild West Companions. Chicago: Henneberry, 1893.

Buffalo Bill's Wild West and Congress of Rough Riders of the World. Chicago: Blakely Print, 1893.

Burdett, Charles. *Life of Kit Carson, the Great Western Hunter and Guide.* Philadelphia: J. E. Potter, 1860.

Burk, Martha Cannary. *Life and Adventures of Calamity Jane.* 1896.

Burnett, W. R. *The Dark Command: A Kansas Iliad.* New York: Knopf, 1938.

Carter, Forrest. *The Outlaw Josey Wales.* New York: Leisure Books, 1973.

Cattermole, E. G. *Famous Frontiersmen, Pioneers, and Scouts.* Chicago: Coburn & Newman, 1883.

Cordley, Richard. *A History of Lawrence, Kansas, from the First Settlement to the Close of the Rebellion.* Lawrence, Kans.: E. F. Caldwell, Lawrence Journal Press, 1895.

——. *Pioneer Days in Kansas.* New York: Pilgrim Press, 1903.

Cowgill, Flora K. *Never Forgotten Memories of a Kansas Childhood.* Lawrence: University of Kansas Press, 1965.

Crump, S. A. *Speech of Hon. S. A. Crump of Macon, Ga. Delivered at the Reunion of the North Carolina Confederate Veterans. Greensboro, N.C., Aug. 20th, 1902.* Macon, Ga.: Macon Evening News, 1902.

Cummins, Jim. *Jim Cummins: The Guerilla.* Excelsior Springs, Mo.: Daily Journal, 1908.

——. *Jim Cummin's Book: Written by Himself.* Denver: Reed, 1903.

Dacus, J. A. *Illustrated Lives and Adventures of Frank and Jesse James and the Younger Brothers, Noted Western Outlaws.* Cincinnati: Cincinnati Publishing, 1882.

Daggett, Thomas F. *Billy LeRoy, the Colorado Bandit, or, the King of American Highwaymen.* New York: R. K. Fox, 1881.

——. *Outlaw Brothers, Frank and Jesse James.* New York: R. K. Fox, 1881.

Dalton, Kit. *Under the Black Flag.* Memphis, Tenn.: Lockard, 1914.

Donald, Jay. *Outlaws of the Border: A Complete and Authentic History of the Lives of Frank and Jesse James.* Cincinnati: Foresee & McMakin, 1882.

Dowdey, Clifford, and Louis H. Manarin, eds. *The Wartime Papers of R. E. Lee.* New York: Bramhall House, 1961.

Duncan, Charles V. *John T. Hughes: From His Pen.* Modesto, Calif.: C. V. Duncan, 1991.

Eakin, Joanne C. *Recollections of Quantrill's Guerrillas: As Told by A. J. Walker of Weatherford, Texas, to Victor E. Martin in 1910.* Shawnee Mission, Kans.: Two Trails Genealogy, 1996.

——. *Warren Welch Remembers: A Civil War Guerrilla from Jackson County, Missouri.* Shawnee Mission, Kans.: Two Trails Genealogy, 1997.

Early, Jubal A. *A Memoir of the Last Year of the War for Independence.* Augusta, Ga.: Steam Printing Press of Chronicle and Sentinel, 1867.

Edwards, John Newman. *John N. Edwards: Life, Writings and Tributes.* Kansas City, Mo.: Jennie Edwards, 1889.

——. *Noted Guerrillas, or, The Warfare of the Border.* Saint Louis, Mo.: Bryan, Brand, 1877.

——. *Shelby's Expedition to Mexico: An Unwritten Leaf of the War.* 1872. Reprint, Austin, Tex.: Steck, 1964.

Ellis, Edward S. *The Camp-Fires of General Lee, from the Peninsula to Appomattox Court-House.* Philadelphia: Henry Harrison & Co., 1886.

Eve, F. Edgeworth. *Address Delivered before the Confederate Survivors' Association of August, Georgia, upon the Occasion of Its Seventeenth Annual Reunion, on Memorial Day, April 26th, 1895.* Augusta, Ga.: Chronicle Job Printing Co., 1895.

Fable, Edmund. *Billy the Kid, the New Mexican Outlaw, or, the Bold Bandit of the West!* Denver: Denver Publishing, 1881.

Fisher, George A. *The Yankee Conscript.* Philadelphia: J. W. Daughaday, 1864.

Fiske, Samuel W. *Mr. Dunn Browne's Experiences in the Army.* Boston: Nichols & Noyes, 1866.

Frank James Tells the Story of the Centralia Fight. Columbia: Columbia Missouri Herald, 1897.

Freeman, Douglas S. *The Last Parade.* Richmond, Va.: Whittet & Shepperson, 1942.

Garrett, Patrick F. *An Authentic Life of Billy the Kid, the Noted Desperado of the Southwest.* Santa Fe: New Mexican Printing & Publishing, 1882.

Glazier, Willard. *Three Years in the Federal Cavalry.* New York: R. H. Ferguson, 1871.

Goodman, Thomas M. *A Thrilling Record: Founded on Facts and Observations Obtained during Ten Days' Experience with Col. Wm. T. Anderson.* Des Moines, Iowa: Mills, 1868.

Grisham, Howard C. *Centralia and Bill Anderson.* Jefferson City, Mo.: H. C. Grisham, 1964.

Grover, George S. *Civil War in Missouri: Address of Capt. George S. Grover of Warrensburg, Mo., Nov. 4, 1893.* Columbia: State Historical Society of Missouri, 1913.

Hale, Donald R. *Bloody Bill Anderson Scrapbook.* Lee's Summit, Mo.: D. R. Hale, n.d.

——. *Branded as Rebels: Volume II.* Lee's Summit, Mo.: D. R. Hale, 2003.

——. *Branded as Rebels: Volume III.* Lee's Summit, Mo.: D. R. Hale, 2007.

——. *Jesse and Frank James Scrapbook: Volume I.* Lee's Summit, Mo.: D. R. Hale, n.d.

——. *Jesse and Frank James and Cole Younger Scrapbook: Volume I.* Lee's Summit, Mo.: D. R. Hale, n.d.

——. *"Little Archie": The Death of Archie Clement, Missouri Civil War Guerrilla.* Independence, Mo.: Blue & Gray Book Shoppe, 2001.

——. *The Cole Younger Scrapbook.* Lee's Summit, Mo.: D. R. Hale, 2002.

——. *The William Clarke Quantrill Men Reunions, 1898–1929.* Independence, Mo.: Blue & Gray Book Shoppe, 2001.

Hale, Donald R., and Joanne C. Eakin, eds. *Branded as Rebels: A List of Bushwhackers, Guerrillas, Partisan Rangers, Confederates and Southern Sympathizers from Missouri during the War Years.* Lee's Summit, Mo.: J. C. Eakin & D. R. Hale, 1993.

Hansen, Duncan E., and Donald R. Hale. *A Reunion in Death.* Independence, Mo.: Two Trails, 2002–2006.

Harris, Joel C. *Uncle Remus His Songs and Sayings: The Folk-lore of the Old Plantation.* New York: D. Appleton, 1880.

——. *Uncle Remus and the Little Boy.* Boston: Small, Maynard, 1910.

Harris, N. E. *The Civil War: Its Results and Losses.* Macon, Ga.: J. W. Burke, 1906.

Hepworth, George H. *Whip, Hoe, and Sword; or, The Gulf-Department in '63.* Boston: Walker, Wise, 1864.

Hildebrand, Samuel S. *Autobiography of Samuel S. Hildebrand, The Renowned Missouri Bushwhacker,* ed. Kirby Ross. Fayetteville: University of Arkansas Press, 2005.

Hill, A. F. *Our Boys: The Personal Experiences of a Soldier in the Army of the Potomac.* Philadelphia: John E. Potter, 1865.

Historical, Pictorial and Biographical Record of Chariton County, Missouri. Salisbury, Mo.: Pictorial and Biographical Publishing, 1896.

History of Howard and Chariton Counties, Missouri. Saint Louis, Mo.: National Historical, 1883.

The History of Jackson County, Missouri. Kansas City, Mo.: Union Historical, 1881.

Kennedy, Flora Cowgill. *Never Forgotten: Memories of a Kansas Childhood.* Lawrence: University of Kansas Press, 1965.

Lawrence: Today and Yesterday. Lawrence, Kans.: Lawrence Daily Journal-World, 1913.

Lee Jr., Robert E., ed. *Recollections and Letters of General Robert E. Lee.* New York: Doubleday, Page, 1904.

Lewis, Charles B. *Field, Fort, and Fleet: Being a Series of Brilliant and Authentic Sketches of the Most Notable Battles of the Late Civil War, Including Many Incidents and Circumstances Never Before Published in Any Form.* Detroit: Detroit Free Press, 1885.

Lieber, Francis. *Guerrilla Parties: Considered with References to the Laws and Usages of War.* New York: D. Van Nostrang, 1862.

Life and Adventures of Sam Bass: The Notorious Union Pacific and Texas Train Robber. Dallas: Dallas Commercial Steam Print, 1878.

Lloyd's Battle History of the Great Rebellion. New York: H. H. Lloyd, 1866.

Lumpkin, Katherine Du Pre. *The Making of a Southerner.* Foreword by Darlene Clark Hine. Athens: University of Georgia Press, 1991.

Magruder, Henry C. *Three Years in the Saddle: The Life and Confession of Henry C. Magruder.* Louisville, Ky.: Major Cyrus J. Wilson, 1865.

Martin, George W. *The First Two Years of Kansas, or, Where, When and How the Missouri Bushwhacker, the Missouri Train and Bank Robber, and Those Who Stole Themselves Rich in the Name of Liberty, Were Reared and Sired.* Topeka, Kans.: State Printing Office, 1907.

McCorkle, John, and O. S. Barton. *Three Years with Quantrill: A True Story Told by His Scout.* Notes by Albert Castel. Commentary by Herman Hattaway. Norman: University of Oklahoma Press, 1992.

McElroy, John. *The Struggle for Missouri.* Washington, D.C.: National Tribune, 1909.

Miller, George. *The Trial of Frank James for Murder with Confessions of Dick Liddil and Clarence Hite and History of the "James Gang."* Columbia, Mo.: Press of E. W. Stephens, 1898.

Minutes of the Annual Reunion of the United Confederate Veterans. New Orleans: Rogers, 1934.

Minutes of the Thirty-Second Annual Meeting and Reunion of the United Confederate Veterans. New Orleans: Rogers, 1921.

Monks, William. *A History of Southern Missouri and Northern Arkansas: Being an Account of the Early Settlements, the Civil War, the Ku-Klux, and Times of Peace.* Edited by John F. Bradbury Jr. and Lou Wehmer. Fayetteville: University of Arkansas Press, 2003.

Mosby, John S. *Mosby's War Reminiscences and Stuart's Cavalry Campaigns.* New York: Dodd, Mead, 1887.

———. *Take Sides with the Truth: The Postwar Letters of John Singleton Mosby to Samuel F. Chapman.* Edited by Peter A. Brown. Lexington: University of Kentucky Press, 2007.

Nott, Charles C. *Sketches of the War: A Series of Letters to the North Moore Street School of New York.* New York: Anson D. F. Randolph, 1865.

Noyes, George F. *The Bivouac and the Battle-Field.* New York: Harper & Brothers, 1863.

Orders U.C.V.: General and Special Issued by General J. B. Gordon during His Term of Office, June 10, 1889, to January 9, 1904, Volume I. New Orleans: United Confederate Veterans, 1911.

Past and Present of Saline County, Missouri. Saint Louis: Missouri Historical, 1881.

Peacock, Thomas B. *Poems of the Plains and Songs of the Solitudes.* New York: G. P. Putnam's Sons, 1889.

———. *Rhyme of the Border: A Historical Poem of the Kansas-Missouri Guerrilla War.* New York: G. W. Carleton, 1880.

Philpott, William Bledsoe, ed. *The Sponsor Souvenir Album and History of the United Confederate Veterans' Reunion, 1895.* Houston: Sponsor Souvenir, 1895.

Porter, D. D. *Incidents and Anecdotes of the Civil War.* New York: Appleton, 1885.

Portis, Charles. *True Grit.* New York: Simon & Schuster, 1968.

Proceedings of the Twenty-Seventh Annual Reunion of the Confederate Veterans. Washington, D.C.: Government Printing Office, 1918.

Roberts, Samuel. "Letter to His Brother" in Alan Conway's "The Sacking of Lawrence." *Kansas Historical Quarterly* 24, no. 2 (Summer 1958): 144–150.

Roosevelt, Theodore. *Hunting Trips of a Ranchman: Ranch Life and the Hunting Trail.* New York: Charles Scribner's Sons, 1924.

Shea, John C. *Reminiscences of Quantrill's Raid upon the City of Lawrence, Kansas.* Kansas City, Mo.: Isaac P. Moore, 1879.

Sheridan, Richard B. *William Clarke Quantrill and the Civil War Raid on Lawrence, Kansas, August 21, 1863, An Eyewitness Account by Rev. Richard Cordley.* Lawrence, Kans.: Richard B. Sheridan, June 1999.

Six, Fred N., ed. "Eyewitness Reports of Quantrill's Raid: Letters of Sophia Bissell and Sydney Clarke." *Kansas History: A Journal of the Central Plains* 28 (Summer 2005): 94–103.

Snead, Thomas L. *The Fight for Missouri: From the Election of Lincoln to the Death of Lyon.* New York: Charles Scribner's Sons, 1886.

Sons of Confederate Veterans (Virginia Division). *Stars and Bars* Vol. 1, No. 1. Richmond, Va.: Service Press, 1923.

Sylvester, Edward. *The Life of Kit Carson, Hunter, Trapper, Guide, Indian Agent, and Colonel U.S.A.* New York: New York Publishing, 1899.

Todd, W. C. *The Centralia Fight.* n.p., 1883.

Trow, Harrison. *Charles W. Quantrell.* Edited by John P. Burch. Vega, Tex.: J. P. Burch, 1923.

United Daughters of the Confederacy. Reminiscences of the Women of Missouri during the Sixties. Missouri Division, United Daughters of the Confederacy, 1913.

U.S. Sanitary Commission. Narrative of Privations and Sufferings of United States Offi-cers and Soldiers while Prisoners of War in the Hands of the Rebel Authorities. Phila-delphia: King & Baird, 1864.

Violette, E. M., and C. N. Tolman. *History of Adair County.* Kirksville, Mo.: Dens-low History Co., 1911.

The War of the Rebellion: A Compilation of the Official Records of the Union and Con-federate Armies, 128 vols. Washington, D.C.: Government Printing Office, 1880–1901.

Watts, Hampton. *The Babe of the Company: An Unfolded Leaf from the Forest of Never-to-be-Forgotten Years.* Fayette, Mo.: Democrat-Leader Press, 1913.

Wharton, H. M. *War Songs and Poems of the Southern Confederacy, 1861–1865.* Phila-delphia: American Book & Bible House, 1904.

Williams, Burton J. "Erastus D. Ladd's Description of the Lawrence Massacre." *Kansas Historical Quarterly* 29, no. 2 (Summer 1963): 113–121.

Winchell, Shalor Eldridge. *Recollections of Early Days in Kansas, Volume II.* Topeka: Kansas State Printing Plant, 1920.

Woodrell, Daniel. *Woe to Live On.* New York: Holt, 1987.

Woodson, W. H. *History of Clay County, Missouri.* Topeka: Historical Publishing, 1920.

Younger, Cole. *The Story of Cole Younger, by Himself.* Chicago: Henneberry, 1903.

Dissertations and Theses

Beilein Jr., Joseph M. "Household War: Guerrilla-Men, Rebel Women, and Guer-rilla Warfare in Civil War Missouri." PhD diss., University of Missouri, 2012.

Fialka, Andrew W. "Reassessing Guerrillas: A Spatial and Temporal Analysis of Missouri's Civil War." MA thesis, West Virginia University, 2013.

Foster, Terry G. "Altered Destinies: Quantrill's Guerrillas and the Civil War in Western Missouri." MA thesis, University of Western Ontario, 1999.

Gerlach, Russel L. "Rural Ethnic and Religious Groups as Cultural Islands in the Ozarks of Missouri: Their Emergence and Persistence." PhD diss., University of Nebraska, 1974.

Hulbert, Matthew C. "Politics of the Black Flag: Guerrilla Memory and Southern Conservatism in the New South." MA thesis, North Carolina State University, 2010.

Marshall, Anne E. "A Strange Conclusion to a Triumphant War: Memory, Iden-tity and the Creation of a Confederate Kentucky, 1865–1925." PhD diss., Uni-versity of Georgia, 2004.

Miller, Jeremy B. "Unconventional Warfare in the American Civil War." MA the-sis, U.S. Army Command and General Staff College, 2004.

Myers, Barton A. "Rebels against a Rebellion: Southern Unionists in Secession, War, and Remembrance." PhD diss., University of Georgia, 2009.

Secondary Sources

Adamson, Hans C. *Rebellion in Missouri, 1861: Nathaniel Lyon and His Army of the West.* Philadelphia: Chilton, 1961.

Alonso, Ana Maria. "The Politics of Space, Time, and Substance: State Forma-tion, Nationalism, and Ethnicity." *Annual Review of Anthropology* 23 (1994): 379–405.

Anderson, Paul C. *Blood Image: Turner Ashby in the Civil War and the Southern Mind.* Baton Rouge: Louisiana State University Press, 2002.

Anderson, Vicki. *The Dime Novel in Children's Literature.* Jefferson, N.C.: McFarland, 2005.

Anderson, Vincent S. *Bald Knobbers: Chronicles of Vigilante Justice.* Charleston: History Press, 2013.

Arenson, Adam. *The Great Heart of the Republic: St. Louis and the Cultural Civil War.* Cambridge, Mass.: Harvard University Press, 2011.

Arenson, Adam, and Andrew Graybill, eds. *Civil War Wests: Testing the Limits of the United States.* Berkeley: University of California Press, 2015.

Astor, Aaron. *Rebels on the Border: Civil War, Emancipation, and the Reconstruction of Kentucky and Missouri.* Baton Rouge: Louisiana State University Press, 2012.

Athearn, Robert G. *The Mythic West in Twentieth-Century America.* Lawrence: University Press of Kansas, 1986.

Ballard, Sandra L., and Leila E. Weinstein, eds. *Neighbor to Neighbor: A Memoir of Family, Community, and Civil War in Appalachian North Carolina.* Boone, N.C.: Center for Appalachian Studies, 2007.

Barber, E. Susan, and Charles F. Ritter. "'Physical Abuse . . . and Rough Handling': Race, Gender, and Sexual Justice in the Occupied South." In Whites and Long, *Occupied Women*, 49–66.

Barrett, Jenny. *Shooting the Civil War: Cinema, History, and American National Identity.* London: Tauris, 2009.

Bartels, Carolyn M. *The Civil War in Missouri: Day by Day, 1861–1865.* Independence, Mo.: Two Trails, 2003.

Bederman, Gail. *Manliness and Civilization: A Cultural History of Gender and Race in the United States, 1880–1917.* Chicago: University of Chicago Press, 1995.

Beilein Jr., Joseph M. "The Guerrilla Shirt: A Labor of Love and the Style of Rebellion in Civil War Missouri." *Civil War History* 58, no. 2 (June 2012): 151–179.

———. "'Nothing but Truth Is History': William E. Connelley, William H. Gregg, and the Pillaging of Guerrilla History." In Beilein and Hulbert, *Civil War Guerrilla,* 207–229.

Beilein, Joseph M., and Matthew C. Hulbert, eds. *The Civil War Guerrilla: Unfolding the Black Flag in History, Memory, and Myth.* Lexington: University Press of Kentucky, 2015.

Benson, Ivan. *Mark Twain's Western Years.* Stanford, Calif.: Stanford University Press, 1938.

Bernath, Michael T. *Confederate Minds: The Struggle for Intellectual Independence in the Civil War South.* Chapel Hill: University of North Carolina Press, 2010.

Berry, Stephen J. *All That Makes a Man: Love and Ambition in the Civil War South.* New York: Oxford University Press, 2003.

Binnington, Ian. *Confederate Visions: Nationalism, Symbolism, and the Imagined South in the Civil War.* Charlottesville: University of Virginia Press, 2013.

Bird, Roy. *Civil War in Kansas.* Gretna, La.: Pelican, 2004.

Blair, William. *Cities of the Dead: Contesting the Memory of the Civil War in the South, 1865–1914.* Chapel Hill: University of North Carolina Press, 2003.

Blight, David. *American Oracle: The Civil War in the Civil Rights Era.* Cambridge, Mass.: Harvard University Press, 2011.

——. *Race and Reunion: The Civil War in American Memory.* Cambridge, Mass.: Harvard University Press, 2001.

Blyth, Lance R. *Charicahua and Janos: Communities of Violence in the Southwestern Borderlands, 1680–1880.* Lincoln: University of Nebraska Press, 2012.

Boddie, William W. *Traditions of the Swamp Fox: William W. Boddie's Francis Marion.* Spartanburg, S.C.: Reprint Co., 2000.

Bodnar, John E. *Blue-Collar Hollywood: Liberalism, Democracy, and Working People in American Film.* Baltimore: Johns Hopkins University Press, 2003.

——. *The "Good War" in American Memory.* Baltimore: Johns Hopkins University Press, 2010.

——. *Remaking America: Public Memory, Commemoration, and Patriotism in the Twentieth Century.* Princeton, N.J.: Princeton University Press, 1992.

Bold, Christine. *Selling the Wild West: Popular Western Fiction, 1860 to 1960.* Bloomington: Indiana University Press, 1987.

Boman, Dennis K. *Lincoln and Citizens' Rights in Civil War Missouri: Balancing Freedom and Security.* Baton Rouge: Louisiana State University Press, 2011.

Bosel, Anke. *Homogenizing History: Accomodationist Discourse in Ken Burns' The Civil War.* Trier, Germany: Wissenschaftlicher Verlag Trier, 2003.

Bowen, Don R. "Guerrilla War in Western Missouri, 1862–1865: Historical Extensions of the Relative Deprivation Hypothesis." *Comparative Studies in History and Society* 19, no. 1 (January 1979): 30–51.

——. "Quantrill, James, Younger, et al.: Leadership in a Guerrilla Movement, Missouri, 1861–1865." *Military Affairs* 1, no. 41 (February 1977): 42–48.

Breihan, Carl W. *Quantrill and His Civil War Guerrillas.* New York: Promontory, 1959.

——. *The Complete and Authentic Life of Jesse James.* New York: Frederick Fell, 1953.

Brown, Thomas, ed. *Remixing the Civil War: Meditations on the Sesquicentennial.* Baltimore: Johns Hopkins University Press, 2011.

Brownlee, Richard S. *Gray Ghosts of the Confederacy: Guerrilla Warfare in the West, 1861–1865.* Baton Rouge: Louisiana State University Press, 1958.

Brumgardt, John R. *Civil War Nurse: The Diary and Letters of Hannah Ropes.* Knoxville: University of Tennessee Press, 1980.

Brundage, Fitzhugh. *The Southern Past: A Clash of Race and Memory.* Cambridge, Mass.: Harvard University Press, 2008.

Burnett, Robyn, and Ken Luebbering. *German Settlement in Missouri: New Land, Old Ways.* Columbia: University of Missouri Press, 1975.

——. *Immigrant Women in the Settlement of Missouri.* Columbia: University of Missouri Press, 2005.

Bynum, Victoria. *Long Shadow of the Civil War: Southern Dissent and Its Legacies.* Chapel Hill: University of North Carolina Press, 2010.

Campbell, Jacqueline Glass. *When Sherman Marched North from the Sea: Resistance on the Confederate Homefront.* Chapel Hill: University of North Carolina Press, 2003.

Carmichael, Peter S. *The Last Generation: Young Virginians in Peace, War, and Reunion.* Chapel Hill: University of North Carolina Press, 2005.

Cashin, Joan E. *The War Was You and Me: Civilians in the American Civil War.* Princeton, N.J.: Princeton University Press, 2002.

Castel, Albert. *A Frontier State at War: Kansas, 1861–1865.* Ithaca, N.Y.: Cornell University Press, 1958.

——. "Quantrill's Bushwhackers: A Case Study in Partisan Warfare." *Civil War History* 13, no. 1 (March 1967): 40–50.

——. *William Clarke Quantrill: His Life and Times.* New York: Frederick Fell, 1962.

Castel, Albert, and Thomas Goodrich. *Bloody Bill Anderson: The Short, Savage Life of a Civil War Guerrilla.* Lawrence: University of Kansas Press, 1988.

Catton, Bruce. *The Coming Fury.* New York: Doubleday, 1961.

——. *Never Call Retreat.* New York: Doubleday, 1965.

——. *Terrible Swift Sword.* New York: Doubleday, 1963.

Chadwick, Bruce. *The Reel Civil War: Mythmaking in American Film.* New York: Knopf, 2001.

Chapman, Carl H. *The Archaeology of Missouri, I.* Columbia: University of Missouri Press, 1975.

——. *The Archaeology of Missouri, II.* Columbia: University of Missouri Press, 1980.

Childers, Christopher. *The Failure of Popular Sovereignty: Slavery, Manifest Destiny, and the Radicalization of Southern Politics.* Lawrence: University Press of Kansas, 2012.

Clark, Kathleen A. *Defining Moments: African American Commemoration and Political Culture in the South, 1863–1913.* Chapel Hill: University of North Carolina Press, 2009.

Clinton, Catherine, and Nina Silber, eds. *Divided Houses: Gender and the Civil War.* New York: Oxford, 1992.

Cloyd, Benjamin. *Haunted by Atrocity: Civil War Prisons in American Memory.* Baton Rouge: Louisiana State University Press, 2010.

Cobb, James C. *Away Down South: A History of Southern Identity.* New York: Oxford University Press, 2005.

Connelly, Thomas L. *The Marble Man: Robert E. Lee and His Image in American Society.* New York: Knopf, 1977.

Connelley, William Elsey. *Quantrill and the Border Wars.* New York: Smithmark, 1909.

Cook, Michael. *Dime Novel Roundup.* Bowling Green, Ohio: Bowling Green State University Popular Press, 1983.

Cox, J. Randolph. *The Dime Novel Companion: A Source Book.* Westport, Conn.: Greenwood, 2000.

Cox, Karen. *Dixie's Daughters: The United Daughters of the Confederacy and the Preservation of Confederate Culture.* Gainesville: University of Florida Press, 2003.

Cozzens, Peter. *Shenandoah 1862: Stonewall Jackson's Valley Campaign.* Chapel Hill: University of North Carolina Press, 2008.

Crofts, Daniel W. *Reluctant Confederates: Upper South Unionists in the Secession Crisis.* Chapel Hill: University of North Carolina Press, 1999.

Cullen, Jim. *The Civil War in Popular Culture: A Reusable Past.* Washington, D.C.: Smithsonian Institution Press, 1995.

Cushman, Stephen. *Belligerent Muse: Five Northern Writers and How They Shaped Our Understanding of the Civil War.* Chapel Hill: University of North Carolina Press, 2014.

Cutler, Bruce. *A West Wind Rises.* Lincoln: University of Nebraska Press, 1962.

Davidson, Mary Richmond. *Buffalo Bill, Wild West Showman.* Champaign, Ill.: Garrard, 1962.

Davis, William C. *The Lost Cause: Myths and Realities of the Confederacy.* Lawrence: University Press of Kansas, 1996.

Dearing, Mary R. *Veterans in Politics: The Story of the G.A.R.* Baton Rouge: Louisiana State University Press, 1952.

Denning, Michael. *Mechanic Accents: Dime Novels and Working-Class Culture in America.* New York: Verso, 1987.

Deverell, William. *A Companion to the American West.* Malden, Mass.: Blackwell, 2004.

Dickson, Keith. *Sustaining Southern Identity: Douglas Southall Freeman and Memory in the Modern South.* Baton Rouge: Louisiana State University Press, 2011.

Dinan, John A. *The Pulp Western: A Popular History of the Western Fiction Magazine in America.* San Bernardino, Calif.: Borgo, 1983.

DiSilvestro, Roger. *Theodore Roosevelt in the Badlands: A Young Politician's Quest for Recovery in the American West.* New York: Walker, 2011.

Doherty, Thomas. *Cold War, Cool Medium: Television, McCarthyism, and American Culture.* New York: Columbia University Press, 2003.

Downs, Gregory. *After Appomattox: Military Occupation and the Ends of the War.* Cambridge, Mass.: Harvard University Press, 2015.

———. "Three Faces of Sovereignty: Governing Confederate, Mexican, and Indian Texas in the Civil War Era." In Arenson and Graybill, *Civil War Wests,* 118–138.

Earle, Jonathan, and Diane Mutti-Burke, eds. *Bleeding Kansas, Bleeding Missouri: The Long Civil War on the Border.* Lawrence: University Press of Kansas, 2013.

Edwards, Laura. *Gendered Strife and Confusion: The Political Culture of Reconstruction.* Chicago: University of Illinois Press, 1996.

Etcheson, Nicole. *Bleeding Kansas: Contested Liberty in the Civil War Era.* Lawrence: University Press of Kansas, 2004.

Eyerman, Ron. "The Past in the Present: Culture and the Transmission of Memory." *Acta Sociologica* 47, no. 2 (June 2004): 159–169.

Fahs, Alice. *The Imagined Civil War: Popular Literature of the North and South, 1861–1865.* Chapel Hill: University of North Carolina Press, 2001.

Fahs, Alice, and Joan Waugh, eds. *The Memory of the Civil War in American Culture.* Chapel Hill: University of North Carolina Press, 2004.

Faust, Drew Gilpin. *This Republic of Suffering: Death and the American Civil War.* New York: Knopf, 2008.

Feimster, Crystal N. *Southern Horrors.* Cambridge, Mass.: Harvard University Press, 2009.

Fellman, Michael. *In the Name of God and Country: Reconsidering Terrorism in American History.* New Haven, Conn.: Yale University Press, 2010.

———. *Inside War: The Guerrilla Conflict in Missouri during the American Civil War.* Oxford: Oxford University Press, 1989.

Fenin, George N., and William K. Everson. *The Western: From Silents to Cinerama.* New York: Orion, 1962.

Folsom, James K. *The American Western Novel.* New Haven, Conn.: College and University Press, 1966.

Foner, Eric J. *Reconstruction: America's Unfinished Revolution, 1863–1877.* New York: Harper, 2002.

Foote, Shelby. *The Civil War: A Narrative.* Alexandria, Va.: Time-Life Books, 1998.

Forbes, Robert P. *The Missouri Compromise and Its Aftermath: Slavery and the Meaning of America.* Chapel Hill: University of North Carolina Press, 2007.

Foster, Gaines M. *Ghosts of the Confederacy: Defeat, the Lost Cause, and the Emergence of the New South, 1865–1913.* New York: Oxford University Press, 1987.

Frank, Lisa Tendrich. *The Civilian War: Confederate Women and Union Soldiers during Sherman's March.* Baton Rouge: Louisiana State University Press, 2015.

Frazier, Donald S. *Blood and Treasure: Confederate Empire in the Southwest.* College Station: Texas A&M University Press, 1996.

Frizzell, Robert. *Independent Immigrants: A Settlement of Hanoverian Immigrants in Western Missouri.* Columbia: University of Missouri Press, 2007.

Gallagher, Gary. *Causes Won, Lost, and Forgotten: How Hollywood and Popular Art Shape What We Know about the Civil War.* Chapel Hill: University of North Carolina Press, 2004.

Gallagher, Gary T., and Alan T. Nolan, eds. *The Myth of the Lost Cause and Civil War History.* Bloomington: Indiana University Press, 2010.

Gallagher, Gary T., and Kathryn Shively Meier. "Coming to Terms with Civil War Military History." *Journal of the Civil War Era* 4, no. 4 (2014): 487–508.

Gannon, Barbara. *The Won Cause: Black and White Comradeship in the Grand Army of the Republic.* Chapel Hill: University of North Carolina Press, 2011.

Garrett, Richard. *Famous Characters of the Wild West.* London: Arthur Baker, 1975.

Garrison, Webb. *Civil War Hostages: Hostage Taking in the Civil War.* Shippensburg, Pa.: White Maine Books, 2000.

Geiger, Mark W. *Financial Fraud and Guerrilla Violence in Missouri's Civil War, 1861–1865.* New Haven, Conn.: Yale University Press, 2010.

Genovese, Eugene. *Roll, Jordan, Roll: The World the Slaves Made.* New York: Vintage Books, 1972.

Gerlach, Russel L. *Immigrants in the Ozarks: A Study in Ethnic Geography.* Columbia: University of Missouri Press, 1976.

Gerteis, Louis. *The Civil War in Missouri: A Military History.* Columbia: University of Missouri Press, 2012.

Gilmore, Donald. *Civil War on the Missouri-Kansas Border.* Gretna, La.: Pelican, 2006.

Gilmore, Glenda. *Gender and Jim Crow: Women and the Politics of White Supremacy in North Carolina, 1896–1920.* Chapel Hill: University of North Carolina Press, 1996.

Goodrich, Thomas. *Black Flag: Guerrilla Warfare on the Western Border, 1861–1975.* Bloomington: Indiana University Press, 1995.

Gordon, Lesley J., and John C. Inscoe, eds. *Inside the Confederate Nation: Essays in Honor of Emory D. Thomas.* Baton Rouge: Louisiana State University Press, 2005.

Greenberg, Kenneth S. *Honor and Slavery.* Princeton, N.J.: Princeton University Press, 1996.

Hahn, Steven. *A Nation under Our Feet: Black Political Struggles in the Rural South, from Slavery to the Great Migration.* Cambridge, Mass.: Harvard University Press, 2003.

Halbwachs, Maurice. *The Collective Memory.* New York: Harper & Row, 1980.

Hale, Donald R. *They Called Him Bloody Bill: The Life of William Anderson Missouri Guerrilla.* Clinton, Mo.: Printery, 1975.

——. *"We Rode with Quantrill."* Clinton, Mo.: Printery, 1975.

Hall, Jacqueline Dowd. *Revolt against Chivalry: Jesse Daniel Ames and the Women's Campaign against Lynching.* New York: Columbia University Press, 1979.

——. "'To Widen the Reach of Our Love': Autobiography, History, and Desire." *Feminist Studies* 26, no. 1 (Spring 2000): 231–247.

——. "'You Must Remember This': Autobiography as Social Critique." *Journal of American History* 85, no. 2 (September 1998): 439–465.

Hanna, Alfred J. "A Confederate Newspaper in Mexico." *Journal of Southern History* 12, no. 1 (February 1946): 67–83.

Hardeman, Nicholas P. "The Bloody Battle That Almost Happened: William Clarke Quantrill and Peter Hardeman on the Western Border." *Civil War History* 23, no. 3 (September 1977): 251–258.

Harmon, George D. "Confederate Migration to Mexico." Hispanic American History Review 17, no. 4 (November 1937): 458–487.

Harper, Kimberly. *White Man's Heaven: Lynching and the Expulsion of Blacks in the Southern Ozarks, 1894–1909.* Fayetteville: University of Arkansas Press, 2010.

Harris, Charles F. "Catalyst for Terror: The Collapse of the Women's Prison in Kansas City." *Missouri Historical Review* 89, no. 3 (April 1995): 290–306.

Hendershot, Cyndy. *I Was a Cold War Monster: Horror Films, Eroticism, and the Cold War Imagination.* Bowling Green, Ohio: Bowling Green State University Popular Press, 2001.

Hoberman, J. *An Army of Phantoms: American Movies and the Making of the Cold War.* New York: New Press, 2011.

Hobsbawm, Eric J. *Primitive Rebels: Studies in Archaic Forms of Social Movement in the 19th and 20th Centuries.* New York: Norton, 1965.

——. "Social Bandits: Reply." *Comparative Studies in Society and History* 14, no. 4 (September 1972): 503–505.

Hobsbawm, Eric J., and Terrence O. Ranger. *The Invention of Tradition.* New York: Cambridge University Press, 1983.

Hoganson, Kristin L. *Fighting for American Manhood: How Gender Politics Provoked the Spanish-American and Philippine-American Wars.* New Haven, Conn.: Yale University Press, 1998.

Horwitz, Tony. *Confederates in the Attic: Dispatches from the Unfinished Civil War.* New York: Vintage Books, 1999.

Hulbert, Matthew C. "Constructing Guerrilla Memory: John Newman Edwards and Missouri's Irregular Lost Cause." *Journal of the Civil War Era* 2, no. 1 (March 2012): 58–81.

——. "How to Remember 'This Damnable Guerrilla Warfare': Four Vignettes from Civil War Missouri." *Civil War History* 59, no. 2 (June 2013): 142–167.

——. "Killing 'Bloody Bill' Anderson." *New York Times, Opinionator, Disunion,* October 2014.

——. "The Lawrence Massacre." *New York Times, Opinionator, Disunion,* August 2013.

——. "Memory in the Re-Making: Larkin Skaggs and the Massacre(s) at Lawrence." In Myers and McKnight, *Guerrilla Hunters* (forthcoming).

——. "The Regularly Irregular War: Domestic Violation, Women, and Remembrance in Missouri's Guerrilla Theater." *Common-Place* 14, no. 2 (Winter 2014), http://www.common-place-archives.org/vol-14/no-02/hulbert/#.Vp2Eo TbtJUQ (accessed January 16, 2016).

——. "Texas Bound and Down: An Untold Narrative of Missouri's Guerrilla War on Film." *Journal of the West* 50, no. 4 (Fall 2011): 27–33.

——. "William 'Bloody Bill' Anderson." *Essential Civil War Curriculum* (June 2012): 1–10.

Hutton, T. R. C. *Bloody Breathitt: Politics and Violence in the Appalachian South.* Lexington: University Press of Kentucky, 2013.

Inscoe, John C. *Race, War, and Remembrance in the Appalachian South.* Lexington: University Press of Kentucky, 2008.

——. "Guerrilla War and Remembrance." In Ballard and Weinstein, *Neighbor to Neighbor*, 45–70.

Inscoe, John C., and Robert Kenzer, eds. *Enemies of the Country: New Perspectives on Unionists in the Civil War South.* Athens: University of Georgia Press, 2001.

——. "Irregular Warfare 1861–1865." *North and South* 11, no. 3 (June 2009): 16–33.

Janney, Caroline E. *Burying the Dead but Not the Past: Ladies' Memorial Associations and the Lost Cause.* Chapel Hill: University of North Carolina Press, 2008.

——. *Remembering the Civil War: Reunion and the Limits of Reconciliation.* Chapel Hill: University of North Carolina Press, 2013.

Jaquette, Henrietta S., ed. *Letters from a Civil War Nurse: Cornelia Hancock, 1863–1865.* Lincoln: University of Nebraska Press, 1998.

Jones, Daryl. *The Dime Novel Western.* Bowling Green, Ohio: Bowling Green State University Popular Press, 1978.

Kachun, Mitchell J. *Festivals of Freedom: Memory and Meaning in African American Emancipation Celebrations, 1808–1915.* Amherst: University of Massachusetts Press, 2006.

Kamensky, Jane. *The Exchange Artist: A Tale of High-Flying Speculation and America's First Banking Collapse.* New York: Viking, 2008.

Kammen, Michael. *Mystic Chords of Memory: The Transformation of Tradition in American Culture.* New York: Vintage Books, 1993.

Kapsis, Robert E., and Kathie Coblentz. *Clint Eastwood: Interviews.* Jackson: University Press of Mississippi, 1999.

Kastor, Peter J. *The Nation's Crucible: The Louisiana Purchase and the Creation of America.* New Haven, Conn.: Yale University Press, 2004.

Kelman, Ari. *A Misplaced Massacre: Struggling over the Memory of Sand Creek.* Cambridge, Mass.: Harvard University Press, 2013.

Kinnard, Roy. *The Blue and the Gray on the Silver Screen: More than Eighty Years of Civil War Movies.* Secaucus, N.J.: Carol, 1996.

Knapp, Frank A., Jr. "A New Source on the Confederate Exodus to Mexico: The Two Republics." *Journal of Southern History* 19, no. 3 (August 1953): 364–373.

Knight, David B. "Identity and Territory: Geographical Perspectives on Nationalism and Regionalism." *Annals of the Association of American Geographers* 72, no. 4 (December 1982): 514–531.

Koblas, John J. *The Great Cole Younger and Frank James Wild West Show.* Saint Cloud, Minn.: North Star, 2002.

Kukla, Jon. *A Wilderness So Immense: The Louisiana Purchase and the Destiny of America.* New York: Knopf, 2003.

Laughlin, Sceva Bright. *Missouri Politics during the Civil War.* Salem, Oreg.: S. B. Laughlin, 1930.

Lavery, Ray. "The Man Who Made a Folk-God Out of Jo Shelby and Created a Legend for Jesse James." *Trail Guide* 6, no. 4 (December 1961): 1–15.

Le Goff, Jacques. *History and Memory.* New York: Columbia University Press, 1992.

Lepore, Jill. *The Name of War: King Philip's War and the Origins of American Identity.* New York: Knopf, 1998.

Leslie, Edward E. "Quantrill's Bones." *American Heritage,* July-August 1995. http://wesclark.com/jw/quantril.html (accessed January 2, 2016).

LeSueur, Stephen. *The 1838 Mormon War in Missouri.* Columbia: University of Missouri Press, 1990.

Library of Congress. *The American Civil War: A Centennial Exhibition.* Washington, D.C.: Library of Congress, 1961.

Limerick, Patricia. *The Legacy of Conquest: The Unbroken Past of the American West.* New York: Norton, 1987.

Lowndes, Joseph E. *From the New Deal to the New Right: Race and the Southern Origins of Modern Conservatism.* New Haven, Conn.: Yale University Press, 2008.

Mackey, Robert R. *The Uncivil War: Irregular Warfare in the Upper South, 1861–1865.* Norman: University of Oklahoma Press, 2004.

Manning, Chandra. *What This Cruel War Was Over: Soldiers, Slavery, and the Civil War.* New York: Vintage Books, 2007.

Marshall, Anne. *Creating a Confederate Kentucky: The Lost Cause and Civil War Memory in a Border State.* Chapel Hill: University of North Carolina Press, 2010.

Marten, James A. *Sing Not War: The Lives of Union and Confederate Veterans in Gilded Age America.* Chapel Hill: University of North Carolina Press, 2011.

Mattson, Stanley J. "Mark Twain on War and Peace: The Missouri Rebel and 'The Campaign That Failed.'" *American Quarterly* 20, no. 4 (1968): 783–794.

McConnell, Stuart. *Glorious Contentment: The Grand Army of the Republic, 1865–1900.* Chapel Hill: University of North Carolina Press, 1992.

McCullough, David G. *Mornings on Horseback.* New York: Simon & Schuster, 1981.

McDermott, John. "The Mystery Man of Quatsino Sound: The Second Life of William Clarke Quantrill." *American West* 10, no. 2 (March 1973): 12–16, 63.

McKnight, Brian. *Confederate Outlaw: Champ Ferguson and the Civil War in Appalachia.* Baton Rouge: Louisiana State University Press, 2011.

McPherson, James M. *Battle Cry of Freedom: The Civil War Era.* New York: Oxford University Press, 1988.

McVeigh, Stephen. *The American Western.* Edinburgh: Edinburgh University Press, 2007.

Mihm, Stephen. *A Nation of Counterfeiters: Capitalists, Con Men, and the Making of the United States.* Cambridge, Mass.: Harvard University Press, 2007.

Mills, Cynthia, and Pamela H. Simpson, eds. *Monuments to the Lost Cause: Women, Art, and the Landscapes of Southern Memory.* Knoxville: University of Tennessee Press, 2003.

Monaghan, James. *Civil War on the Western Border, 1854–1865.* Boston: Little, Brown, 1955.

Moore, Beth S. *Bones in the Well: The Haun's Mill Massacre, 1838: A Documentary History.* Norman, Okla.: Arthur H. Clark, 2006.

Morris, Edmund. *The Rise of Theodore Roosevelt.* New York: Coward, McCann, & Geoghegan, 1979.

Moses, L. G. *Wild West Shows and the Images of Native Americans, 1883–1933.* Albuquerque: University of New Mexico Press, 1996.

Murphy, Paul V. *The Rebuke of History: The Southern Agrarians and American Conservative Thought.* Chapel Hill: University of North Carolina Press, 2001.

Mutti-Burke, Diane. *On Slavery's Border: Missouri's Small-Slaveholding Households, 1815–1865.* Athens: University of Georgia Press, 2010.

Myers, Barton. *Executing Daniel Bright: Race, Loyalty, and Guerrilla Violence in a Coastal Carolina Community, 1861–1865.* Baton Rouge: Louisiana State University Press, 2009.

Neely, Jeremy. *The Border between Them: Violence and Reconciliation on the Kansas-Missouri Line.* Columbia: University of Missouri Press, 2007.

———. "The Quantrill Men Reunions: The Missouri-Kansas Border War, Fifty Years On." In Earle and Mutti-Burke, *Bleeding Kansas,* 243–257.

Neely, Mark. *The Civil War and the Limits of Destruction.* Cambridge, Mass.: Harvard University Press, 2007.

Neff, John R. *Honoring the Civil War Dead: Commemoration and the Problem of Reconciliation.* Lawrence: University Press of Kansas, 2005.

Nelson, Megan Kate. *Ruin Nation: Destruction and the American Civil War.* Athens: University of Georgia Press, 2012.

———. "Death in the Distance: Confederate Manifest Destiny and the Campaign for New Mexico." In Arenson and Graybill, *Civil War Wests,* 33–52.

———. "Indians Make the Best Guerrillas: Native Americans and the War for the Desert Southwest, 1861–1862." In Beilein and Hulbert, *Civil War Guerrilla,* 99–122.

Nixon, Raymond B. *Henry W. Grady: Spokesman of the New South.* New York: Knopf, 1948.

Noe, Kenneth W. "Who Were the Bushwhackers? Age, Class, Kin, and Western Virginia's Confederate Guerrillas, 1861–1862." *Civil War History* 49, no. 1 (2003): 5–26.

Nolan, Alan T. *Lee Considered: General Robert E. Lee and Civil War History.* Chapel Hill: University of North Carolina Press, 1991.

Nolan, Frederick. *The Lincoln County War: A Documentary History.* Norman: University of Oklahoma Press, 1992.

Nora, Pierre. "Between Memory and History: Les Lieux de Mémoire." *Representations,* no. 26, Special issue: Memory and Counter-Memory (Spring 1989): 7–24.

Oates, Stephen B. *A Woman of Valor: Clara Barton and the Civil War.* New York: Free Press, 1994.

Oertel, Kristin T. *Bleeding Borders: Race, Gender, and Violence in Pre–Civil War Kansas.* Baton Rouge: Louisiana State University Press, 2009.

Paludan, Phillip Shaw. *Victims: A True Story of the Civil War.* Knoxville: University of Tennessee Press, 1981.

Patterson, T. W. "I Can Prove I Am Quantrill by John Sharp." *Real West* 9, no. 48 (July 1966): 10–11, 54–56.

Petersen, Paul, and David Jackson. *Lost Souls of the Lost Township: Untold Life Stories of the People Buried in the Smith-Davis Cemetery, Kansas City, Jackson County, Missouri.* Kansas City, Mo.: Orderly Pack Rat, 2011.

Phillips, Christopher. *Damned Yankee: The Life of General Nathaniel Lyon.* Columbia: University of Missouri Press, 1990.

———. *Missouri's Confederate: Clairborne Fox Jackson and the Creation of Southern Identity in the Border West.* Columbia: University of Missouri Press, 2000.

———. "'The Chrysalis State': Slavery, Confederate Identity, and the Creation of the Border South." In Gordon and Inscoe, *Inside the Confederate Nation,* 147–164.

Piston, William G. *Wilson's Creek: The Second Battle of the Civil War and the Men Who Fought It.* Chapel Hill: University of North Carolina Press, 2003.

Proctor, Nicholas W. *Bathed in Blood: Hunting and Mastery in the Old South.* Charlottesville: University of Virginia Press, 2002.

Rable, George C. *But There Was No Peace: The Role of Violence in the Politics of Reconstruction.* Athens: University of Georgia Press, 2007.

———. *Civil Wars: Women and the Crisis of Southern Nationalism.* Urbana: University of Illinois Press, 1989.

Ragsdale, Bruce A., and Kathryn Allamong Jacob. *Biographical Directory of the United States Congress.* Washington, D.C.: Government Printing Office, 1989.

Reddin, Paul. *Wild West Shows.* Urbana: University of Illinois Press, 1999.

Rhyne, J. Michael. "'A Blood Stained Sin': Slavery, Freedom, and Guerrilla Warfare in the Bluegrass Region of Kentucky, 1863–1865." *Register of the Kentucky Historical Society* 112, no. 4 (Autumn 2014): 553–587.

Richardson, Heather Cox. *West from Appomattox: The Reconstruction of America after the Civil War.* New Haven, Conn.: Yale University Press, 2007.

Rister, Carl C. "Carlota, a Confederate Colony in Mexico." *Journal of Southern History* 11, no. 1 (February 1945): 33–50.

Robertson Jr., James I. *The Civil War.* Washington, D.C.: Library of Congress, 1961.

Rose, Kenneth D. *Myth and the Greatest Generation: A Social History of Americans in World War II.* New York: Routledge, 2008.

Rotundo, Anthony. *American Manhood: Transformations in Masculinity from the Revolution to the Modern Era.* New York: Basic Books, 1993.

Rowan, Stephen, ed. *Germans for a Free Missouri: Translations from the St. Louis Radical Press, 1857–1862.* Columbia: University of Missouri Press, 1983.

Rubin, Anne S. *Through the Heart of Dixie: Sherman's March and American Memory.* Chapel Hill: University of North Carolina Press, 2014.

Russell, Don. *The Wild West, or, a History of the Wild West Shows.* Fort Worth, Tex.: Amon Carter Museum of Western Art, 1970.

Russell, William B. *Civil War Films for Teachers and Historians.* Lanham, Md.: University Press of America, 2008.

Sandoz, Mari. *The Battle of Little Big Horn.* Philadelphia: Lippincott, 1966.

Saults, Dan. "Let Us Discuss a Man: A Study of John Newman Edwards." *Missouri Historical Society Bulletin,* January 1963, 150–160.

Sayers, Isabelle S. *Annie Oakley and Buffalo Bill's Wild West.* New York: Dover, 1981.

Sayre, Nora. *Running Time: Films of the Cold War.* New York: Dial, 1982.

Scharff, Virginia, ed. *Empire and Liberty: The Civil War in the West.* Oakland: University of California Press, 2015.

Schickel, Richard. *Clint Eastwood: A Biography.* New York: Knopf, 1996.

Schultz, Duane. *Quantrill's War: The Life and Times of William Clarke Quantrill, 1837–1865.* New York: St. Martin's, 1996.

Seal, Graham. *The Outlaw Legend: A Cultural Tradition in Britain, America, and Australia.* Cambridge: Cambridge University Press, 1996.

Sensing, Thurman. *Champ Ferguson: Confederate Guerilla.* Nashville: Vanderbilt University Press, 1942.

Settle, William A. *Jesse James Was His Name.* Columbia: University of Missouri Press, 1966.

Sheridan, Richard B. "A Most Unusual Gathering: The 1913 Semi-Centennial Raid Memorial Reunion of the Survivor's of Quantrill's Raid on Lawrence." *Kansas History* 20, no. 3 (Autumn 1997): 176–191.

Siddali, Silvana. *Missouri's War: The Civil War in Documents.* Athens: Ohio University Press, 2009.

Silber, Nina. *The Romance of Reunion: Northerners and the South, 1865–1900.* Chapel Hill: University of North Carolina Press, 1997.

Singal, Daniel. *The War Within: From Victorian to Modernist Thought in the South, 1919–1945.* Chapel Hill: University of North Carolina Press, 1982.

Slatta, Richard W., ed. *Bandidos: The Varieties of Latin American Banditry.* Westport, N.Y.: Greenwood, 1987.

Slotkin, Richard. *Gunfighter Nation: The Myth of the Frontier in Twentieth-Century America.* New York: Atheneum, 1992.

Smith, Andrew B. *Shooting Cowboys and Indians: Silent Western Films, American Culture, and the Birth of Hollywood.* Boulder: University Press of Colorado, 2003.

Spencer, Thomas M. *The Missouri Mormon Experience.* Columbia: University of Missouri Press, 2010.

Starr, Stephen Z. *Jennison's Jayhawkers: A Civil War Cavalry Regiment and Its Commander.* Baton Rouge: Louisiana State University Press, 1973.

Stiles, T. J. *Jesse James: Last Rebel of the Civil War.* New York: Vintage Books, 2003.

Strong, Pauline T. *Captive Selves, Captivating Others: The Politics and Poetics of Colonial American Captivity Narratives.* Boulder: Westview, 1999.

Sutherland, Daniel, ed. *Guerrillas, Unionists, and Violence on the Confederate Home Front.* Fayetteville: University of Arkansas Press, 1999.

——. *A Savage Conflict: The Decisive Role of Guerrillas in the American Civil War.* Chapel Hill: University of North Carolina Press, 2003.

——. "Guerrilla Warfare, Democracy, and the Fate of the Confederacy." *Journal of Southern History* 68, no. 2 (May 2002): 259–292.

——. "Sideshow No Longer: A Historiographical Review of the Guerrilla War." *Civil War History* 46, no. 1 (March 2000): 5–23.

Tai, Hue-Tam Ho. "Remembered Realms: Pierre Nora and French National Memory." *American Historical Review* 106, no. 3 (June 2001): 906–922.

Thelen, David. "Memory and American History." *Journal of American History* 75, no. 4 (March 1989): 1117–1129.

——. *Paths of Resistance: Tradition and Dignity in Industrializing Missouri.* New York: Oxford University Press, 1986.

Thiessen, Thomas D., Douglas D. Scott, and Steven J. Dasovich. "'This Work of Fiends': Historical and Archaeological Perspectives on the Confederate Guerrilla Actions at Centralia, Missouri, September 27, 1864." Prepared for Friends of Centralia Battlefield and Missouri Civil War Heritage Foundation. Lincoln, Nebr., 2008.

Thomas, Emory M. *The Confederate Nation, 1861–1865.* New York: Harper & Row, 1979.

Tibbetts, John C. "Riding with the Devil: The Movie Adventures of William Clarke Quantrill." *Kansas History: A Journal of the Plains,* Autumn 1999, 182–199.

Toplin, Robert Brent. *History by Hollywood: The Use and Abuse of the American Past.* Urbana: University of Illinois Press, 1996.

——, ed. *Ken Burns's The Civil War: Historians Respond.* New York: Oxford University Press, 1996.

U.S. War Department. Bibliography of State Participation in the Civil War, 1861–1866. Washington, D.C.: Government Printing Office, 1913.

Utley, Robert M. *Billy the Kid: A Short and Violent Life.* Lincoln: University of Nebraska Press, 1989.

——. *High Noon in Lincoln: Violence on the Western Frontier.* Albuquerque: University of New Mexico Press, 1987.

Van de Water, Frederic F. *Glory-Hunter: A Life of General Custer.* Lincoln: University of Nebraska Press, 1988.

Varon, Elizabeth. *Appomattox: Victory, Defeat, and Freedom at the End of the Civil War.* New York: Oxford University Press, 2013.

Verhoeff, Nanna. *The West in Early Cinema: After the Beginning.* Amsterdam: Amsterdam University Press, 2006.

Walle, Alf H. *The Cowboy Hero and Its Audience: Popular Culture as Market Derived Art.* Bowling Green, Ohio: Bowling Green State University Popular Press, 2000.

Wallis, Michael. *Billy the Kid: The Endless Ride.* New York: Norton, 2007.

Warren, Louis S. *Buffalo Bill's America: William Cody and the Wild West Show.* New York: Knopf, 2005.

Warren, Robert Penn. *The Legacy of the Civil War.* Lincoln: University of Nebraska Press, 1998.

Watson, Thomas S. *Confederate Guerrilla Sue Mundy: A Biography of Kentucky Soldier Jerome Clark.* Jefferson, N.C.: McFarland, 2008.

——. *The Silent Riders: A WAKY News Documentary.* Louisville, Ky.: Beechmont, 1971.

White, Richard. "Outlaw Gangs of the Middle Border: American Social Bandits." *Western Historical Quarterly* 12, no. 4 (October 1981): 387–408.

Whites, LeeAnn. *The Civil War as a Crisis in Gender: Augusta, Georgia, 1860–1890.* Athens: University of Georgia Press, 1995.

——. "Forty Shirts and a Wagonload of Wheat: Women, the Domestic Supply Line, and the Civil War on the Western Border." *Journal of the Civil War Era* 1, no. 1 (March 2011): 56–78.

——. "The Tale of Three Kates: Outlaw Women, Loyalty, and Missouri's Long Civil War." In Stephen Berry, ed., *Weirding the War: Stories of the Civil War's Ragged Edges* (Athens: University of Georgia Press, 2011), 73–94.

Whites, LeeAnn, and Alecia P. Long. *Occupied Women: Gender, Military Occupation, and the American Civil War.* Baton Rouge: Louisiana State University Press, 2009.

Williams, Burton J. "Quantrill's Raid on Lawrence: A Question of Complicity." *Kansas Historical Quarterly* 34, no. 2 (Summer 1968): 143–149.

Wills, Brian S. *Gone with the Glory: The Civil War in American Cinema.* New York: Rowman & Littlefield, 2001.

Wilson, Charles Reagan. *Baptized in Blood: The Religion of the Lost Cause, 1865–1920.* Athens: University of Georgia Press, 1986.

Witt, John Fabian. *Lincoln's Code: The Laws of War in American History.* New York: Free Press, 2012.

Woodward, C. Vann. *Origins of the New South, 1877–1913.* Baton Rouge: Louisiana State University Press, 1974.

Wright, Will. *Sixguns and Society: A Structural Study of the Western.* Berkeley: University of California Press, 1975.

Wyatt-Brown, Bertram. *Southern Honor: Ethnics and Behavior in the Old South.* New York: Oxford University Press, 1982.

York, Neil Longley. *Fiction as Fact: The Horse Soldiers and Popular Memory.* Kent, Ohio: Kent State University Press, 2001.

INDEX

UnCivil Wars